A Specter Haunting Europe

A Specter Haunting Europe

THE MYTH OF

JUDEO-BOLSHEVISM

Paul Hanebrink

THE BELKNAP PRESS OF

HARVARD UNIVERSITY PRESS

Cambridge, Massachusetts
London, England
2018

Library of Congress Cataloging-in-Publication Data

Names: Hanebrink, Paul A., author.
Title: A specter haunting Europe : the myth of Judeo-Bolshevism / Paul Hanebrink.
Description: Cambridge, Massachusetts : The Belknap Press of Harvard University
Press, 2018. | Includes bibliographical references and index.
Identifiers: LCCN 2018005089 | ISBN 9780674047686 (alk. paper)
Subjects: LCSH: Communism and Judaism—Europe—History—20th century. |
Socialism and antisemitism—Europe—History—20th century. | Prejudices—Religious
aspects—Judaism. | Communism—Europe—Public opinion—History—20th century. |
Jews—Europe—Public opinion—History—20th century.
Classification: LCC HX550.J4 H36 2018 | DDC 320.53/208992404—dc23
LC record available at https://lccn.loc.gov/2018005089

Contents

A Specter Haunting Europe

Introduction

The recent surge in political activity on the far right in Europe and North America owes much of its strength to the circulation of language and ideas among ethnonationalist extremists on both sides of the Atlantic. In Charlottesville, Virginia, where white supremacists and neo-Nazis gathered in August 2017 to demonstrate against the removal of a statue of Confederate general Robert E. Lee, they waved Nazi swastikas next to the Confederate battle flag. Equally significant, they chanted a slogan—"You will not replace us!"—devised originally by far-right intellectuals in France to demonize immigrants whose presence, they believed, would ruin the supposed purity of French culture, erode the sovereignty of Europe's nations, and ultimately replace (white) Europeans in their own homes.[1] Three months later, far-right activists from across Europe gathered in Warsaw on the occasion of Poland's Independence Day. Some were Poles calling for a "pure Poland, white Poland." Others came from countries like Sweden, Hungary, and the United Kingdom to celebrate a "white Europe of brotherly nations." All of them demanded that refugees "get out."[2]

One more element was common to both events, beyond anti-immigrant sentiment and invocations of white power. Demonstrators in Charlottesville and Warsaw alike declared that "Jewish power" was another threat to the pure communities they wanted to defend. "Remove Jewry from power!" one participant in the Warsaw rally told an interviewer.[3] Others carried symbols of 1930s-era antisemitic organizations.[4] "Jews will not replace us!" shouted marchers in Virginia, inventing an antisemitic variation on the original anti-immigrant theme. When asked what they meant by this, white nationalists responded with angry screeds against Jews in the media, Jews who controlled banks, and Jewish liberals who wanted to force their morality on "real" Americans. And they also aimed their vitriol at one more face of the Jewish enemy: the Jewish Communist.[5]

Across Europe, neofascists similar in age and outlook to white nationalists in America rally to defend their "own" culture against the forces of globalism, which they associate with Jews. Like the racist militants in Charlottesville, Europe's new far-right movements freely associate distorted elements of the local past to find connections with racist histories borrowed from elsewhere. And they also include Jewish Communists—or, more abstractly, "Judeo-Bolshevism"—among the enemies who threaten their nations. When the World Jewish Congress held an international conference in Budapest in 2013, the far-right Jobbik Party staged a rally to protest the "sale" of Hungary to Jewish investors and to commemorate Hungarian victims of "Bolshevism and Zionism."[6] In Poland and Romania, right-wing extremists blame "Jewish Communists" for promoting homosexuality and multiculturalism. They also associate Judeo-Bolshevism with attacks on traditional religion and morality, which they blame for their declining birth rates.[7] Similar rhetoric can be heard from far-right groups and parties in the Baltic states, Ukraine, and Russia. And these ideas are by no means current only in the former Soviet bloc. In Greece, the neofascist Golden Dawn accuses Communists of wanting to destroy the ethnic purity of the Greek people, and associates Communism with "Zionist world conspiracy."[8]

Contemporary far-right movements in Europe and North America have also appropriated older fascist accounts of so-called Judeo-

Bolshevik plots and integrated them into their ideological imagination. Of course, translations of Adolf Hitler's *Mein Kampf* can be
found on every far-right website, but these forums also nurture the
legends of more obscure figures. In the aftermath of the August 2017
Charlottesville violence, newspapers across the United States published the photograph of one white nationalist leader who took part
in the racist demonstration wearing a t-shirt that displayed the portrait of the interwar Romanian fascist Corneliu Codreanu. In his life-
time, Codreanu (who was executed for sedition in 1938) warned his
countrymen that Bolshevism and liberalism were both Jewish plots
against the nation. Today, neo-Confederates in the United States re-
vere him for these ideas. So does the far right in Poland, even though
there was no connection in the 1930s between Polish and Romanian
right-wing radicals.[9] Extreme-right websites in Hungary sell reprints
of anti-Bolshevik propaganda from World War II as well as books by
fascist and antisemitic émigrés who blamed Jews for the Communist
regime that took power in their country after the war. They also feature discussions of historical figures from the 1920s and 1930s whose
fusion of antisemitism and anti-Communism made them leading personalities at the time. Across the former Soviet bloc, far-right groups
also consistently identify long-dead Communists as Jews in order to
"prove" their theories about an international Jewish plot to rob their
nations of sovereignty. Some of these "unmasked" Jewish Bolsheviks,
like Leon Trotsky, are icons of antinational conspiracy in many different countries. Others—like Jakub Berman, head of the secret police in Stalinist Poland, or Mátyás Rákosi, head of the Communist
Party in Hungary in the early 1950s—appear as demonized enemies
only in specific national contexts.

Mátyás Rákosi died in 1971, Jakub Berman in 1984. Communism
collapsed across Eastern Europe in 1989. The young men and women
active today in many of the far-right groups, movements, and parties
in Europe and North America were infants when the Berlin Wall fell.
Some were not even born yet. Few of the young activists in Eastern

Europe's new extreme right have any conscious experience of Communist rule, nor do Communist parties exert any significant influence on political life in most places in Europe and North America. Nevertheless, nationalist extremists and far-right movements on both sides of the Atlantic have made the idea of Judeo-Bolshevism—the belief that Communism was a Jewish plot—a prominent element of their worldview. They have interpreted different episodes in the history of Communism in the twentieth century as proof of a transhistorical global conspiracy by Jews to destroy Western civilization. And they have revived the memory of prominent antisemites from the decades between 1914 and 1945 to celebrate them as anti-Communist heroes and defenders of national culture. Communism is gone, but the idea of Judeo-Bolshevism refuses to go away. This book is an attempt to understand why.

Over the course of the twentieth century, the belief that Communism was created by a Jewish conspiracy and that Jews were therefore to blame for the crimes committed by Communist regimes became a core element of counterrevolutionary, antidemocratic, and racist ideologies in many different countries. The association of Jews with Communism was used to justify violent pogroms, especially in times of revolutionary upheaval, state breakdown, or regime change. During the decades between the two world wars, the idea of Judeo-Bolshevism inspired a variety of countries to enact policies that discriminated against Jews or placed them under surveillance. When Nazi Germany went to war with the Soviet Union in 1941, its leaders told themselves (and the men they commanded) that the Judeo-Bolshevik threat required them to wage war on the Eastern Front with relentless and barbarous cruelty. They also made the idea of Judeo-Bolshevism a crucial element in the origins of the Holocaust. Today, nationalist extremists and far-right movements across Europe embrace this history and make its memory central to their own political identity. Given the history of discrimination, exclusion, and violence that the idea of Judeo-Bolshevism inspired in the past century, its persistence in the present one is deeply troubling. How should historians respond?

Some have tried to separate fact from fiction. How many Jews were Communists? Were they overrepresented among party members or party leaders? Did Jews in particular places and at particular times vote for or support Communism in high numbers, and if so, why? How many Jews joined the Communist secret police forces, what did they do, and why? This book draws on the many studies that have tackled these questions carefully and responsibly.[10] Nevertheless, assessing the idea of Judeo-Bolshevism as a matter to be verified or falsified is profoundly misleading for several reasons. It requires historians to impose rigid ethnic categories on men and women whose sense of themselves was always more complex and multifaceted. It reduces the complicated intellectual, emotional, and existential attachments that Communism inspired in so many—Jews and non-Jews alike—to a simplistic question of "belief." It focuses disproportionate attention on one political choice that some Jews made, ignoring the much richer diversity of Jewish politics in the twentieth century. Most important, it reproduces a strategy undertaken many times before. Again and again, scholars, political liberals, and members of the Jewish community have debunked the claim that "Jews were responsible for Communism." They have convincingly and authoritatively exposed the "myth of Judeo-Bolshevism" as an ideological construct that has no bearing on the complex realities of Jewish encounters with Communism. Still, none of their efforts has caused the idea of Judeo-Bolshevism to disappear from the ideological arsenal of right-wing nationalists. Given this history, the purpose of studying the Judeo-Bolshevik myth must be not to determine how true it is, but to understand why it has been and remains so powerful.

One way to do this is to treat the construct of Judeo-Bolshevism as one among many forms of antisemitism.[11] There are good reasons for this approach. One does not have to spend much time reading the writings and speeches of well-known modern antisemites, from Adolf Hitler to the Frenchman Charles Maurras to the Romanian Corneliu Codreanu, to see that Communism and global capitalism always functioned in their minds as two faces of the same international (and antinational) Jewish evil. In their paranoid fantasies, Jewish Communists and Jewish financiers invariably worked together to pursue world domination, each feeding off the power of the other. Historians of antisemitism have also shown that hysteria over Judeo-Bolshevism is closely related to much older fears of Jewish plots and conspiracies.[12] In many ways, the figure of the Jewish Bolshevik is a modern-day version of medieval fables about Jewish devils intent on subverting the Christian order. Understanding the idea of Judeo-Bolshevism helps us see how malleable that image was and how easily it circulated from one place and time to another. Yet treating the idea of Judeo-Bolshevism alongside other kinds of antisemitism runs the risk of flattening it into just another variation in transhistorical Jew hatred. It blurs the specific meanings that Judeo-Bolshevism had at certain times and places. And it obscures the power that the figure of the Jewish Bolshevik had, in particular contexts, to crystallize a wider set of political and cultural anxieties in ways that other antisemitic stereotypes did not. The specter of Judeo-Bolshevism loomed larger at some times and in some places than in others. To understand the power and longevity of this specific fear, we have to ask why this was so.

Israeli historian Shulamit Volkov once proposed thinking of antisemitism as a cultural code. She meant to draw attention with this phrase to the ease with which stereotypes about Jews have been used in the modern world to generate associations and linkages among a variety of complex and disparate social phenomena. She argued that in the context she studied—nineteenth-century Germany—antisemitic language offered its users a way to interpret the multiple dislocations caused by economic modernization, democratization, and cultural pluralism; it reduced all aspects of dislocation to a single

"Jewish question" and mobilized supporters around its solution. Antisemitism functioned as a sign of "cultural identity, of one's belonging to a specific cultural camp." Volkov insisted that understanding anti-Jewish rhetoric in this way did not diminish appreciation of its violent potential. Instead, it highlighted the interaction at a given historical moment between the specific content of antisemitic thought and its function as a tool to organize political worldviews, imagine and justify state policies, and even incite violence. Long continuities across centuries shaped the tropes used and reused in anti-Jewish language. But the cultural logic of antisemitism functioned differently from one historical context to another.[13]

This is the approach to the idea of Judeo-Bolshevism that I take in this book. What did the idea of Judeo-Bolshevism mean in different political contexts? How did it circulate across borders and from one regime to another? How was it transformed over the course of the twentieth century? When was it used instrumentally as an ideological tool to advance the interests of specific groups or actors? And when did it function more generally as a phantasmagoria that crystallized broader sets of political and cultural anxieties? To answer these questions, I begin with the emergence of Judeo-Bolshevism as a feature of anti-Communist politics in the crucible of war, civil war, revolution, and imperial breakdown in Europe between 1914 and 1923. I then look at how fascist movements made use of the Judeo-Bolshevik enemy during the interwar era, as well as how traditional conservatives, including especially the Christian churches, tried to mobilize (or neutralize) it for their own purposes. This leads into an analysis of the role that the idea of Judeo-Bolshevism played in the unfolding of the Holocaust. In the second half of the book, I ask how the function of Judeo-Bolshevism changed after the destruction of Nazi Germany. How was the idea transformed under Communist rule in Eastern Europe after 1945? What happened to it in the West during those same years? And finally, how was the idea of Judeo-Bolshevism resurrected after 1989 as an element in the contested memory of war, genocide, and Communism on both sides of the Atlantic? What legacy has it left for the present?

Throughout the twentieth century, the idea of Judeo-Bolshevism embodied threats to national sovereignty. Nationalists in many different countries across Europe imagined the Jewish Bolshevik as a malevolent agent who worked tirelessly to subordinate the nation, which they imagined as a monoethnic community, to an international revolutionary order that had no place for "true" national belonging or "real" national identity. This fear took a variety of forms. At moments of revolutionary upheaval or regime change, Jews were often accused of supporting Communism, misleading the "native" working class, subverting national unity, and aiding and abetting Soviet rule. At other times, an antinational Jewish Bolshevik threat expressed more general anxieties. After World War I, the specter of Judeo-Bolshevism fueled hostility toward Jewish refugees, who were fleeing imperial collapse and state breakdown in the borderlands of Eastern Europe and were seen as unassimilable and infected with a revolutionary virus. And Judeo-Bolshevism crystallized concerns about state security, especially in countries, like Poland and Romania, that shared a border with the Soviet Union. Throughout the twentieth century, the figure of the Jewish Bolshevik was imagined as an ethno-ideological zealot, a destructive border-crosser intent on mobilizing local Jews and other discontented groups to overturn the social and moral order. After the fall of Communism, memories of these fears were used by Europe's new Right to justify a new hostility toward international liberal norms derided as cosmopolitan and Jewish.

Ethnonationalists imagined the specter of Judeo-Bolshevism as a threat to their own nations. They also believed that it endangered a wider cultural community: Europe, or Western civilization. In the first years after 1917, when Bolshevik revolution seemed poised to spread westward to Germany and beyond, counterrevolutionaries everywhere cast "Judeo-Bolshevism" as a threat to European civilization. Many of them imagined Europe as a community of Christian nations, and likened Bolshevism to earlier invasions from the east. The perceived threat of Judeo-Bolshevism made collective memories of past wars against barbarians, Mongols, and Ottoman Turks seem relevant to circumstances in the early twentieth century. During the interwar decades, a wide variety of Europeans associated Judeo-Bolshevism with a more general cultural crisis facing the West and with the possibility that European civilization might be swept away by more powerful ideological forces. Some turned to fascism in response and then celebrated the Nazi-led invasion of the Soviet Union in 1941 as a crusade to defend Christendom from Judeo-Bolshevism and Asiatic barbarism. Today, nationalist intellectuals across Europe insist that "Europe" has meaning and value only as a community of nations bound together by a common Christian culture, and that each nation in it must be free to develop its own distinct culture and to cherish the heroes of its own particular past. Debates about these issues now center on anxieties that Muslim migrants and the growing presence of Islam in Europe engender. As this book demonstrates, these fears have a powerful precursor in the history of the Judeo-Bolshevik myth.

The nature of Judeo-Bolshevism as a transnational threat took shape within equally transnational networks of anti-Communist thought and practice. Writers feature prominently in this book, as translators and journalists who circulated accounts about Jews and revolutionary terror, and as travelers who took an interest in revolutionary events elsewhere to lend a veneer of authenticity to their own speculations about the relationship between Jews and Communism. So too do émigrés, who breathed life into the Judeo-Bolshevik myth with firsthand accounts of their own experiences with revolutionary terror. More profoundly, the ideological power of Judeo-Bolshevism in specific national contexts was shaped and reshaped throughout the twentieth century by shifts in what might be called international regimes of anti-Communist politics. The shock caused by the triumph of the Bolsheviks in Russia set the conditions in which fears of Judeo-Bolshevik perfidy could flourish across Europe. The rise of Nazi Germany, and the claim that it made after 1933 to lead a grand European anti-Communist front, changed the political valence of the Judeo-Bolshevik myth. The destruction of Hitler's empire and the division of Europe into a Communist-dominated East and a West led by the United States changed it yet again. Most recently, the collapse of Communism in Eastern Europe and the emergence of global Holocaust memory as a powerful sign of liberal values have infused the issue of Judeo-Bolshevism with new meaning, ensuring that it remains a potent image in the arsenal of nationalists who believe their nation's sovereignty is under assault by nameless cosmopolitan forces.

To capture the simultaneously transnational and national dimensions of the Judeo-Bolshevik myth, I focus most closely on the history of this idea in Central and Eastern Europe. The image of the Jewish Bolshevik was a powerful stereotype in the politics of Hungary, Romania, and Poland after World War I, and it remained so across the many political ruptures and transformations of the twentieth century. The enduring power of the Judeo-Bolshevik menace, as well as its subtle shifts from one period to another, can be observed especially closely in these cases. I focus on the history of Judeo-Bolshevism as a political idea in Germany as well, not only because of its crucial importance to Nazi ideology, and ultimately to Nazi genocide, but also because its radical refashioning into a different kind of anti-Communism after 1945 was one of the more astonishing twists in the history of the Judeo-Bolshevik myth. At the same time, I follow the ideological exchanges among Central and Eastern Europe and Russia or the Soviet Union to the east, Western Europe, and the United States, for it is precisely within those wider political and geographical contexts that the specter of Judeo-Bolshevism acquired its full imagined meaning as a threat to European civilization or, more simply, the West.

1

The Idea of Judeo-Bolshevism

In April 1919, Eugenio Pacelli was papal nuncio in Munich. It was a turbulent time in Bavaria and throughout Germany. In November 1918, revolution had broken out in the city. The socialist Kurt Eisner had formed a government and declared Bavaria a republic. Three months later he was assassinated by a right-wing aristocrat. After a chaotic interlude, a new group of revolutionaries, led by the Russian Max Levien, arrived in Munich to take charge of the workers' and soldiers' councils. Sent by the Communist Executive in Berlin, Levien and his associates declared a dictatorship of the proletariat. They imprisoned bourgeois hostages, imposed censorship, requisitioned homes and even food from those they called "class enemies," and began to seize property from embassies and consulates in the city. Their arrival seemed to foretell a coordinated effort by Communists across Europe to spread the revolution from Russia to Central Europe. Labor militancy in Germany's industrial regions only added to this fear. So did the establishment in March of a Hungarian Soviet Republic in Budapest. In the midst of all this, Pacelli communicated his impressions of the political situation in Munich to Vatican officials in Rome. In one letter to Rome, Pacelli wrote about what happened when he sent his aide to pay a visit to the headquarters of Bavaria's new Soviet regime.

"The scene that presented itself at the palace was indescribable." Revolutionaries issued a stream of instructions and commands about every possible aspect of life, their frenzied activity expressing a shared determination to bring a new revolutionary dawn to Catholic, conservative Bavaria. The "new" men and women who met with Pacelli's envoy had risen to the heights of power from obscure origins, and their triumph seemed to foreshadow a more complete transformation of the social order in the future. Pacelli knew none of them, but he claimed to know their type. One group had made a particularly strong impression on his assistant: "a gang of young women, of dubious appearance, Jewish like all the rest of them." The sight of these independent and politically radical women, as comfortable in power as their male counterparts, shook the churchmen deeply. Far out of his depth, the emissary who reported back to Pacelli could make sense of what he had seen only by imagining that the excitement of revolutionary activism unfolding before him was in reality a scene of sexual debauchery dominated by the revolutionary leader, Max Levien. Pacelli wrote: "The boss of this female rabble was Levien's mistress, a young Russian woman, a Jew and a divorcée." Levien himself seemed a sinister and repulsive figure. "This Levien is a young man, of about thirty or thirty-five, also Russian and a Jew. Pale, dirty, with drugged eyes, hoarse voice, vulgar, repulsive, with a face that is both intelligent and sly." He embodied the revolution, in Pacelli's eyes. Munich's Bolsheviks were grimy and ugly, sexually debased, and devoid of any moral conscience. One other feature seemed to stand out. According to Pacelli, they were all Jews.[1]

When this letter, signed by the man who would later become Pope Pius XII, was discovered in the 1990s, these lines caused a minor scandal. Critics of Pius, opposed to efforts to have him canonized as a saint, heard echoes of Nazi antisemitism and took them as one more reason that Pacelli had not resisted Nazi tyranny more vigorously after he became pope. Pius's defenders argued, in turn, that they were only a few short lines in one document written in 1919 and they should not be taken as the key to understanding his thought or his actions two decades later. They also pointed out that Pacelli had based his letter entirely on the observations of his aide, who had supplied him not only with the details of the encounter but perhaps also the language that Pacelli used to describe them to the Vatican. These are entirely reasonable objections. They are also beside the point. The letter is not significant because it is a magic key that unlocks hidden truths about a historically important person. It matters because it is so utterly typical of its time. The letter reflected what many Europeans believed: Jews were the face of the revolution.[2]

After 1917, a wide variety of groups and parties across the continent and even across the Atlantic shared the belief that Bolshevism was caused or led by Jews. Germany's extreme right demonized Bolsheviks, alongside socialists and democrats, as agents of the "Jewish revolution" that had birthed the Weimar Republic. So did Bavaria's Catholics, who denounced the Bolsheviks ruling in their capital as Jews and declared the revolution to be the product of "Jewish" secularism. French Catholics who had fought bravely to defeat Germany in the war expressed their postwar fears of Bolshevik revolution in much the same way. So too did many Protestants, from conservative Lutherans in eastern Germany to the dour Presbyterian Robert Lansing, the American secretary of state, who believed that Jews in New York's Lower East Side intended to bring the evils of revolution across the Atlantic to the United States. In Great Britain, Winston Churchill noted that Jewish revolutionaries had "gripped the Russian people by the hair of their heads."[3] In Munich, Thomas Mann reflected in his diary on the "Russian Jewish type" that seemed to stand at the forefront of international revolution.[4] In Hungary, Miklós Kozma, who directed the propaganda office of the counterrevolutionary army gathering in the French-occupied south, wrote in his diary that the active and lively participation of Jews in the revolution there had caused a violent backlash against them.[5] And in Eastern Europe, the civil war that raged across the lands of the former Russian empire fueled the belief that Jews were responsible for Bolshevism. Between 1917 and 1923, that belief was used to justify the mass slaughter of Jews in Ukraine by the anti-Bolshevik counterrevolutionaries known as the Whites, Ukrainian nationalists, rag-tag peasant militias, and other armed groups.

Judeo-Bolshevism—the idea that Jews had created and supported Bolshevism and were therefore responsible for its crimes—was an explosive charge that had dangerous and often lethal consequences for Jews across Europe. But it seemed to contain a kernel of truth. Certainly the many counterrevolutionaries who took it upon themselves to catalog the ethnic origins of local and internationally prominent revolutionaries thought so. The wave of political and social unrest that swept across Europe after 1917 inspired the zealous "unmasking" of Bolsheviks, in order—it was said—to understand them better and to neutralize the threat that they posed. These efforts often took the form of published "rogues' galleries." One German pamphlet promised a complete list of "Russia's gravediggers."[6] Its authors, all of them close to Adolf Hitler and the fledgling Nazi Party, filled its pages with antisemitic doggerel, apocalyptic philosophizing, and cartoons of men like Leon Trotsky and Grigorii Zinoviev. In Hungary, counterrevolutionaries produced innumerable descriptive lists of the most prominent Bolsheviks in Béla Kun's Hungarian Soviet regime, invariably noting that most of them were Jews. Efforts like these typically juxtaposed a revolutionary's commonly known name with his (and occasionally her) Jewish family name. Early in his life, for example, Lev Davydovich Bronstein had changed his name to Leon Trotsky. After 1917, counterrevolutionaries around the world insisted on changing it back. They did the same with secretary of the Comintern Karl Radek, who was born Karol Sobelsohn and who often appeared in right-wing publications as "Radek (Sobelsohn)." The Hungarian Bolshevik leader Béla Kun was similarly transformed into the hyphenated Béla Kun-Kohn. His commissar of war became "József Pogány (Weiss)." Repeated often enough, these genealogical facts seemed to offer privileged insight about the deeper realities of Europe's revolutions.

Sometimes, though, the unmaskers got it wrong. The Munich Communist Eugene Leviné, who was Jewish, was frequently confused with Max Levien, who was not. Eugenio Pacelli made this error, and he was not the only one. Nor did the description of Levien that Pacelli sent to the Vatican ring true. A French journalist who met with Levien around the same time found a man who was not "pale, dirty, with drugged eyes," as Pacelli described him, but "more slavic than semitic."[7] There were other mistakes. Rosa Luxemburg was Jewish, but her comrade, Karl Liebknecht, was not, although the men who murdered them both believed otherwise.[8] The fear of "Jewish revolution" also cast a shadow over men and women who were neither Jews nor Bolsheviks. In Germany the extreme right tried to delegitimize the January 1919 elections to the new National Asssembly by circulating posters that featured cartoons of prominent Bolsheviks, like Karl Radek, alongside socialists and democrats, like the Catholic politician Matthias Erzberger. All were "unmasked" as Jews, their distorted and leering faces framed by stars of David and the slogan: "Their star is subversion! Make Germany free for Germans!"[9] In Russia, the Whites associated Alexander Kerensky, prime minister of the first Russian Provisional Government, with the Jewish Bolshevik plot, alongside Trotsky and Zinoviev, despite the fact that Kerensky was not himself Jewish.[10] Kerensky's Hungarian counterpart, Count Mihály Károlyi, received similar treatment from counterrevolutionary nationalists there.

These are revealing mistakes. Eugenio Pacelli, like so many others, looked at the revolution and saw only Jews at the center of the action. His perception of Jews as revolutionary leaders, and of Jews as the revolution's principal beneficiaries, was overwhelming. It was also culturally constructed. His immediate experience of "seeing" Jews as

Bolsheviks was shaped by his beliefs about what revolution was and why it was happening. Some Bolsheviks were Jews. But this "fact" by itself signified nothing. Its meaning had to be made.

The association of Jews with postwar revolution worried Germany's Jewish leaders deeply. During the war, extreme-right nationalists had slandered German Jews with rising intensity, accusing them of shirking military service and exploiting the black market for their own profit. By the autumn of 1918, the largest of these groups was vowing with stunning candor to make "Jews the lightning rods of all injustice." After the November armistice brought down the old empire, these radical nationalists made good on their promise, denouncing the young Weimar Republic as a "Jewish republic" (*Judenrepublik*), blaming Jews for inflation, and "unmasking" them as leaders of the workers' movements that frightened Germany's middle class. Faced with these threats, the Central Union of German Citizens of Jewish Faith (generally called the Central Union, or Centralverein), which represented the interests of the majority of liberal and middle-class German Jews, pushed back hard. They asserted their patriotism, demanded legal protection, and tried to disprove the lies about Jews that were staple items in the newspapers of the extreme right. They also spoke directly to the revolutionaries. Editors of the Centralverein's newspaper knew all too well how the far right would manipulate the fact that some of Germany's most notorious revolutionaries were Jews. Eager to neutralize this "kernel of truth" in the panic over Judeo-Bolshevism, they pleaded with the radicals. "Through your high-handed conduct . . . you endanger the whole community."[11]

Hungarian Jewish leaders shared these worries. If anything, the problem they faced was more acute. By some counts, thirty of the forty-eight people's commissars in the 1919 Hungarian Soviet regime were Jews. These included Béla Kun, the head of the Bolshevik regime, as well as lieutenants like Ottó Korvin, the chief of the political police, and Tibor Számuelly, the leader of the Bolshevik paramilitary guard, all of them reviled by the counterrevolutionary press as enemies of the Hungarian nation. Even before Kun came to power, the nationalist Right had blamed Jewish influence in the country's first postwar government for abandoning the country's borders and allowing neighboring states to seize great chunks of historically Hungarian land. After Kun was toppled, they easily added Bolshevism to the list of Jewish sins against Christian Hungary. In response, the Pest Israelite Community, the most important liberal Jewish congregation in Hungary, met weeks after the collapse of the Kun regime in August 1919 to draft a public statement about recent events.

In their statement they expressed their joy as patriotic Hungarians at the collapse of Bolshevism in Hungary. They also cast themselves as victims of Soviet misadventure, noting that the anticapitalist zeal of the Bolsheviks had hit Hungarian Jews especially hard. And like their counterparts in Germany, they felt compelled to address the fact that many of Hungary's Bolshevik leaders had been "men of Jewish origin," in an attempt to contain the damage that Hungarian antisemites could do with it. Their strategy was to put this fact in context. They insisted that Hungary's Jewish Bolsheviks were neither Hungarians nor Jews in any meaningful sense. "Almost without exception, [they] had betrayed first their religion and then their country." These "non-Jewish" Jewish revolutionaries had also been a vanishingly small minority. "Against every single Communist of Jewish origin stands at least 1000 Jewish Hungarian patriots, faithful to the Hungarian homeland and nation in peace and war . . . who stood as far from the teachings and mores of Communism as anyone else." By framing the problem in this way, Hungary's liberal Jewish leaders hoped desperately to convince a fair-minded public to see Hungary's "Jewish Bolsheviks" as outliers with no connection whatsoever to the rest of Jewish Hungary.[12]

Analysts who dared to venture a more nuanced interpretation of the relationship between Jews and Communism quickly found themselves in a minefield. In late spring 1919, Leopold Greenberg, a journalist and editor of the British *Jewish Chronicle,* wrote two articles on the topic. In them, he lamented the evident failures and horrible destruction that Bolshevism had already brought to Europe. But he also conceded that poor Jewish immigrants in London's East End might see Bolshevism as a legitimate response to the oppression and persecution that they had experienced in Russia. He even hypothesized that the utopian ideals of Bolshevism might be somehow "consonant" with the ideals of Judaism, although he immediately qualified this assertion by noting that the two were very different in origin. Despite his analytic care, Greenberg's essay caused a furor. On the right, British conservatives, long suspicious about the loyalty of East End Jews, declared the text to be a public declaration of the affinity of Jews, and especially London's Russian Jewish immigrants, for Bolshevism and demanded that British Jews denounce the traitors in their own community. In response, some of the most notable Anglo-Jewish elites, including Lionel de Rothschild, prominent member of the Rothschild banking family in Britain; Sir Israel Gollancz, professor of English language and literature at King's College, London; and Claude G. Montefiore, great-nephew of Moses Montefiore, published an open letter in the right-wing *Morning Post,* where essays and articles about the Jewish Bolshevik peril had been standard fare for months. In their "Letter of the Ten," the signatories publicly disassociated themselves "absolutely and unreservedly from the mischievous and misleading doctrine" of Bolshevism and urged all British Jews to do the same. Of course, this gesture did little to appease Britain's far right, which simply used the letter as a foil to highlight the activities of Jewish radicals in London and abroad, thereby ensuring that the Judeo-Bolshevik menace remained a topic of public debate.[13]

These three cases recall a comment that the great Israeli historian Jacob Talmon once made about the association between Jews and revolution. He described the problem as a "foundling, a waif, an abandoned child" that no one was willing to claim; Jews could not ignore it, but many wished "they had never heard of it."[14] From Germany to Hungary to Great Britain, liberal Jewish leaders tried to neutralize, explain, or deflect attention away from debates about the Jewishness of prominent revolutionaries because they saw clearly how it could be used as a weapon to deny Jews their place in the national communities with which they identified so deeply. For them, and for many Jewish diplomats on both sides of the Atlantic, making peace after the destruction of World War I required stabilizing the international order of liberal nation-states across Europe and ensuring the legal security of Jews within them.[15] Minority treaties were one tool to this end. But liberal Jewish leaders in Central and Eastern Europe knew that defending the hard-won gains of political emancipation also meant combating the widespread slander, reborn amid the breakdown and reconstruction of states across the region, that Jews were aliens among the nations of Europe.

Of course, theirs were not the only responses to the charge of Judeo-Bolshevism. On both sides of the Atlantic, Jewish activists mobilized to document and condemn attacks on Jews committed in the name of anti-Communism, and to organize relief aid for the victims. The massive wave of pogroms in the Ukraine, which claimed the lives of 50,000 to 200,000 Jews, dominated their attention, but Jewish organizations tried to publicize violence against Jews in Poland and Hungary as well.[16] Postwar anti-Jewish violence also inspired important debates about how to situate the claim of Judeo-Bolshevism in the longer history of hostility toward Jews in Eastern Europe.[17] At the same time, some Jewish leaders found it possible to find specific uses for the racist association of Jews with revolution. Chaim Weizmann, for example, knowingly played on this fear when he suggested to officials in the British Foreign Office in 1917 the possibility that Jews in Russia could turn either to Germany or to revolution if Britain did not support the Zionist cause. His message, so credible to diplomats who believed that a "world Jewry" always acted as one, helped to generate support for the Balfour Declaration at a crucial moment in the last years of World War I. Judeo-Bolshevism might be a myth, but it could also be a dubious means toward a desired end.[18]

Despite the variety of responses to idea of Judeo-Bolshevism, it is worth considering the arguments made about it by a smaller set of liberal Jewish leaders. Their patient and analytically sound strategies to defuse the myth anticipated the efforts of later scholars, both Jewish and non-Jewish, to wrestle with Judeo-Bolshevism as an idea that contained a horrible power to justify anti-Jewish persecution but also seemed to have a measure of truth at its core. In the aftermath of world war and revolutions, antisemites across Europe won audiences for their views by unmasking different Communist revolutionaries as Jews. Although sometimes they were completely wrong, the stubborn fact remained: Some Jews were Communists.

Leopold Greenberg insisted in 1919 that Jews in Eastern Europe might have rational political reasons for becoming revolutionaries. Across the region, above all in the Russian Empire but also to different degrees in Romania and Hungary, the nineteenth century had brought Jews incomplete opportunities for integration into the societies around them. Secular education and a willingness to take risks in newly dynamic economies gave some Jews a chance at social advancement—up to a point. Russia, in particular, remained an autocracy whose elites were deeply opposed to real democratic change. Indeed, their belief that Jews were subversive exploiters of the Russian people reflected their own inability to produce social reforms or to address widespread poverty. Caught amid these social and political contradictions, some Jews (and other people too) found hope in movements and ideologies that promised a complete transformation of society. Persecution—above all, murderous pogroms like those carried out in Kishinev in 1903 and Odessa in 1905—and discrimination (for example, Romanian Jews did not receive citizenship rights until 1919) also drove some Jews to seek security in the ideal of international revolution. The wave of anti-Jewish violence that engulfed Ukraine during the Russian Civil War further reinforced the image of the revolutionary state as a safe haven for Jews, even though antisemitism was by no means absent from the ranks of the new Red Army. Finally, some Eastern European Jews did fashion new forms of Jewish socialism in a cultural and religious idiom of their own, suggesting, as observers like Greenberg hypothesized, that a creative relationship could exist between Jewish tradition and revolutionary politics, albeit with results very different from the Bolshevism of Vladimir Lenin and Leon Trotsky.[19]

The critical word in this account is "some": *Some* Jews embraced Bolshevism in particular places at particular times for particular reasons. How many were some? In the new Poland, for example, 20–40 percent of the members of the Polish Communist Party in the 1920s were individuals of Jewish origin. But only about 7 percent of Polish Jews voted for the Communist Party during this time. According to the most thorough analysis of the electoral data from this period, "Jews were no more Communist than Catholic Poles."[20] In the east and southeast of the country, a much greater part of the party's support in the 1920s came from Belarussians (43 percent of the Communist vote in central and eastern Poland) and Ukrainians (46 percent of the Communist vote in the south) looking for a political outlet to express resentment about their treatment in the Polish nation-state. These dry statistics belie the dizzying complexity of Jewish politics in the interwar Polish republic. In the wake of the Russian Revolution, a generation of Jewish intellectuals embraced Communism, inspired by the intellectual and aesthetic possibilities of Marxism and bound by friendships made and broken over the course of the twentieth century. But many more were Zionists, Bundists, Yiddishists, and socialists, all of whom imagined different ways to chart a particularly Jewish modernity. Finally, there were of course those who avoided politics altogether, whether because of religious conviction or personal inclination. Fixating on those Jews who declared themselves Communists, however spectacular their intellectual life or dramatic the political choices they later made, inevitably mistakes the part for the whole.[21]

Even among Jewish socialists, Bolshevism was only one choice among many, and by no means the most popular one. The array of political possibilities was especially dramatic in the lands of the former Russian Empire. There, legal restrictions on Jewish civic participation vanished with the fall of the Romanov dynasty in February 1917. Jewish political and cultural life exploded. By far, the majority supported Zionist parties; of those who turned to socialism, most chose alternatives to Lenin, opting instead for the Mensheviks or the Party of Socialist Revolutionaries (SR) or the Jewish Bund. In 1917 Jews made up 50 percent of the leadership of the Mensheviks, a far higher figure than that for the Bolsheviks (six of twenty-one Bolshevik leaders were Jewish, according to historian Oleg Budnitskii). These parties were deeply divided. In Ukraine, where nationalists hoped to build an independent republic, Jewish socialists, working with Ukrainian leftists, saw a chance for far-reaching cultural autonomy within the new nation-state. Zionists in Ukraine opposed them, suspicious of their internationalist politics. At a May 1917 Jewish Congress in Kiev, a rabbi asked all present to stand in honor of the Torah. Members of the socialist Bund refused. Shocked, the writer S. A. An-sky insisted that the Torah was not only a religious symbol but also a "symbol of Jewish culture." Soon thereafter, Zionists and leftists broke with each other.[22]

In the revolutionary centers of Central Europe, Bolshevism was a far more marginal phenomenon in Jewish politics. In Vienna, the leader of the Austrian Social Democratic Party, Otto Bauer, who was the son of a prosperous and politically liberal Jewish family, helped fashion a distinctive Austro-Marxism that was always more radical in theory than in practice. When the Bolsheviks seized power in Hungary in 1919, Bauer resolutely opposed the efforts of the tiny Austrian

Communist Party to do the same in Vienna. Bauer and his colleagues marginalized the Bolsheviks and ensured that Vienna's working class remained loyal to the new republic and to the remarkable experiment in urban community that was attempted in 1920s "Red Vienna."[23] In Germany, the socialist theoretician Eduard Bernstein, who was born to a Reformed Jewish family in 1850 but who left the community when he was twenty-seven, also believed that the Russian example threatened the true aims of socialism. The revolutionary Rosa Luxemburg derided his moderation as nothing more than a hope to change "the sea of capitalist bitterness into a sea of socialist sweetness by progressively pouring into it bottles of social reformist lemonade."[24] In 1919, Bernstein and Luxemburg stood on opposite sides of the barricades. While Rosa Luxemburg, a leader of the Communist Spartacus Union, fought and died, Eduard Bernstein tried to find common ground between moderate and militant socialists. After 1919 he devoted his intellectual talents to the fragile German democracy, for which the radical right vilified him as a leader of the "Jewish Republic" that they despised.[25]

Jewish liberals from Britain to Hungary also insisted that Jewish revolutionaries were not really Jews. In Hungary, Jewish leaders launched a campaign to remind the Hungarian public that Jews had been an integral part of the nation for a very long time. Variations of this argument could be also found in the pages of the German Jewish Centralverein newspaper and heard in the denunciations of Communism made by liberal Jewish leaders on both sides of the English-speaking Atlantic. The assertion rested on assumptions about the relationship between (and the separation of) private faith and public citizenship that had driven the politics of Jewish emancipation in Europe in the nineteenth century.[26] These ideas suggested that having religious faith in private meant that Jews, like Christians, would possess the moral virtue to act as loyal citizens in public. One corollary to this proposition was that a person with no faith at all was dangerous. No one could expect political loyalty from a figure who lacked the moral compass of positive faith. Hungary's Jewish leaders put this plainly: The Bolshevik Béla Kun had denied God. Therefore he could be neither Jewish nor Hungarian.

More recent explorations of Jewish identities have revealed this be- lief in the secular separation of private religion and public citizen- ship to be more political program than descriptive analysis.[27] Even so, the Jewish Hungarian liberals who denied Béla Kun's Jewish iden- tity had a point. It was not at all clear what role Kun's Jewish family background had in making him a revolutionary. Kun was born Béla Kohn, in a Transylvanian village, to a Calvinist mother and a Jewish father, a village notary who was mainly absent from the boy's life. Like any Hungarian-speaking Transylvanian boy of talent, Kohn (who later changed his name to Kun because it sounded more Hungarian) attended Hungarian Calvinist schools, which were steeped in a pro- gressive nationalist tradition defined by a deep cultural memory of opposition to Catholic Habsburg rule. At school, he had the tremen- dous good fortune to be mentored by the greatest Hungarian poet of the age, Endre Ady, who was making a name for himself as a rad- ical democrat bitterly critical of Hungary's semifeudal social struc- ture. Inspired by Ady, and by the progressive milieu of his school, Kun gravitated—with the fits and starts and distractions common to all teenagers—toward socialism.

After graduation Kun became a journalist for the Social Demo- cratic newspaper *Népszava*. But Hungary's Social Democratic Party was no hotbed of radicalism. The party was small and moderate in its demands. If the war had not intervened, Kun probably would have become a senior editor and lived a comfortable life in Budapest, writing for a newspaper that was critical of the government but firmly committed to democratic norms and institutions. However, war did break out. Kun was called up, sent to the Russian front, and taken captive. Revolution freed him from a prisoner-of-war camp. Whether he was gripped by ideological conviction in those turbulent months or simply captivated by the sheer spectacle of dramatic events is difficult to say. But something changed in him: Kun, who had gone to Russia as a Social Democrat, was swept up by Russia's Bolshevik revolution and returned to Hungary determined to bring the revolution to his homeland. What had made Kun a revolutionary? The force of events? His time writing articles for socialist newspapers? His Calvinist teachers? Had there been anything meaningfully "Jewish" about Kun's early life? According to his biographer, nothing at all.[28]

Similar stories could be told about many other Jewish revolutionaries. These men and women gravitated toward Bolshevism for the same reasons that so many other Jews in the Russian Empire and across Europe embraced Zionism or assimilationist nationalism: to slip the bonds of traditional communities, to embrace the social and cultural opportunities that modernity offered, or to feel themselves part of the sweep of history.[29] Many, like Béla Kun, took new names in the process. Some came from humble backgrounds and knew the misery of poverty at first hand; others came from privileged families and turned to socialism to find a remedy for the pervasive injustice that they saw. Some grew up in families that observed Jewish law, but others did not. As they turned to Communism, all broke with the Jewish milieu of their grandfathers, some with a twinge of regret, others with only a feeling of liberation. All believed in the power of ideas to transform the world; all saw a future filled with limitless possibility; all were convinced in the rightness of their beliefs. Truly understanding the hopes, fears, and motivations of any particular Jewish revolutionary in all their irreducible complexity is ultimately a task best undertaken by a biographer.

Scholarship on the problem of Jews and revolution highlights an array of variables that include region, class, generation, gender, educational background, and the incalculable intrusive force of historical events. Useful generalizations are hard to come by. This complex of factors is entirely at odds with Judeo-Bolshevism as a form of paranoia that simply blames "the Jews" for Bolshevism. Understanding its power requires the historian to ask what the idea meant to those who used it and treated it as "real," not to investigate to what extent it was or was not true. War and revolution made Judeo-Bolshevism seem an utterly new danger. But the fear and loathing it excited derived from a particular set of much older anti-Jewish prejudices.

In July 1920, Poland's Catholic bishops sent a cry of distress to their fellow bishops around the world. After more than a century, Poland had been reborn. Erased from the map of Europe in the late 1700s, a new Polish state now emerged from the ruins of three East European empires. But the battles fought to secure the borders of the new Poland were part of the bloody civil war that raged across the lands of the old Russian empire. To Poland's east, the new Bolshevik state in Russia had gained the upper hand at last over its counterrevolutionary rivals and now hoped to spread the revolution westward. After initial successes, the Polish army had been forced to retreat all the way to the outskirts of Warsaw, and now Poland's fate hung in the balance. If Warsaw fell the state would vanish once again, and the Red Army could well begin to march on Berlin. In this crisis, the leaders of Poland's Catholic Church wanted to remind Europe that Poland fought on the front line in its defense and to warn of the danger that would spread if that line broke. The letter read in part: "Bolshevism is striding toward the conquest of the world. The race that has led Bolshevism has already made the world subject to gold and banks, and today, driven by the eternal imperialist desire that flows in its veins, turns to the last campaign of conquest in order to force the nations under the yoke of its regime. . . . Bolshevism is truly the living embodiment and manifestation of the Antichrist on earth."[30]

The Polish line held, and the Red Army retreated eastward. The "miracle on the Vistula" entered Polish national memory as a moment when divine grace intervened in human events to protect one of God's chosen nations. However, the specter that the Polish bishops had seen looming over Warsaw in the summer of 1920 did not disappear. In their letter, Poland's Catholic leaders had put a specific face on the doom that their country and all of Europe faced if the Red Army should triumph. Jews were the agents and leaders of the Bolshevik peril. They personified the rising power in the East that threatened all of European Christendom. And Judeo-Bolshevism also breathed new life into older versions of anti-Jewish hatred. Indifferent to the logical absurdity, the bishops tied "Jewish" revolution against capitalism to the power of modern finance capitalism itself, a force associated with Jews since the nineteenth century. Both, in turn, were signs of Jews' unslakable thirst for power and their ability to manipulate all kinds of rulers to their advantage, a narrative of Jewish evil that had roots in early modern fears of Jewish power and misrule. The bishops proclaimed Judeo-Bolshevism to be the manifestation of the Antichrist, an even older form of anti-Judaism with roots in the earliest days of Christianity. Without question, the bishops' fear and hatred of Jewish Bolshevism was connected to many other older varieties of anti-Jewish hate. Responding to an utterly new and unprecedented political threat, Bolshevism, the bishops gave it a very old name: the Jew.

A search for the origins of Judeo-Bolshevism can easily lead to a series of near-infinite regressions, from the Russian revolutions of 1905–1906, when Jews were also associated with political unrest, to the nineteenth century, when fears of global Jewish power seemed real to Europeans across the Continent, and back to the Middle Ages and ultimately to the time of the Gospels, when Jews were first marked as evil and hostile to the Christian order on earth. The Judeo-Bolshevik myth was one type of antisemitism among many. It bled easily into other anti-Jewish stereotypes, like that of the malevolent Jewish cabal that had plotted Christianity's downfall for centuries, or the cunning and malicious Jewish financier who only seemed, at first, to be diametrically opposed to Bolshevik revolution. The Judeo-Bolshevik peril was constructed from the raw materials of anti-Judaism, recycled and rearranged to meet new requirements. But that

does not mean it was the same as any other kind of anti-Jewish hatred. Judeo-Bolshevism foregrounded certain stereotypes about Jews
and not others and loaded them with new meaning.

The idea of Judeo-Bolshevism rested on three venerable pillars of
anti-Jewish thought. First, the concept was built on a long history of
associating Jews and Judaism with heresy, misrule, and social dishar-
mony. Jews (as rhetorical constructs) were symbolically rich and malleable figures, useful in defining both the nature and the boundaries
of the well-ordered Christian state in historical-cultural eras ranging
from the Spanish Inquisition to Reformation Germany to revolution-
era France torn between Enlightenment and Counter-Enlightenment.
Exactly how the figure of the Jew was put to use and (more important) what consequences this had for Jews at the time varied, of
course. In the long and complex history of Christian-Jewish relations,
however, the suggestive power of the Christian-Jewish binary remained a constant, available to a wide variety of political and social
theorists who wanted to clarify their thoughts about the perils of
secularism, the rights of a Christian ruler, and the foundations of
social order. Much like witches and witchcraft in Renaissance Europe,
Jews and Judaism gave coherence to a variety of cultural visions by
suggesting what their inversion might look like. Conjuring a dystopia
in which Jews had social or political power made the ideal of the ordered Christian polity simultaneously more concrete and more beleaguered. Even as it was imagined, Christian civilization seemed in
dire need of defense.[31]

The threat of Judeo-Bolshevism rested on this conceptual history. Over the course of the nineteenth century, as Jews moved—
unevenly—from the margins of Christian European society into
new roles in economic and social life, new concerns arose about Jews
acting as, or one day becoming, a "state within the state." In imperial
Russia, tsarist officials worried about the loyalties of a generation of
newly assimilating Jews. Imagining a rising tide of Jewish power, they
imputed to Jews an "arrogance" that was manifest in revolutionary

movements intent on destroying the state. By the late nineteenth century, violent nationalist groups had formed for the purpose of defending Russia by teaching Jews a "lesson." In republican France, Édouard Drumont declared in *Jewish France*, one of the first "classics" of modern antisemitic literature, that Jews had already succeeded in taking power within the French state. When accounts of so-called Jewish Bolshevik rule in 1919 Hungary began to circulate in France, antisemitic reviewers received the news as proof of the "truth reported by Drumont."[32] Against the backdrop of the long association of Jews with political misrule and subversion, Jewish commissars were easily seen as the architects of a strange new world in which terror and decay replaced Christian order. In 1918 the Hungarian Catholic bishop Ottokár Prohászka warned that Jews were using the war to transform Hungary (Magyarország) into "Jew-country" (*Zsidóország*), by shirking military duty and consolidating their power at home. In 1919 he denounced the Bolshevik revolution in his country as the culmination of those plans and proof that he had been right to warn the Hungarian public about them.[33]

Second, the idea of Judeo-Bolshevism drew on well-established beliefs in an international Jewish conspiracy. Fear that revolution might spread across Europe and North America, which seemed plausible against the backdrop of widespread labor unrest, prepared a new generation of readers to find truth in the *Protocols of the Elders of Zion*. After 1917 this preposterous forgery, which purported to unmask a plot among Jewish leaders around the world to provoke disorder in many countries at once and then seize power amid the chaos, circulated like wildfire. Anti-Bolshevik émigrés from Russia brought copies to Germany. Catholic presses in France and Italy published new editions of the tract and claimed it was one more sign of an organized assault on Christian order and morality. One 1921 article in the Roman Jesuit journal *Civiltá Cattolica* concluded its (favorable) analysis of the *Protocols of the Elders of Zion* with this assertion: "Bolshevism is at base the old Judaism that tightens, with audacity and with the zeal that comes from having the better cause, the strings of world revolution in order to extend its plutocratic reign and to take advantage of Christian peoples."[34] Newspapers in Great Britain (the *Morning Post*) and the United States (Henry Ford's *Dearborn Independent*) published extensive commentaries on the *Protocols*, presenting the text to their readers as a reliable guide to world events. These commentaries were, in turn, translated into other languages for readers on the European continent, who ascribed special credibility to antisemitic paranoia when it came from Anglo-American sources. Adolf Hitler considered Henry Ford an authority on Jews. British commentaries in the *Morning Post* were collected and republished in Hungary by the antisemitic United Christian National League, under the title *Underground Conspirators*. The ultranationalist editors boasted in the foreword that their little book told a story that Hungarians, who had suffered through a "Jewish" Bolshevik regime of their own, knew intimately.[35]

Third and finally, the figure of the Jewish Bolshevik embodied in secularized form much older fears of Jewish fanaticism. For centuries, the paranoid belief that Jews performed bizarre religious rituals with fanatical and inhuman zeal resurfaced periodically across Europe, reinforcing religiously inspired connections to the idea that Jews were evil and fueling blood libel accusations. In late imperial Russia, the belief that Jews were religious fanatics who murdered Christian children for ritual purposes contributed to violent pogroms. It also took root in the minds of Nicholas II and his entourage, and imperial elites more generally, as a suspicion that Jews were driven to join revolutionary movements by a particularistic zeal for disorder.[36]

Echoes of this logic could be heard across Europe after 1917. In Hungary, the conservative intellectual Cécile Tormay described the leader of the Bolshevik paramilitary guard, Tibor Számuelly, as an executioner who was "brought up in the secret rites of hatred and belongs to an ultra-Orthodox sect of oriental Jews which is stricter in the observance of its ceremonies than any other. This . . . sect shuns the light of the sun. . . . [A]n 'eye for an eye, a tooth for a tooth' is the foundation of its creed. Számuelly's degenerate soul has been formed and shaped by these rites and teachings. . . . In [him] the revolution has found an executioner . . . who is blood of its blood and soul of its soul."[37]

In other places, an older language of Jewish fanaticism found updated expression in the understanding of revolution as a secularized version of Jewish messianism. This was especially true within Catholic intellectual circles. Before he broke with the fascist group Action Française, the philosopher Jacques Maritain understood the association of Jews and revolution in this way. Jews, he insisted, were "an essentially messianic people" who inevitably played a "subversive role in the world" because their peculiar "messianic hopes and passion for justice" became the "most active ferment of revolution" when they were brought down from the "supernatural to the national level."[38]

The long history of anti-Judaism made Judeo-Bolshevism a coherent idea. It combined a specific set of old anti-Jewish stereotypes and transformed them into something that looked new. But Judeo-Bolshevism did not become the ideological issue that it did simply because it translated fast-moving and bewildering political events into more familiar language. The connection between Jews and revolution became self-evident to so many when it was debated in many different national contexts all at once. After 1917, the ubiquity of Judeo-Bolshevism made it seem "real."

The idea of Judeo-Bolshevism circulated across the borders of postwar Europe in newspaper accounts, thought pieces, books of reportage, and the tales of émigrés who described the reality of Jewish Bolshevik terror with the voice of "authentic" experience. Everywhere, readers were encouraged to make connections between faraway upheavals and domestic threats to social and moral order. Judeo-Bolshevism gave local fears of political upheaval and cultural dislocation a pan-European significance. In this lay its formidable political power. It gave an international perspective to parochial anxieties about the nation and its enemies. Examples of Judeo-Bolshevik power were endlessly cross-referential: the "unmasking" of Jewish revolutionaries in one place gave credibility to accusations of Jewish subversion in another. This circulation and mimetic reproduction had a "reality effect." Through constant repetition, in multiple countries and languages simultaneously, the specter of the Jewish Bolshevik came to seem real. After 1917, the image went "viral."

Fear of Judeo-Bolshevism circulated through a variety of different networks. The letter that Poland's bishops wrote to their fellow leaders of the Roman Catholic Church was reproduced in Catholic publications and shared among Catholic publics primed by the "culture wars" of the nineteenth century to see distant assaults on Christian order as signs of an impending assault on the faith at home. Though Catholics had fought and died in the trenches on both sides in World War I, Catholic publication networks throughout Europe spread fears about Bolshevik disorder and the Jewish conspiracy that might lie behind it. Catholics in France and Italy shared wisdom about the *Protocols of the Elders of Zion* and the insight that it gave into the dangers of the postwar world in journals like *The International Review of Secret Societies*, edited by the conspiracy theorist Monsignor Ernest Jouin. News of Bolshevik power in Hungary or the threat of Soviet invasion in Poland was only more grist for their mill. Similarly, the Viennese Catholic publicist Joseph Eberle filled the pages of his new journal, *Das neue Reich* (The new empire), with explorations of the relationship between Bolshevism and the Jewish question. Eberle's journal also brought together images of Judeo-Bolshevism produced in a variety of regional Catholic cultures. In 1919 he published several essays by the Hungarian Catholic bishop and rabid antisemite Ottokár Prohászka. He also found space for pieces written in Bavaria by like-minded Austro-German Catholics, such as Franz

Schrönghamer-Heimdal, a virulent racist who joined the Nazi Party just months after Adolf Hitler because he blamed Jews for the collapse of order in Germany and the rise of revolutionary government in Munich. French and German Catholics may have been divided by the war, but conservative and nationalistic publicists on both sides of that political gulf still found remarkably similar uses for the same anti-Bolshevik material.[39]

Journalists also wrote about the Judeo-Bolshevik threat. One was the British journalist Robert Wilton. When revolution broke out in Russia, Wilton was the chief correspondent for the *Times* of London stationed in Saint Petersburg. Wilton had lived and worked in Russia since the 1880s and knew the country and its imperial elites well. Throughout 1917 Wilton followed revolutionary events closely, filing detailed and highly influential reports for the prestigious British newspaper. He also took sides. Before the October Revolution, he supported military efforts to suppress the Bolsheviks. When Lenin seized power, Wilton fled the capital for Siberia, where Admiral Alexander Kolchak led a counterrevolutionary (White) government. After Kolchak's defeat, the British journalist left Russia for good and made his way to Paris. Throughout this time, Wilton tried to understand the causes of the revolution and why the Bolshevik Party had taken it in such a radical and (to his mind) disastrous direction.

Robert Wilton always insisted that Bolshevism had no roots in Russian culture at all. He concluded that it was the work of a Jewish conspiracy. He expanded on this idea in a book-length account of the Russian Revolution that he published in 1919. According to Wilton, the "seething mass of Jewish pauperdom" had reached eagerly for the teachings of Karl Marx ("a German Jew"). As Jews from imperial Russia's Pale of Settlement migrated throughout Russia and abroad, they carried Marx's teachings with them, "decocted in their quintessence." The result was a violent and destructive revolution, "carried out by a handful of pseudo-Jew Extremists" who wished to destroy every trace of traditional order and impose a cruel and twisted dictatorship of

their own in its place.[40] Wilton pursued this theme in other books
about the Russian Revolution for British readers, including a lovingly
sympathetic account of the last days of the Romanovs. Their deaths,
he insisted, had been an act of Jewish ritual murder.[41]

Wilton's views perfectly mirrored the prejudices of imperial Russia's toppled elites, whom he admired so much. During the war the
empire had forcibly relocated between half a million and a million
Jews from the western borderlands because they believed that Jews
would betray the war effort. After the empire collapsed, imperial loy-
alists formed the counterrevolutionary White Army, which named
Jews as allies or agents of the Bolshevik enemy. Wilton's journalism
resonated with a broad spectrum of *Times* readers immediately after
the war in surprising ways, even if nothing about life in postwar Britain
bore the slightest resemblance to the imperial collapse, political upheaval, or intensity of violence in Russia during the revolution and
ensuing civil war. Suspicions of Jewish disloyalty, especially among
Russian Jewish immigrants in London's East End, had been common
in Britain during World War I. After the war, increased labor activism
at home and anticolonial unrest overseas dismayed conservatives, who
wanted to restore imperial order at home and abroad as if nothing had
happened and the war had not touched every aspect of British life.

Conspiracy theories flourished in this climate. Extremist newspapers like the *Morning Post* ran widely discussed analyses of world
unrest that blamed Jews for upheavals in Russia, Ireland, and India.
Well-born conspiracy theorists like Nesta Webster enjoyed a moment
of notoriety with their denunciations of Jewish Bolsheviks as "modern
Illuminati" whose campaign of destruction "led many people to believe in the theory of a Jewish conspiracy to destroy Christianity."[42]
Webster's arguments impressed the young Winston Churchill, who
marveled at the power of Jewish nationalism in Palestine but was
deeply troubled by the role he believed Jews had played in the destruction of the Russian Empire. "Mrs. Webster," he wrote, had "ably
shown" that Jews had played a central role in the Bolshevik revolution.[43] Even among responsible policy makers, it was generally ac-

cepted that the prominence of Jews in the Russian Revolution was a factor that had to be considered in any discussion condemning the Whites for anti-Jewish violence.[44]

Political émigrés carried stories of Jewish revolutionary terror with them into exile. After the Russian Civil War, adherents of the White cause fled westward to safety, dreaming of returning one day to overthrow the Bolshevik usurpers. Some found refuge in Romania, where they made contact with young antisemitic activists like Corneliu Codreanu, the future leader of the fascist Iron Guard.[45] Others fled to France, where their dire warnings about the evils of Bolshevism found a warm welcome in Catholic and monarchist circles.[46] Still others ended up in Germany. After 1917 Germany was a magnet for refugees fleeing Bolshevik rule in Russia. German intervention in the Baltics in 1919 created another point of contact, when Baltic Germans acted as intermediaries between White Russian forces and German paramilitary troops fighting in Latvia. When this campaign failed, many Russian counterrevolutionaries escaped to Berlin, Munich, and other cities, where they dreamed impossible fantasies of a racist German–White Russian alliance that could topple the Weimar Republic, defeat Bolshevism in Russia, and then remake all of Eastern Europe. They also encountered local German nationalists, to whom they expressed their fervent belief that a sinister Jewish Bolshevik conspiracy had destroyed imperial Russia, and offered as proof a variety of texts, including a version of the *Protocols of the Elders of Zion.*[47]

One prominent émigré who claimed to speak about the Bolshevik cataclysm from bitter personal experience was Alfred Rosenberg, who later became one of the leading ideologues of the Nazi movement. Born in Reval (today, Tallinn in Estonia), the Baltic German émigré impressed local radicals in Germany with firsthand accounts of the Jewish Bolshevik enemy: "From 1917 to February 1918, I traveled Russia from Petersburg to the Crimea," he wrote in 1920. "Wherever Bolsheviks appeared, 90 out of 100 were Jews."[48] Publishing houses and newspapers on the German far right published these works and analyzed them at length. Soon Rosenberg was writing for the *Völkische*

Beobachter, the newspaper of the fledgling Nazi Party. Partly under the influence of these émigrés, Adolf Hitler became more interested in the events of the Russian Revolution in the second half of 1920.[49] But Hitler, and the extremists who followed him, did not need the Russian émigrés to demonstrate that revolution at home and abroad was a Jewish plot. They came to that conclusion on their own, and then took the news that men like Rosenberg brought them from Russia as proof that they had been right all along. Using tales of revolutionary disorder and Jewish tyranny in Russia as signs of their own credibility, they deliberately stoked fears of a Bolshevik coup by linking strikes and worker unrest to the political activities of Russian revolutionaries like Grigorii Zinoviev, who traveled Germany in 1920 exhorting workers to embrace the global revolutionary vision of the Communist International. To Germany's newly empowered far right, these were clear signs of a "final violent test of power between order-loving Germans and Communists incited by Jewish slave-drivers."[50]

Vienna was another city where different strands of anti-Bolshevik thought converged. After Béla Kun took power in neighboring Hungary, Hungarian conservatives fled across the border to the Austrian capital. They found the city at the center of an ideological contest for control of the young Austrian republic. Socialists dominated the Viennese municipal government, while the Christian Social press denounced Marxist, cosmopolitan, and Jewish power in the city. In this climate, the Christian Social Party's daily newspaper happily offered Hungary's counterrevolutionary exiles a forum in which to discuss the evils of Bolshevism. In a series of articles published in March and April 1919, unnamed authors, described by the editors as concerned Hungarians, routinely described the Bolshevik regime in power in their homeland as a horrible plot led by Jews that in no way reflected the beliefs and hopes of "true" Hungarians.[51] At the same time, Austrian analysts interpreted their tales of woe as an ominous warning about what could happen in Austria. When a railway workers' strike failed in late March 1919, one writer contrasted that happy turn of events to the catastrophe unfolding across Austria's eastern border, arguing that Austria must remain ever vigilant against threats to civilization coming from the East.[52]

Rhetorical similarity disguised the fact that the meaning of "Jewish Bolshevik" changed in translation, despite the short distance between Vienna and Budapest. In Hungary, a Bolshevik party had seized power, sweeping aside or co-opting other leftist groups. After their defeat, counterrevolutionaries faced the task of undoing everything their enemies had done and rendering it illegitimate and antinational. A new language of Christian nationalism sharpened these dichotomies. In Austria, by contrast, it had been socialists, not the Right, who had forcefully marginalized the Communist Party. Self-styled Christian conservatives did not have the possibility of rebuilding a society to their liking in the aftermath of a failed revolution. Instead, they faced a well-organized Socialist camp that had deep electoral support and a confident cultural vision for the future of Austrian society. The specter of Judeo-Bolshevism did not reference fears of revolution. Instead, it projected anxieties about the prospect of Red Vienna ascendant: the cultural and social hegemony of a (nonrevolutionary) Marxist formation. In both places, the meaning of the Jewish Bolshevik was used to delegitimize political alternatives. But the enemies were very different.

Circulation and repetition breathed new life into old anti-Jewish themes, configuring them for a rapidly changing ideological context. One more aspect gave the idea of Judeo-Bolshevism a fierce hold on the imaginations of Europeans in these years. The association of Jews with Russian Bolshevism was closely connected to fears that a bestial threat had arisen in the East and now threatened civilization itself.

In the summer of 1920, two French writers, Jérôme and Jean Tharaud, toured Hungary for four months to research a book. The country offered them dramatic material. The Austro-Hungarian monarchy had collapsed. Hungary had lost more than two-thirds of its territory to its neighbors and was now a small country; it had also seen two revolutions in rapid succession. The second of those revolutions had brought Hungary's Bolsheviks to power. Their rule had been brief but eventful, aiming at nothing less than the complete transformation of Hungary's semifeudal society. After the Bolsheviks were ousted, the country's old elites returned, riding a wave of paramilitary violence that targeted anyone associated with the hated revolution. It was, in short, a good story, one certain to interest readers in France. Boarding a train bound for Budapest, the Tharauds went to collect impressions about the Bolshevik revolution in Hungary. Their book appeared in France the following year. It bore the title *Quand Israël est roi* (*When Israel Is King*).[53]

The argument of the book was in the title. According to the Tharauds, Bolshevism in Hungary was essentially Jewish. Its leader, Béla Kun, was "a small-time Jewish clerk, round like a ball with huge bulging lips and a lizard head." Its chief police officer, Ottó Korvin, was "a small, hunchbacked, scrofulous Jew—from what sewer had he come to light?" The French brothers also found other Jews in the Bolshevik regime, serving as its leading theoreticians and chief ministers as well as commanders of security detachments created to intimidate and terrorize "class enemies." The rise of these Jewish radicals from obscurity to the heights of power fascinated the Tharauds, who devoted much of their book to telling a long story of Hungary's decline as a nation that ended in the catastrophe of Bolshevism. Migrant Jews, they wrote, had come from the East over many years. As their numbers grew, they began to change the character of the society around them. A traditional Christian society, protected across the centuries by a nobility that embodied the nation's proud history, was replaced by an alien and disorienting modernity at odds with everything old and true. The Bolshevik revolution had nearly been the death blow: "A few weeks in Budapest sufficed to overthrow a society built up over centuries. On the banks of the

Danube a new Jerusalem arose, sprung from the mind of Karl Marx and built by Jewish hands on ancient [messianic] thoughts."[54]

All the drama of the book came from the vivid contrast between the old and new regime. The Tharauds eulogized Hungary's traditional aristocratic society for its elegance and nobility. In the medieval past, they wrote, Hungary had fought to defend Christian Europe ("our civilization") in "battle against the Orient." Its contacts with Latin civilization had given it a refined, beautiful, and "Western appearance." Long after the medieval glories had faded, this legacy continued to define Hungarian society. Hungary's Bolshevik revolution was so momentous, and thus relevant to the Tharauds' French readers, because its leaders had done more than seize power. They had deliberately attacked the culture that Hungary shared with Europe and replaced it with a harsh and brutal dystopia.[55]

What and who lurked on the edges of civilization transfixed the Tharauds throughout their long joint career. The two brothers built their literary reputation on lyrical and essayistic depictions of peoples on the margins of Europe whose strange "otherness" contrasted so vividly with the Tharauds' sense of what it meant to be French and European. Typically they cast these reflections—as in *When Israel Is King*—in the form of literary travelogues that portrayed the Jews of Eastern Europe and the Arabs of North Africa in colorful and exotic detail as the antitheses of Christian European culture. In an earlier book, for example, the two had meditated on the eternal strangeness of the Hasidic Jews who lived in the Carpathian Mountains, at that time the northeasternmost part of the Hungarian half of the Austro-Hungarian monarchy.[56] Sometimes they rendered these alien people as picturesque and sympathetic. In more than one book, the Tharauds contrasted the spiritual richness of Eastern European Jews with an increasingly materialistic West. But in other books, such as *When Israel Is King*, the Tharauds imagined this difference in menacing terms, warning readers of the profound threat that these outsiders posed to Europe's civilization and way of life.[57]

Jérôme and Jean Tharaud were disciples of Maurice Barrés, whose vision of an integral French nation rooted in the soil of its ancestors fired the imaginations of several generations of French intellectuals. The two even dedicated *When Israel Is King* to Barrés, their "master and friend." No doubt their old teacher liked the book, since he spoke about Bolshevism in the same way they did. When the wave of mass strikes in 1920 failed to overturn the political order in France, Maurice Barrés exulted: Bolshevism "will not overthrow civilization here. . . . France . . . will not take orders from the muck of Asiatic saboteurs."[58] The word "Asiatic" was no accident. Judeo-Bolshevism was not only a new way to refashion old fears of Jewish conspiracy or Jewish fanaticism. Its rich symbolic power was also easily harnessed to a style of cultural pessimism that flourished across Europe after 1918 among both the winners and losers of the war. Beset by anxieties about the vitality of European civilization, nationalist intellectuals, like Barrés and the Tharauds, projected their fears and fantasies about the decline of the West onto a stylized (and geographically imprecise) East that embodied a brutal and primitive vitality alien to the more refined, but also more fragile, Europe.

One version of this fantasy resurrected ancient histories of invasions from the East by Tatars, Mongols, or Islam, casting Europe's fight against Bolshevism as the latest "clash of civilizations." Still another cast Russia as Europe's eastern "other," and understood Bolshevism as the inevitable product of a barbarous place inhabited by a variety of uncivilized races. Another cast Jews as the quintessentially "Eastern" (read: un-European) people, occasionally admired for their spiritual vitality but more frequently abhorred for their promiscuous border crossing and their disregard for the traditions and order customary in those places where they settled. The idea of Judeo-Bolshevism brought all these strands of thought into an image that represented the dangers to Europe's cultural order as a primitive and brutal force, bred in the uncivilized "muck" beyond the eastern limits of Europe and carried by eastern Jews to the West, where it threatened the foundations of a tottering civilization. The Bolshevik was at once a rootless migrant Jew, the sign of an invading horde from the East, and an Asiatic beast.

In Eastern Europe, the threat of "Asiatic Bolshevism" fit neatly into historical memories of earlier invasions from the East that began with the Mongols and Tatars but more often invoked the wars against the Ottoman Empire and Islam. Polish nationalists remembered the first Polish republic's long wars against Islamic Ottoman invaders in the sixteenth and seventeenth centuries. It had been the Polish army that had lifted the Turkish siege of Vienna in 1683 and pushed the Ottoman Empire into perpetual retreat. For this, Poland had won accolades and the title *antemurale Christianitatis*, the defense wall of Christendom. This legacy seemed especially meaningful in 1920, as the Red Army advanced on Warsaw and deep into the heart of Europe. Polish defeat would expose all of Central Europe to Russian Bolshevik invasion. When the Polish line held outside Warsaw, the battle became known in Poland as the miracle on the Vistula to suggest that divine intervention had saved both the nation and Europe from the godless hordes. One Polish newspaper explained that "Bolshevism is not, as we have already emphasized, a renewal in the history of humanity. The steppes of the Turanian nomads of Asia are its cradle. From the swarming heap, the hordes of Attila and Tamerlan swashed into Europe."[59]

This language, at once deeply Christian and also orientalizing in equal measure, alternated with depictions of the Red Army as a mob of inhuman beasts. During the war, the Polish military circulated posters exhorting its soldiers and the public to defend Poland to the end. In one image, entitled "Beat the Bolshevik!" a dashing Polish cavalier with raised sword drives an ape in a Red Army uniform before him. The dashing Polish cavalier recalls historical memories of earlier wars to defend the freedom of Christian Europe from invaders to the East. With noble figure and determined mien, he presents a clear contrast to the brutish black ape, whose eyes betray fear and whose cap, too large for his head, looks simply ridiculous. Bolshevism was not only an ideological threat. The racial and evolutionary contrast in the poster's image suggested it was also a threat to culture and civilization.

Another Polish anti-Bolshevik poster, circulated by Poland's Ministry of Military Affairs to counter Red Army propaganda during the 1920 war, tied these themes together. In this image, Leon Trotsky appears as a naked red devil, perched on a pile of skulls with a pistol in one hand and a bloody dagger in the other. The figure stares intently ahead while Death whispers in his ear from behind; in the near background, Red Army troops (again with vaguely Asian facial features) club a body with their rifles as the skulls mount around them. In the far distance, a village burns. Above the scene, the poster reads: "Bolshevik Freedom." The text at the bottom describes Bolsheviks as liars and warmongers who bring only hunger and slavery. Depicting Leon Trotsky like this was a deliberate choice. Trotsky was the founder and commander of the Red Army that was fighting to bring the revolution westward. He was also the most prominent and best-known Jewish Bolshevik, a man whose Jewish origins had been pointed out again and again in the press, from one end of Europe to the other. Picturing Trotsky in devil form captured the widespread and very real fear of Russian Bolshevik occupation. It also drew on a long tradition of representing Jews as demons and Jewish designs as evil. In this poster, the Jewish Bolshevik Trotsky looks on intently as the Asiatic horde that he has created unleashes its fury on the Polish countryside.

Many officers in the new Polish army had begun their careers in the Imperial Russian Army, where the belief that Jews were responsible for Bolshevism was widespread.[60] This may partly explain why the "Bolshevik Freedom" poster bears such a striking similarity to anti-Bolshevik propaganda circulated by the counterrevolutionary White Army fighting in Russia. During the Russian Civil

War, the White Army created an information agency to influence popular opinion about the revolution.[61] To that end, a propaganda department designed posters to undermine popular support for the Bolshevik enemies. Leon Trotsky was "enemy number one." In one well-known poster, titled ironically "Peace and Freedom in Sovdepia"— a term coined by the Whites to mean the lands of Russia under Bolshevik control—Trotsky appears as a gigantic naked red beast. He straddles the walls of the Kremlin, a Star of David around his body, his hands and feet dripping with blood. Atop the city's cathedrals, flags have replaced crosses. Below the looming Trotsky, Chinese Red Army soldiers—symbolizing the "Asiatic" horde sweeping across Russia—execute captive prisoners. All around them, a sea of skulls and bones give evidence of Bolshevik cruelty. The figure of Trotsky represents Jewish power, which has swept away traditional authority and made an alien force the master of Russia. The Soviet flags flying from the Kremlin while soldiers from East Asia execute Russian prisoners tell the tale in one way. The physical ease with which the monster reclines languorously against the buildings of the Kremlin—his nakedness hidden by a strategically placed turret; the blood of his victims running slowly down the wall—tells it in another. The image suggests an animal sated after violating the most sacred Russian places. With his abnormally thick and hairy limbs splayed over the Kremlin walls, the Jewish Bolshevik figure in the poster is in every sense of the word a monster: abnormal, rapacious, implacable, and utterly alien to the Russian nation. To the peasants who were the intended audience, this horrific vision would indeed have been an illustration of the apocalypse.[62]

The imperial Russian context was not the only one that gave meaning to Poland's fight against "Asiatic" and "Jewish" Bolshevism. Shared memories of defending Europe from eastern or Islamic invaders were prominent in other national traditions as well. Hungarians remembered their wars with the Ottoman Empire and believed that the heroism of their forebears in both defeat and victory had proven Hungary also to be one of Christendom's protective walls. After 1919, many compared the Ottoman occupation of Hungary in the sixteenth century to the modern tragedies of territorial loss and revolutionary upheaval. Hungarian Catholics, in particular, found inspiration in the historical role of their Church in re-Christianizing Hungary after the Turks had been expelled, and called for a new "counterreformation" to heal the wounds of Bolshevik rule.[63] These historical memories of civilizational clashes merged easily with racial understandings of what the rebirth of Christian Hungary after revolution meant. Before the war, the Roman Catholic Bishop Ottokár Prohászka had described socialism as "a new Islam." After 1919, he declared Communism to be a Jewish ideology. The Bolshevik regime had been a "Russian-Jewish invasion" akin to earlier barbarian invasions from the East. A new eastern horde, not of Turks or Tatars this time, but of Bolsheviks and Jews, had marched into the West, spreading terror and the "brutality of entirely alien elements." Hungarians had taken its measure and seen "in the dark red glow of the proletarian dictatorship . . . the madness of racial imperialism."[64] They responded by raising their nation's banners against the enemy. They had fought to defend Christian Europe.[65]

Across Europe, the fears and anxieties triggered by revolution were crystallized in the figure of the Jewish Bolshevik. For many, the triumph, however short-lived, of Bolshevik regimes in the heart of Central Europe and the newfound militancy of the workers' movement throughout the Continent gave rise to the nightmarish thought that revolutionary unrest was like a disease that respected no borders. In this climate, Judeo-Bolshevism revived old anti-Jewish themes of disorder, conspiracy, and fanaticism and reshaped them into a critique of Bolshevism that was broadly persuasive, and not only to those who stood on the fringes of the far right. Described and debated so often and in so many different media, the equation of Jews and Bolshevik revolution was transformed from a paranoid generalization into an "objective" fact. Judeo-Bolshevism came to seem real.

The raw materials of the Judeo-Bolshevik idea circulated freely across Europe from east to west and back again. In Eastern Europe, however, they seemed especially salient. There, war and revolution had destroyed the great land empires that had dominated the region before 1914. A new state order emerged slowly and painfully, born amid an explosion of violent conflicts that pitted a variety of nationalist forces against one another and all of them against the Bolsheviks. Often Jews bore the brunt of this violence because it was said that they supported Bolshevism. In Eastern Europe, the idea of Judeo-Bolshevism was inseparable from violence against Jews.

2

The Greater War

Today, Khmelnytsky is a city of more than 250,000 people on the banks of the Southern Bug River in the western part of Ukraine. Located in the historic region of Podolia, its name recalls Bohdan Khmelnytsky the seventeenth-century Cossack leader revered as a national hero in Ukraine for heading a rebellion against Polish rule in 1648. The fact that Khmelnytsky's uprising also sparked a massive wave of attacks by Christian peasants against Jews that claimed the lives of tens of thousands of people went unmentioned in 1954, when Soviet officials gave Khmelnytsky its current name. Before then, the city was called Proskurov (Ukrainian: Proskuriv; Polish: Płoskirów). At the turn of the twentieth century it was a much smaller town, with perhaps one-tenth of the population that it would come to have after World War II. Jews, almost 40 percent of the population then, were prominent in the city, as they were in towns all across the Pale of Settlement. When the Russian empire collapsed and revolution broke out, Ukrainian cities like Proskurov found themselves at the center of a vicious civil war. A new Ukrainian national government claimed the region. So did the Bolshevik Red Army. Soon a counter-revolutionary White Army eager to restore the tsarist autocracy would enter the fray, as would various unaffiliated bands of peasant marauders. Though Proskurov's Jews rejoiced at the demise of the repressive and frequently antisemitic tsarist autocracy, they quickly found themselves caught in the middle of the struggle between the parties warring to replace it. In February 1919, their precarious situation turned deadly.

Early in February, soldiers fighting for the fledgling Ukrainian national government of Symon Petliura entered Proskurov. Their commander, the ataman (or warlord) Semesenko, quickly placed the city under martial law and issued a formal warning addressed to the town's Jews ("Wretched nation, troubling poor people"), ordering them to refrain from "anarchist demonstrations."[1] Soon after, local Communists decided to launch an uprising against Ukrainian power across the whole of Podolia, beginning in Proskurov. Their uprising was hastily planned, poorly conceived, and a dismal failure. Semesenko's troops quickly stamped out all armed resistance. In the aftermath, however, Semesenko resolved to exact retribution for the Communist plot by ordering his troops to murder the local Jewish population. (Very few of the town's Jews were involved in the local Communist Party in any way. However, Semesenko considered all Jews Communists or Communist sympathizers.) Semesenko's men hunted Jews down in the streets, invaded their homes, and slaughtered entire families. At first, they followed orders not to loot Jewish property, but by the first evening they had completely forgotten this command. In all, Semesenko's troops killed 1,500 Jews, including the elderly and children, over the course of two days.[2]

The pogrom in Proskurov was not an isolated atrocity. Nor was it even the bloodiest massacre of Jews in the civil war that raged across the lands of the former tsarist empire. Between 1918 and 1921, there were more than 2,000 pogroms, most of them in Ukraine. Even the Red Army units attacked Jews, especially in the early stages of the civil war. But most of the violence was committed by anti-Bolshevik forces, especially by the counterrevolutionary Whites who wanted to restore

the Romanov dynasty, and by rival armed groups loyal to the Ukrainian national government, who fought to establish an independent
and sovereign Ukraine. Sometimes these groups attacked Jews
simply to plunder their belongings. More often, they justified their
attacks by accusing Jews of Communist political activity or of helping
the Red Army by hiding weapons, undertaking acts of sabotage, or
generally sympathizing with Bolshevism. The precise number of
victims is difficult to determine. According to one recent study,
30,000 Jews were killed directly and another 150,000 died because
of mortal wounds or diseases that were the results of the violence.
Across Ukraine, Jewish communities were in ruins. Half a million
people were homeless. Thousands of children became orphans. A
wave of refugees fled across the borders into Romania and the newly
created states of Poland, Latvia, and Lithuania.[3]

Around the world, Jewish communities mobilized to meet the humanitarian crisis. *Landsmanshaftn*, or mutual aid societies in the diaspora, held public rallies to call attention to the slaughter and to
raise money to help the victims. Relief workers from groups like the
Joint Distribution Committee, working on their own or in coopera-
tion with the International Red Cross, rushed to the region to distribute food and medical aid to the wounded and to provide shelter
and assistance to the displaced. Jewish journalists traveled within the
war zone, sending back impressions and reports for newspapers in
New York and London. Jewish relief agencies and activists also worked
closely with local communities in Ukraine to collect information.
They interviewed survivors, held community meetings in larger towns
and cities, and gathered public documents issued by the different parties to the civil war. On one level, their work was meant to chronicle
what was already understood at the time to be one of the greatest ca-
tastrophes in Jewish history. But it was also political. By establishing
the facts of the slaughter and bringing them to light, they hoped to
draw international attention to the special vulnerability of Jews in the
new Eastern Europe. More ambitiously, they hoped to influence de-

bates among diplomats of the victorious Western powers about how best to guarantee their security.[4]

Many reports of the humanitarian catastrophe were written in Yiddish and transmitted (and translated) by diaspora Jewish publics into broader circulation. Others were written in the languages of the Great Powers and intended for non-Jewish audiences. One such work was *The Slaughter of the Jews in the Ukraine in 1919*, by Elias Heifetz. A lawyer, Heifetz was chairman of the All-Ukrainian Relief Committee for the Victims of Pogroms, a humanitarian organization with ties to the Red Cross. In his book, Heifetz wrote about pogroms like the one at Proskurov. He also described harrowing personal testimony from survivors of the violence, who spoke of ransacked homes, family members hacked to pieces before their eyes, and friends and neighbors falsely accused of spying for the Bolsheviks, cruelly tortured, and murdered. These gruesome stories stirred Jewish memories of the devastation wrought by the Khmelnytsky uprising centuries earlier. But Heifetz insisted that the current crisis could not be explained simply as the latest expression of an ancient hatred that Jews in the diaspora had always faced. He argued that violence against Jews had become a form of "political warfare" in 1919 Ukraine.[5]

The pogroms, Heifetz wrote, had nothing to do with choices that Jews had made or not made. Instead, they were a political tool that helped different warring parties to unify their disparate forces and whip up popular support for their cause. The loosely organized Ukrainian forces fighting for the Ukrainian National Republic headed by Symon Petliura waged war against the Judeo-Bolshevik enemy in order to associate their actions with the loftier common goal of establishing a secure and sovereign Ukrainian nation-state. The counterrevolutionary White Army invoked the same enemy for different reasons. They fought not to establish a new state but to restore an old one. Divided by factionalism and leadership conflicts, the Whites could agree on very little—except that Judeo-Bolshevism was the enemy. Fighting this menace created a common political purpose. It also allowed them to postpone difficult choices about the goals of the counterrevolutionary movement. For Heifetz, recognizing the fungible utility of the pogrom was crucial to understanding the scope and scale of violence against Jews during the Russian Civil War. Bitterly divided by their stated agendas, Ukrainian forces and the counterrevolutionary White Army were nevertheless bound together into one "continuous system" of violence that included reprisals against Jewish Bolsheviks and paranoid searches for Jewish Bolshevik partisans and spies. Whether committed by men fighting for a warlord like Ataman Semesenko or by soldiers in the White Army, these acts of violence had the same function: to identify and punish an enemy and to establish dominion over contested territory. The near universal panic over Judeo-Bolshevism had to be understood as a problem of political sovereignty.[6]

Elias Heifetz's interpretive approach to the 1919 pogroms in Ukraine was analytically sophisticated. It was also explosive, because it cast violence against Jews as a deliberate and illegitimate political act. Even as conflict continued to rage across Eastern Europe, Western peacemakers met in Paris to redraw the map of the Continent. Both Russian and Ukrainian diplomats lobbied desperately to influence the outcome in their favor, respectively. They also strenuously disputed the conclusions of men like Heifetz in meetings with representatives of the Western powers. Though the causes they served were utterly incompatible, Ukrainian diplomats and envoys from the White movement made similar arguments about the pogroms. They both denied that the violence against Jews was deliberate and found Jewish spokesmen willing to vouch for their tolerance. Both explained the pogroms as brutality carried out by rogue warlords who ignored the orders of the leaders they claimed to serve. And both insisted that if they could only establish a stable and wholly sovereign state, they would quickly put an end to the terror of such irregular warfare. Above all, they claimed that Judeo-Bolshevism was real. They reasoned that the undeniable presence of some Jews on the side of the Bolsheviks inevitably provoked violence during times of civil war. The bloodshed might be lamentable, but it did not diminish the legitimacy of their (separate, if similar) goals: to defeat Bolshevism and to create a national state. After the Russian Civil War was lost, exiled leaders of the White movement living in cities like Berlin and Paris made the idea of Judeo-Bolshevism central to the memory of the war that they constructed for themselves. So did exiled Ukrainian nationalists, who continued to fight against the charge that their efforts to establish a free and independent Ukraine in the face of a powerful Bolshevik enemy had been irredeemably tainted by antisemitism.[7]

Elias Heifetz's proposition—that anti-Jewish violence in 1919 Ukraine had a *political* rationale—is crucial for understanding how the idea of Judeo-Bolshevism functioned across Eastern Europe during the "long World War I" and why the memory of Jewish Bolshevik "enemies" cast such a long shadow in the decades that followed. War did not end here in November 1918 when the Germans signed the armistice in a railway car in Compiègne, France. Instead, it continued for several years in border wars, bloody cycles of revolutionary and counterrevolutionary violence, and security panics over shifting and porous national lines. Amid these upheavals, Judeo-Bolshevism loomed in political imagination throughout the region as a powerful transnational enemy. Fear of the Judeo-Bolshevik threat fueled violence in 1919 Ukraine. It also shaped political life in the new or newly formed states of Poland, Hungary, and Romania. As war bled into postwar life across Eastern Europe, wartime security concerns about saboteurs and traitors bred new anxieties about Jews and revolution.

Fears of spies and saboteurs had flourished in wartime Russia. Unlike the grinding battle for position on the Western Front, fighting in Eastern Europe during World War I swept mercilessly back and forth across the vast borderland shared by the Russian, German, and Austro-Hungarian Empires, an ethnically diverse area that covered much of the Pale of Settlement, where the Russian Empire had historically confined its Jewish subjects. As they devised strategies to defend this sensitive region, Russian military authorities identified Jews (as well as other ethnic minorities across the empire more generally, including Germans, Hungarians, Roma, and Turks) as unreliable elements disposed toward treason and espionage. Within the Russian army, reports that Jews communicated with the Germans through secret telephones, fabricated weapons "in their basements and slums," and sent money to the enemy were taken as entirely credible. Even more fanciful stories received due consideration: a priest in Volhynia believed that local Jews had hidden a telephone linked to the German command in the stomach of a cow; several reports from towns along the western border accused Jews of hiding messages to and from the Germans in the eggs of their chickens. The superficial similarity between German and Yiddish also seemed suspicious. Acting on these fears, Russian military authorities organized a series of mass deportations of "all Jews and suspect individuals" from the border regions. Between 1914 and 1917, Russian military authorities forcibly relocated between five hundred thousand and one million Jews. In some towns, army commanders also seized prominent local Jews, such as rabbis, as hostages who would vouch on pain of death for the good behavior of their entire community.[8]

Anti-Jewish violence accompanied these strategic measures. When the Russian army invaded Austrian Galicia in the summer of 1914, Cossack units incited pogroms in newly captured towns like Brody, Lwów (L'viv), and Radziłów. Military policies also opened the door to the looting of Jewish property. When orders went out to expel four thousand Jews from the area around Warsaw, the directive denied the affected Jews access to carts. The Jews fled their homes and businesses with only what they could carry, and local Poles immediately took what they left behind. Scenes like these were repeated on a wider scale the next year, when the Russian army was forced to retreat from its westernmost positions and military authorities imposed forced expulsions more systematically and on a wider scale. The accompanying pogroms were never official military policy, but expulsion orders again gave cover to Cossack units, which were almost always the ones that incited looting and violence in towns from Vilna (Vilnius today, in Lithuania) to Grodno (Hrodna, in Belarus). Often local peasants joined in plundering the property of Jewish "spies." Their zeal to seize the "illegitimate" property of "treasonous" Jews reflected the fevered circulation throughout the empire of rumors about Jewish plots that involved great wealth, shadowy international connections, and revolutionary insurrection. Such rumors only multiplied as the Russian Empire tottered under the economic strain of fighting a modern total war. One infamous circular from a high-ranking police official to all local governors and chiefs of police explained the wartime "Jewish" threat: "Knowing that neither military setbacks nor revolutionary agitation will have any lasting effect on the masses, the revolutionaries, the Jews that inspire them, and their secret German supporters now intend to incite discontent and protests against the war through the methods of famine and hyper-inflation."[9]

Romanian military officials were also obsessed with fears of Jewish espionage and betrayal. Romania did not enter the war until the summer of 1916, when it joined the side of the Allied powers in hopes of seizing territory from the Austro-Hungarian monarchy. But even before Romanian forces took the field, the Romanian parliament passed a law empowering military authorities to intern or remove foreigners from border regions when this was deemed necessary to maintain security and order. From the outset, military officials applied the law indiscriminately to all Jews in border areas, displacing whole families on the flimsiest of pretexts. The newspaper *Adevarul*, a rare voice of sympathy in the Romanian press, described their plight: "Wandering columns of refugees fill the country's roads," it reported, "dying of hunger and thrown on the mercy of the gendarmerie." Once Romania began fighting, anti-Jewish prejudice in the military intensified. General Constantin Prezan, chief of the General Staff, was notorious for filling his daily reports with reports of Jewish spies and saboteurs. Like his Russian counterparts, he too was suspicious of Yiddish, which he understood to be a German code. His views were echoed in the Romanian right-wing press, where articles about Jewish treason were common. This rhetoric encouraged local army commanders to flagrantly abuse their powers. Jewish organizations recorded numerous accounts of officers or soldiers seizing Jewish property or extorting money from Jews on the pretext that they had been spying for the enemy. Jewish soldiers in the army were also frequently accused of disloyalty and singled out for arbitrary punishment or mistreatment. In isolated cases, local commanders interned Jews for a time, subjected them to forced labor, and even sentenced some to death for alleged espionage. Jewish refugees fleeing across Romania's eastern border to escape the violent forced resettlements in the Russian Empire told of cruel mistreatment by Romanian army units. None of this was as lethal as the persecution of Jews in the Russian Empire, but it nevertheless left a powerful legacy for Romanian politics in the decades to come.[10]

War and the hysteria about Jewish reliability that it produced brought tremendous misery to Jewish communities across the historic Pale of Settlement. Some shtetls in Galicia were conquered and re-conquered a dozen times or more during the course of the war. Those caught up in the advance and retreat of the Russian army were subjected to the chaos of evacuation orders that were hastily carried out amid the fog of war. One witness to the misery that ensued was the Jewish writer S. Ansky. Familiar with the region from his prewar trips to study Jewish folklore, Ansky returned in 1915 as a political activist, intent on helping Jews in this borderland between warring armies and on getting word of their situation to the wider world. As war raged around him, Ansky desperately lobbied military and civilian officials on behalf of Jewish refugees and worked with local Jewish communities to raise money and distribute aid. In his memoirs of the time, published posthumously in 1925, certain scenes recur again and again:

numbingly regular looting and pogroms, the devastation of starvation and disease, recalcitrant authorities and hostile mobs. In the town of Vladimir-Volinsk (today, Volodymyr-Volynskyi in northwestern Ukraine), Ansky found "the Jews in dire straits because of a typhus and cholera epidemic. . . . Not a single doctor was left, and the only pharmacy was being evacuated." In Kobrin (Kobryn, in Belarus), he found the courtyard of the local synagogue "brimming with home-less Jews. The sick and the healthy were thrown together pell-mell, and all were marked by the bitterest want, poverty, and desolation." Panic at the train station followed as he negotiated space for these people on railroad cars that would take the refugees and their belong-ings away from the front. Ansky recalled having a difficult confron-tation with the station master when he tried to "wangle" more cars out of him. He also remembered "Gentiles, guffawing at these ghastly scenes."[11]

The more fortunate escaped to the west. Some 75,000 Jews fled war-torn Galicia for Vienna, the capital of the Austro-Hungarian monarchy. Another 25,000 sought shelter in Budapest, the empire's other capital. There they received the charity of imperial officials and private Jewish groups, who tried to provide the refugees with a min-imum of care and shelter. However, most of the people in both cities had little sympathy or understanding for the refugees and recoiled from their unwelcome presence. Soon Galician Jews were linked to worsening social tensions. In Vienna they were blamed for wartime food shortages; in Budapest, for the acute and growing lack of housing. In both places, the Jewish refugee came to symbolize profiteering, criminality, and black marketeering in the pages of the right-wing press and in the speeches of rabble-rousing politicians. The furor over the "flood" of refugees even provoked a debate in Hungary's most prominent sociological journal about whether or not Jews could truly assimilate into Hungarian society. The editors invited responses from leading intellectuals and tried to maintain a dispassionate tone, but the episode fueled ever more toxic anti-Jewish language. By 1918, doubts about the willingness of Jews to fight were being voiced in Hungarian newspapers. Soon, right-wing newspapers spoke darkly of "another Hungary" on the home front that had betrayed the real Hungary. Mounting anti-Jewish hostility soon forced the same liberal Jewish groups that had been generous with their charity to issue statements to the public reaffirming their patriotism and distancing themselves from the strange and foreign "eastern Jews" (*Ostjuden*). Their protests had little effect.[12]

Revolution erupted in 1917 on ground already shaped by wartime fears of Jewish treason and paranoia about "floods" of alien Jewish refugees. Russia's military policy of deporting Jewish "spies" from border areas forced imperial officials to abandon the legal restrictions that had confined the empire's Jews to the historic Pale of Settlement since the late eighteenth century. Their actions shattered the basic geography of Jewish life in Eastern Europe. Jews now seemed to be "everywhere," in part because so many of them were simply homeless. Some two-fifths of Jews forcibly displaced from their homes during war wound up in towns and cities in Russia where no Jews had ever lived. Others were displaced within the area of the former Pale, living in desperate circumstances in unfamiliar towns, dependent for survival on Jewish charity, and surrounded by local people who resented the newcomers as aliens and undeserving beggars. This hostility lingered long after the imperial authorities who had ordered the evacuations had vanished. When revolution toppled the tsar in March 1917 (February, according to the Julian calendar), monarchists linked the political turmoil to their paranoid belief in Jewish ubiquity. Wartime panic over masses of unsettled, suspect, and "out of place" Jews gave force to the embryonic White movement's propaganda, that Jews—regardless of ideological distinctions between Bolsheviks, Mensheviks, or other types of socialists—stood behind every twist in the course of the revolution. "Just a short time ago," read one pamphlet that circulated in 1917 Kiev, "the sun shone in Kiev and the tsar often came here. Now the Jews are everywhere! We want to throw off this yoke, we cannot bear it any longer! They will destroy the Fatherland. Down with the Jews! Give us back the tsar!" Their hysteria soon turned violent as the ideological chasm between revolutionaries and counterrevolutionaries widened.[13]

Wartime fears of spies and saboteurs who passed secrets to the enemy and poisoned the public mood shaped reactions to revolution elsewhere as well. Particular suspicion fell on Jews, despite the bravery with which many of them fought for their countries. When revolution came, it was easily understood as an act of sabotage committed by Jews. The panic over Judeo-Bolshevism that ensued flourished in ground that had been prepared by wartime paranoia about Jewish loyalty.

Polish troops in the town of Pinsk (Polish: Pińsk) had every reason to be on edge in early 1919. Today an industrial city of 130,000 in southwestern Belarus near the border with Ukraine, Pinsk in 1919 lay in a contested borderland that no one fully controlled. The newly reborn Poland claimed it. So did the Bolshevik regime in Russia. Between 1919 and 1921, the two states fought a bloody war, one of the many conflicts in the wider civil war that engulfed the lands of the former Russian Empire.[14] The strategic aims of the Polish government were clear: establish its existence as a state, define and secure its borders, and assert its sovereignty over ethnically, linguistically, and religiously heterogeneous territories. As the situation in and around Pinsk showed, these were not easy tasks. Pinsk was a largely Jewish town (74 percent of the population), surrounded by poor communities of Orthodox Slavic peasants. Only a small minority of townspeople identified themselves as ethnic Poles. In addition, there had been fierce clashes in the region between Polish troops and Bolshevik sympathizers. Thus, Polish control of Pinsk was by no means completely secure. For all these reasons, the commander of the local Polish garrison was inclined to believe reports he received in early April that Jewish revolutionaries were meeting to plot a rebellion. (In fact, Zionists had met only to discuss how to distribute charity baskets they had received from the United States.) Acting swiftly, he ordered his men to arrest some eighty Jews, whom they accused of being Bolshevik spies. The next day, the soldiers executed thirty-four of them.[15]

Rumors of armed Jewish collaboration with the Bolsheviks fueled violence against Jews in other places where Polish forces clashed with the Red Army. A few weeks later, Polish troops fought a pitched battle in Lida, some 250 kilometers north of Pinsk. On their first foray into the town, Polish troops searched the synagogue and the Jewish hospital for insurgents. After a brief reversal, they entered the town again, this time amid rumors that Jews had shot at Polish troops from windows and had even mutilated the bodies of dead Poles. Enraged Polish soldiers looted Jewish shops and homes, arrested dozens of Jews on suspicion of collaboration with the enemy, and then impressed local Jews into forced labor. Thirty-eight Jews were killed. Similar accusations accompanied the Polish soldiers' entry into the city of Vilnius (Polish: Wilno; Yiddish: Vilna). According to a report compiled by the local Jewish Committee and presented to Polish authorities, Jewish victims of reprisals were identified as Bolsheviks by strangers, sometimes even by children, according to their physical appearance. At least sixty Jews were killed. The authors of the report noted that Polish forces made little effort to learn much about what Jews had done or not done under Bolshevik rule before they imprisoned them. The fate of Leib Jaffe, poet and president of the Lithuanian Zionist Association, was typical. Polish authorities held him in prison on suspicion of being a Bolshevik sympathizer even though his newspaper had been suppressed by the Bolsheviks as counterrevolutionary propaganda.[16]

These attacks on Jewish civilians reflected the persistence of violence in a region where the First World War evolved into a series of interlocking regional wars that unfolded against the backdrop of revolution. As the war evolved, so too did wartime fears about Jewish spies and saboteurs. These were reframed and linked to a new threat: the Jewish partisan. Elusive enemies, partisans (or *francs-tireurs*) were imagined in military cultures across Europe as savage warriors who attacked their victims without any consideration for the rules of civilized warfare.[17] They were generally understood to be cowards who attacked from behind and then hid among civilians. They were even thought to recruit women and children to fight for them, further blurring the lines between combatants and innocents. Obsessions like these made partisans into enemies whose treachery justified both harsh repression and preventive action. As war in Eastern Europe was replaced by a state of revolution and civil war, fears of partisan treachery often fixed on the supposed menace of Jews believed to be taking up arms on behalf of their Soviet masters.

Polish soldiers were not the only ones in a region rocked by wars to imagine that Jews had fired on them from their homes or from behind their lines. Fantasies of Jewish regiments, of Jews who shot at enemies of the revolution from their windows, or who poured boiling water or tar on soldiers in the streets below, influenced Ukrainian troops loyal to the government of Symon Petliura to commit pogroms against Jews. Similar rumors became the pretext for massacres of Jews by counterrevolutionary White troops. Needless to say, these accusations were invariably groundless. Sometimes, as in Pinsk, commanding officers fundamentally misunderstood why a group of Jews had gathered in public, mistaking Zionist meetings for Bolshevik plots. Often, suspiciously, rumors of Jewish sniper fire centered on buildings with well-stocked stores, so that suppressing Judeo-Bolshevik sabotage became an excellent opportunity for looting. Sometimes Jewish self-defense units, formed to protect their communities from plunder and murder, were attacked as Red Army units. Most often, wild rumors were conjured from thin air and then spread by word of mouth and through anti-Bolshevik propaganda. These became the basis for interpreting the smallest details as proof of treason. In one case, Petliurist soldiers captured a Jewish tailor and his two daughters. The elder child, a girl of fourteen, was holding a pair of scissors, which immediately was taken as proof of her involvement in cutting telegraph lines. The soldiers cut out her eyes and tongue, did the same to her sister and father, and then killed all three.[18]

The violence committed by the Polish military was nothing like that in Ukraine in scope or scale, but it was no less politically important.[19] As they staked out their place in the political landscape of the new Polish republic, those on the right in Poland framed violence committed by the military against Jews as a matter of national defense. Their views were widely popular. In parliamentary elections held in January 1919, Polish voters had made the National Democrats, a political movement that espoused an ethnonationalist vision of Poland, the largest party in the Polish parliament. Its éminence grise was Roman Dmowski, a brilliant polemicist who had for decades preached a grim vision of Poland's struggle against other ethnic groups. Jews occupied a central place in his thinking, because he believed their sympathies for Poland's many enemies changed constantly—they were pro-Russian, then pro-German, then pro-Bolshevik, according to the imperatives of the moment. Local National Democratic politicians echoed his ideas in the new political landscape, following his lead in repurposing wartime suspicions of Jews that had enjoyed currency between 1914 and 1918 for the military realities of the new border wars. "In my opinion," one wrote, "the Jewish menace is hostile to us, and socialism—also hostile to us—is supported mainly by the Jews. During the war we saw the Jews as they betrayed us and supported the Germans." The right-wing press echoed these views, airing wild theories of Jewish conspiracies and then, after the anti-Soviet war began, constantly identifying Jews with the Soviet enemy. "Jews," explained one, "demonstrate their antagonistic position towards the Polish army . . . they spread Bolshevik appeals and cheer for Lenin and Trotsky." Their hostility required constant surveillance and even vigorous countermeasures.[20]

By the summer of 1920 these dire warnings were no longer rhetorical. By then, Polish military fortunes had dramatically reversed. From the victories in 1919 at Pinsk and Vilnius, Polish forces had advanced eastward. In late May 1920 they even entered Kiev. But the Red Army counterattack drove them back along the entire front. By August, Bolshevik troops stood before Warsaw. As the defeats mounted, anxieties in Poland about Jews and Bolshevism reached a point of near hysteria. The Ministry of War circulated posters to mobilize popular support for the war that associated the Red Army and its promises of freedom with images of Leon Trotsky as a bloodthirsty demon. The sharp-edged propaganda campaign openly drew on long-standing anti-Jewish stereotypes current in the right-wing press. Military authorities did not stop at propaganda. They carried out preventive arrests of Communists, trade unionists, and Jews. The Jewish Bund was proscribed. On August 6, 1920, the War Ministry set a 5 percent cap on Jewish participation in the military. Jews were removed from office staffs. The army even confined Jewish soldiers in the vicinity of Warsaw to an internment camp at Jabłonna. Similar camps were set up in the towns of Wyszków, Piotrków, Szczakowa, Dąbie, and Tuchola. Speaking afterward before the Polish parliament, the Polish minister of war, General Józef Leśniewski, justified these actions as necessary counterinsurgency efforts: "Unfortunately, I must declare that the Jewish population stood on the side of the Bolsheviks with weapons in hand."[21]

The measures taken by the Polish government against Jewish civilians at the crisis point of its war with the Soviet state reflected broader anxieties about the sovereignty of the new state. Poland was independent, but its existence was precarious in these early years. In Paris, diplomats debated Poland's place in the new postwar international order. The decisions made there would dramatically shape the strategic fortunes of the new republic. At the same time, Poland's leaders began to imagine ways to project their political and cultural authority over the ethnically mixed borderlands where fighting still raged in 1920. Their nationalizing project inevitably raised concerns about the loyalties of people whom they defined as the new state's ethnic minorities. This was by no means an exclusively Jewish problem. Throughout the interwar years, Polish authorities also worried about the challenges posed by Lithuanian and Ukrainian nationalists.[22] But Jewish political loyalty was a special concern, especially in the tense early years. Obvious cultural and communitarian ties linked Jews in the new Polish state with their brethren across the borders that now crisscrossed the old Pale of Settlement. In addition, Zionist politics connected Polish Jews to activists in other successor states, as well as to supporters in the West. And Jewish charitable organizations in the United States sent aid packages to express their solidarity with destitute Polish Jews suffering the effects of war and civil war, an act of generosity interpreted by Polish nationalists as subversive favoritism. In all these ways, the fundamentally transnational nature of Jewish political and cultural life made it easy to associate Jews with the circulation of ideologies that directly threatened the sovereignty of the new Polish nation-state.[23]

In the last phase of the "long World War I" in Eastern Europe, these anxieties about state insecurity fueled the idea of Judeo-Bolshevism and propelled it into the center of Polish national politics. Rumors of Jewish Communist sympathizers in various towns in the *kresy* (Poland's eastern borderlands) or even—in August 1920—within the ranks of the Polish army suggested that Jews might be more loyal to their brethren in Soviet Russia than to Poland. Even as Polish authorities desperately tried to mobilize society to fight for the state, they feared that a foreign power might rally elements within to destroy it. The Jewish Bolshevik, like the earlier figures of the Jewish spy and Jewish saboteur, represented an enemy who could slip across lines and over borders. It was a threat perceived to move back and forth between the "outside" and the "inside" of a state, undermining the power of authorities to control their own territory. Fear of this threat gave meaning to the violence at Pinsk and Lida. It also produced the gross infringement on the rights of Jewish civilians during the battle for Warsaw. However, sovereignty panics were a feature of political life in other Eastern European states as well—as were fears of Judeo-Bolshevik subversion.[24]

Weeks after the Polish army had miraculously defeated the Red Army outside of Warsaw, the autumn term began at Romania's universities. The atmosphere on campuses across the country was tense, nowhere more so than at the prestigious University of Iaşi. The city of Iaşi was a major center of Romanian cultural and artistic life, home to some of the foremost nationalist intellectuals in the country. During World War I it had even been Romania's capital for a brief time. Iaşi was also a border city, located just a few miles from the Prut River that had once divided the Kingdom of Romania from the Russian Empire. Now Romania's borders had shifted to the east to encompass an entire region—Bessarabia—that had once been Russian. Even so, Iaşi remained a city of borders and border crossings, since it was there that Romania's political and cultural elites encountered their new compatriots from the eastern borderland most immediately. Iaşi was also a large Jewish city. Perhaps one-third of Iaşi's inhabitants were Jews, a number that exploded as pogroms erupted in Ukraine and Jews fled across the border into Romania. The arrival of so many Jewish migrants worried state authorities, whose views of the refugees were shaped by wartime fears of Jewish espionage and by anxieties that the newcomers would bring with them an epidemic of disease. In many ways, Iaşi in 1920 was a city primed for a culture war. The clash that ensued played out most dramatically at the university.[25]

By 1920 a large number of young Bessarabians, now freshly minted citizens of Romania, had come to study at Iaşi. Only one-third of the newcomers were ethnic Romanians. About 44 percent of them were Jews. The university had also become a center of leftist student activism, and many student societies were led by Communists.

Government officials worried openly about Bessarabian Jewish agitators turning Iaşi into a "Bolshevik nest." So did some Romanian nationalist students. One of these was Corneliu Codreanu, a passionate young nationalist who would soon become the leader of Romania's fascist movement. Years later, Codreanu recalled that he and his ("true Romanian") classmates had felt outnumbered and besieged at the university, overwhelmed by the "immense mass of Jewish students . . . from Bessarabia, all communist agents." In response, Codreanu organized like-minded students into a gang. Shouting anti-Bolshevik and antisemitic slurs, they attacked the Bessarabian students, swiping the Russian-style caps from the heads of their enemies and then, in an act of symbolic violence, burning them on the main square. University administrators disapproved of such hooliganism, and Codreanu was expelled. But the clashes were a harbinger of things to come.[26]

Compared with the attacks on Jewish civilians in the Polish *kresy* and elsewhere in Eastern Europe, the hooliganism of antisemitic students at the University of Iaşi might, at first glance, seem trivial. But it was another symptom of anxiety across the region about Jews as a threat to fragile or insecure national sovereignty. Before the war, Romania had been a small, agrarian, and economically underdeveloped kingdom. Its population was almost 90 percent ethnic Romanians, most of whom were peasants. After 1918 the country doubled in size and population. The country's elite began to dream of policies to modernize the economy and society of the new Greater Romania. But postwar Romania was a much different place. Ethnic Romanians now made up only two-thirds of the population, a demographic fact that spawned widespread fears about the erosion of Romanian power in the country. In the new territories, urban elites were typically not Romanian at all. Bessarabia exemplified this starkly. According to the 1897 census, only 47.6 percent of Bessarabians were ethnic Romanians. Almost 20 percent were Ukrainians, and more than 11 percent were Jews. Romanian and Ukrainian peasants dominated in the countryside; the cities were predominantly Russian and Jewish. Russian, not Romanian, was widely considered the language of polite society. Alarmed by the new demographic reality, Romania's state builders moved swiftly to change it, producing a raft of policies that discriminated in favor of Romanians in employment, cultural policy, the awarding of government contracts, and admission to institutions of higher education.[27]

The panic over Judeo-Bolshevism at Iaşi University in the autumn of 1920 arose from these broader anxieties. Students like Codreanu felt entitled to a bright future among Romania's new elite, and they looked down at their fellow Russian and Jewish students as "eastern anti-Romanian Yids." But they also feared them as competitors. Most ethnic Romanian students came to the university from village schools and were woefully underprepared for the leap into higher education. On campus, facilities were underfunded and classes were overcrowded. Most Romanian students eventually failed out. (University graduation rates hovered around 10 percent for much of the interwar period.) Competition for jobs after graduation was intense. Students without elite connections generally came up short. Frustration with these conditions bred ethnonationalist activism. Popular lectures by antisemitic professors, who warned darkly of the Jewish invasion that was taking over Romania, stoked their rage. (A. C. Cuza, one of the country's most prominent far-right political theorists, taught law at Iaşi.) After the 1920 demonstration, radical nationalist students continued their campaign against Jews, organizing lockouts and strikes at universities around the country as well as physically intimidating Jewish students in lecture halls. A December 1922 nationwide general student strike demanding limits on the number of Jews admitted to study was celebrated by Romanian fascists for years afterward as the moment a new generation of young nationalists was born. During this period of upheaval, Romanian students (joined by Russian refugees from the counterrevolutionary White armies) forcibly expelled Jewish students from their dormitories. These later demonstrations mixed the fear of Judeo-Bolshevism into a farrago of national enemies that included Jews, liberals, and freemasons. But Judeo-Bolshevism remained a central image in the ideological arsenal of Romanian fascists throughout the interwar years.[28]

Students' fears about Jewish Bolsheviks mirrored the panic of army and security officials about Jewish subversion, especially in the new Bessarabian borderland. Unlike Poland, Romania did not fight a border war with the Red Army. Romanian troops had annexed the region in 1918 without much of a fight. However, the Soviet Union never formally recognized Romanian control of Bessarabia. For this reason, the Romanian security service was consumed by fears of Communist agitation and infiltration in the territory. Inevitably, their suspicions fell most heavily on Bessarabia's Jewish communities. (Although the Communist Party in Bessarabia attracted supporters from all ethnic groups that resented or feared Romanian rule, including Jews, the vast majority of politically active Jews in the region were Zionists.) Throughout the interwar years, police and security officials kept Jews under close surveillance. Army intelligence consistently produced risk assessments that declared Jews responsible for all Communist activity in the region. One typical report stated that "there is no case of corruption, Communist propaganda, or espionage, etc., where the Jews were not discovered to be the leaders, the organizers, and they form the majority of the members of these subversive organizations." Another claimed that Jews were "fomenters of the dissolution of the state." The army worked closely with the Ministry of Education in the early days of the annexation to nationalize formerly Russian schools and to place in them a cadre of nationally conscious Romanian teachers. In the years that followed, far-right parties recruited heavily among civil servants like these. They made impressive gains in Romanian villages by identifying Jews as enemies of the state whose assets should rightly be confiscated to benefit the Romanian people. When Romania went to war against the Soviet

Union in 1941, this political work bore fruit in mass anti-Jewish violence across Bessarabia.[29]

The threatening image of Judeo-Bolshevism also surfaced in Romania's early efforts to nationalize its western borderland. Hungarian culture dominated the newly acquired territory of Transylvania, which had been an integral part of the historic Kingdom of Hungary. Nearly three-quarters of town dwellers in the region were ethnic Hungarians and Jews. Most Transylvanian Jews strongly identified with Hungarian language and culture. Long resentful of Hungarian dominance, Romanian activists in Transylvania declared the province part of Romania in November 1918, and the Romanian army quickly occupied the region. But military officials and local nationalists worried constantly about Hungarian resistance. They also nervously watched the political turbulence across the border in Hungary. One response to these perceived threats was a stream of stories in the Romanian press about Hungarian atrocities and terror in Transylvania. Another was anti-Bolshevik panic. "This province is full of Bolshevism," declared the Romanian premier in November 1918, "and we would be guilty if we remained indifferent." When Bolsheviks did take power in Hungary some months later, military officials worried openly about the country's encirclement by Soviet forces, while nationalist leaders painted black pictures of the submersion of Romanian culture. The tense border conflict between Hungary and Romania reached a climax in July 1919, when Hungary's Red Army attempted an attack. The assault failed, Hungary's Bolshevik rulers fled into exile, and the Romanian army marched all the way to Budapest. In the wake of victory, the Romanian government consolidated power by making the Hungarian Soviet experiment into a symbol of antinational danger and Judeo-Bolshevik perfidy. State propaganda urged Romanians to remain vigilant against the "red beast." Authorities circulated posters and photographs of Hungarian Bolsheviks that identified them as Jews.[30]

Romanians celebrated the occupation of Budapest as a triumph of nationalist aspirations and a victory over Bolshevism. Hungarians saw it very differently. Setting the two cases side by side shows the sheer malleability of Judeo-Bolshevik hysteria in Eastern Europe after 1918. In Romania, it took root in a country that was unquestionably one of the greatest "winners" of the war. In Hungary, the course of events showed that it also flourished in defeat.

The war that had given birth to a Greater Romania double its former size also reduced the Kingdom of Hungary to a tiny country and threw it into political turmoil. When the Austro-Hungarian monarchy collapsed, a radical democratic government took power in Hungary. Led by Count Mihály Károlyi, a wealthy aristocrat with an old and prestigious family name, the new regime dreamed optimistically of transforming Hungarian society by leveling political and social inequalities. But their ambitious plans for reform collided with the harsh realities of territorial loss. After November 1918, neighboring states (like Romania) occupied more than two-thirds of Hungary's historic lands. Defeat left the country's economy in ruins, and the army, belatedly mobilized to defend the borders, collapsed. Refugees from the occupied territories flooded into the capital. Once-comfortable provincial administrators now lived with their families in railway boxcars. Meanwhile, groups of officers began to form paramilitary groups, declaring themselves intent on restoring "Christian" Hungary and undoing the revolutionary and "un-Hungarian" reforms that the Károlyi regime had tried to enact.[31] In March 1919, the ongoing crisis forced Mihály Károlyi to resign. In his wake, the Communist revolutionary Béla Kun brought Hungary's Bolsheviks to power.

During their short rule, the Bolsheviks tried to mobilize Hungarian society by terrorizing elite groups, identifying them as enemies of the people. They nationalized property and repurposed churches. They solved a housing shortage by placing factory workers in the apartments of the urban bourgeoisie. And they tried to remake the country's educational system along secular-materialist lines. The Romanian occupation ended their revolution. After the Romanians withdrew, a band of paramilitary fighters that called itself the National Army rode into Budapest, led by a former Habsburg admiral named Miklós Horthy. They came to liberate the city and cleanse it of the "filth of the nation all converging here," he declared.[32] The counterrevolution had begun.

Horthy's National Army played no role in toppling the Bolshevik regime in Hungary. Instead, his soldiers waited safely in the southern Hungarian city of Szeged in the French-controlled zone. When danger had passed, squads of paramilitaries fanned out across western and southern Hungary. They called themselves officers, but many were not. Some came from gentry families that had fallen in the world. Many more had humble origins but liked to pretend otherwise. Under the pretext of eradicating Communism and redeeming Hungary as a Christian nation, these paramilitary troops unleashed an orgy of opportunistic violence that quickly came to be known as the White Terror. In village after village, they attacked people suspected (often entirely wrongly) of being Communists or Communist sympathizers. They also settled personal scores, punished peasants who had forgotten their station, raped and looted, and extorted money and property from those who could not defend themselves. Many of their victims were Jews, whom they saw as self-evidently antinational and pro-Bolshevik.[33]

After a new counterrevolutionary government formed, some of the men in Horthy's National Army continued to terrorize their enemies. In 1920, members of a group called the Association of Awakening Magyars assassinated the editor of Hungary's leading Social Democratic newspaper, a man they demonized as a ringleader of the

antinational "Jewish-Bolshevik-liberal" media. Others served as security officers in the new government or worked as associates of the new
government to arrest tens of thousands of people suspected of subversive activities and to seize property from many others. At the same
time, the right-wing media were saturated with accounts both real
and spurious of atrocities committed by the Communists: upstanding
men of the community arrested and tortured; homes invaded; churches
made into movie theaters; schoolchildren taught that marriage was
a sham and patriotism a lie; aristocratic women molested; and innocents executed by Red terror squads. In these accounts, the Bolshevik
perpetrators were invariably identified as Jews.[34]

The fury of the Hungarian counterrevolution was terrible. Perhaps
3,000 people were killed, of whom roughly half were Jews. Some
70,000 were interned in jails and camps, sometimes for years. At least
100,000 more were driven into exile.[35] To the paramilitaries and their
political backers, all of this was a natural response to Bolshevik crimes.
Speaking in the country's new National Assembly, the ascendant
Right contemptuously dismissed liberal critics who complained that
the "paramilitary scourge" was illegal and uncivilized. "It is not the
rule of law that must be saved, but Christian Hungarians," declared
Bishop Ottokár Prohászka, who was now an elected representative as
well as a man of the cloth.[36] More moderate conservatives, who were
eager to restore order, admitted that the White Terror was excessive
and destabilizing. But they also blamed the Bolsheviks, whom they
accused of starting a civil war that inevitably provoked an even more
violent backlash. If Jews were now vulnerable targets, then this was
due entirely to their prominence in the Bolshevik regime. In the years
that followed, this interpretation became political wisdom. "We have
to consider that what unfolded in Hungary in 1918–1919 was basically
a civil war," wrote one conservative historian nearly ten years later.
"And where has there been a civil war in which innocent people did
not lose their lives?"[37]

Powerless to restore their country's borders, Hungary's counter-revolutionaries turned their impotent rage on the scourge of Judeo-Bolshevism. However, the figure of the Jewish Bolshevik functioned as more than just a scapegoat. Judeo-Bolshevism folded the Bolshevik revolution into a more general assertion about the rise of "Jewish power" in Hungary. After the revolution was crushed, right-wing intellectuals debated the causes of the political and territorial catastrophe that had befallen the nation. Many concluded that the country's decline had begun long before the start of the First World War. They argued that Hungarian liberals had permitted a destructive and modern "Jewish spirit" to take root in the decades before 1914. Over time, this "spirit" had distorted the country's traditional economic, cultural, and moral order.[38] Defeat and revolution made the consequences of an empowered "Jewish spirit" plain for all to see. It had filled the heads of democrats with fantasies of a liberal international order and seduced them into abandoning military defense when the borders were in greatest danger. And it had driven the Bolsheviks to pursue a proletarian dystopia that would have severed Hungary from its history.

In this fantasy of historical decline, Jewish Bolsheviks came onstage only in the last act. Nevertheless, Judeo-Bolshevism exerted an outsized hold on the nationalist imagination throughout the years that followed. After 1920 it was an article of faith that Bolshevism was an alien force with no roots in national tradition. Bishop Prohászka called it a "Russian-Jewish invasion" and likened it to the barbarian invasions of the Middle Ages.[39] Agents within, united by a common Jewish identity, embraced the ideological enemy, despite their superficial political differences. "A thin wall separated radicalism from social democracy, and this wall collapsed at the point where the Jews found each other," wrote one contributor to an early counterrevolutionary assessment of Hungary's "proletarian dictatorship."[40] This analysis recalled wartime fears of Jews as saboteurs or an "inner front." It also crystallized in a powerful way the confluence of external and internal threats that had toppled Hungary's prewar political order and ripped apart the historical integrity of the state.

Just as in Poland and Romania, the belief that "Judeo-Bolshevism" was a hostile and subversive force became a central element in Hungary's national politics after 1918. In each of these places, the figure of the Jewish Bolshevik came to embody widespread fears that the nation was not sovereign in its own home. The issues shifted from one state context to another, but in all three, nationalists associated Judeo-Bolshevism with threats that loomed from without and within. Local events—revolutions, border wars, the failures of nationalization policy—fueled their anxieties. So did the fundamental reshaping of the European order that was taking place in Paris. This confluence of national and international politics in postimperial Eastern Europe would give the Judeo-Bolshevik menace its full meaning.

As Hungary's counterrevolutionaries prepared their campaign of terror in the summer of 1919, the Hungarian general Károly Soós had some words of advice for the eager and ambitious paramilitary leaders who (in theory, at least) answered to him. Soós was a highly decorated officer in the Austro-Hungarian army who had served on the Russian and Italian fronts. Without question, he was also a fierce anti-Communist. After the monarchy that he had served so loyally collapsed, he joined the growing anti-Bolshevik community in the southern (and French-occupied) Hungarian city of Szeged. There, he became the chief of general staff in Admiral Miklós Horthy's newly created National Army, responsible for welding the different groups of zealous anti-Bolshevik rebels into a reliable force. Soós was eager to remove every trace of Bolshevism from the country and to replace it with a "Christian nationalist" regime. But his long years of service also gave him an insight into the relationship between military tactics and political calculation that the paramilitary squad commanders lacked entirely. As the detachments prepared to ride north from Szeged to hunt down the Judeo-Bolshevik enemy, he gave some words of advice to one of the most ruthless of the commanders: "Don't kill too many Jews, since this can also cause problems."[41]

Soós's blunt words captured an important truth. The White Terror in Hungary unfolded against the backdrop of efforts by the peacemakers assembled in Paris to create a new European order. The decisions they made would shape the future of Hungary and every other state in Eastern Europe. The counterrevolutionary regime that Soós served wanted desperately to revise the borders that were fast becoming reality. Hungary needed friends abroad who would declare it a "good actor" on the international stage. Admiral Horthy's new regime had some friends. Western conservatives spoke warmly of Hungary for its anti-Communist stance. Some with positions in the British Foreign Office produced a White Paper titled *Report on Alleged Existence of "White Terror" in Hungary*, which dramatically minimized the violence taking place in the country.[42] A few ultraconservative British aristocrats, the tabloid magnate Viscount Rothermere (Harold Sidney Harmsworth) foremost among them, even became lifelong advocates for Hungarian border revision.[43]

But the violence against Hungary's Jews also drew critical attention. Throughout the autumn of 1919, Jewish community offices in Budapest collected and published eyewitness accounts of Jews in the provinces who had been assaulted, robbed, and lynched.[44] They shared this information with press agencies abroad. In Washington, D.C., president of the American Jewish Committee Louis Marshall lobbied the State Department to take this into account: "When [Hungary] is seeking to rehabilitate herself and expects to be relieved from the obligations which she is about to assume under the Treaty of peace, an indication from the Great Powers . . . that these anti-Semitic demonstrations must cease, will not be disregarded."[45] Leftist émigrés fleeing counterrevolutionary Hungary also circulated accounts of their experiences through an international network of socialists and labor activists. In time, international inspectors came to Hungary to investigate. American Jewish organizations took a keen interest. So did a delegation from the British Labour Party. Their critical assessments would certainly cast a shadow over Hungary's international reputation.[46]

Several considerations shaped the deliberations about postwar Europe. Led by U.S. president Woodrow Wilson, the peacemakers in Paris believed that a future without war depended on ridding the Continent of autocratic and repressive empires (like Austria-Hungary) and replacing them with an international order that rested on the principle of national self-determination—a world, in Wilson's words, that was "safe for every peace-loving nation that wants to live its own life and determine its own institutions." They were also determined to contain Bolshevism. French policymakers, in particular, imagined that new states in Eastern Europe like Poland and Romania could be a *cordon sanitaire* that would prevent the spread of revolution from Russia to the west. Finally, legal experts from both sides of the Atlantic debated ways to protect the rights of ethnic minorities in the new Europe. They placed their hopes in a set of minority treaties that would require the governments of Eastern Europe to respect certain norms of behavior and empower ethnic minorities to bring their grievances before the League of Nations if they did not.[47]

How these goals might be balanced was an open question, with important consequences for the currency of Judeo-Bolshevism as a political idea. Diplomats in Paris often sent ambiguous signals. At times, they lectured their Eastern European partners about excessive nationalist zeal and worried openly that countries like Romania and Poland were exploiting the postwar crisis to expand their borders beyond limits that the Paris peace conference deemed reasonable. Western peacemakers also dreamed of building a new world order that embedded humanitarian norms, for fair treatment of ethnic minorities, for example, within an international legal framework— norms that would become benchmarks of political maturity against which the new states of Eastern Europe (and also the peoples in former German colonies and Ottoman holdings outside Europe who were governed after World War I by the League of Nations mandates system) could be measured. Seen in this light, reports of pogroms and other acts of violence against Jews were crude anachronisms that cast doubt on the ability of Eastern Europeans to conduct themselves properly on the world stage. Yet Western diplomats also needed the new nation-states of Eastern Europe as partners in the fight against Bolshevism. The revolutionary threat loomed over the Paris peace talks, as Red Army successes in the east and Soviet regimes in Central Europe (however short-lived) fueled anxieties about Bolshevik expansion across the Continent. Anti-Bolshevism dominated the postwar strategic calculations of the victorious Western powers and frequently led Western diplomats to temper loftier humanitarian visions with hard-nosed assessments about how to contain or roll back Communism. At such moments, claims made by Eastern European leaders that anti-Jewish violence was a (lamentable) reaction to the role that Jews played in revolutionary subversion were comfortingly plausible.[48]

Jewish humanitarian groups tried to maneuver within this shifting political and diplomatic terrain, embracing the language and proposed structures of international law as mechanisms that could guarantee the safety of Jewish lives. They vocally condemned fears of Jewish subversion across the region as the latest manifestation of a backward prejudice that had long plagued less-civilized Eastern Europe. The Paris-based Alliance Israélite Universelle made these arguments especially forcefully. For decades the group had condemned the Romanian state for denying citizenship rights to the country's Jews. After 1918, it renewed this effort. (Under intense international pressure, Romanian Jews were finally emancipated in 1919.) The alliance also reported on the open hostility toward Jews at Romanian universities. And it denounced Romanian efforts to expel refugees from the pogroms in Ukraine as inhumane, justified by a specious equation of Jews with Bolshevism that could not withstand sober examination.[49]

The French military stationed in the region sent no such mixed signals. From the first days of November 1918, French commanders in southeastern Europe watched the formation of the Hungarian democratic republic with trepidation, concerned that it was a natural haven for Bolshevik revolutionaries. The fact that some members of the new Hungarian government were Jews only magnified their un-ease, as the Hungarian emissaries who tried to negotiate with French military authorities bitterly recalled years later. While Hungarian do-mestic politics grew ever more volatile, the French army gave sanc-tuary to counterrevolutionaries like Admiral Horthy and General Soós, in the hope that they might someday take power in Budapest. Even more important, French military officials embraced the Roma-nian government as an ally in the fight against Communism. Ro-mania, General Henri Berthelot declared, was "the best French colony in the world." Throughout 1918 and 1919, Berthelot encour-aged his Romanian partners to take a hard line against the revolution in Hungary. He also fully supported the country's efforts to transform Bessarabia into a reliable buffer zone against Soviet Russia. Roma-nian policy-making elites understood, in turn, that their nationaliza-tion policies would earn them no more than a cautionary note from Paris, so long as they advertised them as necessary anti-Communist measures. Romania had become the "gendarme of the Entente on the Danube." In this climate, attacks against "Jewish Bolsheviks" were not violations of humanitarian norms. They were rational acts of counterinsurgency.[50]

The Great Powers' strategy to contain Communism shaped the po-litical function of Judeo-Bolshevism in the newly created Polish state even more dramatically. The peacemakers in Paris agreed that a sov-ereign Poland must be part of the new international order in Europe. Its contested border with Russia ensured that it would figure promi-nently in the fight against Bolshevism, although exactly how remained unclear. The counterrevolutionary White armies still enjoyed Allied support, and their plans to restore an undivided Russia had implications for the location of Poland's eastern frontier. Even so, French, British, and U.S. policy makers all assigned Poland an important role in preventing the westward expansion of Bolshevism—as "a barrier against [a] Russian Bolshevism dangerous for all European civilization," according to one French formulation.[51] Here too the French military was the most direct in its pursuit of regional allies against Communism. Early in 1919, Marshal Ferdinand Foch even thought of using Poland as an operational base for an offensive against the Red Army. Over time, the French government settled on a regional strategy that made Poland the linchpin in an Eastern European *cordon sanitaire* that would contain Communism and also serve as a check on German aggression. France's British and American allies reached the same conclusion. But they also worried that the Polish government would use the fight against Bolshevism as a pretext for pushing its borders far to the east. In his Fourteen Points outlining principles for peace, Woodrow Wilson had imagined a Polish state made of territories "inhabited indisputably by Polish populations."[52] Fully aware that this declaration did not describe the multiethnic eastern borderlands claimed by the government in Warsaw, British and American policymakers labored to find ways to encourage Poland in its anti-Soviet war while also raising concerns about the instability of nationality politics in the region.

Jewish diplomats at the Paris peace conference shared their concerns. Though they represented no state, delegations of Jewish legal experts from France, Britain, the United States, and Eastern Europe convened there to speak for the Jewish communities in Eastern Europe so devastated by war and revolution. The First World War had created new opportunities for Jewish politics. The Zionists were eager to build on the promise of a homeland made in the British government's Balfour Declaration. But the West's alliance with tsarist Russia—widely seen as the land of pogroms—had been a bitter pill, especially for Anglo-Jewish leaders used to aligning their own interests with those of the liberal imperial British state. In London, activists associated with the Jewish immigrant community in the East End openly resented this state of affairs. British conservatives, in turn, took their writings as proof that Jews secretly supported the German enemy. The collapse of the tsarist autocracy was a cause for celebration, and Jewish leaders everywhere anticipated the expansion of Jewish civil rights in a liberal and democratic Russia. That hope soon crumbled also. The massive violence of the ensuing civil war alarmed Jewish communities throughout the diaspora and left leaders on both sides of the Atlantic facing a new political reality: Jews who had once been subjects of a single empire were now caught in the middle of a war between Bolshevik internationalism and several different nationalizing states. In an Eastern Europe of nation-states, Jews would always be a minority group. As they gathered in Paris in 1919, Jewish diplomats considered ways to defend the communitarian rights of Jews in this new world.[53]

They were divided in their approach. Liberal and assimilationist Jewish leaders from Western Europe wanted to obligate the nation-states of Eastern Europe to grant equal rights to Jews as individuals. Others found this insufficient and pointed to the horrific violence against Jews in Eastern Europe as proof. "There is only one way in which the civil equality of the Jews can be preserved," wrote the pro-Zionist journalist Israel Cohen, "and that is by their being given the rights of a national minority."[54] Cohen and other activists traveled across Poland to give voice to the suffering of Jews in the region. Often their initial estimates of Jewish victims were wildly inflated and had to be revised downward. (The first reports of the November 1918 pogrom in Lemberg [Lviv] put the number of dead at 3,000. Subsequent investigations put the number in the hundreds, and contemporary historians debate numbers even lower.) But their vivid accounts of the violence and interviews with eyewitnesses to what came to be known in the media as the Polish pogroms cast doubt on Poland's ability to treat its minorities fairly. Diaspora Jewish communities in cities like London and New York organized mass demonstrations throughout 1919 to protest the persecution of Jews in Poland. Their activism gave support to diplomats in Paris (Jewish and non-Jewish) who favored international legal protections for Eastern Europe's minorities as distinct national groups rather than as individual citizens. Labour Party activists in Britain also cited reports of the "Polish pogroms" as further proof that their government's anti-Soviet policy was reactionary and unjust.[55]

At a moment when the peacemakers in Paris were themselves uncertain about how to marry their dreams of national self-determination and minority rights with their strategic goal of containing Communism, news that Polish soldiers had killed Jews as Communist partisans in Pinsk and other places touched an especially sensitive nerve. Several weeks after the incident in Pinsk, Jewish press agencies began to report on evidence that showed the executed Jews had been wrongly accused of Bolshevism. They also suggested that the victims had been killed simply "to intimidate the Jewish population."[56] The news sparked mass demonstrations. In New York, Jewish protesters marched on the Lower East Side to demonstrate their solidarity with Polish Jews. Crowds thronged Madison Square Garden, where a rally was held calling for international action to stop anti-Jewish violence. They urged the media to devote more attention to the problem, and accused the press of being silent about the bloodshed so that—in the words of financier and philanthropist Jacob Schiff—Poland might be established as a "self-determining, clean nation, even if the Jews are destroyed in cold blood."[57] Schiff and many of the other speakers that evening demanded that Poland be excluded from the new League of Nations until it committed itself to protecting Jewish lives.

Outraged, the Polish government pushed back at the criticism. To support their position, Polish officials relied on evidence collected by one of the international groups that had been in the area—a Christian humanitarian group led by a Polish-American named Francis

Fronczak—and ignored evidence collected by another group, a team sent by the Jewish Joint Distribution Committee. According to Fronczak, Jews in Pinsk had been Bolshevik allies. Government spokesmen issued statements insisting that the men killed in Pinsk had been "Bolshevist plotters" and not the victims of a pogrom. Reports to the contrary had been "deliberately distorted . . . for the purpose of discrediting Poland," they claimed.[58] In interviews, Polish prime minister (and renowned pianist) Ignacy Paderewski made the same argument. Speaking to the *New York Times*, Paderewski insisted that the shooting of Jews in Pinsk had been a "matter of pure Bolshevism. We executed the people responsible for that crime, and they happened to be Jews."[59] The reports of a pogrom that had fueled demonstrations in New York and given new urgency to debates in Paris about how to guarantee security to ethnic minorities were signs, Paderewski said, that "German agents [were] still active in New York and Paris to undermine the world's faith in the Polish State." He offered the same explanation in his private diplomatic conversations. When British foreign secretary Arthur Balfour asked Polish authorities to do more to protect Jews, Paderewski replied huffily that Poland was already doing everything it could and that the racial violence was a "provocation both from within and without the country."[60] Amid the crisis, Lucien Wolf, an Anglo-Jewish liberal who favored assimilation, warned Paderewski that reports of the killings had aroused indignation in London and that Polish diplomats would do well to drop the insinuations that the Jewish victims in places like Pinsk, Lida, and Vilnius had been Bolsheviks.[61]

Some Western diplomats, like the first American minister plenipotentiary to Poland, Hugh Gibson, sided with Paderewski. Convinced of the Bolshevik danger both in Eastern Europe and in the United States, where the Red Scare raged, Gibson concluded in his reports on the situation in Poland that the Jewish community there was rife with "spies" and "provocateurs."[62] Other members of the American political establishment demurred. At the protest rally held in Madison Square Garden in May 1919, the former Supreme Court justice and future secretary of state Charles Evans Hughes thrilled the crowd with his vigorous defense of the ideal of international justice: "We hear from time to time of some attempts to make excuses for this ruthless barbarity. But there is not, and in this day less than at any time in the world's history, any excuse for letting the spirit of violence have play, and for the dethronement of the institutions of justice."[63] As public pressure mounted, American officials felt compelled to form a new commission to investigate violence against Polish Jews, this time one led by the lawyer and former U.S. ambassador to the Ottoman Empire Henry Morgenthau, whom President Woodrow Wilson trusted. Zionist leaders on both sides of the Atlantic were dissatisfied with many aspects of this group's report too. But the Morgenthau Commission did address the issue of Judeo-Bolshevik rebellion that had sparked the violence in Pinsk. It concluded that the Polish commander had shown "reprehensible and frivolous readiness" to believe unsupported (and ultimately false) charges against "reputable citizens whose loyal character could have been immediately established by a consultation with any well-known non-Jewish inhabitant."[64]

In the end, the Polish government was compelled to sign a minority treaty. Concluded in the summer of 1919, in the wake of the furor over the killings at Pinsk, the treaty granted certain collective rights in matters of religion, culture, and education to ethnic minorities, such as Jews. It also made the League of Nations the ultimate guarantor of those rights and empowered that body to enforce them if the Polish state would not. A model for similar treaties signed by other Eastern European states, the Polish Minority Treaty symbolized the power (in theory, at least) of the international community to intervene in the domestic ethnic politics of Eastern Europe's new nation-states. It was bitterly opposed in Poland for this reason. In vain, Polish officials reminded Western diplomats of their country's history of religious and ethnic toleration. The right-wing nationalist press drew a harsher lesson. For the Right, the treaty was proof that Jewish loyalties were suspect. Poland had won its independence, but the anxieties about national sovereignty and security that had fueled the Judeo-Bolshevik panic persisted long after the Polish-Soviet War ended. So too did the idea of Judeo-Bolshevism in Polish politics.[65]

Amid the violence of imperial collapse, border conflicts, and counterrevolution that marked the last phase of Eastern Europe's "long World War I," wartime suspicions of Jews as spies and saboteurs transformed easily into fears of Jews as revolutionaries. In different national contexts, some shaped by victory and some by defeat, the figure of the Judeo-Bolshevik came to have several interrelated meanings. The idea of Judeo-Bolshevism reflected anxieties about fragile national sovereignty. It embodied fears of internal and external enemies. And it was an argument used to rationalize violence, making incidents internationally condemned as violations of humanitarian norms into legitimate acts of national self-defense. For these reasons, the threat of Judeo-Bolshevism was a central feature of the political turmoil that produced a new Eastern Europe of nation-states. In the years that followed, the Judeo-Bolshevik threat remained a potent symbol in nationalist politics across the region. Soon, however, these nationally specific versions of the idea would come to intersect with another variation on the theme: the vision of Judeo-Bolshevik menace espoused in Nazi Germany.

3

Refashioned by Nazism

Judeo-Bolshevism made Adolf Hitler. The former corporal, who claimed to have perceived the full truth of Jewish evil at the end of World War I while recovering in a military hospital from a gas attack, began his political career in Munich, a city profoundly shaken by its experience of revolution. The political upheavals that began in November 1918 culminated in a very brief period of Communist rule in May 1919. Though the Bavarian Republic of Councils, as the Communist government called itself, existed for only a few days, it was indelibly associated in the public imagination with alien rule, anarchy, and violence. Several of Munich's revolutionaries were Jewish, one was Russian, and all declared fidelity to the Bolshevik revolution in Russia, proof in the eyes of many that the revolution had been a Russian-Jewish plot. The Bavarian Soviet's decision to execute some ten prisoners, including a woman, two captured soldiers, and a handful of extreme-right activists held as hostages, symbolized for many Bavarians the reign of terror (*Schreckensherrschaft*) that revolutionary power had inflicted on them. And the role that paramilitaries played in chasing Munich's revolutionaries from power and unleashing a wave of retributive violence convinced a broad spectrum of Bavarians that the threat of Bolshevik power must be met with firm and determined force. Thereafter, Munich became a center of activity for the extreme German Right. The Nazi Party, and its leader, Adolf Hitler, emerged in this political milieu, drawing on the memory of the Bavarian revolution to justify their ideological belief in the Jewish threat to German society.[1]

But Bolshevism did not make Hitler an antisemite. The threat of Judeo-Bolshevism did not become a constant theme in his speeches until the summer of 1920, possibly influenced by Baltic German émigrés who had gathered in Munich, as well as the constant press coverage of the Russian Civil War. Hitler's personal fixation with Jews predated the war. In the context of Germany's defeat, the German revolution of 1918, and the political turbulence that ensued, his hatred became an ideology. Hitler's conviction that Bolshevism was a Jewish plot, a fixed vision once formed, gave substance and intensity to his ideas about the Jewish enemy. Similarly, it was several years before Hitler's conception of Bolshevik Russia, which he understood as a Jewish-ruled Asiatic realm that must be destroyed for Germans to expand and thrive, took coherent shape. For several years Hitler had shared the views of anti-Bolshevik Russian émigrés, who distinguished between Jewish Soviet rulers, who were implacable enemies, and oppressed national Russians, who shared innate cultural affinities with Germans. Only as Hitler began to develop his views on German imperial expansion and the importance of "living space" in the East did he begin consistently to describe the Soviet Union as a racial and ideological enemy that represented both an implacably hostile Judeo-Bolshevik system and, at the same time, a reservoir of brutal Asiatic subhumanity. All these ideas crystallized gradually in Hitler's thinking. Once they gelled, however, they never changed, remaining central to Nazi ideology to the last hours of the Third Reich in 1945. Jewish Bolsheviks were bloodstained terrorists. They had inspired the "November criminals," who had stabbed the German people in the back in 1918. And they were deceitful enemies on a mission to impose

Jewish rule over the world. Hitler believed it was the German people's historic calling to protect the world from Judeo-Bolshevik evil. German annihilation would leave the entire world helpless before this great enemy. As he wrote in *Mein Kampf:* "If, with the help of his Marxist creed, the Jew is victorious over the other peoples of the world, his crown will be the funeral wreath of humanity and this planet will, as it did thousands of years ago, move through the ether devoid of men."[2]

Nazism's roots in Bavarian counterrevolutionary politics connected the image of the Jewish Bolshevik demonized by Hitler and his fellow party members to the specter of Judeo-Bolshevism imagined across Europe in the years between 1917 and 1923. From the Vatican to Paris salons to paramilitary barracks in the south of Hungary, the history of Munich's Republic of Councils seemed proof of a Jewish plot to overthrow civilization and impose foreign rule on the nations of Europe. The language that Hitler used in Munich beer halls in the early 1920s to thunder against Jewish Marxism would not have seemed out of place in anti-Bolshevik circles in many other countries. Indeed, Munich soon became a gathering place for counterrevolutionaries across east-central Europe for precisely this reason.

There was, however, an important difference that loomed ever larger once Hitler seized power. Even in defeat, Germany remained a central player in the politics of international order in Europe. After 1933, the Nazi vision of Judeo-Bolshevism, fused with broader dreams of German dominance in Europe and racial imperialism in the East, was transformed. Once a language of antidemocratic and antiliberal opposition to a republic seen as un-German, it became instead a strategic vision for a reborn Germany that could in fact be realized. As Nazi Germany began to project its power eastward and to revise the state order that had been established after World War I, the Nazi vision of Judeo-Bolshevism, now inseparable from the prospect of German hegemony, collided with other understandings of "Jewish

Bolshevik power" that were deeply rooted in local nationalist politics. The confluence of different racist idioms convinced some that Europe was embroiled in a vast civil war and that they should make common cause with Nazi Germany against the Bolshevik enemy. Others were less sanguine about a Europe under Nazi domination. The meaning of Judeo-Bolshevism changed over the course of the interwar years as it became ever more closely associated with Hitler's Germany.

In Nazi mythology of the *Kampfzeit*, the "period of struggle" between 1919 and 1933 when the Nazi Party fought for power, there was no greater martyr than Horst Wessel. Son of a Protestant pastor and military chaplain, Wessel came of age in an intensely nationalistic milieu; after 1918 Wessel's father had a brief career as a political agitator, moving from the pulpit to the public square to denounce Germany's defeat, the Treaty of Versailles, Jews, and the Bolshevik menace, before he died in 1921.[3] After his father's sudden death, Wessel took part in various right-wing student organizations before joining the Nazi Party and the Sturmabteilung (SA), or Storm Troopers, also known as the Brownshirts. He soon displayed talents as a speaker and organizer, taking charge of an SA Storm section in the working-class district of Friedrichshain in Berlin, challenging the Communist Party for control of the streets in the neighborhood, and working to "redeem" truly German workers from the foreign and degenerate ideology that had seduced them. In 1930, he was shot by Albrecht Höhler, a member of the local Communist Party. When Wessel died three weeks later, Joseph Goebbels orchestrated a provocative and imposing funeral procession through the working-class districts of Berlin. This was the first act in Wessel's "resurrection." In the years that followed, the story of the life and death of Horst Wessel became central to the Nazi cult, and the regime ritually commemorated its comrade as a victim of Communist brutality who still—in the words of the "Horst Wessel Song"—"marched in their ranks in spirit."[4]

Albrecht Höhler was not a Jew. But this did not prevent Goebbels and other Nazis from working to give Wessel's killer a Jewish face. As Wessel lay in the hospital in Friedrichshain, Goebbels denounced the "subhuman" and "murder-crazed, degenerate Communist bandits" who had shot him.[5] Soon after, Hanns Heinz Ewers, best known until then for writing erotically charged horror tales, was commissioned to write a biographic novel about Wessel, after impressing Hitler in a personal meeting. In *Horst Wessel: A German Fate* (1932), Ewers describes a network of villains who had conspired to betray and kill Wessel: "The string-pullers in the Karl Liebknecht House played their little game and played it well." Wessel's killer in the novel was a pimp named Höhler, incited to act by a Jewish girl named Else Cohn ("an anti-fascist girl, a small, ugly person") who in turn was following the orders of "Kronstein," the leader of the Reds in Warsaw. Those who cared to read this novel did not need to be told that Cohn and Kronstein were agents of an international Jewish conspiracy.[6] Ewers also wrote the script for a film, *Hans Westmar: One of Many*, that was based on the details of Wessel's life. In this work, too, many of the Communist leaders are embodiments of ideological and racial menace: a Russian commissar sent by Moscow, a mannish woman, and a wildly stereotypical Jew with a shock of tangled white hair, dark round glasses, bushy eyebrows, and a large nose, who incites the Berlin workers to acts of violence, but who flees from it himself.[7]

In the end, neither the novel nor the film was successful. (Nazi Party ideologues found Ewers's earlier works distasteful and ultimately banned many of them.) Nevertheless, these early attempts to canonize Wessel reflected the zeal with which Nazi Party leaders tried to cast general fears of working-class activism and Communist militancy as a racial threat. For many Germans, the tense political situation of the early 1930s recalled the tumultuous years immediately after 1918, when revolutionaries had briefly ruled in Munich and the Communist

Spartacists, led by Karl Liebknecht and Rosa Luxemburg, had vied
for power in Berlin. Bourgeois Germans across the country had feared
the contagion of revolution. In some cities they had formed civil defense groups to protect themselves and their property. Nationalist newspapers had fed their fears with headlines that proclaimed an impending
"flood" of Bolshevik violence, the virulent spread of "Russian chaos,"
and the prospect of a bloodbath in the streets. After the first turbulent postwar months, the chance of an actual civil war evaporated,
but the fears remained, reinforced by detailed and highly politicized
accounts of revolutionary terror in Munich and other places, and
by press coverage of state repression in the Soviet Union. As the Weimar
Republic descended into crisis once again after 1929, Nazi Party activists preyed on memories of postwar revolutionary upheaval, warning
that Germans must defend themselves against a new wave of revolutionary unrest or else become slaves to alien masters.[8]

The political unrest of the early 1930s afforded many opportunities
to stoke those fears.[9] Young men in the Nazi SA and the Communist
Red Guard clashed in the streets over symbols and public spaces,
nowhere more intensely than in Berlin. The city was the capital of
the Weimar Republic and of a Prussian state still governed by democratic parties. It was also a stronghold of the organized working
class. The Nazi Party worked tirelessly to present street fights there
as a sign that the republic was rotten to the core everywhere. It
blamed Communist strength on the cowardice of bourgeois politicians and presented the Nazi Party's own acts of violence as a justified response to leftist provocations that could redeem Germany
from the humiliation of November 1918 and prevent a new revolutionary reign of terror. And they harnessed generalized public fears
about a destructive civil war to their own belief in the treachery of
the Jewish enemy. In this campaign, Berlin was both a Communist
stronghold and a center of illegitimate Jewish power. Easily conflating
the two, Goebbels wrote in 1930: "The key to power over Germany
lies in Prussia. . . . And the way to power in Prussia goes through the

conquest of Berlin." Throughout the last years of the Weimar Republic, antisemitic articles filled the pages of *Attack*, the Nazi newspaper for Berlin founded by Joseph Goebbels. Goebbels and other writers for the paper routinely tied Jewish Communists to Prussian state and Berlin municipal authorities: all were faces of the "Jewish-Marxist power" that ruled over Germany. No one was a greater target for Nazi slander than the vice president of the Berlin police, Bernhard Weiss (always called by the false and Jewish-sounding name of "Isidor" in the newspaper), a German-Jewish liberal who was routinely defamed as an agent of Jewish Bolsheviks and Jewish capitalists. Such men were the true enemies who had killed Horst Wessel, "soldier of the German revolution," as he fought to conquer Berlin for the Nazi movement. The memory of Wessel's death, Goebbels prophesied after his funeral, would inspire Germany's awakening and sweep them all away.[10]

After Hitler came to power in 1933, Nazi Party leaders kept alive the memory of Communist violence during the "time of struggle."[11] According to the myths they told about themselves, Germany had almost been destroyed in November 1918. The criminals who had seized power built a regime that bred revolutionary uprisings and allowed the Communist Party and other anti-German movements to flourish. Only the Nazi Party had resisted these dangers with the necessary force and commitment of purpose. This brave legacy, crowned by political triumph in 1933, was used to legitimize everything the party had done in the past and would do in the future. In his 1935 address to the Nuremberg Party Congress, Joseph Goebbels rehearsed this history to mobilize party members. He began by denouncing the "criminals" of November 1918. He retold the depredations committed by Jewish Communist revolutionaries in Munich in 1919 and even reprised the false accusation that a Jewish girl named Else Cohn had played an important role in the murder of Horst Wessel. All this was background to the great transformation that 1933 had brought. Now, he said, "we have completely overcome this menace . . . [W]e know

how to cope with these insidious forces." Adolf Hitler had "set up a
barrier against world Bolshevism against which the waves of this vile
Asiatic-Jewish flood break in vain." History would give him credit for
"having saved Germany . . . by overthrowing Bolshevism and thereby
saving the whole civilization of the West."[12]

Officials at the Ministry of Propaganda elaborated on this premise,
explaining the widespread support of German workers for Communism before 1933 in racial terms. Beginning in 1933, the Institute for
the Study of the Jewish Question, under the direction of Eberhard
Taubert, the top ministry specialist for anti-Bolshevik propaganda,
produced a series of studies that "revealed" the Jewish Communist
leaders who had colonized workers' minds in Germany. The foreword
to one such work, *Jew and Worker,* asserted that the problem was not
one of "leader and follower, but of seducer and seduced," "the most
unnatural partnership and political parasitism of a racially alien element, in every respect unequal to the German worker." In keeping
with the narrative of redemption through National Socialism, the racial "expert" F. O. H. Schulz, who wrote the book, concluded optimistically that "in this era of national [*völkisch*] upheaval," the
German worker had recognized that the "opium of Judo-Marxism"
could lead only to the "atomization of the people [*Volk*]," and had thus
begun to "free himself."[13] Nazi vigilance against the Judeo-Bolshevik
enemy had prevented a second November 1918.

But the fear of Judeo-Bolshevism was more than a powerful tool to
mobilize party members. The Nazi Party used anti-Communism
to win over to their vision of a new Germany those who had hitherto
kept their distance. During the Weimar years, the image of the Jewish
Bolshevik had aroused fear far outside the circles of committed Nazi
voters. The presence in German cities of Jewish refugees from Eastern
Europe, especially in the early 1920s, fueled speculation that they had
brought revolutionary destruction with them. The Nazi regime nul-
lified Weimar-era efforts to liberalize Germany's naturalization laws.[14]
Conservative intellectuals obsessed in the 1920s with the survival of

authentic German culture in the modern world had identified Jews with the ravages of materialism and mass culture, coining a new phrase—"culture Bolshevism" (*Kulturbolschewismus*)—to express their concerns. After 1933, the Nazi Party promoted a vision of authentic German culture with a series of popular exhibitions demonizing "Jewish art Bolshevism." These efforts culminated in the massive show of "degenerate art" that toured Germany in 1937.[15] Finally, many Christians, both Catholic and Protestant, associated Jewish Bolsheviks with the dangers of secularization and the inversion of moral and social order. Once in power, the Nazi Party made anti-Communism an important element of Nazi church policy, serving to subordinate the churches to the state while also appealing to the concerns of religious Germans. "Where can our interests," Hitler declared in 1934, "be more convergent than in our struggle against the symptoms of degeneracy in the contemporary world, in our struggle against cultural bolshevism, against the Godless movement, against criminality . . . and for the conquest of class war and class hatred, or civil war and unrest, strife and discord. These are not anti-Christian, but rather Christian principles!"[16]

Most important, the Nazi regime in power embraced tough "law and order" tactics, such as widespread house searches, brutal interrogation procedures, and imprisonment in concentration camps, to deliver on its promise to restore order and eliminate subversive elements. At the same time, a compliant press trumpeted arrests of Communist "terrorists." These reports had a powerful effect, offering many Germans a sign that a corner had been turned while also reinforcing their paranoia about subversives within. In Braunschweig, Elisabeth Gebensleben, wife of a city planning officer, expressed the thoughts of many middle-class Germans when she worried in a letter to her daughter: "Bolshevism has taken far, far deeper anchor than one suspected." She welcomed the tough course that Hitler's government was taking against their political enemies. Even among those still skeptical of the new Nazi order, the police crackdown seemed a good thing. In Dresden, Victor Klemperer wrote in his diary about an acquaintance whose husband had once been factory director but was now reduced to working as a traveling salesman: "They are not well-disposed to the Nazis, but even they repeat the nonsense that is hammered into everyone. . . . After them there would be the Communists and that would be even worse!"[17] In this way, anti-Communism, reinforced by memories of the *Kampfzeit* and the "lessons" that Nazi propagandists drew from them, helped to generate broad consensus for the party's racialized vision of internal security and domestic order.

Hounded by the Nazi state, the Communist Party soon ceased to be a political force in Germany. The purpose of anti-Communism began to change. In 1935 Heinrich Himmler reimagined the role of the security services as "preventive defense" in anticipation of a future war. From that point on, a more powerful Schutzstaffel (SS) could move against a wide range of ideological and racial foes by justifying their actions as preemptive strikes against enemies whom the German people would inevitably meet in battle sooner or later. Reinhard Heydrich, head of the Security Police, explained this "transformation" in broad ideological terms for a 1935 article in the SS journal *Schwarzes Korps:* "When our short-term objective was suddenly achieved, most of our fellow combatants believed . . . our opponents had simply disappeared. . . . Unfortunately our fellow combatants have actually only seen and fought oppositional parties. They do not realize that these parties are merely the external forms of intellectual forces . . . that want to exterminate Germany with all its powerful forces of blood, spirit, and soil. . . . [T]he form of battle has changed. The driving forces of the enemy remain eternally the same." In this eternal struggle for national survival, Bolshevism was clearly "one of the most important instrumental creations of the Jews."[18] Judeo-Bolshevism became a symbol of the need to wage a ruthless war of preemptive defense against racialized threats to national security. In 1941, this ideology would come to drive a murderous onslaught against Jews across the Soviet Union.

Germany was not yet at war in 1936. Even so, the ideological transformation of Judeo-Bolshevism in Nazi Germany had an international dimension. By 1936 many observers in Nazi Germany were
watching events in Spain and France with growing concern. The rise
of Popular Front governments there seemed to be signs of a rising
Communist tide across Europe. Nazi leaders had used fears of civil
war and criminal Jewish saboteurs to win broad support and to con-
solidate their power at home. Now they internationalized this linkage.
Judeo-Bolshevism had been neutralized within, but it remained a
menace abroad. To Hitler and those around him, the course of European politics justified more aggressive measures to protect Germany's
"blood, spirit, and soil." In response, the Nazi regime started to ready
itself for war. At the same time, it also began to promote a vision of
Europe united under German leadership against a common enemy:
Judeo-Bolshevism.

In July 1936, military officers led by General Francisco Franco rose
in Madrid against the Republican government of Spain. Five years
earlier, Republicans had overthrown the monarchy and established
a fragile democracy filled with promise for urban workers and the
rural poor. The Right—a coalition of monarchists that included
landowners, the military, the clergy, and the fascist Falange Party—
denounced the Republic as an international conspiracy to destroy
the "true Spain." The rebellion had multiple causes: the end of the
monarchy had energized separatist movements in Catalonia and
the Basque region that threatened the historical unity of Spain; the
Catholic Church feared a wave of secularization; plans for land reform threatened the power of wealthy landowners; monarchists
hated the Republican government on principle; and all feared the
power of a united Republican Popular Front, which had won a huge
electoral victory earlier in 1936. But across the anti-Republican, or
nationalist, coalition, one belief was common: the civil war that soon

consumed the entire country was a "crusade" against a "Jewish-Masonic-Bolshevist" conspiracy. For all parties in the nationalist coalition, the idea of the Jewish Bolshevik threat crystallized long-held antipathies to liberalism and republicanism into a clearly "visible" enemy. General Miguel Cabanellas, president of the military junta, denounced "freemasons, Jews, and similar parasites." Falangists told the readers of their party newspaper that they "had the obligation to persecute and destroy Judaism, Masonry, Marxism, and separatism." And in his first statement after the civil war began, Cardinal Isidro Gomá, archbishop of Toledo and primate of Spain, asserted that "Jews and masons had poisoned the national soul with absurd doctrines."[19]

The ubiquity of Judeo-Bolshevism talk among Spanish nationalists is remarkable, since there were only perhaps 6,000 Jews living in Spain in the 1930s. The number of Jews in the Spanish protectorate of Morocco was somewhat larger, about 13,000.[20] In addition, some German Jews found their way to Spain after the Nazis seized power. And when the danger to the Republican government became an international cause, antifascists from around the world came to fight for it. Some, like the photographer Robert Capa, who produced some of the most enduring images of the conflict, came from Jewish families; others, like writer George Orwell, did not.[21] All in all, however, the number of Jews in Spain in the years before and during the Spanish Civil War was tiny indeed.

None of that mattered. For nationalists, the specter of a Judeo-Masonic-Bolshevik conspiracy was so powerful precisely because it effectively demonized both their internal and their external enemies. Republican and Catalan leaders alike were portrayed in the pages of the nationalist press as Jews. Nationalists also saw Jewish Bolsheviks as controlling the Soviet Union, which was supplying the Republic with arms and military advisers. Marcel Rosenberg, the Soviet ambassador to the Republic, was a popular target, frequently derided as the "real dictator of Spain." Finally, nationalists denounced France as a country controlled by Jews, after a Popular Front government led by the socialist Léon Blum came to power there in 1936. Although right-wing opposition forced Blum's government to maintain a non-interventionist stance, this fact did not prevent Spanish nationalists from accusing the Blum government of funneling arms to Republicans. In the words of one: "The national uprising [i.e., the anti-Republican war] is bound to be a ruthless war, a heroic crusade against what is going on in France under Mr. Léon Blum." Facing an array of enemies both within and without, Spanish nationalists saw themselves as fighting a holy war to preserve the true nature of Spain as a Catholic monarchy.[22]

The idea of Judeo-Bolshevism that circulated among the different parties to the nationalist coalition in Spain was not identical to the image of the Jewish Bolshevik demonized in Nazi ideology. There were important points of comparison. German veterans of the postwar paramilitary violence on the Baltic borderlands had come to identify Jews with the revolutionary dangers they had fought against during the war and after. The Nazi fusion of anti-Communism, antisemitism, and colonialism in Eastern Europe had an obvious appeal for them.[23] Similarly, accounts of Jewish conspiracy circulated especially widely among military officers, most notably among the so-called Africanistas who manned the garrisons in Spanish Morocco, who believed in Spain's colonial mission in North Africa and who played a central role in Franco's coup d'état in 1936.[24] But the Jewish Bolshevik menace perceived by Spanish nationalists was profoundly shaped by Catholic traditions of anti-Jewish thought that fused Latin Christian ideas about monarchy, nationalism, and the state with Catholic traditions of anti-Freemasonry, antisecularism, and antisemitism.[25] For this reason, Spanish nationalists invariably described Communism as a Jewish-Marxist-*Masonic* plot with an emphasis on all three parts of an unholy trinity that would have sounded strange in the German context, even if Nazi ideologues did also vilify Freemasonry.[26] And Spanish anti-Communists invested the Judeo-Bolshevik enemy with meaning by embedding it in a distinctly Spanish narrative of national history. Many Spanish nationalists believed that the Popular Front and the Republican government that preceded it were a conspiracy to punish Spain for expelling the Jews and defeating the Moors in 1492, and then upholding a traditional Catholic monarchy in the centuries that followed. As General Emilio Mola, a chief plotter of the 1936 coup, had written as early as 1922, Jews hated Spain "because they blame it for their dispersion throughout the world."[27] Vanquished in the reign of Ferdinand and Isabella, this age-old enemy of all Spaniards had returned again in the guise of Communism. Needless to say, this account held no significance at all for Hitler and his colleagues in Germany.

Nevertheless, the Nazi regime saw an opportunity in the Spanish crisis to reshape the international order in Europe. Events in Spain (as well as the Popular Front victory in France that same year) allowed Hitler to project his obsessions with German expansion and racial survival onto an ideologically polarized and dramatically fluid European stage. During the time of struggle, Nazi leaders had shoehorned domestic fears of disorder and civil war into their own vision of the eternal struggle between Germany and its racial enemies. Now, in 1936, fears of Communist power were once again widespread. This real political contest provided a tangible point of reference for Nazi fantasies about war, the clash of races, and Germany's global future. The common image of a Judeo-Bolshevik enemy, shared by Nazi leaders and Spanish Francoists, even if expressed in different idioms, added emotional and ideological substance to this vision.

At the closing session of the Nazi Party's 1936 Nuremberg Rally, dubbed the "Party Rally of Honor" to signify the symbolic power of the remilitarization of the Rhineland in March of that year, Hitler spoke at length about his determination to destroy the Bolshevik threat that had reared its head most recently in Spain. He declared to the assembled party members and to the international public at large: "We will fight [Moscow Bolshevism] as a world power, if it wants to try with new and more violent methods to spread the Spanish misfortune also over Germany." He insisted that the threat was pan-

European: "Bolshevism has attacked and put into question the bases of our human state and social order, our conception of culture, our foundations of belief, our moral views." In the face of this ideological menace, every European nation would have to set aside liberal bourgeois scruples, he declared, as Germany had done. Indeed, Europeans would witness to German resolve in this time of crisis: "For you can count on this in this time of international revolution: In Germany, the German people will remain master in their own house! And not Judeo-Bolshevik Sovietism."[28]

Nazi propagandists developed this pan-European vision still further. In 1937 the publishing house of the Anti-Comintern, the agency within the Propaganda Ministry responsible for anti-Soviet propaganda, released the *Red Book on Spain*, a collection of documents, pictures, and eyewitness accounts, to show the cruelties perpetrated by the Republicans and especially by the Soviet forces sent by Stalin to support them. In the foreword, Eberhard Taubert, the head of the Anti-Comintern, wrote that "just as the puppet masters of this campaign of destruction consciously and methodically fight peace, so does the great pack of those tiny Jews and Bolsheviks around the world . . . who work as the disguised vanguard of Moscow." These fiends preach peace, which is in reality a call to war, he said, conceived in an "atmosphere of bloody and fanatical hatred against national states."[29] Taubert also commissioned books by other authors. He assigned the Dutch writer Maria de Smeth, an enthusiastic supporter of Nazi Germany who had made her name with her account of four months spent in a Soviet prison, to tour Spain to collect proof of Soviet involvement in the Spanish Civil War. After seven months in Spain, from November 1936 to May 1937, de Smeth returned to Germany to write *Viva España! Arriba España! Eine Frau erlebt den spanischen Krieg* (Long live Spain! A woman experiences the Spanish War), in which she presented her impressions of Spain in prose shot through with denunciations of Communism and the Jews who pulled its strings. She too was convinced of the international importance of Spain: "The battle in Spain is no private affair of the Spanish. That is only the front line of the moment. The Spanish people are fighting against the international mercenaries of the most closed people on the planet: against the Jewish idea of world domination, called—Bolshevism!"[30]

Soon the Nazi regime was supplying nationalist forces in Spain with arms and military personnel, including air power. Airmen in the so-called Condor Legion, celebrated in Germany for their gallantry and courage, began to rehearse the tactics of terror bombing that would be widely used during World War II, most infamously using them on April 26, 1937, at Guernica in the Basque country of northern Spain.[31] At the same time, Hitler proposed new diplomatic arrangements based on a shared stance against Communism. In these years, the Nazi regime tried to construct an "anti-Comintern" out of formal partnerships built, at least publicly, on a shared anti-Communist agenda.[32] First to sign was Japan, in November 1936. It was followed in November 1937 by Italy, a country whose relations with Nazi Germany grew ever closer as the Italian Fascist regime deepened its support for nationalist forces in Spain. Hitler explained these coalition-building efforts in his closing speech to the Nazi Party's 1937 Nuremberg Rally. "We have a serious interest in making sure that this Bolshevik plague does not spread further over Europe . . . [f]or I believe that we cannot leave out or wish away any of the real European culture-nations. We owe each to each not only some trouble and sorrow, but also a huge mutual enrichment. . . . Jewish Bolshevism is an absolute alien body in this community of European culture-nations."[33] It seemed that Nazi Germany was proposing a Europe united in an anti-Bolshevik crusade.

On the same day in September 1936 that Adolf Hitler spoke about the evils of Judeo-Bolshevik Sovietism at the Nazi Party's annual Nuremberg Rally, Pope Pius XI received a large number of Catholic clergymen at the Castel Gandolfo, the historic papal summer residence fifteen miles southeast of Rome. The visiting priests were from Spain, where the Catholic Church was under attack by Republican forces. Across Europe, Catholics had been following the persecution of their church with keen interest. In the months that followed, they devoured articles in their confessional newspapers about the destruction of churches in Spain, the seizure of church property, and the imprisonment or murder of priests and nuns. Now, in the autumn of 1936, as the civil war in Spain rapidly escalated, this delegation of Spanish priests had come to Rome to bear witness to their suffering. They also hoped to hear the Vatican fully identify itself with the nationalist cause, which they believed was a holy war against Communism.[34]

When the pope spoke to them—in an address generally titled "La vostra presenza"—Pius described the Spanish Civil War as a warning to all of Europe. He said that the suffering of the Catholic faithful in Spain proved to all that "satanic" forces had lit the "flames of hatred" and unleashed the "wildest persecutions." He also declared that the foundations of "order, civilization, and culture" were under immediate and extreme threat. After these rousing words, he concluded with a prayer that Spain would someday once again be guided by the principles of religion, social justice, the sanctity of the family, social authority, and order.[35] It was a resoundingly anti-Communist message. Yet the Spanish visitors were disappointed. The pope had not called the conflict in Spain a "crusade" or a "holy war." Nor had he demonized their enemies with the violent language against Judeo-Masonic-Bolshevism that was common among nationalists in Spain. Instead, he had spoken about hatred and persecution in the most general terms and then prayed for peace and order.

Back in Spain, Catholic and nationalist journalists carefully edited the speech. Glossing over the nuances, they simply highlighted the most anti-Communist sections of the text in ways that allowed their readers to believe that the Vatican supported their crusade after all. The following year, the Spanish episcopate sent a "collective letter" to fellow bishops around the world that also emphasized the war in Spain was a holy war against Communism. The Vatican never endorsed the letter's text, but other Catholics did. Just as they had at the height of the Polish-Soviet War in 1920, Poland's bishops made their own statement about the international danger of Bolshevism. They proclaimed solidarity with their Spanish brethren and completely identified with the conviction in Catholic Spain that the civil war was a holy war between good and evil. Bolshevism, the Polish bishops declared, was an evil Satanic "plot." Anti-Christian enemies were on the march in Spain and Poland alike.[36]

The coincidental timing of the papal audience in Rome and the Nazi Party rally in Nuremberg exposed a dilemma that became more acute for Christians across Europe by the second half of the 1930s. In Germany, the regime in power made anti-Communism a centerpiece of its elaborately staged ceremonies. Its leaders spoke at length about the dangers of Communism, and its propaganda offices produced a growing mass of images, books, and exhibition materials that targeted the Soviet Union and its allies in Western Europe as dangerous and destructive forces. In every case, Nazi Germany identified the Communist enemy as "Judeo-Bolshevism," which they defined as a threat to order and civilization everywhere. This was familiar language to Europe's Christians. Catholics and Protestants alike had routinely associated Communism or Bolshevism with the "Jewish" evils of secularism, atheism, and materialism. They had also identified Jews as the leading revolutionaries and labeled them the enemies of Europe's Christian nations. But these ideas were now being championed loudly by Nazi Germany, whose leaders believed that state power should be absolute and that German hegemony should extend over the entire continent. Increasingly, the idea of Judeo-Bolshevism was becoming associated with Nazi power. Embracing the first meant supporting the second.

The dilemma was greatest in Germany. Since 1933, Christian churches there had struggled to defend their institutional autonomy against a regime intent on eliminating independent civic activity and imposing state authority over religious life. Church youth groups were dissolved, the Catholic-aligned Center Party was banned, and clergy were monitored for antistate activity. In this repressive climate, anti-Communism promised to be a point of consensus that church leaders could use to gain some breathing room. Two months after the 1936 Nuremberg Rally, Cardinal Michael Faulhaber journeyed to Hitler's retreat in Berchtesgaden to congratulate him on his powerful speech. There, he was treated to a long diatribe about Bolshevism and Jews. "How the subhumans, incited by the Jews, created havoc in Spain like beasts," Hitler declared. Their victory "would mean the end of Christianity and the Churches in Europe." Faulhaber agreed and compared Hitler's "great speech at the Nuremberg Party Rally" to the pope's address to the Spanish clergy. While Hitler had "impressively explained the cultural and economic consequences of Bolshevism (it can only destroy, it is led by Jews . . .)," he said, the pope had "described atheism, godlessness, and blasphemy" as the root and essence of Bolshevism. Faulhaber presented the two positions as mutually compatible and urged Hitler to revise his church policy so that the Catholic Church could be an ally to the National Socialist state. A month later (on Christmas Eve), Faulhaber released a pastoral letter titled "On the Defense against Bolshevism" that made this claim even more strongly: "Adolf Hitler saw the march of Bolshevism from afar and turned his mind and energies toward averting this enormous danger from the German people and the whole Western world. The German bishops consider it their duty . . . to support the leader of the Reich with every available means in this defense." Such pandering gravely compromised the church's moral authority, and it got Faulhaber nowhere politically. Hitler ignored the cardinal's institutional concerns, and state discrimination against the church continued unabated.[37]

Elsewhere, European Catholics could debate the threat that Hitler's version of anti-Communism posed to their church more openly.

As they watched Nazi encroachment on traditional church authority
with growing alarm, some of them began to develop novel theories
of church-state relations that equated Communism and Nazism as
equally dangerous systems of secular political power. They called
these systems "totalitarian." The French Catholic theologian and philosopher Jacques Maritain is the best example of this shift. In the
early 1920s Maritain had still been a follower of the proto-fascist Action Française who believed that Bolshevism had arisen from the
radical strangeness of the Jewish faith. "An essentially messianic
people such as the Jews," he wrote in 1921, "from the instant when
they reject the true Messiah," inevitably become "the most active
ferment of revolution."[38] By the 1930s Maritain had broken with fascism and begun to explore the dangers that secular politics in all its
forms posed to the dignity of the human person. He rejected Nazism
and Communism alike as political theologies that wrongly elevated
material categories (class, race) to divine status and endowed the
state with powers over matters of faith and conscience that it should
not have. Most important, he also began to see Judaism differently.
He believed that its strangeness, which he now called the "mystery
of Israel," should inspire Christians to defend human dignity against
the totalitarian evil emanating from Moscow *and* Berlin.[39]

Maritain was not alone. Others also rejected the "ideological division of the world into Bolshevik and anti-Bolshevik in the spirit of the
Nuremberg Party Rally as false," to take the words of the German
Catholic philosopher Dietrich von Hildebrand.[40] Hildebrand had fled
Germany for Vienna, where an authoritarian Catholic state was desperately trying to resist popular enthusiasm for Nazism within and
German political pressure from without. While Austria remained independent, Hildebrand and a small group of like-minded Catholics
there wrote trenchant critiques of the Nazi and Soviet states, Hitler's
deification of blood and race, and the irreducible dignity of the human
person in the face of all these secular perils.[41] Their intellectual work
in Vienna, together with the writings of Maritain and others in France

and elsewhere, represented a new and comparative understanding of Communism within Catholic Europe, ultimately expressed in two papal encyclicals issued within days of each other in March 1937. The encyclicals, *Mit brennender Sorge* (written to address the "painful trials of the church" in Germany) and *Divini Redemptoris* (on "atheistic Communism"), defended human dignity against the predations of the collective. Without question, their critique of Communism was more forceful than their critique of Nazism, but the Pope condemned both for the same reasons. The contrast with Nazi anti-Communism was stark.[42]

A similar debate about Communism gripped Europe's Protestants.[43] Again German churches were at the epicenter. Some German Protestants, calling themselves German Christians to emphasize their racial identity, enthusiastically echoed state ideology on matters of race and politics: "Bolshevism in Soviet Russia," declared the editor of *The Gospel in the Third Reich*, "has spilled streams of Christian blood. . . . Bolshevism in Spain, works the same way—it all follows the same approach: it is the Jewish-Bolshevik war of annihilation against the Christian church."[44] Others worried about state control over religious life, and tried to defend themselves and their autonomy by insisting on their bona fides as anti-Communists and patriots who had fought against "culture Bolshevism" and "godless atheism" throughout the Weimar era. In November 1936, Germany's Protestant bishops declared that they "stood with the Führer in the German Volk's life-and-death fight against Bolshevism," but also insisted that the church needed "internal freedom . . . to do its work."[45] One Protestant group (the Confessing Church) went even further, declaring that the state had no right at all to intervene in internal church affairs and no authority to decide who was a Christian and who was not. In response, they were targeted as traitors by the regime and accused of serving "Jewish masters." Some, like Confessing Church leader Martin Niemöller (a conservative nationalist, decorated war veteran, and member in 1920 of the paramilitary Freikorps), were arrested and imprisoned in concentration camps. A Confessing Church leader in Schleswig-Holstein fumed at the irony that Protestant nationalists who had remained fiercely loyal to the German people and the German state were now lumped into the "same front with Jewish-led Bolshevism!"[46]

The travails of the German church riveted Protestants on both sides of the Atlantic. Of course, there could be no authoritative declarations of the sort that Pope Pius XI issued in 1937. Nevertheless, many Protestants in Europe and North America found their way to a similar understanding of Communism and Nazism. That same year, a long-anticipated ecumenical congress was held at Oxford University. The gathering was powerfully shaped by the Anglo-American Protestants who were prominent among the organizers. Responding to a travel ban imposed by the Nazi regime on their German colleagues, the conference issued a powerful letter in support of the Confessing Church. Working groups of participants also articulated points of consensus on core matters of faith shared by Christians of all denominations. The relationship between state, community, and individual believer was one of the most intensely discussed topics. Conference delegates agreed that secular "pseudo-religions" were a rising threat to Christian communities around the world. With one eye firmly on Germany, they listed radical nationalism alongside Communism as contemporary examples. Both were materialist creeds that denied individual dignity and subordinated the human person to ideological categories. The "deification of nation, race, or class, or of political or cultural ideals, is idolatry," the delegates declared. "Communism may differ theoretically, but does not differ practically from other contemporary totalitarian movements."[47]

The emerging totalitarian consensus did not signal the end of Christian antisemitism. The struggle of Christians to confront the legacy of anti-Jewish thought within their doctrines and their churches has been well documented, as has the silence of many Christians during World War II in the face of the Holocaust. Nor did the new theories of totalitarianism displace the firm conviction held by many Christians, even leaders in the hierarchies of national churches, that Communism was uniquely associated with Jews. Nevertheless, the idea that Communism and Nazism were comparable threats to Christian faith and to the independence of the Christian believer reimagined anti-Communism in ways that were utterly distinct from the crusade against Judeo-Bolshevism that Hitler proclaimed at Nuremberg. After 1945, antitotalitarianism would come into its own. In the 1930s, however, it was still just one of the possible ways to oppose the Soviet experiment. The Christian churches were struggling to adapt to a new Europe in which Nazi Germany was the preeminent anti-Bolshevik power and the vision of a crusade against Communism was inseparable from the spread of Nazi ideology. Other Europeans were far less ambivalent.

Always quick to capitalize on dramatic international developments, French writers Jean and Jérôme Tharaud devoted their attention to the ideological struggles that divided 1930s Europe. Having visited Budapest in 1920 to research a book on Jews and Bolshevism (*When Israel Is* King), they traveled to Hitler's Germany in 1933 to collect notes for another of their "travelogue novels." They gave this one the title *Quand Israël n'est plus roi* (When Israel is no longer king). It became their most controversial book. The brothers were astonished by the transformation that an uncultured, intellectually unimpressive former corporal had wrought in Germany. "Where are these realities that seemed so indestructible? Where are the Communists? Where are the Socialists?" they wrote.[48] Before January 1933, Germany had been politically unstable and divided by ideological tensions so great that many Germans wondered if the country were not on the brink of a civil war. Those fears had seemingly vanished. The Tharauds insisted that reports of anti-Jewish persecution were overblown, although they were also understandable, because Jews had

exercised so much cultural and economic power during the years of
the Weimar Republic. They described Adolf Hitler's antisemitism as
coming from hard-won experience, the result of having seen Jewish
revolutionaries in power in Munich in 1919. Germans, the Tharauds
insisted with not a little condescension toward their neighbors across
the Rhine, were a people congenitally attracted to abstract systems like
Communism. To save themselves, Germans had turned to Hitler. Now
(the Tharauds imagined), Hitler offered comfort to the nation: "Rest
easy. . . . First let us begin by protecting you from the Jews, because,
as you know, Jewry and Bolshevism are the same thing."[49]

When the Spanish Civil War erupted across France's southern
border, the Tharauds pivoted to that new turn of events, and traveled
to Spain to see the war for themselves. Since writing their account of
Hungary's Bolshevik revolution, they had viewed Jewish Bolshevism
as a threat to all of European civilization. For the Tharauds, lurid stories about Jewish revolutionaries from Eastern Europe destroying
the moral order elsewhere were important mainly for the power they
contained to shock and urge Western readers into action. The upheaval in Spain presented them with new material to fashion into a
cautionary tale. Their tour through the Spanish theater of war inspired
them to reflect on the similarities between Communism and Islam.
They believed both were cruel and tyrannical systems with no regard
for spirit or morality. Spain, they concluded, was doubly cursed,
because long centuries of Muslim rule had bequeathed a culture of
violence that Communist revolutionaries had revived. They ended
their novel *Cruelle Espagne* (Cruel Spain) with a prayer to Saint
Martin: "Pray for unfortunate Spain! And . . . pray for us, you, the
great patron of this Occidental Christian Europe. . . . And do not let
us fall, not to Marx and not to Lenin, under the Gospel of a German
Jew as interpreted by a Mongol!"[50]

The writers Robert Brasillach and Henri Massis also spent time in
Spain during the civil war, tying events there to their broader con-

cerns about the state of French culture. They were deeply moved by the saga of General Moscardo, who led the defense of the Alcázar of Toledo, in the face of a far larger Republican force, until the siege could be lifted. In a novelistic account, Brasillach and Massis celebrated this victory as a triumph for all Europe: "Twice, against the Moor and the Turk . . . Spain has saved Western civilization from a peril originating in the East. Today she is rising up against another peril, against a more insidious and perhaps more domineering East."[51] Charles Maurras, leader of Action Française, found similar meaning in the capturing of historic Spanish cities that were under Republican rule, writing, in the preface to an account of the Spanish war by a fellow Catholic royalist, that Franco's forces came as liberators to return them to Rome and the Latin West, and to prevent their decline into "cosmopolitan cities" like Moscow, Jerusalem, or—Maurras was ever a Germanophobe—Berlin.[52]

The French Right followed events in Spain so avidly, and took such hope from nationalist victories, because they feared that the civil war to the south was a harbinger of upheavals that would soon take place in France itself. In 1936 the antifascist Popular Front, comprising liberal, socialist, and Communist parties, won elections in France only three months after the Popular Front had come to power in Spain. In their euphoria, workers across France launched a general strike. They soon won an astonishing set of social rights that included the right to strike and to organize freely, the right to collective bargaining, the forty-hour work week, and the right to paid vacations. "Everything is possible!" exulted French socialist Marceau Pivert. The Right agreed with him and denounced the strike as a clear act of treason organized by "Soviet leaders." The pages of Maurras's journal *Action Française* were filled with denunciations of the "*bolchevisante* and Judeo-Marxist rabble" who threatened law and order.[53] Meanwhile, many wealthy French citizens made plans to transfer their assets out of the country and beyond the reach of the Blum government.

As premier of the new Popular Front government, Léon Blum, a French Jew and a socialist, immediately became a magnet for fears, prominent in rightist circles since Édouard Drumont had first artic- ulated them in the 1880s, of a "Jewish France" cut off from its roots and its identity. In Blum, whose proper family name right-wing writers insisted on "unmasking" as Karfunkelstein, the nationalist right saw a man whose ethnic breeding could only make him a "state-destroyer," in the tradition of the revolutionaries who had destroyed the Russian Empire.[54] In this climate, new accounts of the Jewish stranglehold on power in the Soviet Union circulated widely in the newspapers and publishing houses of the far right.[55] At the same time, Blum became a target of unparalleled vitriol. Speaking on the floor of the Chamber of Deputies, the extreme rightist Xavier Vallat described Blum's rise to power as the last act in a long national decline. For the first time, he said, "this ancient Gallo-Roman country will be governed by a Jew."[56] Writing a few months later in Action Française, the far-right journalist Léon Daudet linked all these themes in vulgar fashion, comparing Blum to a dog whose "ethnic fate" was his master, a master who had "taken him for a Hebraic tinkle and a Communist shit." Others scoured Léon Blum's publications for evidence to prove both his personal perversity and his long-held plans to subvert French cul- ture.[57] Many took his 1907 book on marriage, in which Blum argued that both men and women needed to have a variety of premarital sexual experiences for a marriage to be happy and stable, as proof that Blum planned nothing less than an assault on the moral fabric that underlay French civilization. In one such analysis, Judaïsme et Marx- isme by Louis Massoutié, the author tied Blum's views to Soviet di- vorce laws, which were an affront to fundamental Christian values. Massoutié concluded that Marxism was a plot to destroy "occidental civilization" and bring about "the triumph of the Jewish people," and warned: "It is clear that nations, perceiving the danger that threatens them, will sooner or later take a defensive position that will bring the most dire calamities on Israel."[58]

Fears of civilizational decline loomed large in France in these years and shaped discussions of Communism and Judeo-Bolshevism. In 1927 Henri Massis had set the tone for a generation with a powerful depiction of Western civilization in crisis. In *Défense de l'Occident* (*Defence of the West*), Massis argued that the West was no longer able to assert its superiority over the nonwhite peoples of the world. Beset by an "Asiatic crisis" that included Bolshevik revolution, but also Eastern mysticism and modernity more generally, Europeans had abandoned the cultural values that defined them at the moment of greatest crisis: "Our ideas no longer belong to us," he lamented.[59] In the years that followed, a Young Right took Massis's account of the decline of the West as inspiration, embracing the apocalyptic tone of his analysis as the point of departure for their own cultural critique, which they believed pointed the way to a renewal of France, and with it, European civilization.[60] For intellectuals on the extreme right, this sense of crisis found expression in acute fears of eroding boundaries. Throughout the last years of the 1930s, the pages of newspapers like *Je suis partout* and *Gringoire* were filled with visions of a France brought low by Judeo-Bolshevik power, racial and sexual contamination, and French emasculation.[61]

Extreme rightists also connected the idea of Judeo-Bolshevism to fears of eroding French colonial power. Just as the Africanista officers at the heart of the nationalist revolt in Spain maintained that theirs was a struggle against the Jews and Moors who aimed to overturn the victories of the *reconquista*, French intellectuals on the extreme right argued that Bolshevism was a harbinger not only of rising Jewish power but also of broken racial hierarchies. In his 1937 screed *Bagatelles pour un massacre*, Louis-Ferdinand Céline may have notoriously fashioned the French as "natives" colonized by "Negroid Jews," but he was not the only one to do so.[62] In Algeria, French settlers believed in a vision of a French Algeria that excluded Jews, *indigènes*, and Marxists. Support for the nationalists in Spain was widespread; right-wing combat leagues like the Croix de

feu dominated local politics, drawing support because they offered
settlers a powerful weapon against an Algerian Left that was gaining
popularity among Muslims. For many French settlers, and not only
those on the far right, the Popular Front victory was a catastrophe;
Léon Blum's selection of Maurice Violette as minister of state,
charged with implementing electoral reforms in Algeria that would
promise citizenship to the French-educated Muslim elite, seemed a
harbinger of further challenges to racial and social order. In the
weeks that followed, rightist leagues reacted to an upsurge in labor
activism and Popular Front rallies with protests of their own. In Oran,
the right-wing mayor responded to Jewish socialist demonstrators
with a Hitler salute; two days later, Croix de feu members vandalized
a local bar and then went to the Jewish quarter, shouting "Down with
the Jews!" "Blum to the gallows!" and "Long live fascism!" Throughout
the last years of the 1930s, the fusion of racial hierarchy, antisemitism, and anti-Leftism that defined French Algeria only became
more entrenched in wide circles of European settlers in Algeria.[63]

The French Right's vision of national redemption, against which
was invariably juxtaposed the threat of Judeo-Bolshevism, led the
Right to see possibilities in a deeper collaboration with Germany.[64]
Nazi ideology could be an ally in the Right's opposition to the un-
loved republic and the Popular Front government that seemed to embody its worst aspects. In the East, such calculations were far more
complicated. Local variations on the fusion of anti-Communism and
antisemitism had long histories in countries like Hungary, Romania,
and Poland. They resonated in many ways with the rhetoric proclaimed at Nuremberg. But an anti-Communist crusade in the East
necessarily meant the spread of Nazi political, economic, and cultural
power. Without question, there were fascists in some places who were
eager to join the ideological fight on those terms. Others, both traditional conservatives and more extreme rightists, had reservations precisely because Nazi anti-Communism was so tightly tied to German

imperial ambitions. In 1930s Eastern Europe, doing battle with Judeo-Bolshevism could never be divorced from questions of national sovereignty and German hegemony.

The specter of Judeo-Bolshevism was deeply entrenched in the political language of the Polish Right. In right-wing nationalist and Catholic publications, it remained an article of faith, long after the signing of the Treaty of Riga, that Poland's Jews had supported the Red Army during the Polish-Soviet War. So did the belief that Jews exercised undue influence within the Soviet state. In one 1927 novel, *A gdy komunizm zapanuje . . . Powieść przyszłości* (If Communism prevails . . . : A novel of the future), the writer Edmund Jezierski imagines a Soviet occupation of Poland twenty years in the future. Jews figure in this dystopia as the vanguard of an anti-Polish civilization.[65] Writers for the Polish Catholic daily *Mały Dziennik* (Little journal) routinely reminded their readers that "factually Soviet Russia is ruled by Jews," focusing particular attention on the role they believed Jews played in the Soviet secret police. Other extremists, such as Father Stanisław Trzeciak, repeated the argument that Jews had betrayed the Polish army during the 1920 Polish-Soviet War and thus jeopardized the existence of the Polish state. Convictions like these disposed Catholic publicists to interpret world events in light of recent national history as they understood it. The Catholic press in Poland published detailed reports of atrocities committed by Republican forces against priests and nuns in Spain, connecting them to Poland's own experience of anti-Bolshevik struggle.[66] The constant association of Jews and Bolshevism in rightist and Catholic circles became the context in which many people heard pronouncements by ethnonationalist politicians, that—in the words of the 1937 Ideological Declaration issued by the authoritarian Camp of National Unity (Obóz Zjednoczenia Narodowego, or OZN) that governed Poland from 1936 to 1939—"a

Communist Poland would cease to be Poland."[67] The nationalists in Spain fighting with Franco might have said the same thing about their own country.

But Polish nationalists had little enthusiasm for a German-led international crusade against Judeo-Bolshevism. Certainly the Polish government remained staunchly anti-Communist throughout the interwar years, not least because of the territorial implications that went with supporting the Soviet Union to the east. Inevitably, "the communist choice meant supporting the immediate partition of Poland and the attachment of its eastern lands to the Soviet Union."[68] Polish security forces kept a close watch on Communist Party activity. By the 1930s, they had rendered Communism in Poland politically irrelevant. Poland and Germany even signed a nonaggression pact in 1934. Despite all this, the Polish government had every reason to be wary of German intentions. Throughout the interwar years German nationalists on both sides of Poland's western border denounced Polish cultural imperialism in Upper Silesia, Danzig, and other areas of the borderland that had German-speaking minorities. After 1933 the Nazi regime supported these efforts, thereby fueling political tensions between the two states.[69] Poland's political leaders saw the Anti-Comintern Pact in this light, as an instrument of German hegemony. (When asked to sign, the Polish government declined, declaring only that "Poland would never be found in the Bolshevik camp."[70]) Even Polish fascists, who hoped to transform Poland into a prototo-talitarian state like Germany, remained wary of German plans for ethnic domination in Eastern Europe.[71]

Hungary's government should have been more receptive to a German-led crusade against Communism. The country had been ruled since 1919 by a counterrevolutionary regime that had made the idea of Judeo-Bolshevism central to its political identity and that commemorated the defeat of the Bolshevik regime as the rebirth of "Christian Hungary." Many of the most ardent anti-Communists of 1919 had risen to prominent positions of political power in the years that followed. They had suppressed the Left, arrested some Communist Party members and driven others into exile, and reduced Hungary's Social Democratic Party to political irrelevance. Many of them openly admired Hitler's Germany for its vision of national unity, its dramatic economic revival, and its open desire to redraw borders that had been established at the postwar Paris peace talks. Hungary's political establishment applauded Germany on this last point especially loudly, because it hoped to regain territory that had been lost to neighboring states, in this case in the 1920 Treaty of Trianon. There should have been no more enthusiastic supporter of the new German vision of a Europe united against the Judeo-Bolshevik menace.

Yet Hungary also refused (at first) to sign the Anti-Comintern Pact. When German and Italian diplomats asked the Hungarian government to join them in signing the agreement, Hungary's prime minister, Kálmán Kánya, declared, "Hungary is always willing, even in the international field, to take up a position openly alongside the anti-Communist states." But nothing tangible came from those words, simply because Hungary's political leaders did not see that signing the pact would be in the national interest. Territorial revision remained the alpha and omega of Hungarian diplomacy. For much of the 1930s, most responsible Hungarian politicians still felt that British and French support were crucial to any hope of revision. So long as they believed this, they would not do more than declare their anti-Communist sympathies. In frustration, Count Ciano, the Italian minister of foreign affairs, expressed his irritation at his Hungarian counterpart's "occasional Anglophile slips." For his part, Hitler complained of Hungary's ability to "get lost in matters of minor political importance." Only after Germany began to forcibly redraw the map of Europe through annexation and to draw the states of Eastern Europe more closely into its economic orbit did the Hungarian government change its position. In November 1938 Hitler awarded Hungary a tiny sliver of Czechoslovakia that had once been Hungarian. Two months later, Hungary signed the Anti-Comintern Pact. It was a "formal gesture of political and diplomatic obeisance to Berlin" that had nothing to do with the Soviet Union at all.[72]

Fear of an international Judeo-Bolshevik conspiracy played no role in these calculations. The Hungarian Right continued to believe that the 1919 Béla Kun regime was a Jewish conspiracy, and Hungarian analysts of the "Jewish question" continued to interpret the revolution as one important manifestation of Jewish power over Christian Hungary.[73] But Bolshevism no longer threatened the political and social order in Hungary. After the defeat of his revolution, Béla Kun had fled to the Soviet Union. (In 1937 he was accused of Trotskyist deviations and executed some months later, a victim of Stalin's purge trials.) Others who tried to take his place, such as the young Mátyás Rákosi, leader of the Hungarian Communist Party after 1945, were in Hungarian jails. Throughout the interwar period, the police kept working-class organizations under careful surveillance. By 1935, Prime Minister Gyula Gömbös, himself a veteran of the counterrevolutionary White Terror of the early 1920s, was absolutely justified in declaring: "The time of socialism, as a party, is over."[74] In this climate, Jewish economic power seemed a more pressing topic to Hungarian rightists. Impressed by Nazi measures against German Jews, they clamored for similar laws that would force Jews from their jobs, transfer Jewish wealth, and promote a "Christian middle class." In 1938 Hungary's parliament passed an anti-Jewish law that began to do all those things. A year later, it passed another. Neither had anything to do with anti-Communism or the Soviet threat.

At the same time, claims that a "national revolution" had empowered Germany to meet the racial-ideological threat of Bolshevism wherever and whenever it might appear did resonate with some Hungarians. One of them was the antisemitic journalist and editor Zoltán Bosnyák. In radical right-wing newspapers like A Cél (The goal), Bosnyák published his own columns along with carefully edited snippets of news from across Europe in order to make a consistent argument for tough new laws to strip Jewish Hungarians of their rights and property and to make Hungary "free" for Hungarians. By the mid-1930s, Bosnyák and many of the antisemitic publicists active since the earliest days of the counterrevolutionary "Christian-national course" begun in the aftermath of the 1919 Bolshevik revolution had become discouraged. Indeed, one of the leading "race defenders" of the 1920s, Gyula Gömbös, had become prime minister in 1932 (and then died unexpectedly in 1936). And Hungary's numerus clausus law, passed in 1920 to restrict the number of Jews receiving professional diplomas, had had a measurable effect on admissions policies at Hungarian universities, even if the law itself had been rewritten and then quietly shelved. Nevertheless, Bosnyák and his allies felt that Christian nationalism had become little more than an empty phrase, as Hungarian political leaders made arrangements of convenience with Hungary's financial and cultural elites. In this cozy climate, Bosnyák believed, Hungary's Jews, who had nearly brought the nation to its knees in 1919, had once again become comfortable. In the space of less than twenty years, the nation had sunk back into the state of abjection that enemies like Béla Kun had exploited once before, with nearly catastrophic results.[75]

In 1936 Bosnyák took a break from his busy life as a newspaper editor to translate a German work that he found timely and ideally suited for a Hungarian audience: Hermann Fehst's 1934 *Bolschewismus und Judentum* (Bolshevism and Jewry).[76] Fehst's "exposé" of Jewish power in the Soviet Union was one of the first products of Nazi Germany's Institute for the Study of the Jewish Question, founded by Eberhard Taubert in 1934 under the aegis of the Ministry of Propaganda. (In 1943 Bosnyák would become director of a similarly named institute in Hungary.) The book was thoroughly typical of Nazi anti-Communist and anti-Soviet propaganda in those years. In making this work (and a preface that he added) available to his Hungarian readers, Bosnyák adapted Nazi anti-Communist propaganda to a specifically Hungarian context. In Germany, he argued, the Nazi regime, "led by Hitler's political and organizational genius," had dealt Bolshevism a "deadly blow." In response, the forces of world revolution had begun "ever more feverish activity," opening contacts with "Western European Jewish radical and freemasonic" circles, cajoling bourgeois liberal parties to join them in an alliance, and spreading their shadow so widely that the nightmare of Bolshevik rule had awoken even in Spain. In light of this, the work of Hermann Fehst was all the more valuable, because he showed exactly who stood behind the Soviet threat, and who had the most to gain from the fragmentation of Europe and Western civilization. No people, Bosnyák argued, needed to be reminded of the truths that Fehst told more than the Hungarians. The feeling of "national self-esteem" that had driven the Hungarian people to fight so implacably against the Jewish Bolshevik "mob" that had ruled over Hungary in 1919 had "completely died out of us," Bosnyák lamented. Once more the "revolutionary mob" had donned "white togas" and was speaking freely in the "Hungarian forum." The flames of counter-revolution had died out, and Hungarians would do well to take instruction from the desperate struggles for national life and death that were being waged elsewhere in Europe.[77]

Romania provides an even more vivid example of both the ideological excitement and the diplomatic calculation that Nazi Germany's transnational crusade against Communism provoked. On February 11, 1937, thousands of uniformed members of Romania's fascist Legion of the Archangel Michael, also known as the Iron Guard, assembled at the train station in Bucharest to meet a train carrying the coffins of two fallen comrades, Ion Moța and Vasile Marin. Three months earlier, the two men had led an elite group of seven legionaries to Spain, where they had paid honor to the Francoist cause and been killed fighting for it. In death, they were translated into martyrs. With much pomp and circumstance, the train carrying their caskets returned to Bucharest, passing first through Berlin, where SS and SA units, including a detachment of Hitler's personal guard, paid their respects, before traveling a circuitous route from the Romanian border through all regions of Romania. At each stop, crowds gathered to honor them. When the funerary train finally arrived in Bucharest, the assembled legionaries accompanied the funeral procession to the church of Sfântul Ilie Gorgul, while tens of thousands looked on. There the bodies lay in state for two days before they were placed in a mausoleum near the legion's headquarters. At every stage of this ritual drama, Romanian legionaries proclaimed their loyalty to their comrades who had fallen in Spain with an oath composed by their leader, the Captain, Corneliu Codreanu. In time, they even adopted a hymn to the martyrs. The song begins darkly—"There are pyres and flames. Spain is in ashes"—but ends with a promise of redemption: "Death we tighten to our chests, so that the Legion may grow more proudly;/So that the Captain may make the Country like the holy sun in the sky."[78] In death, the nation would live.

Only seven Romanian legionaries fought in Spain. They did not alter the course of events there, either in life or in death. Nor did their actions signal a new direction in Romanian foreign policy. By the mid-1930s, most leading Romanian political figures, including King Carol II, openly supported a closer relationship with Nazi Germany. But they did not do so because they wanted to take part in an ideological crusade across the continent. Indeed, the Romanian government did not sign the Anti-Comintern Pact until 1941, when war with the Soviet Union created a new and very different geopolitical reality. Instead, Romania's leaders correctly judged after 1936 that Germany's power was rising in the region, and that German favor would be crucial in any border disputes with their Hungarian neighbor. They also hoped that the Nazi regime would help them retain Bessarabia, a northeastern territory that Romania had acquired after World War I and that the Soviet Union refused to recognize as Romanian. Strategic considerations, rather than anti-Communist fervor, dictated a pro-German course. Finally, the events in Spain did not unleash a new anti-Communist campaign at home. The Romanian Parliament had already outlawed the Communist Party in 1924 and made Communist agitation punishable even by death. Under the so-called Mârzescu Law, the government had arrested hundreds of Communist leaders, holding them in the notorious Doftana prison. By the 1930s Communism posed little threat to state order. The number of active Communist Party members in Romania was reduced to 1,000 by 1944.[79]

Nevertheless, the deaths of Ion Moţa and Vasile Marin acquired an outsize importance in Romania, precisely because Romania's fascists believed that the Spanish Civil War was one part of the broader struggle between Communist atheism and Christianity. The nation's future—its rebirth or its death—depended on the outcome of that struggle. "If the Cross will fall in Spain," Moţa wrote shortly before his death, "its foundations will be shaking in Romania as well, and if communism wins there today, it will come against us tomorrow." For this reason, admirers found their deaths rich with symbolic meaning. An editorial that appeared in one of the leading Iron Guard newspapers lamented: "The Bolshevik demon has torn two archangels from us." Mircea Eliade, who would become internationally renowned after 1945 as a philosopher and historian of religion but was a journalist and critic openly sympathetic to the Iron Guard in the 1930s, wrote at length about their deaths as a sacrifice: "The voluntary death of Ion Moţa and Vasile Marin has a mystical meaning: sacrifice for Christianity. . . . When he felt that Lucifer was again preparing to fight Christ, Ion Moţa, the Orthodox crusader, went out boldly, with peace in his heart, to sacrifice himself for the victory of the Savior." The two dead legionaries became symbols of a nation redeemed and renewed. Codreanu, leader of the Iron Guard, cemented their place in the legion's mythology when he composed the Moţa-Marin oath, which read in part, "I swear before God, before your holy sacrifice . . . for the resurrection of my people, to be ready for death at any time." In their memory Codreanu also created an elite Moța-Marin Order, to comprise 10,000 "new men" who would be ready, like the two martyrs who went before them, to die for the rebirth of their nation. Moved by these gestures, Eliade declared, "Never before has the Romanian soul wanted to be more . . . Christian," and pronounced the legionary movement "a Christian revolution . . . never before known in the history of Europe."[80]

The longing for redemption so evident in these paeans to the fallen legionaries made sense only when set against the widespread sentiment across the nationalist Right that Romania had fallen into a state of profound abjection. In the decades following World War I, disappointed nationalists believed that the Romanian state was dominated by a liberal elite in thrall to powerful business interests, with no understanding at all of the needs of the Romanian people. Parliamentary liberalism, they declared, was nothing more than the tool of an international conspiracy led by Jews and Freemasons to rule Romania. Since the nineteenth century, when international humanitarian groups put the question of Jewish citizenship in Romania at the center of diplomatic debates about the post-Ottoman state order in the Balkans, the place of Jews in Romanian society had been entangled with anxieties about national sovereignty. Although Romania had emerged from World War I a territorial "winner," many nationalists continued to denounce liberal politicians as too subservient to Western economic and legal norms. They insisted instead that a better course for national development lay in the rediscovery of the nation's unique ethnic and cultural traditions. The nightmare of national "slavery" loomed over this rhetoric, allowing intellectuals on the far right to fuse Jews, Freemasonry, and Bolshevism into interchangeable symbols of national oppression. Writing in one of the leading newspapers of the Iron Guard, one member wrote plainly that Bolshevism had "satanic" origins and meant a "return to the state of barbarism"; all humanity would be "reduced to slavery" and condemned to serve a "closed caste of terrorists, of sadistic criminals, of maniacal kikes."[81] But the Iron Guard had no monopoly on this rhetoric. In his diary, the writer

Mihail Sebastian recorded a conversation he had with his fellow writer and intellectual Camil Patrescu. "What else," Patrescu asked, "is Communism but the imperialism of the Jews."[82] It was in the context of these views that legionary leader Corneliu Codreanu called for "new men," free from "politicking" and the infection of "Jewish influence," who would lead Romania as it strove to fulfill the "highest and most sublime goal for which a nation can strive": "national resurrection."[83]

Adolf Hitler made the image of the Jewish Bolshevik central to Nazi ideology from the earliest days of the movement. Memories of struggle—against revolutionaries in Munich; against Communists in the streets of Berlin—animated party members and justified Nazi leaders in calling for extreme measures to guarantee domestic order and internal security, concepts they always understood in racialized terms. After the Nazis took power in the 1933, they crushed their Communist opponents. Consequently, the location and meaning of the Judeo-Bolshevik menace shifted, becoming a powerful symbol for external, rather than internal, defense. As the Nazi regime began to assert itself more aggressively on the international stage, the idea of Judeo-Bolshevism helped to crystallize a useful and exceedingly flexible vision of a Europe of nations, united by German example and under German leadership, in a common struggle against the Communist enemy. Events like the election of the Popular Front government in France or the civil war in Spain could be adduced to support this thesis. So too could accounts of state repression in the Soviet Union.

Hitler's bid for leadership of an international anti-Communist front challenged Europeans, West and East. Some radical nationalists welcomed the example set by the new Germany, idealizing it as a model according to which they too might lift their nations from decline and stagnation. For them, the concept of Judeo-Bolshevism provided a shared language for a broader set of beliefs about national culture and the kind of Europe in which it might flourish. But other Europeans worried about the implications of the Nazi-led crusade against Bolshevism for their own strategic state interests. Although they might associate Jews and Jewishness with the Soviet threat, they could not ignore the fact that joining the partnership that Hitler offered would also mean abetting his expansionist ambitions. Finally, the promise of an anti-Communist crusade forced European Christians to consider what sort of crusade a state governed according to a secular political religion could wage, and what its consequences for the future of the faith might be. Some found it easy to reconcile these contradictions. Others were profoundly unnerved by them. By the end of the 1930s, the fight against Judeo-Bolshevism had become indelibly tied to the rise of Nazi power in Europe, a development that forced anti-Communists everywhere to examine their own commitments. The stakes were high. When Nazi Germany invaded the Soviet Union in 1941, they became even higher.

4

A Barbarous Enemy

On August 23, 1939, Hitler signed a treaty of nonaggression with the Soviet Union. The Nazi-Soviet Pact was the prelude to Germany's declaration of war on Poland. In September, German and Soviet occupiers divided Poland between themselves. Freed from the prospect of a two-front war, the Nazi regime then trained its sights on Western Europe. In June 1940, Germany invaded France. The next month, it began the massive aerial bombardment of Great Britain. Meanwhile, Stalin declared war on Finland at the end of November 1939, and the following summer Soviet occupiers seized the Baltic states and the formerly Romanian provinces of Bessarabia and Bukovina.

The profound sense of betrayal that European leftists committed to the antifascist struggle felt when they learned about the terms of the pact has been well documented.[1] But Hitler's sudden abandonment of anti-Bolshevism was no less stunning to Europe's anti-Communists. A regime that had styled itself as the strongest bulwark against Soviet power had now cut a deal with that very enemy. A few found their views of Nazism (and Stalinism) confirmed. "Now the whole world understands," wrote Jacques Maritain, the Catholic theorist of anti-totalitarianism, as he contemplated the official visit to Moscow of the Nazi foreign minister, Joachim von Ribbentrop. "It is sufficient to see Stalin and Ribbentrop shaking hands while they smile at each other the cynical smile of accomplices."[2] In Rome, Vatican officials were more cautious, combining general pleas for peace with continued denunciations of Soviet godlessness. Following this lead, Vatican newspapers distinguished between the Soviet and German invasions of Poland, harshly condemning the former as a brutal assault on a Christian nation while lamenting the latter more neutrally as the "spilling of blood between two peoples" who ought to have resolved their differences without violence.[3]

Elsewhere, the European Right viewed the pact through a nationalist lens. In occupied Poland, the arrival of Soviet forces in the east fueled suspicions there that Jews had betrayed the country by siding with Communist authorities. To the west, in German-occupied Poland, right-wing nationalists active within the broader Polish underground reflected on the destruction of the Polish state and concluded— despite the escalating persecution and ghettoization of Polish Jews by Nazi occupiers during this period—that it proved Jews were openly pro-Soviet *and* secretly pro-German. Poland, they said, was the victim of all three enemies: Soviets, Nazis, and Jews.[4] In Hungary, meanwhile, the rise of the radical right continued unabated, its core message of expropriating Jewish property, promoting Jewish emigration, and purging Jewish influence from culture and education unaffected by the truce between Hitler and Stalin.[5] The pact convinced a few more traditional conservatives, like Count Pál Teleki, that the future depended on the Western powers winning the war. But most of Hungary's Right remained fixated on the country's borders and willing to support anyone who could help Hungary regain territory lost at the end of World War I.[6] The Second Vienna Award of 1940, which reassigned part of Transylvania to Hungary, confirmed the country as a Nazi ally.

In Nazi Germany, the impact of the nonaggression pact was dramatic and immediate. Alfred Rosenberg, who had influenced Hitler's anti-Bolshevik views in the early 1920s but had long since fallen from favor believed that Germany would suffer a "moral loss of respect" because of the move.[7] Undeterred, Joseph Goebbels's Ministry of Propaganda ceased its anti-Soviet campaign as soon as the treaty was signed.[8] The Anti-Comintern saw its budget cut by 30 percent and its staff reduced or seconded to other corners of Goebbels's vast propaganda empire. Some of Eberhard Taubert's men, so active in the 1930s chronicling the iniquities of the Judeo-Bolshevik enemy in Moscow, Spain, and elsewhere, were transferred to an office of the organization Antisemitic Action, where they worked in concert with other propaganda experts on a different but related anti-Jewish project: demonizing the Jewish plutocrats who pulled the strings behind Germany's enemies to the West.[9] Those who remained behind in the silent offices of the Anti-Comintern could do little more than monitor the Soviet press and follow international responses to the Nazi-Soviet Pact.[10]

The unexpected turn of events did little to diminish the conviction, held by Anti-Comintern members, that Bolshevism was a dangerous Jewish plot. During the long months of forced inaction, they dreamed grandiosely of freeing their organization from state control and remaking it as an independent mass movement that could mobilize Germans around the real truth about the Soviet Union.[11] As fanciful as this vision was, it nonetheless demonstrated how firmly committed Nazi anti-Communist experts remained to their original purpose. The same could be said for Adolf Hitler himself, for whom anti-Bolshevism remained a "lodestar" in his global thinking.[12] He always understood the nonaggression pact with Stalin as a temporary stratagem that would allow Germany to dispense with its enemies in the West before it turned east again and delivered a crushing blow to the Soviet Union. By the summer of 1940 German war planners were already preparing an attack on the Soviet Union, originally scheduled for the autumn of that year but then postponed to the next year.[13] Preparations took place in secret, without any propaganda buildup. When the German army launched Operation Barbarossa in June 1941, Joseph Goebbels reflected in his diary on the task before him: "Now it is time to put on the anti-Bolshevik record again. Gradually, so that the transformation does not seem too sharp."[14]

As German soldiers poured across the Soviet border, Nazi propagandists revived the anti-Bolshevik language of the 1930s and remade it for a Europe at war. Germany's fight in the east, they said, was a crusade to defend Germans and all Europeans from a barbaric and cruel racial-ideological enemy. But the diversity of responses to the surprise of the Nazi-Soviet Pact of 1939 shows that Nazi Germany did not have a monopoly on anti-Communism or on ways to imagine the Judeo-Bolshevik threat. When the Nazi regime launched its war of annihilation against the Soviet Union, the intensity of its propaganda against Judeo-Bolshevism and the Soviet state fired the imaginations of anti-Communists in some parts of Europe and encouraged them to think of their part in the war against the Soviet Union in similar terms. Elsewhere, however, the Nazi propaganda did little to build common ground with other states or nationalist actors, despite a shared antipathy to Communism and a similar conviction that Jews were behind its evils. And in some places, the local fear of Judeo-Bolshevik terror took on a form and life of its own. The Nazi invasion of the Soviet Union returned the idea of Judeo-Bolshevism to European politics. This chapter examines where and how it had the greatest impact.

One of the most prominent experts on the Soviet Union in Nazi Germany was the pseudoscholar Hermann Greife. In 1936 Greife called for a new kind of Soviet studies that would take seriously "the special position of the Soviet Union as a land that has been conquered by international Jewry." He argued that Jewish Bolsheviks had used Marxism to construct a "complex system that enabled them to rule and exploit enormous masses of people." A "national socialist racialist

perception of reality," he claimed, would enable scholars to understand exactly how this system operated.[15] Inspired by this ludicrous
notion, Greife wrote a number of books about the Soviet Union that
"undermined the standards of Russian studies established in Weimar
Germany."[16] In each of them he assembled a variety of facts about
political repression or standards of living in the Soviet Union, gleaned
from sources available in Germany, and then repackaged them in a
racist framework that connected every example of brutality or terror
to a single cause: Judeo-Bolshevism.

One of Greife's most infamous books, a short study entitled
Forced Labor in the Soviet Union, put this approach on full display.
In it, Greife claimed to analyze the regime of terror that Jewish Bolsheviks had used to exercise power in the Soviet Union over an "en-
slaved and mentally and morally degenerate population." Soviet
terror, he argued, was motivated by a racial mentality: the Jews who
held the real power in the Soviet Union knew they could not succeed unless they systematically destroyed the "most valuable racial
elements" in society. In the fifty-some pages that followed (complete
with nearly two dozen mug shots that identified leading figures in
the Soviet secret police as Jews), Greife described how Jewish secret
police officers used their power to imprison their enemies in labor
camps and at construction sites like the infamous White Sea Canal
project, where from 1931 to 1933 some 170,000 prisoners were
forced to work with primitive tools in chaotic and brutal conditions
to build a waterway that would connect the White Sea to the Baltic.
Using a pastiche of photographs, statistics, official Soviet texts, and
quotes from persecuted victims (generally taken from Nazi information agency sources), Greife described the punishing labor, miserable living conditions, and high death rates to which millions of
prisoners in the Soviet Union's vast system of gulags were subjected.
At every turn, he insisted that Jewish Bolshevik terror had caused
all the suffering. He concluded: "Millions of people have already
been destroyed in the world's first Marxist state. Countless more

will lose their lives under Jewish rule, so long as this diabolical system persists."[17]

Greife was one of many practitioners of a nazified Soviet studies. After 1933 a new Institute for Scientific Research on the Soviet Union was created and charged with producing scholarship on Bolshevism and the Soviet state from a "militant national socialist" perspective.[18] Such works were then published and circulated inside Germany and across Europe by publishing houses that worked closely with the Anti-Comintern office within the Ministry of Propaganda. Some studies analyzed the role Jews played in the Russian Revolution, rehearsing the same racist accounts of the revolution that Baltic German émigrés like Alfred Rosenberg had written a generation earlier, but this time giving them a superficially impressive pseudoscientific conceptual apparatus. Others detailed the power that Jews held behind the scenes in Stalin's Russia, within the Communist Party and in the secret police, and assessed the implications of this for the future of the Soviet Union. ("Can the Soviet Union develop into a national state?" asked Hermann Greife in one essay.[19] No, he answered, because Jewish Bolshevism was incapable of evolution.) Still other studies interpreted the Red Army as an instrument of Jewish power and studied the Comintern as a key feature of the international Jewish plot to overthrow sovereign governments around the world. Throughout all of the institute's publications, one idea predominated. Nazi Germany was—in the words of Hermann Greife—the "antipode" of the "Juden-Bolshevik system" that had been erected in the Soviet Union.[20] Hitler's triumph, these works insisted, was a source of unending frustration to the Soviet rulers, goading them into their relentless and implacable hatred.[21]

The vivid material that German Soviet experts produced about the miseries of life in the Soviet Union was immediately useful to Nazi diplomats. Propagandists in the Anti-Comintern office had used their work to justify the Nazi regime's bid in the mid-1930s to lead an international anti-Communist alliance, but that was only part of the ideological significance of Soviet studies in Nazi Germany. Analyses showing that the Soviet Union was a land ruled by and through a "Judeo-Bolshevik system" magnified the strategic threat to Germany and crystallized it in racial and ideological terms, charging fears of military encirclement with deeper anxieties about national death. When "experts" like Hermann Greife described Soviet labor camps and collectivization drives as policies devised by Jewish Bolshevik rulers to establish and maintain their power, the ideological implications of their work were clear. Such scholarly descriptions (of the way things were in Russia) were also dystopian prophecies (of the way things could have been in Germany). According to Nazi propaganda, Hitler had crushed the Bolshevik enemy in Germany and saved the country from a civil war far worse than the one in 1918.[22] Studies of "Jewish terror" in the Soviet Union painted a frightening picture of an alternative Germany, had he failed. Finally, Nazi Soviet studies also presented a model of the relationship between Soviet rulers and the peoples of the Soviet Union. Invariably, the former appeared as Jewish puppet masters; the latter were typically a degenerate and faceless mass, brutalized by terror and slaves to the whims of Jewish rule. The fusion of Jewish power and Eastern savagery resonated powerfully with well-worn stereotypes of Eastern Europe as a backward and barbarous region dependent on Germans for models of civilized culture and honorable conduct.[23] The "knowledge" produced by these so-called experts on the Soviet Union and the East reflected two important premises of Nazi ideology about the Soviet Union. Germany's rival to the east was a land peopled (mainly) by the racially unworthy, who lived in squalor and knew nothing about culture and civilization. It was also a state governed by a Judeo-Bolshevik system. Together, these tenets cast the Soviet Union as a barbarous and deadly enemy.

Nazi propaganda offices scrupulously avoided these themes during the nearly two years that the Nazi-Soviet Nonaggression Pact was in force. Once that truce was broken, they returned to their old work

without missing a beat. Adolf Hitler set the tone. Three months before Operation Barbarossa began, Hitler told his generals that a "war
of annihilation" against the Soviet Union demanded the ruthless extermination of the "Bolshevist commissars." Reflecting general Nazi
assumptions about how Soviet society functioned, Hitler singled out
these particular enemies for destruction because he believed they
held the power to mobilize the Slavic masses into a marauding horde
fighting to spread the "asocial criminality" of Bolshevik ideology. He
told his military leaders that this was a matter of Germany's life or
death: "We do not wage war to preserve the enemy." If the Judeo-
Bolshevik system survived, the enemy might return again in thirty
years. Hitler understood the invasion as a war of "preventive defense,"
to destroy the enemy before it destroyed Germany, and he under-
scored this point even more clearly in the proclamation he issued to
all the soldiers on the Eastern Front as the invasion was launched.
Germany, he reminded them, had been the target in 1918 of a "plot
between Jews, Democrats, Bolsheviks, and reactionaries" to destroy
the country "within and without." Since then, he said, the "Jewish-
Bolshevik rulers in Russia have constantly tried to impose their rule
on us and other European peoples." They had tried to set Germany
and the rest of Europe "on fire." Hitler claimed that his decision to
invade had been difficult but necessary. Faced with an implacable and
deadly foe, Germany had no choice but to wage war.[24]

Of course, this was a lie. The invasion of the Soviet Union was a
premeditated war of choice, not a necessary preemptive strike. Yet
the vision that Hitler outlined—of a grim and necessary war of annihilation against the Soviet Union and the Judeo-Bolshevik rulers
who led it—became a point of consensus that cut across the different
institutions of the Nazi state. Officials in the Propaganda Ministry
eagerly promoted the idea of the war as an act of "preventive defense" against a foe that threatened German and European culture.
They explained war against Stalin as a war against degenerate Jewish
power.[25] They also promised that the war would expose the sham of

Soviet propaganda. The "German reckoning with Moscow," Goebbels declared, "would expose the greatest Jewish swindle of all time."
The Soviet Union was no "workers' paradise." Instead, it was a dirty
and backward land whose (racially inferior) peoples had been reduced to "animalistic dullness" and exploited by a cruel system of
terror unknown before in human history. But the German invasion
had "ripped the mask from the face of this deception," proclaimed
Goebbels. "The fight in the East means the liberation of mankind
from these crimes."[26]

As the general staff prepared for war, military leaders prepared
guidelines for troop conduct in the east. "Bolshevism," they declared,
was "the archenemy [*Todfeind*] of the National Socialist German
people." Soldiers were instructed to carry out "ruthless and energetic
measures against Bolshevik agitators, partisans, saboteurs, Jews,
and . . . any active or passive resistance." These general principles
were reflected in the orders given to individual army units. One general instructed the tank group under his command to fight against
"Jewish Bolshevism" and the "Muscovite-Asiatic flood." Even more
important, the army issued a decree authorizing the summary execution of "political commissars" because they were the progenitors
of "barbaric and Asiatic fighting methods" and because—following
Hitler—German military leaders expected them to treat any Germans
they captured "with hate, cruelly, and inhumanely." These orders sig-
naled the kind of war that the German army was prepared the fight
and the nature of the enemy that it expected to encounter.[27]

Most fatally, the security apparatus embraced and promoted the
idea that a Judeo-Bolshevik system held power in the Soviet Union
and that its representatives were Germany's "objective" enemies. Once
the invasion was under way, Reinhard Heydrich listed in writing
the groups preselected for execution by the Einsatzgruppen, mo-
bile killing units of the Security Service of the SS. They included:
"Jews in Party and state posts" and "other radical elements (saboteurs,
propagandists, snipers, assassins, agitators, etc.)."[28] In another set

of orders issued at the same time to the Einsatzgruppen security squads, Heydrich expressed himself more clearly: "It goes without saying that cleansing actions primarily apply to Bolsheviks and Jews."[29] These were not (yet) orders to murder all Jews in the Soviet Union, let alone Jews elsewhere in Europe. But they were clear signs that German security forces had already identified Jews as key carriers of Bolshevik power and a core enemy group that embodied the "biological substance of the Soviet system."[30] In the coming war of worldviews, it was common wisdom within the SS that Jews would resolutely line up with the enemy. That belief would play a crucial role in the origins of the Final Solution.

Operation Barbarossa was conceived as a "preventive strike" against a Soviet state that was ruled by an implacably cruel Judeo-Bolshevik system. This ideology crystallized a variety of long-standing beliefs about the Soviet Union and transformed them into a strategic imperative that shaped how German forces would fight the war in the East and how they would treat the enemy groups that they found there. The implications for Soviet Jews were especially dire.

For three months, the German army raced eastward. In September 1941, the Germans captured Kiev. That same month, German forces encircled Leningrad to the north. And weeks later they would begin to march on Moscow. For Germany, these stunning advances bred euphoric visions of total victory and dreams of a vast colonial empire in the East. Yet anxieties persisted. The Soviet state had not collapsed, and its army, which had fled headlong before the German assault in the first days of the invasion, fought bitterly even in retreat. Now deep inside Soviet territory, the German army was overextended, vulnerable, and paranoid about Soviet atrocities and partisan reprisals.[31] When bombs planted by retreating Soviet engineers destroyed the German army's headquarters in Kiev (along with part of the city center), German authorities cited sabotage and the threat of partisan warfare as reasons to murder the city's Jews. On September 29 and 30, killing squads shot 33,771 Jews in a ravine called Babi Yar, northwest of the city. Just over a week later, the commanding general in Kiev, Walter von Reichenau, issued a general order to his troops about their conduct on the Eastern Front. In it, he explained the massacre as a necessary action in the war against the "Judeo-Bolshevik" enemy.

Reichenau began his general order with a warning. The battle against the enemy behind the front line was "still not taken seriously enough." Partisan groups loomed everywhere, he said, threatening German positions with diabolical cunning and deadly force. He went on to remind the troops that this was an ideological threat as well as a strategic challenge. "The fundamental goal of the campaign against the Jewish-Bolshevik system," he wrote, "is the total defeat of its means of power and the extermination of the Asiatic influence in the European sphere of culture." The threat it posed justified extreme violence. Judeo-Bolshevism was the source of "all the bestialities inflicted on German and racially related races." German troops could not afford to fight with restraint against an enemy who was without conscience or humanity and who desired nothing less than Germany's destruction. For this reason, Reichenau instructed his soldiers to fight without pity and to accept the "hard but just punishment" meted out to "Jewish subhumans." Such measures protected the army's rear from revolts that were—"according to experience"—incited or led by Jews. The German soldier had only two duties: to destroy "false Bolshevik ideas, the Soviet state, and its army" and to "annihilate racially alien (*artfremd*) perfidy and cruelty without mercy." Only through extreme and unrestrained violence could the German army fulfill its historic mission "to free the German *Volk* from the Asiatic-Jewish danger once and for all."[32]

The Reichenau Order reflected the ideological conception of the invasion as a war to the death against the Judeo-Bolshevik system in

the Soviet Union. This vision of warfare conditioned German invaders from the very first days of the attack to carry out operations
against targeted racial-ideological enemy groups with ruthless violence. Army commanders systematically executed captured Soviet
political officers—the so-called political commissars whom Hitler had
said were the authors of the Soviet army's unrestrained "Asiatic cruelty." And they treated prisoners of war abysmally. By early 1942, of the
3.3 million Red Army soldiers captured by the Germans, 2 million
were dead of starvation or disease or had been shot.[33] The same ideological rationale drove security operations carried out behind the
lines against "Judeo-Bolshevik subversion." Instructed to eradicate
"Jewish Communists" and the ideological influence of the "Jewish
intelligentsia," in the first weeks of the war the SS and German Order
Police (Ordnungspolizei) organized shootings of Jews (at first, primarily
Jewish men) in occupied areas. Labeled Jewish Communists, the
victims were selected and executed arbitrarily.

One SS Einsatzkommando team operating in western Ukraine
reported shooting 300 people in late June in the town of Sokal, individuals it classified as "Communists" or "Jewish Communists." The
same unit then moved to the city of Zhytomyr, where its officers carried out similar operations against the "Jewish-Bolshevist leadership
cadre" there. Over the course of several murder operations that
claimed more than a thousand victims, members of the commando
force hunted Jewish Bolsheviks in the city, rounding up ever more
victims until they decided the number was high enough. After the
killing spree was over, unit commanders congratulated themselves in
their report for having "liquidated all of the Jewish intelligentsia"
in the city.[34] Order Police units battled the Judeo-Bolshevik enemy
in similar fashion. One battalion charged with supporting army
efforts to "cleanse" the eastern Polish city of Białystok of Soviet
forces, saboteurs, and "anti-German inhabitants" rounded up nearly
700 Jewish men, locked them in the city's main synagogue, and

then set the building on fire. Afterward the commander wrote in his report that resistance from "Russian soldiers and irregulars" had made this response necessary.[35]

Discoveries of Soviet atrocities also justified the eradication of so-called Jewish Bolsheviks. When the Germans crossed into Soviet territory in June 1941, they immediately found evidence of crimes had committed against civilians. In many cities from eastern Poland to the Baltics, officers from the People's Commissariat of Internal Affairs, or NKVD, had executed prisoners in their jail cells before fleeing eastward with the retreating Red Army, leaving the bodies to rot in the summer heat. At least 5,387 prisoners were murdered in eastern Galicia alone, according to the most reliable sources.[36] Accounts of these murders circulated across the Eastern Front and were readily interpreted as expressions of the enemy's true barbaric nature. Coverage of the incidents in Nazi press sources and in information directed at personnel on the Eastern Front presented them as proof that Hitler's warning about the "Asiatic cruelty" of the Soviet system had been prescient and wise. These reports also identified the Soviet perpetrators as Jews or as agents of the Jewish Bolshevik terror, in stark contrast to the tropes of "German honor" and "German culture" that were also staples of Nazi war propaganda.[37] Images of Soviet atrocities dramatized the existential threat that the Soviet enemy—General Reichenau called it the "Asiatic-Jewish danger"—posed to German security. They justified ruthless antipartisan and counterinsurgency actions, even in areas where there was not yet any resistance activity. And they added a revenge motive to the ideologically determined need to fight the evils of Judeo-Bolshevism.[38]

The diary of one member of a commando unit stationed in eastern Galicia (Poland before 1939; today, western Ukraine) illustrates how the sight of Soviet atrocities was used to justify arbitrary violence. By the time SS-Hauptscharführer Felix Landau arrived in the city of L'viv in early July 1941, the Soviets had already fled. When the city's prisons were unlocked, the corpses of thousands of people killed by the

NKVD were found inside.[39] Fascinated by the grisly spectacle, the SS man toured the prison and found what he saw "almost impossible to describe." The men in his unit were in a vengeful mood, telling themselves of the unspeakable things the enemy had done. As Landau wrote in his diary, "The scum did not even draw the line at children." The commandos killed hundreds of Jews whom they rounded up as partisans, collaborators, or simply as victims of their counterterrorist reprisal.[40]

This outrage cannot be taken at face value. German perceptions of Soviet crimes cannot be separated from their expectation that such crimes existed, waiting to be uncovered. The invasion had been conceived from the outset as a preventive war against a deadly Judeo-Bolshevik system that wielded "Asiatic cruelty" in pursuit of world domination. This idea was a point of consensus among German units across the Eastern Front in 1941, but it was especially dominant in the understanding that SS men in the Einsatzkommando killing squads had of their mission to enforce security behind the lines.[41] Postwar trial testimony of an SS officer in charge of an Einsatzkommando team in western Ukraine reveals how arbitrarily the concept of Judeo-Bolshevism was wielded against predetermined racial enemy groups, and how cynically the idea of "revenge" against Communist crimes was manipulated to ideological ends. One week after the invasion, the commanding officer spoke with SS superiors who informed him that the NKVD had killed many people in a salt mine near the city of Dobromyl, including women, children, and ethnic Germans, in "bestial" fashion. Outraged by the discovery of the bodies, a newly formed local Ukrainian militia had begun rounding up suspects, many of whom were Jews. The SS leaders in the area saw an opportunity to claim the mantle of avenger and instructed the Einsatzkommando to execute some of them. On site, the commando officers selected their victims "according the principle that Jews were the carriers of Bolshevism." The postwar West German court noted that no attempt had been made to establish what any of the approximately eighty selected Jews had done during the period of Soviet rule. They were simply taken at random in the space of a few hours, put on a truck, transported to the nearby salt mine, and shot. Their bodies were dumped down a mine shaft.

Episodes like this one, from the very first days of the invasion, established a murderous dynamic that soon escalated into genocide. Yet the Nazis' Final Solution cannot be reduced to a massive antipartisan operation against Jewish Bolsheviks. Security fears alone did not drive the Holocaust. Instead, they fused with relentlessly murderous calculations about which groups of people should be fed in a time of food shortage, which could be made to work (and thus be allowed to live, at least for a while), and which deserved to die. These factors combined in different ways at different times to drive the course and tempo of the Holocaust across the European continent. At every turn, Nazi racist logic concluded that Jews were the least worthy of life.[42] Nevertheless, there was a straight line connecting the earliest massacres at places like Dobromyl to the horrific slaughter of tens of thousands at Babi Yar a few months later. Security fears about Jewish Bolsheviks and Jewish-Communist partisans played a critical role in the escalation of genocidal violence against Jews in 1941. The idea of Judeo-Bolshevism was crucial to the genesis of the Final Solution.[43]

At the same time, Judeo-Bolshevism was not an exclusively German obsession. Others also associated Jews with Soviet power and harbored fears of Jewish Bolshevik brutality. Sometimes their paranoia aligned with Germans' ideology and interests. Sometimes it deviated from them. Nowhere was this paranoia more prevalent than in the regions of Eastern Europe that were briefly occupied by the Soviet Union.

On the first day of July 1940, the body of a Romanian Jewish soldier, Private Iancu Solomon, was brought for burial to the Jewish cemetery in the northeastern Romanian town of Dorohoi. Days earlier, the Soviet Union had demanded that Romania abandon its easternmost territories (Bessarabia and northern Bukovina) or else face an invasion. The humiliated Romanian army withdrew westward across the Prut River. The withdrawal was chaotic. (Private Solomon fell during one of several unplanned firefights with Soviet troops.) Rumors flew that Jews in the abandoned provinces had betrayed Romania, welcomed Soviet authorities with open arms, and even fired on retreating Romanian soldiers. The wildest (and utterly unsubstantiated) versions of these stories included graphic descriptions of Jews beating or urinating on helpless Romanians. As Solomon's coffin was lowered into the ground, a group of Romanian soldiers attacked the Jewish cemetery. They disarmed the honor guard of ten Jewish Romanian soldiers, stood them against a wall, and executed them. They pursued mourners to a nearby funeral parlor and shot them, too. In the town, Romanian army officers let it be known that Jews were Bolshevik enemies. Grateful for the warning, local Christians drew crosses on their homes and wrote "Romanians live here" on their windows. Soldiers stormed Jewish homes, shouting, "The Bolsheviks are coming!" and raping and killing the people they found inside. The slaughter ended only when a summer thunderstorm erupted. The next day, peasants entered the town and stripped the dead Jews of their clothes. According to an official Romanian investigation, 53 Jews were killed in Dorohoi. Jewish sources put the number of victims closer to 200.[44]

The myth of Jewish Bolshevik treason defined memory of Romania's withdrawal from Bessarabia in 1940. It also set the emotional tenor of the campaign to take the territory back. Nearly one year later, Romania joined the German crusade against Bolshevism. To prepare, Marshal Ion Antonescu ordered his chief of the general staff to "identify all Yids and Communist agents or sympathizers" along the border with the Soviet Union.[45] Officers of the Secret Intelligence Service responded by preparing a pogrom in the city of Iaşi. On June 28, 1941, some 4,000 Jews were killed in the city's streets and at police headquarters. Several thousand more were herded onto trains and shuttled from place to place while the Romanian government debated what to do with them. Most died from starvation or dehydration while on the trains Then Romanian and German forces crossed the Soviet line into Bessarabia and Bukovina. Between July and August, they shot 12,000 to 20,000 Jews in the reoccupied territory. They would also come to deport nearly 150,000 Jews east to a Romanian-controlled no-man's-land or even further, into Nazi-occupied Ukraine. When Romanian Jewish leaders objected, Ion Antonescu replied: "Did you think of what we were going through last year during the evacuation of Bessarabia . . . ?" In the autumn, the combined armies drove on to southern Ukraine. Romania's leaders hoped the campaign would prove to the Germans the glory and worth of Romanian arms. Instead, the stubborn tenacity of the Red Army made it a frustrating and bloody humiliation. Antonescu blamed "Jewish commissars" who drove the Russians with "a diabolical perseverance." When Odessa finally fell in October, Romanian forces slaughtered at least 25,000 Jews in reprisals against the Jewish Bolshevik enemy. Then they threw the bodies into the Black Sea.[46]

The slaughter of Odessa's Jews less than one week after General von Reichenau had ordered his army to fight the Jewish Bolshevik system "without pity" suggests that a shared fear of Jewish Bolshevik treachery helped to align German and Romanian interests in the summer of 1941. But accusations that Jews were traitors and Soviet spies had permeated Romanian political culture long before Hitler came to power. Nazi Germany did not bring the Judeo-Bolshevik paranoia to Romania in 1941, nor did it impose the idea on societies anywhere else in wartime Europe. Instead, Nazi occupiers encountered local variations of the Jewish Bolshevik stereotype that were already fully formed. Judeo-Bolshevism in the summer of 1941 is best understood as a powerful symbol on which independent traditions of anti-Jewish politics converged.

Collective memories of Soviet occupation structured this convergence and gave it content. The 1939 treaty of nonaggression between Nazi Germany and the Soviet Union allowed the Soviet Union to occupy a swathe of Eastern Europe that extended from the Baltic states to the Black Sea. In each of these places (eastern Poland in 1939; the Baltic States, Bessarabia, and Bukovina in 1940), Soviet authorities destroyed the old political establishment and put a new one in its place. As part of its drive to eliminate the Polish political class, the NKVD massacred 20,000 Polish officers and buried them in pits in the Katyn Forest. In the Baltic states, rigged elections ensured that the new governments there would be compliant. NKVD officers also began to identify enemies of the state. About 140,000 Polish citizens were deported to Kazakhstan and Siberia between 1939 and 1941. In June 1941, only weeks before the German invasion, Soviet authorities deported some 17,000 Lithuanians to gulags deep in the Soviet Union. Only perhaps one-third of them ever returned. In the newly acquired territories that they now controlled, Soviet authorities also suspended property rights, suppressed independent religious and civic organizations, and promoted a new pro-Soviet cultural elite. In areas the Soviets did not occupy until summer 1940, the revolution they imposed was sometimes only partial. They carried out just one mass deportation from occupied Romania, for example, several weeks before they were driven out; in eastern Poland, they had enough time for four. Even so, the intentions of the Soviet occupiers were clear.[47]

The imposition of Soviet rule between 1939 and 1941 meant an overturned social order, the obliteration of political elites, ruined lives, and separated families. After the Soviets had gone, Jews were held responsible for the suffering. They were accused of having welcomed the Soviet occupiers and then of collaborating with their reign of terror. In Romania, the nationalist press fomented antisemitic rage among readers in 1940 with tales of Jews desecrating Christian churches and spitting on retreating Romanians. Many believed what they read. "The first items of news to reach us are very sad," wrote King Carol II during the summer of 1940 as Romanian troops withdrew from Bessarabia. "The behavior of the population . . . especially of the Jews, leaves much to be desired."[48] In Poland, Nazi and Soviet occupation destroyed the free press, along with every other aspect of Polish civil society. Even so, reports from Soviet-occupied Poland to the government-in-exile in London dwelled at length on the problem of Jewish participation in the new Communist regime. Some reports, like those of Jan Karski, were sober and strove for critical objectivity.[49] Most lacked any trace of nuance and labeled Jews collectively as traitors. After the German invasion drove Soviet authorities from all these places in the summer of 1941, local people said they remembered Jews flying red banners and cheering Red Army soldiers as they marched into town. They also accused Jews of directing or supporting the persecution, deportation, and murder of innocent people. The air was filled with demands for revenge.

In fact, most Jews had never been Communists, and many had also suffered miserably under Soviet Communist rule. In eastern Poland, Moscow had quickly replaced the local people recruited to serve the occupation with loyal cadres from the Soviet Union If local Jews had ever been "overrepresented" in the Soviet administration there, it was only briefly and at first. Most important, Soviet authorities had found willing helpers among all ethnic groups, a truth that could prove embarrassing after the Germans arrived.[50] Beneath these social facts lay a deeper issue. Memories of Jews' participation in the Soviet regime, whether recorded as testimony soon afterward or recalled decades later, conflated individual cases, resulting in an unshakeable conviction that "the Jews" as a collective group had been responsible for Soviet terror. Reviewing the testimonies of Poles from the Białystok region who had been deported to the Soviet Union, often used since 1989 as evidence that Jews supported the Soviet occupation in great numbers, the Polish journalist Anna Bikont found only a few concrete examples—and a great many extremely general statements about "the Jews" collaborating with the NKVD.[51] An international historical commission created in Romania in 2003 came to a similar conclusion: "Rich archival sources . . . indicate that some Jews . . . participated in pro-Soviet actions. . . . However, a critical examination of the doc-

uments depicts something quite different than the catastrophic picture presented to the public."[52] Even at the time, officials wrestled
with this anomaly. When the Romanian gendarmerie did a study
soon after the 1941 invasion to determine how many Jews had served
the Soviets, they found the number to be surprisingly low. In one
county, only 3 of 128 local rulers had been Jews. Enraged, the provincial gendarmerie inspector rejected the report as unacceptable and
false. Numbers to the contrary, he said he knew that all Jews were
Communists. "The data," he declared, "contradict the facts."[53]

German security officers had no interest in such complexities. They
saw only confirmation of their prejudices and possibilities for their propaganda efforts. During the period of Soviet occupation, when the
Nazi-Soviet Pact was in force, intelligence officers collected information on the role that Jews played in the Soviet administration.
Some material came from local allies, like members of the extreme-
right Organization of Ukrainian Nationalists (OUN), who believed
that Jews were hostile to their nationalist aspirations and who
shared German fears of Judeo-Bolshevism. Fleeing west in 1939 into
German-occupied territory, members of the OUN connected with
German security officers and shared their impressions of the situation to the east. Their German handlers lapped it up. "Jews enjoy
every privilege as recognized supporters of Communism," wrote the
author of one 1940 German police report on the mood in western
Ukraine. This conclusion perfectly matched Nazi understandings of
Soviet rule and led SS leaders to anticipate the consequences of their
own coming war to end Judeo-Bolshevik terror. Nazi theories about
the Judeo-Bolshevik system predicted that local people would rise up
against the Jewish Bolshevik oppressors when the Germans came.
The sight of such spontaneous pogroms, which German propaganda
crews would be sure to film, would offer convincing proof of the
rightness of the Nazi cause. In late May 1941, SS leaders held a conference to discuss propaganda in Soviet-occupied territory. The participants agreed that "the population will welcome the fact that we

present Jews as the main culprits." Three weeks later, only days before the invasion was launched, Reinhard Heydrich instructed the Einsatzgruppen commanders in this spirit: "Self-cleaning attempts of anti-Communist and anti-Jewish circles in the newly occupied territories are not to be restrained. On the contrary, they should be initiated, but without any traces, intensified if necessary, and channeled in the right directions."[54]

In the summer of 1941, as the Germans and their allies pushed eastward and Soviet rule collapsed across Eastern Europe, violent attacks against Jews broke out in eastern Poland (today western Ukraine and western Belarus), in the Baltic states of Lithuania and Latvia, and in Bessarabia and Bukovina. One of the most dramatic (because of the propaganda uses to which it was put) took place in L'viv, where at least 4,000 people were killed after the corpses of 3,500 people, arrested as counterrevolutionary elements and then killed as Soviet officials fled, were found in the city's prisons.[55] Another mass pogrom took place in the Lithuanian city of Kaunas (Russian: Kovno). There, self-styled militiamen massacred some 1,000 people in the streets of the city's Jewish quarter and tortured and killed another 50 to 60 in a large garage near the German army's headquarters, while a mob looked on.[56] Pogroms took place in smaller towns as well. In the eastern Polish town of Jedwabne, Jews were forced into a barn and burned alive, and Jews were killed in pogroms in other towns nearby, like Radziłów and Wąsosz.[57] All told, between 12,000 and 24,000 people were killed in more than sixty anti-Jewish riots in eastern Poland and the Baltics during the first weeks of Operation Barbarossa.[58] To the southeast, the systematic targeting of Jews in Bessarabia and Bukovina by Romanian gendarmes was accompanied by a wave of spontaneous violence against Jews committed by local people. In the village of Pepeni, gendarmes imprisoned some 200 Jews after Soviet forces had retreated. When the local chief of the gendarmerie found himself without the manpower needed to kill them all, he appealed to the local community for help. Volunteers appeared with clubs, shovels, and other tools, eager to beat the prisoners to death and then steal their clothes and shoes.[59]

German invaders encouraged and provoked acts of "revenge" against Jewish Bolshevik oppressors. They circulated posters that identified Jews as Bolshevik criminals. They set horrific examples of what could be done in the name of anti-Bolshevism—burning Jews alive in the Białystok synagogue; massacring Jews labeled as Bolsheviks in Dobromil; organizing mass shootings of suspected Jewish "subversives" in Vilnius. They also sent clear signals to local officials, such as the mayor of Jedwabne, that such anarchic violence against Jews would be permitted, at least temporarily.[60] Most important, they actively sought out partners. In L'viv, the Wehrmacht made contact with members of the OUN who had formed a local militia after the Soviets fled, and instructed them to force Jews to dispose of the bodies of the prisoners whom NKVD officers had murdered. The sight of Jews being humiliated and punished for NKVD crimes triggered massive attacks against all Jews in the city by civilians and other Ukrainian militiamen. After several days of mob violence, the Einsatzgruppen began killing operations of their own, framing them as "revenge" for NKVD atrocities. In Kaunas, finding local partners proved, according to an Einsatzgruppe report, "at first surprisingly not easy." German intelligence officers were not well-informed about the differences between groups of Lithuanian nationalists, nor were the numbers of Lithuanians prepared to initiate violence as large as the Germans had expected. Mass revenge killings against supposedly Jewish Bolshevik criminals erupted only after the Germans found the right group of extreme nationalists to be their partner.[61]

The idea of Judeo-Bolshevism forged consensus between the Germans and their helpers. But their partners had their own political experiences and goals.[62] In L'viv, radical Ukrainian nationalists eagerly organized themselves into an armed militia ready to attack Jews because they expected that a German victory would make possible a sovereign and independent Ukraine, free from Soviet rule, purified of ethnic minorities (Jews and also Poles), and part of a new (German-led) Europe. Killing Jews was a means to this end, a sign of the common ground they shared with the German occupiers, and—after the Germans dashed their hopes and arranged the administration of Ukrainian territory differently—a way to persuade the Germans to change their minds in the future.[63] Yet consensus about punishing Jewish Bolshevik criminals did not smooth every friction between the Germans and their allies.

Nazi and Romanian officials both detested Judeo-Bolshevism, but they disagreed about what destroying it would mean. In Bucharest, policy makers hoped that recaptured Bessarabia would be an ethnically pure "model province" and a template for the demographic transformation of the entire country. Killing and expelling Jews served that goal—as did robbing and expelling ethnic Ukrainians and discriminating against ethnic Germans. German officials saw things differently. For them, the Soviet army and the Soviets' Judeo-Bolshevik system were the real enemies; Ukrainians were potential allies, and ethnic Germans obviously belonged to the greater German *Volk*. To clear up confusion, Otto Ohlendorf, commander of SS Einsatzgruppe D, which was active in the region, instructed his men to direct Romanian attention toward "Jewish plots" and away from unwanted distractions. "To protect useful Ukrainians, and in particular OUN people, Communists will be put at the disposal of the Romanians." Meanwhile, some of the bloodiest anti-Jewish violence in neighboring Bukovina took place in ethnic Ukrainian villages, where nationalist activists hoped to win German recognition before Romanian authorities could intervene. Killing Jews was part of their political strategy.[64]

Demonizing Jews as Bolshevik criminals who deserved punishment validated other motives for attacking Jews. The mobs who cheered on and joined officially sanctioned "reprisals" against Jews took the opportunity to loot and plunder the homes and bodies of their victims, empowered by the knowledge that their murderous greed would be seen—by officials, by their neighbors—as acts of just violence meant to reassert social order and redistribute wealth "fairly." Mob violence also took ritualistic forms, using anti-Communist symbols to enforce the boundaries of the (Christian) community and return Jews to their "proper" status as outsiders.[65] In Jedwabne, several dozen Jewish men were forced to demolish a statue of Lenin that had been erected during the months of Soviet rule, carry its pieces to a cemetery, and dig a grave for it, all while singing Soviet songs.[66] In Bessarabia, Romanian soldiers dehumanized Jews, just as their German counterparts did, but added acts of shaming or humiliation that were not common among Wehrmacht soldiers, such as forcing rabbis to make the sign of the cross.[67] This action was meant to acknowledge the end of "Jewish power" and the return of moral order to the region. Finally, exacting revenge against Jewish Bolsheviks could be a way to demonstrate one's loyalty to the new order in a time of bewildering regime change. In Bessarabia, Romanian officials knew they could not punish every ethnic Romanian who had served the Soviet regime, so they channeled anti-Communist anger against the Jews. An officer in one village assembled the entire community to witness the execution of five Jews. He told them: "Those who are faithful to Romanian power . . . have to prove it by taking [up] rifles." Two men stepped forward and shot the Jews dead.[68] In Jedwabne, some of the most violent killers in that pogrom had collaborated previously with the NKVD.[69] Murdering Jews labeled as Bolsheviks was one way for the morally flexible to rewrite their biographies.

From the very first weeks of the war, Nazi propagandists strove to turn concrete evidence of Soviet crimes into proof of Judeo-Bolshevik barbarity. Impressed by the scale of the "animalistic" slaughter that NKVD officers had carried out in L'viv, correspondents with the German army reported to Berlin, "We could never have come up with propaganda images like the ones in Lemberg [L'viv]."[70] Minister of

Propaganda Joseph Goebbels immediately dispatched journalists, film crews, and radio men to the city to collect material. "The great campaign against Bolshevism," Goebbels wrote in his diary, "begins at once."[71] Media crews for the newsreel series *Deutsche Wochenschau* carefully edited footage from L'viv into stories that juxtaposed scenes of corpses and weeping women with images of captured prisoners selected to represent different faces of the enemy: the coarse "sub-human" Slav, the grim-faced NKVD agent, and the bespectacled in-tellectual "Jewish Communist." Narrators filled in the rest: "Beasts in human form committed the cruelest acts of murder." The effect was powerful, marking the perpetrators with a racial "essence" and casting them as agents of a demonic and "Asiatic" threat.[72]

German newspapers picked up the story and the ideological line, giving readers daily stories about inhuman, bestial, and "satanic crim-inals" who hacked their victims to death in an orgy of bloodlust and animal instinct. Goebbels wrote about the atrocities in L'viv himself. "The veil had fallen" from the face of the enemy, he claimed. The Soviet Union aimed to bring its system of terror "into the heart of Eu-rope." The war was a clash between civilization and anticivilization. "Human imagination can barely conceive what it would mean," he warned, if the "Jewish-terrorist leaders" who ruled the Soviet Union "flooded Germany and the West with their bestial hordes."[73]

Photographs of mutilated bodies and piles of corpses offered espe-cially compelling visual "proof" of the "Asiatic terror" that Germany was called by history to destroy.[74] Accounts and even photographs from soldiers gave a personal quality to the horrified shock that the regime wanted to provoke and manipulate. Military personnel on site in cities like L'viv were encouraged to see the horrors for themselves. SS officer Felix Landau had been one such atrocity tourist. Another, a Wehrmacht soldier, wrote about L'viv in a letter to his district party leader back home. He described dismembered corpses, bodies nailed to fences, and dead women and children strewn in heaps. "If the road was open for these beasts to come to us and ours at home . . . One shouldn't even think this through."[75] The Ministry of Propaganda published this letter, along with others, in a special collection of "letters from the front" intended for a wider German audience.

Evidence of Soviet atrocities fused with and reinforced widespread prejudices about the Soviet Union as an impoverished, dirty, disorderly, and thoroughly "un-European" land. In his speeches and articles, Goebbels claimed that Germany had torn the mask off the "worker's paradise," revealing the disgusting reality beneath. Letters from the Eastern Front show that these attitudes were common within the Wehrmacht as well. Soldiers wrote home to describe appalling living conditions in the Soviet Union, which they contrasted with the beauty of their German homeland. Often they described how they had recoiled when they entered towns with large numbers of Yiddish-speaking Jews, calling those places "nests," as Nazi propagandists did when they wanted to emphasize the ubiquity of the Judeo-Bolshevik menace in Soviet lands. Many cast the war as a battle between a "Europe of culture" and the subhumanity of Asiatic Bolshevism.[76] One Wehrmacht soldier combined all these themes in a letter he wrote home to his wife, saying he now understood that the depictions of "Red Spain" from a few years earlier had been no exaggeration: "They wanted to let these Jewish-Asiatic hordes loose on our old land of culture." Eyewitness accounts like these depicted vivid nightmare scenarios of what a Red Army victory would mean and dispelled any doubts about the need for a war of "preventive defense" against the Soviet Union. Their message was reflected across all levels of German society. Three months into the invasion, the Roman Catholic bishop Galen of Münster issued a pastoral letter that echoed the official line. "For decades," he warned his flock, "the Jewish-Bolshevik rulers from Moscow have been trying to set not just Germany but the whole of Europe in flames."[77]

The European dimension of the anti-Bolshevik fight was a critical element of Nazi wartime propaganda. Joseph Goebbels believed that German coverage of the war against the Soviet Union "should also

carry along Europe."[78] To accomplish this, the German press was instructed to portray the German war against Moscow as a "European
crusade against Bolshevism."[79] The German Foreign Office shared
press copy and photographs with pro-Nazi journalists across the Continent, who incorporated the material into their own publications
and then supplemented it with enthusiastic praise of Germany's military might and Adolf Hitler's wise strategy. One such newspaper was
the weekly magazine *Magyar Futár* (Hungarian messenger), edited
by the Hungarian antisemite Ferenc Rajniss. It loyally celebrated advances against the Judeo-Bolshevik enemy in the East in elaborate
multipage spreads that combined photos from German sources with
commentary written by Rajniss's staff.[80] German propagandists also
produced their own newsreels that adapted material from the
Deutsche Wochenschau for local audiences. In the occupied zone of
France, for example, the Germans distributed a French-language
newsreel series called *Actualités Mondiales*, which combined German
film stock with on-camera declarations by well-known French rightists. The newsreel addressed local issues, such as the French defeat
in 1940, which it blamed on Jews, Bolsheviks, and Anglo-American
capitalists, and also devoted extensive coverage to the war against the
Soviet Union.[81] Finally, Nazi propagandists produced and promoted
anti-Bolshevik exhibitions across Nazi-occupied Europe that tied the
German-led war to well-established local variations on the Judeo-
Bolshevik theme.[82]

Germany's allies embraced the crusade metaphor enthusiastically.
The Romanian government announced its crusade against Bolshevism in public declarations, films, and even on commemorative
stamps.[83] In France, a Legion of French Volunteers against Bolshevism was created in 1941, so that French soldiers could take part in
the pan-European cause. Cardinal Alfred Baudrillart, rector of the
Catholic Institute of Paris, publicly declared them the "Crusaders of
the twentieth century."[84] But the fact that figures as varied as Marshal Antonescu in Romania and Cardinal Baudrillart in Paris could

both call the war a crusade betrayed how superficial the image really was. The Nazi regime was only halfheartedly committed to the vision of European community that its anti-Bolshevik crusade implied. The demands of war were always paramount. "They say abroad that this is a crusade," Joseph Goebbels wrote in his diary. "We need to use this expression with the world. But it is not exactly right."[85]

Similarly, the language of anti-Bolshevism, however deeply and sincerely felt, was inseparable from naked interests of state across Nazi-dominated Europe. In 1941 German occupiers in France eagerly seized on any evidence, however slight, of Jewish involvement in the nascent resistance as proof that harsh security measures to fight partisans were needed in France as well. Their Vichy partners agreed that Communists should be arrested but balked at their mass execution, fearing popular unrest. Military commanders acknowledged the issue and made it a factor in subsequent debates about the counterinsurgency in France. (One consequence of those discussions: the deportation of a thousand Jews to the East in March 1942, a first step toward the larger deportations of Jews that would follow.)[86]

In 1941 there was also a massive outpouring of official anti-Bolshevism in Hungary, another of Germany's military allies in the war against the Soviet Union. In December an anti-Bolshevik exhibition opened to great fanfare in Budapest. At the opening ceremony, Regent Miklós Horthy praised the strength of Hungarian arms and drew on his own experiences in the post–World War I counterrevolution to warn about the dangers of Bolshevism. The country's prime minister also solemnly intoned that the sacred aim of the war was to "defend Christian culture" against the "demons of godlessness and destruction." The exhibition's organizers drew heavily on Hungary's own history, presenting the Hungarian Soviet Republic of 1919 as a horrifying preview of the dangers that all of Europe now faced. Pictures abounded of Hungarian Bolsheviks, identified explicitly as Jews, and Soviet atrocities that the German army had uncovered in L'viv and the Baltics. The exhibition even praised Hungary's allies in the fight—Finland, Italy, Spain. But it made no mention at all of Romania, which had committed far more troops to the invasion of the Soviet Union, for the simple reason that the two countries were locked in a bitter regional dispute. Winning back lost territory was Hungary's real war aim. By joining the German anti-Bolshevik crusade, the Hungarian government hoped to stake a strong claim to preferential treatment in a German-led postwar settlement in Europe.[87]

Nazi crusade talk had a toxic creative energy, nonetheless. German anti-Bolshevik propaganda promised that annihilating the Judeo-Bolshevik enemy would clear the way for all Europe's nations to re-fashion themselves as "socialist racial communities" (*sozialistische Volksgemeinschaften*) in a "socialist community of races" (*sozialistische Völkergemeinschaft*).[88] Throughout the Continent, fascist intellectuals embraced this vision, finding in it the fulfillment of the racist cultural projects that they had cherished since the 1930s. They too believed that the Soviet Union contained barbaric hordes bent on destroying European civilization. At the same time, belief in the inevitability of German victory allowed them for a time to dream that their nations might be redeemed from the vulgar degradation of the interwar years. Like their German allies, pro-Nazi intellectuals across Europe joined the ideas of Judeo-Bolshevism and Asiatic Soviet barbarity into a powerful vocabulary that spoke at the same time of euphoric national rebirth and apocalyptic national death.

Two examples—one from Hungary, the other from France—reveal how easily this language cut across national boundaries. Throughout the 1930s those on the Hungarian far right had demanded a "changing of the guard" in Hungary, to replace the conservative political establishment—tainted in their minds by too many compromises with "Jewish power"—with a new Christian elite. Deeply disappointed by the outcome of Hungary's postwar counterrevolution, Hungary's extreme right had an inexhaustible list of cultural and social grievances, all of which crystallized around the conviction that their nation might be redeemed from its current state of abjection by a new cultural and social vanguard that could bring their "Christian" nation true sovereignty or freedom. They eagerly hitched their nation's destiny to the German-led war, which they hoped would destroy once and for all Hungary's conservative elites along with the Jewish powers that they said supported them. István Milotay, a leading pro-Nazi journalist, asked his readers if "Hungarian public opinion really understands what this war means for us." War against the Soviet Union would determine the fate of "Europe, human civilization, Christianity, and the freedom of Christian nations," Milotay wrote. A Jewish Bolshevik victory would be more horrible in its "apocalyptic foreign-ness and its brutality" than the Mongol invasions of Europe in the thirteenth century.[89]

French antisemitic intellectuals wrote in a similar key. They used their total support of the German war to promote the vision for France they had forged in heated debates as members of the Young Right in the 1930s. Before the war, anti-Bolshevism had united the entire Right against Léon Blum and the Popular Front. After 1940, it became the "nearest thing to a Vichy common denominator."[90] But extremists feared that the national revolution proclaimed at Vichy was simply a conservative restoration in disguise. They gathered instead in German-occupied Paris, where they wrote and published, dined with German cultural attachés, and angled for real power. One such figure was Lucien Rebatet, whose most significant wartime work was a pamphlet called *Les décombres* (The ruins), in which he blamed Jews and Third Republic politicians for France's downfall and praised Germany as a model for France's rebirth. Rebatet embraced Hitler's crusade against Bolshevism wholeheartedly because he saw it as the central chapter in the renewal of true civilization in France. He expanded on these ideas in another pamphlet he wrote to celebrate the invasion of the Soviet Union. "Moscow's odious plot has been unmasked," he crowed. Bitterly opposed to peace in Europe, he wrote, the Bolsheviks now supported France's enemies everywhere, spreading Gaullist slogans in France, and yoking themselves to the "capitalist imperialism of England" in their desperate campaign to destroy Europe. "Let us recognize," Rebatet concluded, "the great service that national socialist Germany makes . . . to the Christian Occident."[91]

István Milotay and Lucien Rebatet stood on opposite sides of Hitler's Europe, writing diatribes against particular local enemies that mirrored each other to an astonishing degree. It is just imaginable that the Hungarian knew of the Frenchman; even Hungarian fascists prided themselves on their knowledge of French. But nothing of any intellectual substance ever passed between them. Whether their fantasies were compatible was also immaterial. Both wrote about the Judeo-Bolshevik menace in the very same way. Each fervently believed that German victory would restore his own nation's honor, dignity, and greatness. Each also hoped that an anti-Bolshevik crusade would stir up political energies that would sweep away the stultifying rule of conservative elites and clear the ground for a true fascist revolution. And each painted the barely thinkable prospect of German defeat in apocalyptic strokes, as a harbinger of national enslavement and the collapse of European civilization. An idea of Europe renewed and redeemed by a crusade against Judeo-Bolshevism lived in the minds of the far right everywhere.

By 1943 the future for that Europe seemed less bright. The German army had lost the battle for Stalingrad. In July, U.S. and British bombers devastated the city of Hamburg. Meanwhile, Germany's military allies had grown uneasy. Romania continued to fight on the Eastern Front, but the Romanian government had begun to worry about its reputation in the West and had stopped deporting Jews to the ghettos and camps in Transnistria. They also refused to send them to the camps in Poland. Hungarian troops fought on against the Red Army, but Hungary's Second Army had been destroyed at Stalingrad. The Hungarian government was doing its best to seem a loyal German ally while committing as few resources to the anti-Bolshevik "crusade" as possible. It, too, refused German requests for Jewish deportation and would continue to do so until the spring of 1944, when Germany occupied the country. In France, a fierce resistance movement challenged the authority of the Vichy government. A growing number of officials were reluctant to expand the scope of Jewish deportations to include French-born Jews. Civil war loomed in France, and German occupiers turned to a vicious fascist militia (the Milice) to enforce their rule.

As the tide of war began to turn, Nazi propagandists launched a new antisemitic campaign to inspire Germans and allies across Europe to greater sacrifices. The themes remained the same as ever, but the emotional tenor was carefully calibrated to reflect the precarious state of the war. The new campaign began with the speech by Joseph Goebbels in Berlin's Sportpalast in February 1943, when he asked the German people if they wanted "total war." With vividly apocalyptic images, he described what a Soviet victory (and therefore the victory of "international Jewry") would mean for Germany and for Europe: "A Bolshevization of the Reich would mean the liquidation of our entire intelligentsia and leadership, and the descent of our workers into Bolshevist-Jewish slavery." This was a European problem, he insisted, for Bolshevism would surely not stop at the borders of the Reich. "The West is in danger," Goebbels warned, and its governments did not realize the peril. But the German people did, he said. "Behind the oncoming Soviet divisions, we see the Jewish liquidation commandos, and behind them, terror, the specter of mass starvation and complete anarchy." Germany would be a wall that held the barbarians at bay: "We know our historic responsibility." He concluded his long speech with a powerful and infamous exhortation to carry on the fight to the bitter end: "Now, people rise up and let the storm break loose!"[92]

As in the summer of 1941, fresh evidence of Soviet atrocities was a powerful tool. In April 1943 news reached Goebbels that mass graves had been discovered near Smolensk. During the Soviet Union's occupation of eastern Poland, the NKVD had executed more than 20,000 Polish officers it had held as prisoners and buried them in pits in the Katyn Forest. Sensing an opportunity, Goebbels immediately decided to "turn up [*hochkitzeln*] the antisemitic propaganda" and began to weave the revelations into a vision of apocalypse ("Jewish Bolshevik terror" pouring in as barbaric hordes from the Asian steppes) and determination (Germans fighting a total war to its end in victory or death).[93] He took the atrocity at Katyn as proof that his fantasies of "Jewish liquidation commandos" slaughtering their enemies in the wake of Soviet triumph were true. The Nazi press followed suit, describing in graphic detail how "Jewish-Bolshevik murderers working for Stalin" had treated the captured Poles "like animals" and killed them, execution-style, "with a shot to the back of the neck."[94] For the next several months, photographs of atrocities and anti-Jewish articles filled the pages of German newspapers. The broadly conceived propaganda campaign even distorted events like the Warsaw Ghetto Uprising into proof that Jews would destroy Germany if they were not destroyed first.[95]

The German government invited a Red Cross commission to visit Katyn Forest and undertake a massive forensic investigation of the crime. A team of internationally recognized specialists exhumed the bodies, examined the remains, tried to identify the victims, and confirmed that that the Soviet Union was responsible. (This was the "first major forensic inquiry to establish human rights abuse."[96]) The Germans also invited selected journalists to visit the site. One such guest was Robert Brasillach, a long-time colleague of Lucien Rebatet on the editorial board of the most notoriously antisemitic newspaper in France, *Je suis partout*. Part of a team sent by the Vichy government to inspect the anti-Bolshevik Legion of French Volunteers fighting on the Eastern Front, Brasillach viewed the mass graves and published his impressions in July. He concluded his account by warning that France would surely suffer its own Katyn at the hands of Jewish Bolshevik murderers if Germany lost the war.[97] Other antisemitic intellectuals also used the evidence from Katyn to emphasize the apocalyptic consequences of Soviet victory. The Right in Hungary followed the news about Katyn closely.[98] (One of the forensic experts who took part in the international investigation was a prominent Hungarian doctor.) István Milotay raised the specter of cruel Jewish vengeance in terms that echoed Goebbels's Sportpalast speech. "Jewish kosher butchers" working for Stalin had slaughtered the Polish prisoners, he said, foreshadowing the terrible fate they would bring westward if the Red Army were not destroyed: "Siberian horrors, Europe thrown to mass death, mass extermination, massacre, and the depth of mass graves."[99]

Powerful as the images from Katyn were, they did not change political calculations. Since 1939, German propagandists had tried to influence attitudes and neutralize resistance in occupied Poland with posters, films, and exhibitions that identified anti-Jewish and anti-Communist themes as points of common ground. The Katyn revelations seemed especially promising material, and German authorities immediately began to present the Katyn massacre as a sign of the Polish future under "Jewish" Soviet rule. One series of posters produced in 1943, entitled "Who Runs the Soviet Union?" answered that rhetorical question with the slogan: "Jews, Jews, and once again Jews!" Another widely circulated brochure depicted a Red Army soldier, whip in hand, clutching a helpless Polish woman while a lust-filled Jewish male figure looked on over his shoulder. The image was titled: "The Fate of Women under the Jewish-Bolshevik Whip." The campaign undoubtedly resonated with local variations of the Judeo-Bolshevik threat, long a staple in Polish nationalist politics.[100] (Radical nationalists within the underground Home Army consistently described the Warsaw Ghetto as a Communist base. After the Ghetto was destroyed following the uprising, one intelligence bulletin welcomed the outcome because it "caused the premature liquidation of one of the armed positions of the Communists."[101]) It may have even strengthened it. Yet the Nazi propaganda campaign did absolutely nothing to win Polish support for the German cause. Polish national resistance grew only more determined as the war entered its last stages.[102]

Goebbels also hoped that the Katyn revelations would fracture the alliance between the Soviet Union and the Western powers. They did not. In the summer of 1943 the Germans were put on the defensive in the East for good when they lost the massive tank battle at Kursk. One year later, the destruction of the Germans' Army Group Center opened the door for the Red Army to advance into eastern Poland. In March 1944 the German army occupied Hungary in order to mobilize its economic resources and prepare for the Red Army's advance westward from southern Ukraine. On the Western Front, American forces landed at Normandy in June 1944. By the end of August they were in Paris.

The collapse of the Third Reich on two fronts raised two very different visions of what the end of the war might mean for Germany. In the West, Germans feared Allied bombing runs more than anything else and desperately hoped for the day when they would end. Outside of party fanatics, few believed that American or British occupation would mean German death. In the East, by contrast, German defeat would mean certain Soviet occupation. For years Nazi propagandists had deliberately used evidence of Soviet atrocities to inspire fear and hatred of the enemy and to nurture the belief that a Soviet victory would mean the destruction of Germany. As the Eastern Front collapsed and the Red Army drew closer to Germany's eastern provinces, the regime leaned ever more heavily on this message, accepting the possibility that constant atrocity propaganda might demoralize the population in the hope that a vision of their fate under Soviet rule would ultimately drive Germans in the army, the party, and in civilian life to hold out against it, at all costs.

In October 1944 the Soviet army broke through into East Prussia for the first time and briefly occupied a part of the province. After the Soviets were repelled, Joseph Goebbels sent a film crew to the town of

Nemmersdorf, the westernmost point of the Soviet advance, to record what had happened there. Bodies of murdered civilians, mostly elderly men and women but also a few children, lay in open graves, in ditches, or by the roadside. Precise numbers are hard to determine, precisely because of the regime's intense interest in using these events for propaganda purposes. According to the most reliable report, twenty-six bodies were found after Soviet troops had left. In addition, homes had been plundered. Military police recorded testimonies of women who had been raped. The political effect of these atrocities was obvious, and they inspired unverifiable claims of even more lurid atrocities. Some claimed to have seen naked women nailed to barn doors in the crucifix position. All this became the stuff of a propaganda campaign that closely resembled earlier coverage of Soviet atrocities at L'viv in 1941 or Katyn in 1943 in its hysteria. Headlines that shouted "The Raving of the Soviet Beasts" or "Bolshevik Bloodlust" led into stories of plunder, rape, and murder that were intended to provoke shock and outrage. Photographs of dead children featured prominently in the newspaper spreads. Although many Germans blamed party officials for bungling the chance to evacuate the people of Nemmersdorf before these horrors could befall them, the propaganda nevertheless had an effect. For those who faced the prospect of Soviet occupation, there was no alternative to war. Politicized coverage of the atrocities at Nemmersdorf reiterated what the regime had proclaimed all along. In the East, Germany fought a pitiless and barbaric enemy. Surrender would lead to a fate worse than death.[103]

The East-West divide that shaped how Germans saw the end of the war was reflected in attitudes across Europe. How the idea of Judeo-Bolshevism outlived Hitler's empire depended entirely on which army arrived to defeat it. In Western Europe, the U.S. army ended four years of German occupation. As the Germans retreated from Paris, talk of Judeo-Bolshevism evaporated in a final spasm of invective against the world Jewish conspiracy. The French journalists and writers who had cheered the crusade against Judeo-Bolshevism and called for ruthless

action against the Resistance found that the backdrop for their fantasies of national regeneration had collapsed. Lucien Rebatet wrote a
final essay on the topic of "Fidelity to National Socialism" and then
fled with the Vichy regime eastward into Germany, where the French
collaborationist government lived out its final days in Sigmaringen
Castle some twenty-five miles from Lake Constance.[104] Rebatet spent
his time in exile working on a novel, until he was arrested in 1945.
Initially sentenced to death for collaboration, Rebatet was ultimately
released from French prison in 1952.

   In Eastern Europe, the impending reality of Soviet occupation revived fears of Jewish Bolshevik power that had absolutely nothing to
do with Goebbels's last desperate propaganda campaign. By the
summer of 1944 the Red Army had driven the Germans back to the
territory of interwar Poland. A pro-Soviet government was established
in Lublin to challenge the authority and legitimacy of the Polish
government-in-exile in London. The so-called Lublin Committee followed the Soviet line in every respect. It praised the 1943 Warsaw
Ghetto Uprising, which it described as a heroic act of antifascism. But
it was utterly silent in the summer of 1944 about the doomed national
uprising launched in Warsaw by the underground Polish Home Army.
After the Germans had crushed the uprising, extremist nationalists
in the Home Army accused the Lublin Committee of representing
Jewish Bolshevik interests that were implacably hostile to the Polish
cause. Underground pamphlets gave this iconographic form. One featured a Polish coat of arms on which the traditional white eagle was
crowned by a Star of David with a hammer and sickle inside. Others
speculated on the Jewish identities of the individuals on the committee. (There were two; antisemites found more.) Even before the
war ended, the idea that Soviet rule meant Jewish power had reared
its head once more.[105]

   To the south, the idea of Judeo-Bolshevism was also transformed
by looming Soviet victory. Convinced that a Bolshevik conquest
must be prevented at all costs, Marshal Antonescu kept Romania

allied to Germany into 1944. At the same time, his regime reversed its Jewish policy in 1942 to improve its image with the Allies. Romanians resisted German requests to deport Jews and even began to resettle Jews from the ghettos and camps in Transnistria in Romania proper. These decisions saved the lives of Jews but paradoxically added fuel to fears of a Judeo-Bolshevik plot. In 1944 Antonescu reflected on the recent past: "I decided to evacuate all of the Jews of Bessarabia and Bukovina, but . . . I was impeded from doing so. Today, I regret that I did not do this. . . . There has not been a single Communist or terrorist organization discovered by our police in which Jews have not been members, and frequently they are constituted only of Jews."[106] Antonescu was toppled in a coup soon afterward, and the new Romanian government declared war on Germany. Even so, the link between a Soviet takeover and the specter of Jewish power was reestablished well before the arrival of Red Army soldiers in the country.

These new versions of Judeo-Bolshevik terror looked forward to a postwar world in which Nazi Germany was destroyed and the Soviet Union dominated Europe's eastern half. A dwindling number of fascist intellectuals refused to imagine the future. In Hungary, István Milotay remained committed to the doomed crusade against Bolshevism. He welcomed the German army when it occupied Hungary in March 1944 and celebrated when Hungarian and German officials forced Hungary's Jews into ghettos and then deported them to Auschwitz. Lust for Jewish property made this broadly popular, and Milotay described the massive seizure of Jewish property as a great step toward a truly national economy. But he also echoed the government's claims that the war against "Communist world-rule" demanded a last battle against Jewish power on the "inner front" to "ensure the uninterrupted efficiency of the army and the focused and intensified inner resilience of the country."[107] When the despised conservatives tried to escape the alliance with Hitler, he compared them to traitors who had sided with Jews and Bolsheviks against the national interest in

1919. And when the Germans deposed the last conservatives from power and installed the puppet government that would remain loyal to Germany even when the Red Army laid siege to Budapest, he insisted that there was "no other way."[108]

Taking license from imminent defeat, Milotay transposed into the present tense years of editorials that had conjured panic at the triumph of Jewish Bolshevik power. When the Red Army finally broke through Hungary's eastern border, he wrote simply: "They are here." He chastised all his opponents who thought Soviet occupation would not be so bad or hoped in vain for an American-led miracle. Above all, he blamed "Jews, with their huge masses and their impatient hunger for power, terror, and revolution." Fascist newspapers and radio broadcasts offered delusional accounts of German counteroffensives, as the Soviets moved ever closer to Budapest. They also warned Hungarians that the Jews were coming back. Labor servicemen, sentenced by the Hungarian government during the war to unarmed labor brigades and frequently assigned to punishing and dangerous work on the front, were now taking up arms and looking for revenge. They were also working for the Soviet army, guiding it to targets and helping it terrorize the Hungarian people. Above all, they were the signal that the long-invoked storm of Asiatic barbarism had reached Hungary. One government poster showed a Red Army soldier ripping a crucifix from a woman's neck; another invoked the specter of deportations to Siberia that would leave the nation's women and children defenseless. Fascist newspapers associated rumors of Jewish vengeance with reports of mass rape committed by Red Army troops in now-occupied easternmost parts of Hungary. By politicizing accounts of Soviet atrocities even before the war was over, fascist media shaped the way in which Soviet occupation could be discussed. Magdolna Gergely, a young woman in Budapest who kept a diary in 1944–45, wrote in September 1944 with dark humor about a joke making the rounds in Budapest: "Now, even a respectable person can be an antisemite again." Hitler's vision of Europe was collapsing. The idea of Judeo-Bolshevism remained.[109]

For his part, Milotay could only write bitterly that the Jewish Bolshevik enemy had triumphed. In his last editorial, he said he dreamed of an army of one million Hungarians who might drive the Soviets from the land and blamed his fellow Hungarians for lacking the will to make this ultimate sacrifice. Now, the bells of fate tolled for Hungary. Milotay ended his last piece in despair: "The heart must break. . . . Man wails and bangs his fist against the wall."[110] Then he fled west to Austria. He died in 1956 in a Swiss old-age home for Protestants.

German victory over the Soviet Union seemed inevitable in the summer of 1941. Certain that the war would produce a new Europe ordered according to Nazi ideals, would-be state builders, as well as governments of allied regimes who saw a chance to revise their borders or redeem their nations, embraced the Nazi vision of a pan-European crusade against the hated Communist enemy to the east. Cast as a wartime security threat by Nazi invaders and their allies, the idea of Judeo-Bolshevism became the rationale for targeted mass killings of Jews in the occupied Soviet Union in the first phases of the war. Anxiety about Jewish Bolshevik sabotage tightened the associative link between antisemitism, counterinsurgency, and the deportation of unwanted aliens in places as far apart as occupied Ukraine, Romania, and Vichy France. And in the regions of Eastern Europe that experienced Soviet and Nazi occupations in rapid succession, the arrival of German and other anti-Soviet forces triggered numerous instances of mob violence against local Jews, bloody pogroms in which cries for revenge against suspected Jewish Communist collaborators overlay deeper desires to reestablish community boundaries through looting, degradation, and killing. Considered from a local perspective, each of these many forms and instances of anti-Jewish violence involved different sets of actors, German and non-German, who were shaped by different histories, circumstances, and motives. Many of the non-German actors had ideas about Jews and

Communism that owed little or nothing to Nazi example. But the global scope of Nazi Germany's war of annihilation linked all the atrocities committed against Jews in a universe of shared meaning, placing all of them within a larger coherent history of genocide—the history of the Holocaust. The consequences for later European memories of the war were profound.

The prospect of Germany's defeat transformed the idea of Judeo-Bolshevism yet again. Goebbels's calls to defend the West from what he described as hordes of Asiatic barbarians driven relentlessly by Judeo-Bolshevik slave masters were part of a larger effort by the Nazi regime to steel Germans' resolve and, if that failed, to frighten them into holding out for final victory. They also inspired fascists throughout the Continent to remain loyal to the dream of a Nazi new order and all the promises of national regeneration that it enabled. The claims of Nazi propagandists that Europe was threatened by an enemy that fused Asiatic barbarism to the specter of Judeo-Bolshevism revived and redirected a vision, common among Europe's radical right during the interwar era, of Western civilization at war against an ethno-ideological enemy that was motivated by both zealous fanaticism and a savage disdain for Western values and traditions. This image of the West under attack would outlive the Nazi regime in remarkable and unexpected ways. More immediately, however, the impending destruction of Hitler's empire compelled Europeans to imagine futures determined by different armies of occupation. To the west, the arrival of U.S. and British troops would soon propel anti-Communist politics in new directions. To the east, however, the inexorable advance of the Red Army fueled nightmarish visions of Jewish Bolshevik vengeance that had a force and a history independent of Nazi power. Those fears shaped the way that many would understand the Soviet occupation.

5

Under Communist Rule

As the Nazi empire crumbled, partisan wars erupted in the Polish-Ukrainian-Lithuanian borderlands. So did fears of Jewish revenge. During the war, many nationalist partisans had fought bravely against the Germans in the name of ethnic purity. The freedom they imagined involved a future without German occupiers and troublesome ethnic minorities—including Jews. The prospect of trading German for Soviet rule endangered those dreams and revived old fears of subordination to foreign and "Jewish" power.[1] Fighters in the underground Polish Home Army eyed the pro-Soviet government set up in the city of Lublin warily, recognizing the threat that it posed to their vision for postwar Poland. Extreme nationalists among them cast their Moscow-backed rivals as agents of Jewish power intent, as ever, on opposing Polish nationhood.[2]

In Nazi-occupied Lithuania, Soviet partisans recruited young fighters of all nationalities, including Jewish youths who had escaped the ghettos. As German rule collapsed, a "war of nationalities" erupted among the Communist underground, Wehrmacht security forces, the Polish underground, and Lithuanian self-defense units. For all the non-Communist forces, Jews were "others"—enemies of the nation and supporters of Soviet rule—and Jewish partisans who fought with the Soviets became especially dangerous foes. Accounts of Jewish partisan violence, whether invented outright or simply heavily embellished, acquired an outsize importance in nationalist rhetoric and were taken as proof that Jews wanted to destroy the nations struggling for independence and impose Soviet rule over the region.[3]

Similar fears circulated widely in places where there were no such ethnic civil wars. Hungary's fascists had invoked a nightmare of Jewish Bolshevik destruction in a vain attempt to motivate Hungarians to continue the fight against the Soviet Union at all costs. The propaganda did nothing to inspire general enthusiasm for the fascists' own reign of terror, but the stories that they publicized of rape and plunder by Soviet troops increased the foreboding that the approaching Red Army would be a vehicle for Jewish revenge. Promoting such fears were not the exclusive preserve of Hungarian fascists. In 1943, a group of ethnonationalist populist intellectuals, all of them resolutely anti-German, gathered on the shores of Lake Balaton to debate how to chart a "third way" between capitalism and socialism for their country and how to create a democracy that would benefit "true" Hungarians, by which they meant, above all, ethnic Hungarian peasants. One of their number, the writer László Németh, infamously warned the audience that "revengeful Jews" were planning for the end of the war too. They were whetting their knives, the speaker said, "and it is the heart that Shylock wants." It was a powerful metaphor for a dystopian future in which alien and anti-national forces would rule the country.[4]

Similar fears prevailed that same year in neighboring Romania, where many became confused when their government began to repatriate the same Jews it had violently expelled from the country's eastern border regions into camps and ghettos in occupied Soviet Transnistria two years before. The move was a calculated attempt by the Romanian leadership to improve the country's image in the West, but security agents active in villages and towns across eastern Romania reported that many people simply felt betrayed. The expulsion of nearly 150,000 Romanian Jews from the regions of Bukovina and Bessarabia had allowed many Romanians in those areas to enrich themselves at the expense of their vanished neighbors. The 1941 pogroms that had erupted along what had then been the Soviet-Romanian border had also given local people a chance to enrich themselves. Even the return of a handful of families to towns that had been emptied of Jews caused popular outrage. One report filed by security agents in late 1943 captured the mood: people were angry that "so much Romanian blood has been shed at the front while the kikes, who fought against this country by joining up with the Bolsheviks, are being brought back."[5] Romanians had been told that the war against the Soviet Union had been a crusade against Bolshevism, and that the violence that so many had committed against Jews had been justified acts of righteous anger against a treacherous and powerful enemy. The return of the Jews suggested to them that Jewish power might not have been vanquished after all.

The fear that Communism would prove to be a mask for Jewish vengeance was not the dominant theme everywhere in the Soviet Union's new Eastern European "sphere of influence." In Yugoslavia, the Communist Party built its power and prestige on the history of the determined partisan war that it had waged against Nazi occupiers. The Red Army played no role in establishing Communist rule there, and those who were alarmed by the repressive measures taken by the new regime against state and class enemies did not describe them as Jewish. In Czechoslovakia, the Communist Party received the largest number of votes in the 1946 election. There too the prospect of a Communist government, which grew ever clearer in the months that followed, was not widely condemned as the rule of alien Jews. Nor did fear of Judeo-Bolshevism loom over the coup d'état launched in September 1944 by the Bulgarian resistance, which overthrew Bulgaria's pro-German monarchy and replaced it with a Fatherland Front soon dominated by the Communists.

In other places, however—above all, Poland, Hungary, and Romania—deeply entrenched stereotypes that identified Communism with Jews profoundly shaped popular perceptions of Soviet occupying forces and the Communist parties that rose to power with their support. The figure of the Jewish Bolshevik had been a central feature of political life in each of these countries during the interwar era, embodying the threats to both sociocultural unity and state security that nationalists saw in the expansion of Communist power. Wartime propaganda, whether produced by Nazi occupiers, their fascist allies, or right-wing nationalists in the anti-Nazi underground, had reinforced the idea that Communist rule (if and when it came) would amount to a nation-destroying reign of terror by a cadre of fanatical Jewish ideologues. This expectation predetermined the way that many Eastern Europeans in these countries would later understand, discuss, and remember the brutalities committed by Red Army soldiers or the repressive measures used by Communist authorities to establish their power. At the same time, the firm link between Jews and Communism in the popular imagination was a political reality that Communist Party leaders could not ignore. In the years after 1945, they attempted to control the stereotype or to manipulate it to their advantage. In some places they even turned it against one another, identifying enemies within the party as Jewish Communists who were guilty of betraying the people. The Judeo-Bolshevik myth had a long history in some parts of the new postwar Soviet bloc in Eastern Europe. In Poland, Hungary, and Romania, the reality of Communist rule did not extinguish that myth. Instead, it transformed its meaning and function.

The Red Army won the Siege of Budapest in February 1945. The remnants of the German army that survived fled westward, accompanied by Hungary's fascist puppet government, which remained loyal to the end. By April, Soviet forces controlled all Hungarian territory.

To mark their victory, occupation officials prepared to celebrate May Day a few weeks later. Soviet authorities cleared Freedom Square in central Budapest of all the irredentist memorials to Hungary's lost territories that had graced the space throughout the interwar years. In their place they erected a monument to honor the Red Army soldiers who died in the siege. The memorial featured a star at the crown, a frieze of soldiers in battle at the base, and an inscription in Russian and Hungarian that read: "Honor to the liberating Soviet heroes." The monument was like many memorials that Soviet authorities erected across Europe after the war. It commemorated the Red Army soldiers who had fallen in the great antifascist struggle. It also reflected the historical role that the Soviet Union saw for itself in Eastern Europe. In symbolic form, the monument proclaimed that the Red Army had liberated Hungary from fascism. With its help and through its sacrifice, the Hungarian people had been freed from reactionary fascist oppression and been given a chance to build a new and just society in partnership with their Soviet allies. Hungary's Communists adopted this view as well. After 1948 their belief that the Soviet victory had liberated the country from fascism became one of the central ideological pillars supporting and legitimizing Hungary's Communist regime.

Across Eastern Europe, Soviet occupation forces and their local Communist allies made similar claims. It did not ring hollow for everyone. Some people did welcome Soviet forces as liberators without qualification. The Red Army victory saved the lives of Jews trapped in the Budapest ghetto, allowed Jews to emerge from hiding places in basements and haylofts across Poland, freed those still alive in Majdanek (July 1944) and Auschwitz (end of January 1945), and toppled antisemitic regimes in Hungary and Romania. Working-class activists and labor leaders were released from prison or were free to return from exile. Soviet victory also raised hopes for sweeping social reform. A reinvigorated Left—Communist and non-Communist, working together or in competition with each other—openly contemplated measures, such as land reform, that had been nonstarters before the war and that promised to dramatically change the lives of the poorest people in the region. Yet many East Europeans saw Soviet occupation as unwelcome foreign domination, Soviet "liberation" as a cynical and hollow phrase, and Soviet allies in local Communist parties and security services as collaborators with the enemy. In Poland, Hungary, and Romania, these sentiments often coalesced around the idea of Judeo-Bolshevism, condensing the dramatic and dizzying political changes into one simple proposition: Soviet occupation had brought Jews to power.

Three factors shaped the context for this assertion. First, Soviet forces were a foreign occupying power widely seen as hostile to local populations. The systematic liquidation of resistance groups and the arbitrary arrest of civilians played into this narrative. After 1945 the Polish secret police (the Urząd Bezpieczeństwa, or UB), working with the Soviet NKVD, waged war against the Polish Home Army. They arrested its members, hunted partisan groups that remained active, and hounded networks of Home Army veterans. In Hungary, men were indiscriminately arrested in the streets as "prisoners of war." Some were made to clear rubble in Budapest; others were taken to work in the Soviet Union. Many of them returned only years later; some did not return at all. Superficial appearances also played a role. Stories of Soviet soldiers with "Asiatic" features who were frightened by modern toilets, obsessed by the allure of shiny wrist watches, and unfamiliar with "civilized" and "European" behavior reinforced the view (widely broadcast during the war in German-allied countries like Hungary) that the Soviet occupiers were alien, uncivilized, and cruel. Most important, the behavior of Red Army soldiers fueled resentment and hatred. Looting and rape were commonplace in Soviet-occupied Eastern Europe, especially in areas where the fighting had been fiercest and where military discipline was lax.[6] These crimes poisoned attitudes toward the Communist Party from the first postwar moments. In Hungary in February 1945, Communist Party leader

Mátyás Rákosi complained to no less a person than Georgi Dimitrov about mass rape and looting by Soviet soldiers. He tactfully blamed the problem on the "occasional bad behavior of soldiers of the Red Army" but warned Dimitrov that such actions made "our situation more difficult." Local party secretaries gave more blunt assessments. "People blame the communists for what the Russians do," wrote one. "The people live in fear . . . the women are treated most shamelessly. . . . Every day that passes the people have less confidence in the Party," wrote another.[7]

Second, Jews were visible in public again. After their deportation to camps in Poland or across the Dniester into Transnistria, it had been easy to think that the Jews were simply gone. Even where they had not been deported—from regions of the old Romanian kingdom or from Budapest—the combination of anti-Jewish laws and antisemitic terror had made Jews nonpersons. Now, survivors returned from camps. Others came out of hiding. In Hungary, labor servicemen came back from punishing work in forced-labor battalions. Civic organizations were created to provide care for returning Jews and to help them search for family members, make property claims, and document their experiences, for use in war-crimes trials as well as for posterity. International Jewish organizations established offices across Eastern Europe to distribute aid and to assist in emigration. At the same time, the laws and decrees that had separated Jews from their neighbors, excluded them from society, and destroyed their associational life were lifted. Society around them remained hostile and fear remained a constant fact of life, but—in certain places and certain forums—it became possible for some survivors to speak critically and openly about their persecutors.

One letter that made its way into the primatial archives of the Roman Catholic Church in Hungary reveals how strange this altered situation must have seemed. Its author, a fifty-nine-year-old night nurse in Budapest, had felt compelled to write to Cardinal József Mindszenty himself because she was outraged by the bold and open way that the Jewish doctors in her hospital criticized the Church and its priests. Her boss, she said, was a "Jewish son of a bitch" who had said in full voice to anybody who would listen that more priests should be arrested and sent to the secret police headquarters at 60 Andrássy Street in Budapest, because that was where criminals like them belonged. It is impossible to know more about the doctor who spoke those words and what experiences might have made him say them. But the letter writer was clearly shocked that he had dared to utter them aloud, and she devoted the rest of her long letter to defending the Church against "Jewish lies."[8]

Third and finally, Communist parties had sprung back to life across the region. Decimated by the Stalinist purges of the late 1930s, Eastern Europe's Communist parties had been driven underground during the war. In Poland, Communist partisans had been among several groups fighting the German occupation. Other party leaders spent the war in Moscow. In Nazi-allied states, the parties were much weaker. In Romania, for example, the security service had targeted Communists for years; by 1944 only a few hundred members remained. The Hungarian Communist Party was also moribund. Those who had fought alongside Béla Kun in 1919 were dead, in jail, or in exile. A tiny group of party members worked underground to no effect, although later they would be cast as great heroes of the antifascist resistance. Soviet occupation changed their fortunes overnight. As the Red Army advanced into Eastern Europe, Soviet leaders sent émigrés in Moscow back to their home countries to organize Communist parties; other Eastern European Communists emerged from hiding or were released from prison. With Soviet support, they won important ministerial posts, above all in the interior ministries, which controlled police and security services. Soviet power allowed (some would say directed) Communist parties to aggressively attack their rivals as parties of reaction, intimidating, marginalizing, or co-opting their members. The political transformation was swift and stunning. From meager beginnings, Communist parties in Hungary,

Romania, and Poland each had more than a million members by 1948, their ranks swelled by a generation of men and women who were attracted by the party's vision of historical progress, by the power and material opportunities that party membership offered, or by some combination of both. Their prominence and strength announced a new political order.

The fusion of these three factors—fear and anger in reaction to the brutality of Soviet occupation forces; the sudden visibility of Jews; and the new power exercised by Eastern Europe's Communist parties— shaped how the new political reality was understood and interpreted in the popular imagination. The Jewish origins of certain leading Communists quickly attracted attention as proof that Soviet occupation was ultimately Jewish rule; in time, their personal histories assumed an outsize role in the collective memories of Eastern Europe's nations. The figure of Jakub Berman, for example, who ran the secret police in Poland, "has remained a vivid one in Polish memory."[9] So have others: Hilary Minc, minister of industry and architect of Poland's Six-Year Plan; Józef Różański, who joined the NKVD after the Soviet invasion of Poland and then became a top officer (and notorious interrogator) in the Polish Ministry of State Security; Julia Brystygierowa, who oversaw the department that investigated the Catholic Church. In Hungary, the Jewish origins of the four leading Communists—Mátyás Rákosi, the party leader; Ernő Gerő and Mihály Farkas, his powerful lieutenants; and József Révai, the powerful minister of culture—were taken as evidence that Communism was an alien imposition there, as were figures like Gábor Péter, who controlled the Hungarian secret police (the Államvédelmi Hatóság, or ÁVH), and the Communist mayor of Budapest, Zoltán Vas. In Romania, Ana Pauker, the foreign minister and one of the most powerful party officials in the early 1950s, remains a reviled figure, demonized in popular memory as "Stalin in a skirt."[10]

The number of Jews in party cadres, especially in security, foreign relations, and culture and the press, seemed significant. Then and since, a variety of wildly varying figures and percentages have been generated to demonstrate Jewish "overrepresentation" in these positions of power, along with numerous explanations for the size of the numbers.[11] The explanations include the party's need for cadres who were literate (in rural areas like Bessarabia, or Soviet Moldova after 1945, most non-Jewish peasants were illiterate), politically reliable (Jews were excluded from rival ethnonationalist movements and uncompromised by service in the previous anti-Communist and antisemitic regimes), and immediately available (recruiting cadres from the ethnic majority community would take time). Some have advanced psychological hypotheses (Jews wanted revenge). Yet counting the number of Eastern European Jews in powerful party positions is as misleading for the period after 1945 as it is for the period between 1917 and 1923, and the same caveats apply. Individual biographies show Jews and non-Jews alike became Communists, and for a complicated variety of reasons. Finally, and for the period after 1945 most decisively, the Soviet Union was intent on asserting its influence across postwar Eastern Europe. The Communist Party would have flourished throughout the region without any Jews at all.

Nevertheless, the association of Jews and Communism shaped popular opinion about the postwar regimes. The link influenced perceptions of transitional justice especially deeply. Across Eastern Europe, new provisional governments scrambled to staff security offices, the gendarmerie, and the court system, replacing personnel who had served previous pro-German regimes, building new institutions from scratch, or reconstructing old ones destroyed during German occupation. They also established national courts of justice to try collaborators and perpetrators of war crimes in highly public trials that were meant to punish but also to purge and renew society. These developments were quickly labeled "Jewish." In Hungary, newspaper reports of popular violence in the countryside against local representatives of the old government, of former Jewish labor servicemen joining the police to avenge their families, or of angry (presumably Jewish) crowds assaulting guards who had persecuted the labor servicemen under their command during the war all helped to drive this view. So did public trials in 1945 and 1946 of, first, fascist Arrow Cross murderers and then prominent members of the old regime, including those most responsible for working with Adolf Eichmann to deport Jews to Auschwitz. By the summer of 1945 there were reports of demonstrations in provincial Hungarian cities that denounced the new people's courts with slogans such as "Hang the Jews! Down with the People's Courts, stooges of the Jews!"[12]

The truth was very different. Jewish survivors in Poland invariably found the legal system unsympathetic and unresponsive. Focused mainly on punishing ethnic Germans and the members of the so-called blue police who had collaborated with the Germans, state prosecutors were generally uninterested in taking up cases of crimes against Jews. Nor did the police do much about the fierce intimidation of those Jewish witnesses who did step forward. In many cases, witnesses faced tremendous social pressure from their neighbors to give false testimony that exonerated Poles who had taken part (for example, in eastern Poland in 1941) in the murders of Jews. The Hungarian judicial system did a much better job of trying murderers, at least at first. Historian László Karsai counts at least 1,700 "Holocaust-related" cases that came before the People's Court of Budapest in 1945. But he notes a stark decrease after 1946 in the number of trials that had anything to do with the persecution or murder of Jews.[13]

Assertions of vengeful Jewish power also surfaced in acts of violence against Jews. In 1945 and 1946, several pogroms erupted in Eastern Europe, sparked by accusations that Jews had kidnapped or harmed a Christian child. In the northeastern Hungarian village of Kunmadaras, two Jews were killed by a mob that accused the Jews of the village of being murderers and profiteers and denounced Communist Party leader Mátyás Rákosi as "king of the Jews." However, the most significant pogrom by far occurred in the Polish city of Kielce, where rumors of a child's kidnapping spread in July 1946. There, a mob assembled in front of a building that housed the town's Jewish Committee and began shouting denunciations of Jewish "murderers." The militia arrived, ostensibly to keep the peace, but it too turned on the Jews. Shots were fired, unleashing the brutality of the mob, which attacked the town's frightened Jews, beating them and plundering their homes. In the end, forty-two Jews were killed. Eyewitnesses later recalled hearing cries targeting Jews as agents of Communist terror—"A Jew is a Bolshevik!" "They want Communism, so we'll give them Communism!"—in addition to exhortations to finish what Hitler started and to beat all Jews because they were Jews. Similar language drove the fury of mobs in the cities of Rzeszów (June 1945) and Kraków (August 1945).[14]

This violence, so horrifying to urban intellectual elites, resonated widely. When Communist labor leaders in Poland tried to mobilize workers to condemn the violence as a "reactionary" provocation, they found that workers were instead far more eager to take part in strikes and to use anti-Jewish slogans as a way to express their own social and economic dissatisfaction. Opponents of the Communist Party also used the association of Jews and Communism as a way to deflect charges that they were "reactionary" enemies of the people. Soon after the Kielce pogrom, a commission established by the Roman Catholic bishop of Kielce prepared a report that described and also explained what had happened. The commission insisted that Jews themselves were responsible for the violence that they had suffered. Jews were hated, they said, because they were "the main propagators of Communism in Poland, while the Polish nation does not want Communism, which is being imposed on it by force. . . . Ministries are full of Jews. . . . They are in charge of security police offices, and carry out arrests."[15] There were certainly other voices in Poland's Catholic Church. Bishop Teodor Kubina of Częstochowa condemned the pogrom clearly and emphatically. But the commission's rationale was powerful. It separated the violence of the pogrom from anything that had happened during the war and made it simply a reaction to postwar events: Jews supported Communism and so brought hatred on themselves. It was a line of argument echoed by Poland's primate, Cardinal August Hlond, who also issued a statement about the pogrom. He condemned the violence but added that the responsibility for it fell "in great measure . . . to the Jew who has occupied leading positions in the life of the state and who is striving to impose structural forms that the vast majority of the nation doesn't want."[16]

The shocking resurgence in postwar Eastern Europe of anti-Jewish violence triggered by medieval blood-libel accusations has been explained in different ways.[17] One factor was clearly economic and social insecurity, which fueled resentment and revived fantasies of Jewish wealth and advantage. In 1945 and 1946 Hungary was crippled by inflation. In those same years, shifting borders dislocated millions of Poles. Both factors resulted in tremendous social misery. Guilt over the plunder and persecution of Jewish neighbors also stoked fears that the return of the Jews meant that a reckoning would come. Perhaps most significant, if less materially tangible, was the effect of war and genocide on postwar Christian-Jewish relations. The vastly different experiences of Jews and non-Jews during the war produced sharply divergent memories of the recent past and allowed many to remain willfully oblivious to what their Jewish neighbors had endured. This social distancing encouraged the belief that Jews would take advantage of the Soviet occupation to press their own claims and secure their own advantage. The crystallization of these antipathies around the equating of Jews and Bolsheviks hardened social and moral boundaries between Jews ("them") and non-Jews ("us") in ways that mapped neatly onto popular understandings of the new Soviet-backed state as a foreign power: "them." This was a challenge that Communist Party leaders could not ignore.

One month after the Soviet army took Budapest, the Hungarian Communist Party published the first issue of its newspaper, *Szabad*

Nép (Free people). Throughout the war the paper's editors had been forced to work underground, circulating clandestine flyers printed on increasingly scarce paper to a tiny circle of loyal supporters. Soviet victory changed everything for them. With the ideological and financial support of their Soviet backers, the editors of *Szabad Nép* proclaimed the dawning of a new and democratic age and announced the Communist Party's ambition to lead the Hungarian people toward that bright future. The issue featured rousing articles by party leaders, including one by Mátyás Rákosi and another by Ernő Gerő. There were also essays by writers close to the Communist Party but not (or not yet) official members that were meant to signal the party's openness to coalition politics and its desire to broaden its base of popular support. One in particular attracted considerable attention. Its author was József Darvas, who was well known as a writer and activist on the far left of Hungary's peasant-oriented populist movement. (Darvas was a leading figure in the country's National Peasant Party. He would go on to serve the Communist regime after 1948 in ministerial positions.) Darvas gave his full-page essay the title "An Honest Word about the Jewish Question!" Very possibly the first openly antisemitic writing published in Hungary after the Soviet victory, Darvas's essay was an early sign of the complicated role that Jews and antisemitism would play in Communist political strategy in Hungary and across the emerging Soviet bloc.

In his essay, József Darvas allowed that Jews had suffered during the war. Hungary's great landholders and aristocrats and bankers, whom Darvas described simply as the "reaction," had strengthened their rule by spreading antisemitism and dragging Hungary into a futile and destructive war. "The infection was serious," he wrote. "It would be stupid to deny it." But Darvas insisted that Jews were now playing the role of martyrs in order to claim special privileges. "Now that the tables have turned, they want to be the guards." In their thirst for vengeance, he wrote, they were unjustly targeting countless simple Hungarians. The country's poor workers and peasants had been exploited for centuries by an oppressive social system in which Jews had played no small role and had then been blinded by propaganda into supporting the war. They too had suffered. Now, they had a historic chance to heal their wounds by building a new and democratic Hungary with their own honest labor. Even before the war in Europe had ended, Darvas was wondering openly whether Jews would find a place in this new society. He accused Jews of idleness "under the false disguise of their martyrdom." Rather than taking on the hard work of rebuilding, they preferred to indulge themselves in vendettas that would only revive prejudices against them. "In the end," he wrote, "not every Jew is born a democrat and among them there are many with little talent who do not like to work."[18]

"An Honest Word about the Jewish Question!" is interesting as much for where it appeared—in the Communist Party newspaper—as for what it said. Its publication was a deliberate editorial decision that mobilized the prestige of a well-known populist writer to the Communist Party's advantage. The essay did several things for the Communist cause. It affirmed the view that the war (which for Hungary had ended in Soviet victory and Hungarian defeat) had liberated the country from fascism and made possible the transformation of Hungarian society and the improvement of the lives of Hungary's workers and peasants. The essay also positioned Jews outside this transformative vision by consciously invoking well-established anti-Jewish stereotypes. Darvas validated the hysterical wartime fascist rhetoric about Jewish revenge. He identified a particular Jewish "victim" mentality that denied the suffering that non-Jewish Hungarians had endured. And he insinuated that Jews were exploiting their victim status in order to live, like parasites, off the honest work of the Hungarian people. These arguments were so appealing to the editors of *Szabad Nép* because they directly countered one of the greatest challenges to the popular legitimacy of the Communist Party in Hungary and elsewhere in Eastern Europe: after the war, Communism was widely seen as Jewish and antinational.

Communist parties in Eastern Europe tried to inoculate themselves against the stigma of Judeo-Bolshevism in several ways. First,
leaders looked at their own parties through an ethnic lens. They
moved quickly to broaden membership by reaching out to national
majorities, in ways that made a mockery of their own antifascist pre-
tensions. In Romania, Ana Pauker offered amnesty to Iron Guard
legionaries, admitting frankly that "there were more of them, and
especially workers, than I'd imagined."[19] In Hungary, *Szabad Nép*
published articles throughout 1945, by Jozsef Darvas and others, that
distinguished between the majority of so-called little fascists, who
were decent workers pulled by the force of their social circumstances
into the fascist orbit, and the much smaller number of high-ranking
fascist ideologues, who deserved criminal punishment. The articles
sent a clear signal that the party welcomed low-ranking perpetrators
of war crimes if they were willing to commit themselves wholeheartedly
to the new order. Hungarian party leaders also publicly advised Jews
to abandon their demands for justice. In 1946 György Aczél, then a
county-level party secretary, instructed local Jews to "stop turning villages upside down to find your kitchen stools. If you want to live
here, then you have to make peace with people."[20]

Communist parties also instrumentalized manifestations of anti-
Jewish violence to attack their rivals. The 1946 pogrom in Kunmadaras attracted nationwide attention in Hungary, and the case
was quickly transferred to the Budapest People's Tribunal, which had
the authority to try political cases. During the trial, state prosecutors
solicited evidence of anti-Jewish violence. But they were not interested
in understanding the local motives for the attack, nor in establishing
the precise level of culpability of each of the fifty-nine defendants.
Instead, prosecutors presented antisemitism as a symptom of fascist
and antidemocratic politics. They focused particular attention on the
local leader of the Smallholders Party, the main political rival of the
Communists in the early postwar years, and on a village teacher who
had already been convicted in an earlier trial for his involvement in

the interwar "fascist" regime. These men were accused of conspiring against democracy; the testimony against them helped to establish the anti-Jewish violence that ensued as the expression of a deeper hostility to the new postwar order. Lost in the proceedings were the Jewish identities of the three men who died in the attack. As historian Péter Apor argues, the trial erased the Jewish victims in Kunmadaras in order to transform antisemitism into something else. In this way, the trial became a tool the Communist Party could use to discredit its rivals and underscore the illegitimacy of the pre-1944 regime.[21]

Polish Communists considered the Kielce pogrom in a similarly tactical way. Like their Hungarian counterparts, they immediately interpreted the pogroms as a sign that a powerful opposition had formed and was issuing subversive orders. At an August 1945 meeting of the party's Central Committee shortly after a pogrom had taken place in Kraków, the assembled leaders concluded that "attempted pogroms . . . suggest that they have a general character and that they were planned. That they were planned implies that there was a center issuing orders."[22] This useful conclusion, in turn, justified further assaults on rival parties and independent civic organizations. However, Polish Communist Party leaders could not ignore the widespread hostility against Jews. When strikes that featured anti-Jewish slogans erupted in the western industrial city of Łódź, protesting the party's efforts to mobilize workers against "reactionary" pogroms, party leaders scrambled to control the volatile situation. Meetings between visiting delegates from the Central Committee and local Communists accepted the popular anger at "unproductive" and "parasitical" middlemen who avoided honest work and exploited shortages to profit at the expense of the "people." Party leaders hoped to put these old antisemitic stereotypes to new use by transforming them from a specifically anti-Jewish slur into a general image of an enemy. Kielce Communists described the strategy: "During all mass meetings, people transferred their anger from Jews to parasitic elements in general. The action was very successful. . . . A conviction arose that the

Party . . . seeks out and punishes those who prey on the people." Some party officials drew their own conclusions about what this meant for the place of Jews in the new workers' state. At a meeting several weeks after the Kielce pogrom, one member of the Central Committee Secretariat called for an institution that would "facilitate departure of the Jews from Poland." Many others simply hoped that the problem would go away and preferred to focus their attention on generically defined "saboteurs," who could be defined in various ways that had nothing to do with Jews at all. The security police took a similar approach. In the months that followed, they did very little to investigate or punish acts of anti-Jewish violence.[23]

Local Communist activists also exploited popular anti-Jewish prejudices in Hungary, where galloping hyperinflation ravaged the economy. (In July 1946, shortly before the government introduced a new currency, inflation peaked at 41.9 quadrillion percent, the highest monthly rate of inflation in recorded history.) Inevitably, widespread shortages and hoarding stimulated a thriving black-market economy. In response, the Communist Party mobilized its members to demonstrate against black marketeers and "exploiting industrialists," slogans that easily lent themselves to anti-Jewish provocations. A March 1946 protest in the southeastern city of Békéscsaba, originally aimed at discrediting old-regime civil servants as well as the local branch of the rival Smallholders Party, degenerated into a mob that expressed its anger at economic conditions and the "establishment" that did nothing to relieve them by shouting epithets at Jews, priests, and—despite their efforts to organize the demonstration in the first place—the Communists. Fifteen people were injured. Several months later party activists in the northeastern city of Miskolc also organized a demonstration against black marketeers and speculators. There, the manipulation of anti-Jewish stereotypes was much more deliberate. Placards were created that depicted the "enemies" of the people as individuals with stereotypically Jewish features. At the same time, leaflets circulated by the party militants warned these "enemies" that the Left stood ready to fight back against "any among them who see the black market as a better chance, who want to gamble or enter one of the parties in order to satisfy their greed." Language like this was incendiary and was seen as sanctioning anti-Jewish violence. As in Békéscsaba, the Miskolc protests quickly turned violent. Two Jewish merchants were killed in a so-called people's judgment.[24]

Despite their cynical manipulation of antisemitic stereotypes, party leaders in rural Hungary were no more successful than their Polish counterparts in undoing the popular association of Communism with Jewish rule and Soviet occupation. Indeed, Mátyás Rákosi had visited the Miskolc region shortly before violence broke out there. Relatively few came to hear his speech at a special party rally to honor him. Instead, reports accumulated of factory workers complaining that Rákosi was the "king of the Jews" and that he had "sold the country to the Russians." Provincial party leaders complained bitterly that they were seen as Jewish agents. At a meeting of the Central Committee, one county party secretary from eastern Hungary observed that the dissatisfied "working masses" always turned their anger about shortages and speculative prices on the Jews and completely ignored the fact that "greasy peasants" were responsible for most of the black market activity. In the countryside, he said, the antisemitic mood was stronger than it ever had been in 1919.[25] It was a revealing comparison. During the 1919 revolution, rural Communist activists had made dark allusions at the National Congress of Councils to the racial composition of the party leadership, and had accused "urban cosmopolitans" in Budapest of having no understanding of the needs of the Hungarian people.[26] They had also criticized Jews in terms that foreshadowed the tumultuous post-1945 years: as a people indistinguishable from capitalism, whose economic interests automatically made them the agents of speculation, exploitation, and reaction. But in 1919, as later, their protests achieved nothing. The 1919 revolution had collapsed and the counterrevolutionary regime that followed had cemented in the popular imagination the idea that the Bolshevik

revolution had been a Jewish plot. The weight of this legacy profoundly impaired Communist efforts to legitimize the party in
Hungarian society.

In Poland, Hungary, and Romania, especially, Communist Party
leaders struggled to counter the perception that theirs was a Jewish
party. They manipulated debates about postwar antisemitic violence,
downplaying the significance of such acts by casting them as expressions of a much broader and more dangerous enemy: fascism. They
cynically deployed stereotypes of capitalists as "shirkers" and "parasites," knowing full well that those images were commonly understood
as Jewish traits. They made common cause with populists and ethnonationalists, offering their erstwhile opponents the chance to move
from the Right to the Left in exchange for the legitimacy that their
dreams of mono-ethnic hegemony might convey.[27] And they worked
hard to dispel the impression that Jews were overrepresented in the
party by recruiting cadres from ethnic majority communities and
even admitting former fascists into their ranks, so long as they had
not committed major war crimes. These efforts showed how clearly
the leaders of a nominally internationalist party understood the challenges to their rule in ethnic or nationalist terms, and how clearly they
understood, in the years after World War II, that the accusation of
Judeo-Bolshevism was a threat to their consolidation of power in society. Very soon, however, the figure of the Jewish Bolshevik would
acquire a new form and a new meaning. In the late 1940s "the Jew"
would emerge as the face of the enemy within their own ranks.

Czechoslovakia was not an obvious location for an antisemitic show
trial. Unlike its Hungarian, Romanian, and Polish counterparts, the
Czechoslovak Communist Party emerged from the war with genuine
popular support. In the 1946 parliamentary election—the country's
last free election until 1990—the Communists received the most votes
of any party. Nor had the idea of Judeo-Bolshevism been as deeply

entrenched in interwar Czech political life as it had been in Hungary, Romania, or Poland, even if Czechoslovakia did have a tradition of political antisemitism. (The threat of Judeo-Bolshevism was an element, though never the most prominent one, in the ideology of the wartime Nazi-allied Slovak state.[28]) During World War II, Nazi officials spread antisemitic and anti-Bolshevik propaganda and promoted anti-Jewish sentiment in the Protectorate of Bohemia and Moravia (the occupied Czech lands). Historians continue to debate the legacy of Nazi occupation for postwar Czech society, but however significant it may have been, it did not prevent millions of Czechs from voting for the Communists when they had the chance in 1946. As they consolidated power, Czechoslovak Communists did not need to fight the same intense perception of Communism as a Jewish plot that their comrades to the north and south did. Nevertheless, Rudolf Slánský and thirteen other leading figures in the Czechoslovak Communist Party were arrested in November 1952 on charges of conspiracy and made the subjects of an elaborate show trial. Eleven of the fourteen defendants, including Slánský himself, were consistently identified as Jews throughout the proceedings. For several weeks, radio broadcasts and newspaper reports in Czechoslovakia and across the entire Soviet bloc amazed audiences with startling revelations about the endless treachery committed by the defendants against the state and against the party they claimed to love. It would be the last in a series of great show trials that took place across Communist Eastern Europe between 1948 and 1953, and the only one built around the Jewish origins of the defendants.[29]

The Slánský trial was a stunning instance of Communist Party leaders using the figure of the (insincere, cunning, and deceitful) Jewish Bolshevik to attack one another. (In the West, Cold War liberals following the trial from afar took it as proof that Communism was no different from Nazism in its totalitarian hatred of Jews and Judaism.) Once general secretary of the Czechoslovak Communist Party and second in power only to president and party leader Klement

Gottwald, the fallen Rudolf Slánský now abased himself with humiliating self-criticism to prove his deceit, asserting that he had always been a craven opportunist who had only acted like a good Communist to disguise his true intentions. Most important, each of the defendants was coerced by the interrogators to admit to a variety of treasonous acts that were all linked by their supposedly secret and powerful commitment to Zionism. The Jewish origins of Slánský and most of the other defendants were used as proof of their intention to sabotage Communism in Czechoslovakia. Slánský and his colleagues confessed to collaborating with international Zionist networks and to extending those networks into the Czechoslovak Communist Party by promoting and protecting Zionists within it. They were also compelled to admit that they had used campaigns against antisemitism to protect their Zionist agents, an absurd proposition that, as historian Melissa Feinberg observes, made "attacking antisemitism" a "traitorous act."[30] Two weeks after it began, the carefully planned and meticulously staged trial came to an end. Slánský and the other thirteen defendants were found guilty of "Trotskyist, Titoist, Zionist, bourgeois nationalist" conspiracy. Eleven of them, including Slánský, were executed.

The Slánský trial was not initially meant to be a trial of Jews. Faced with demands from Soviet security advisors for a Czech version of a major show trial, the Czechoslovak political police cast about for suitable villains. At first they envisioned a trial that focused on "Slovak bourgeois nationalism." Over time, and with continued and heavy Soviet involvement, the trial evolved into an "anti-Zionist" and "anticosmopolitan" case that featured mainly Jewish defendants.[31] Despite these convoluted origins, the trial resonated with the Czechoslovak public in unexpected ways that mirrored popular opinion in neighboring Poland and Hungary, despite a different history of antisemitism and anti-Jewish violence in the Czech lands. Police reports record an overwhelming number of antisemitic comments made by ordinary people about Slánský and his fellow defendants. They suggest that many found accusations of "Zionist" treason against the people quite plausible, because they resonated with older stereotypes of Jews as antinational cosmopolitans who shirked work and were greedy for power.[32] The trial also drew on local fears that Czech Jews were really crypto-Germans, a suspicion with deep roots in the pre-1945 history of Czech-German nationality politics.[33]

The anti-Jewish, anti-Zionist, and anticosmopolitan themes that dominated the Slánský trial reflected the repressive campaigns directed against Jews in the Soviet Union during the last years of Stalin's life. Nazi Germany's war, fought in pursuit of racist and genocidal goals, had produced a heightened ethnic consciousness among the peoples of the Soviet Union. Soon after it ended, the Communist Party had launched a campaign against "bourgeois nationalism" intended to suppress expression of non-Russian national identities. It also memorialized the heroism displayed in the Soviet people's Great Patriotic War against fascism in ways that allowed no room at all for representations of the particular atrocities that Jewish victims of the Nazis had suffered. In addition, the Soviet Union reversed its initially favorable attitude toward the new state of Israel. In the autumn of 1948 an article in *Pravda*, written by the journalist and propagandist Ilya Ehrenburg, articulated the new ideological direction. It declared that antisemitism was a problem only in capitalist countries, and that Israel was therefore of no concern to Soviet Jews. In February 1953 the Soviet Union broke off its diplomatic relations with Israel. In this climate, official suspicion fell on Jews as a kind of fifth column. The Jewish Anti-Fascist Committee, which had done so much to document the Holocaust as experienced by Soviet Jewry, was purged, and its chairman, Solomon Mikhoels, "died in tragic circumstances," according to the official report. The remnants of Soviet Yiddish culture that had survived the war were decimated. Hundreds of prominent cultural figures were arrested, theaters and publishing houses were shuttered, and in 1952, twenty-five of the most prominent Yiddish-language writers were arrested and tried as "cosmopolitans."

Thirteen of them were executed. Jews were also accused of currency speculation, embezzlement, and economic sabotage. The anticosmopolitan campaign reached a crescendo in 1953, when a group of prominent Moscow doctors, who were publicly identified as Jews, were accused of plotting together and with international Zionist organizations to assassinate top Soviet officials, including Stalin himself. The charges were dismissed only after Stalin's death in March 1953.[34]

The Soviet example inspired a few other much smaller political cases against purported Zionist conspirators in the Eastern bloc in the last months before Stalin's death. In Hungary, Gábor Péter and a number of his colleagues in the Hungarian secret police (many of whom were Jewish) were arrested and charged as Zionist spies, among other crimes. So, too, were the leader of the country's Jewish community and three colleagues. In prison they were beaten, and wild confessions were prepared. (One of Péter's lieutenants in the ÁVH was prepared to declare that he had planned to establish a "center of rabbi-spies" in Budapest.) Stalin's death derailed the proceedings. The charges of Zionist conspiracy leveled against Péter and the other members of the secret police were dropped and the case became one about alleged "economic crimes." (Péter was sentenced to life imprisonment, but his prison term was later shortened and he was eventually released in 1959.) In East Germany, Paul Merker, a high-ranking member of the Socialist Unity Party of Germany (Sozialistische Einheitspartei Deutschlands, or SED, was arrested in December 1952. (Merker was not Jewish, but he stood out among East German Communists for taking the fight against antisemitism seriously.) His name had come up in the course of the Slánský trial, and Stasi interrogators repeatedly pressed him to admit that he was a member of a "Jewish-Zionist organization." However, Merker was not tried until 1955, and then only in a closed session of the East German Supreme Court that remained secret until 1989. (He was declared guilty and imprisoned for eight years.) None of these affairs was as politically important in the history of the Soviet bloc as the Slánský trial, which stood alone among the great Eastern European show trials for explicitly accusing Jewish Communists of betraying the party because they were Jews.[35]

Soviet anti-Zionism, and the damning accusation of "cosmopolitanism" that it inspired, left a legacy for Communist Eastern Europe that outlasted Stalin. The figure of the duplicitous Jewish Communist, so different from a "true" Communist who remained loyal to the people, intersected with nationally inflected associations of Jews with Bolshevism that local Communist parties had struggled to master. When fused, these stereotypes made it possible to discuss reform—how to correct the mistakes and excesses of the Stalinist years and how to implement a more effective "national Communism" in the future— in ethnic terms. In some places, the "Jewish Stalinist," with no "authentic" connection to the working people and no real understanding of the dignity of honest labor, became both a scapegoat and a cudgel that reformers could use to attack their rivals (Jewish or not), demonstrate their populist credentials, and win (they hoped) political support.

Two examples—one from Poland, the other from Romania— illustrate this dynamic. As early as 1945, the Polish Communist Władysław Gomułka warned, "There is a danger that we may come to be seen as Soviet agents. The masses should see us as a Polish party." The overrepresentation of Jews within the party leadership, Gomułka insisted, undermined the party's efforts to control and lead Poland's working class, an ideological category that he understood in exclusively national terms. Gomułka stuck to these views as the Communist Party took power and began to reshape state and society. At a June 1948 plenary session of the party, he raised the theme again, saying an "erroneous national policy" had distorted the ethnic identity of the party. Six months later, he wrote a letter to Stalin himself. "Some of the Jewish comrades do not feel tied by any bonds to the Polish nation or therefore to the Polish working class," he claimed, adding that this was a "serious barrier hindering the expansion of our base." In response, his political rivals accused him of "rightist nation-alist deviation" and expelled him from the party. Gomułka was even imprisoned between 1951 and 1954.[36]

Gomułka returned to power in 1956. Soon he was embroiled in party infighting once more. He took his place at the head of a party divided, after Stalin's death, into rival factions that competed to de-termine the shape of post-Stalinist reforms and to assign blame for the "errors and distortions" of the Stalinist era. The so-called Thaw after Stalin opened up space for economic reform; it also removed barriers to the open expression of ethnonationalist ideas. In this changed political climate, powerful groups fought for position by at-tacking their enemies as "revisionists" and by pinning responsibility for errors on comrades who had no feeling for the needs of "real" Polish workers because of their non-Polish (i.e., Jewish) origins. Amid the jockeying for power, "ethnicity" retained its significance as a tool party leaders could use to undermine their rivals and delegitimize popular attempts at democracy.[37]

In 1968 this tendency erupted into an all-out anti-Jewish campaign in Poland. Faced with student unrest and fearful that its energy would spread to industrial workers, sources within the Communist Party au-thorized the publication of a series of newspaper articles that identi-fied prominent student protesters by name as Jewish and claimed that the Zionists who motivated them were enemies of socialism who bore special "responsibility for the errors and lawlessness of the Stalinist period" and who "openly occupied positions of Jewish nationalism." The campaign snowballed, finding massive popular support and forming the way party members publicly discussed the crisis. In a tele-vised address, Gomułka announced toward the end of a lengthy and wooden speech that Jews who were more attached to Israel than to Poland would probably "sooner or later leave the country. We are ready to give emigration passports to those who consider Israel their Fatherland." At local party meetings around the country, members shouted their rage at the "international Zionist mafia" and demanded that "Zionists" leave the country. Jews were purged from the party and dismissed from their jobs. These events set off a wave of panic among the remnants of Poland's Jewish community. Some 25,000 left the country. By 1970, no more than 10,000 remained.[38]

Communist Party leaders in Romania also found the rhetoric of ethnicity a useful tool to express and frame their own intraparty rivalries. For a time immediately after the war, the Jewish-born Ana Pauker was one of the most powerful figures in the party, having climbed to the position of foreign minister. Pauker was keenly aware that her Jewish background complicated her political position. When Georgi Dimitrov asked her in 1944 to return to Romania and lead the Communist Party, she had demurred on the grounds that she was "a woman, a Jew, and an intellectual." Despite this, she was briefly the nominal party leader, until the autumn of 1945 when she backed Gheorghe Gheorgiu-Dej for the position. In the years that followed, Romanian Communists imposed one-party rule and transformed the country, debating policy and leadership roles by constantly referring to signals emanating from Moscow. Constructing a national Communism without falling victim to "bourgeois nationalist deviation" was an especially perilous undertaking in these years, one that required skillful maneuvering and sheer good luck. It also required figures within the party who symbolized "incorrect" ideological alternatives. For many of her rivals, Pauker served that function because of her ethnic origins. So did other "non-Romanian" party leaders, such as Vasile Luca, who was born an ethnic Hungarian and who never fully mastered the Romanian language. In reality, policy disputes never broke along simple ethnic cleavages. Against Stalin's wishes, the supposedly "Jewish Stalinist" Pauker wanted to slow the pace of forced agricultural collectivization because she thought it would be an unnecessary burden on Romanian peasants. She also favored Jewish emigration when her supposedly "national Communist" rivals worried that the immediate departure of Romanian Jews would disrupt the economy. Despite these complexities, however, it became customary to frame party rivalries as conflicts between a non-Romanian Muscovite faction (Pauker had spent the war years in Moscow) and an indigenous or "national" faction comprising party leaders who had been in Romania (and often in Romanian prison) during the war.[39]

In 1952, faced with Soviet demands for a purge trial, First Secretary Gheorghiu-Dej insinuated at a plenary session of Romania's Communist Party that Pauker was part of a "Zionist conspiracy" because she had intervened to release a number of Zionists from prison. She was expelled from the party and then arrested nearly a year later. Only Stalin's death in 1953 spared her from Rudolf Slánský's fate. Nevertheless, Pauker remained a marginal figure until her death, as the party she had faithfully served her entire life made her into a Jewish Stalinist scapegoat, responsible for all the excesses and errors committed in the years before 1953. Romanian party leaders also openly embraced a nationalist-oriented Communism, charting a course ever more independent of Moscow, and deemphasizing the Russian and Soviet influences on Romanian life that had been a central part of state ideology during the 1950s. In time this policy was expanded to include the rehabilitation of interwar-era right-wing intellectuals and the reintroduction of the xenophobic and nationalist rhetoric that had been commonplace during the 1930s. Nonethnic Romanians were systematically expelled from the party. Meanwhile, intellectuals who enjoyed state support were increasingly free (and even encouraged) to publish writings that demonized Pauker and other so-called Jewish Stalinists as enemies of the people, trafficked in blatant anti-Jewish stereotypes, and treated interwar fascist legionaries as sincere, if misguided, patriots.[40]

Across Eastern Europe, Communist Party leaders embraced nationalist ideology for a variety of reasons. At times they used it to inoculate themselves against the charge that they were "alien" and "cosmopolitan." At others, they used it to discredit and attack their rivals. And they also used it to make strategic choices about how to remember the past—in particular, how to control public memory of the war and the years that preceded it. To construct a usable past from such difficult material, Communist regimes had to decide which national historical events should be celebrated and which should be shrouded in silence. They also had to decide who had been fascists and who were fascism's victims. The conclusions they reached profoundly shaped how antisemitism was understood and how the Holocaust would be remembered.

Within weeks of victory, Soviet occupation officials made plans to erect a war memorial in Berlin. They wanted a monument in the defeated enemy's capital that would shine a "perpetual light of re-membrance on the fallen Soviet soldiers and the enormity of the international liberation mission of the Soviet Army." Construction soon began in Berlin's Treptower Park on a massive war memorial and a military cemetery, where approximately seven thousand So-viet soldiers would be reburied. A statue twelve meters tall of a So-viet soldier was mounted atop a pavilion on a hill, dominating the setting. This figure holds a massive sword in his right hand. In his left, he cradles a baby. (This symbolized a story, widely publicized by Soviet and East German officials throughout the Communist era, of a Red Army soldier who—it was said—heroically braved death during the Battle of Berlin to save a German child from the crossfire.) A broken swastika lies beneath the soldier's feet. A straight path lined with sixteen stone sarcophagi connects this monument to a massive triumphal arch. On each sarcophagus—one for each of the Soviet Union's sixteen republics—visitors can see scenes from the Soviet war against fascism as well as quotations from Stalin, printed in Russian and German. The memorial complex, covering two hun-dred thousand square meters, opened on May 8, 1949, exactly four years to the day after the end of the war. At the inaugural ceremony, attended by Soviet officials and East Germany Communist Party leaders, the Soviet city commander of Berlin explained the meaning of the memorial: "In the center of Europe, in Berlin, this monument will remind the peoples of the world permanently when, by whom, and for what price victory had been gained. . . . This monument in the center of Europe is a symbol of the fight of the peoples of the world for socialism and democracy against the fire raisers of a new war."[41]

Four years after total German defeat, the war memorial in Treptower Park presented Soviet victory as human liberation, not racial destruction. In 1941, Nazi propagandists had declared the invasion of the Soviet Union to be a preventive war to save Germany and all of Europe from the barbaric Asiatic hordes in the East and the cruel Judeo-Bolshevik masters who ruled them. Germany, they said, must prevail or be destroyed. Eight years later, the new memorial was erected to show the war and the post-Nazi future from the Soviet perspective—as a great and ongoing struggle against fascism. According to the inscriptions carved into stone in Treptower Park and the speeches made at the opening of the memorial, the peoples of the Soviet Union had fought a Great Patriotic War against fascist invaders and had made enormous sacrifices to defend humanity against barbarism. As Europe divided into two camps—a West German state was created two weeks after the Treptower Park memorial opened; East Germany was established a few months after that—fears arose across the Soviet bloc that "fascists" and "Hitler's heirs" in the West were preparing to fight a new war to succeed where Hitler had failed. By keeping alive the memory of the sacrifices that the Soviet Union had made to defeat Nazi evil, Soviet leaders and propagandists hoped to inspire antifascist forces around the world to join them in the present struggle for peace and "true" democracy. They meant this message to have a special power for the citizens of the defeated Nazi Germany. This time, they were suggesting, Germans could put themselves on the right side of history.

East Germany's Communist leaders embraced this antifascist ideology and made it central to the way they remembered the Nazi past and the German war in the East.[42] They celebrated Soviet victory in 1945 as liberation rather than defeat. They cast the invasion of the Soviet Union as an aggressive war launched by a "Hitler clique" determined to destroy Communism and exploit working people around the world. And they created a new pantheon of antifascist national heroes that included revolutionaries demonized before the war as Jewish Bolsheviks. Rosa Luxemburg was the most prominent among them. During the decades of Communist rule, Luxemburg became an icon of the German Democratic Republic. State officials held her up as an inspiring example of militant socialism and affixed her name to street signs and factory work brigades. ("Rosa Luxemburg belongs to us!" declared President Wilhelm Pieck in 1951.[43]) At the same time, they refashioned her life's story into a stylized narrative that erased all of its human complexity, including Luxemburg's Jewish identity and the fear that it, combined with her ideological convictions, had inspired in the German radical right. Instead, Luxemburg and other martyrs to the revolutionary cause in Germany, such as her comrade Karl Liebknecht, became inspirational models whose determination in the face of adversity had the power to instruct and mobilize. In life and death, these heroes manifested the unshakeable solidarity of the Communist Party with all victims of fascist and Nazi persecution.

Communist leaders in East Germany and across Eastern Europe used antifascism to signal their commitment to peace and democracy. They soon found that it was a powerful device with which to rewrite the past. State-controlled antifascist commemorations recalled the exploitation of all laboring peoples by fascist oppressors, obscuring the Jewish identity of the victims of the Holocaust. Just as important, antifascism produced a politically useful interpretation of antisemitism. Instead of seeing it as a racial ideology that could be associated with anti-Communism as easily as with anticapitalism, party ideologues transformed antisemitism into a political tactic used by the capitalist classes to distract workers from their revolutionary goals. Antisemitism became a function of capitalist rule, and its remedy was, self-evidently, socialism. In this way, antisemitism could be both a footnote to be ignored and a sin to be projected elsewhere. All of this absolved the citizens of East Germany and other bloc states, like Poland, Hungary, and Romania, of any need to examine their own complicity or involvement in the Holocaust, simply because they lived in a state that was resolutely antifascist. The past was not dead. But its ghosts haunted the capitalist West, not the socialist East.[44]

The potency of the Judeo-Bolshevik myth, and its centrality to much of the violence committed against Jews at certain times and places during the war and in the decades before it, was utterly incomprehensible within this framework. Hungary offers a dramatic example of the way that the history of post–World War I counterrevolutionary antisemitism was manipulated to stunning ends. After 1945 the Hungarian Communist Party had no choice but to identify itself with the country's 1919 Bolshevik revolution. The party included members at all levels who had served the post–World War I revolutionary regime, from party leader Mátyas Rákosi, who had been a commissar for social production, to laborers who had joined and led revolutionary councils in villages and towns across the country. All of them considered the 1919 revolution a harbinger of the triumph of Communism after 1945. However, they were keenly aware that the vast majority of Hungarians understood Béla Kun's Bolshevik regime in terms decisively shaped by two decades of state-sponsored counterrevolutionary propaganda. For this reason, Hungary's Communist rulers developed a complex approach to their historical predecessors. They generally avoided discussing antisemitism at all, except to legitimize their own rule and discredit the counterrevolutionary regime they had replaced. The interwar Horthy regime, they argued, had been founded on the paramilitary massacres of innocent Communists, workers, and (it was sometimes mentioned in passing) Jews.

Against this legacy of bloodshed and exploitation, the Hungarian Communist Party had a historic mission to build a true people's democracy. After 1956 Hungary's Communist leaders redirected this argument to justify crushing the revolution that had briefly toppled the regime. White books were published recounting the criminality of the revolutionaries, who were officially called "counterrevolutionaries." The volumes included reports on antisemitic outbursts, which the editors associated with the fascist spirit that had produced the 1919 White Terror. State prosecutors made similar use of this argument in the high-profile trial of a man who had been a well-known paramilitary in 1919 when he was young and then, decades later, had participated in the 1956 uprising. The years 1919 and 1956, they claimed, were united by a criminal ideology that only Communism could defeat.[45]

A similarly instrumentalized ideology of antifascism was used in Romania to distort the memory of the war against the Soviet Union. There, the Communist Party made August 23, the day in 1944 when the pro-Nazi wartime military dictator Ion Antonescu was toppled in a coup, a national holiday. However, the official commemorative festivities presented Communist revolutionaries as the only actors who mattered and inflated their importance so grandiosely that even the fact that Antonescu had been executed in 1946 as a war criminal receded into the background. (The ensuing public silence around his memory made him an even more attractive candidate for political rehabilitation after 1989.) The Communist regime produced an idiosyncratic and one-sided history of the war in which Romanians had suffered at the hands of impersonal "Hitlerist" fascists while also fighting as heroes against them. The regime celebrated the Romanians who had fought alongside the Red Army at the end of the war—after Romania had switched sides—to push the German and Hungarian armies from the western part of the country. In contrast, the soldiers who had died on the Eastern Front fighting with Germany against the Soviet Union were deemed "victims of dictatorial regimes" and then shrouded in official silence without any serious public reflection on why those men had been fighting on the Eastern Front at all or what they had done while they were there. Nor did the party historians say anything about the acts of anti-Jewish violence that the wartime regime had justified as security measures against the Judeo-Bolshevik threat. After Romania's Communist leaders took a "national Communist" turn, the party conveniently displaced all responsibility for the Holocaust outward onto Hungary and the ethnic Hungarian minority in Romania. In the 1980s the regime launched a revisionist historical campaign to reframe the crimes committed by "Horthyist-fascist" Hungary during the war, as part of the regime's broader anti-Hungarian policy.[46]

The Communist Party in Poland distorted the history of the war even more grotesquely. Anxieties about postwar Poland's new western border fed official discussion of the horrors committed by "Hitler-fascists" during the war. Yet public commemorations typically obscured distinctions between Polish and Jewish fates, describing the victims of German terror as Poles or "Polish citizens" or presenting Polish and Jewish suffering during the war as equivalent. When the regime established Auschwitz as a memorial site, it constructed a narrative of the camp that commemorated the "resistance and martyrdom" of "Poles and citizens of other nationalities." Similarly, the memorial erected in the mid-1960s at Treblinka was praised in the regime's press for commemorating the murder of "800,000 citizens of European nations." At the same time, crimes committed by Soviet forces during the period of occupation between 1939 and 1941—above all, the massacre of Polish officers at Katyn in 1940—remained out of bounds, for obvious reasons. The regime also had to treat the history of the underground Home Army with extreme caution, since it was revered in popular memory as the legitimate expression of Poland's national sovereignty. Initially the regime demonized the Home Army as the tool of bourgeois and reactionary traitors. But in time, as the regime began to promote its own brand of national Communism, it began to distinguish between ordinary soldiers, who were seen as decent patriots, and their superiors, who had misused the heroism of Polish workers and peasants to serve bourgeois class interests.[47]

Communist Party efforts across Eastern Europe to control the memory of the war and shape it to meet the ideological needs of the regime fed historical narratives of national communities victimized by (vaguely defined or exclusively German) fascist perpetrators. The consequences for critical historical understanding of the past were especially apparent in the cases of popular violence against Jews in the summer of 1941, when, amid the chaos of Soviet retreat and German (or German-led) invasion, local people in eastern Poland and in Bessarabia and Bukovina had attacked Jews as traitors and Bolshevik collaborators. During the late 1940s and early 1950s, trials held in Communist Poland did document the extent of anti-Jewish violence committed by local Poles. (Jan Gross used depositions from one such trial to write his book on the pogrom in Jedwabne.) But such evidence often emerged as incidental material in trials that focused more extensively on other matters. State prosecutors were also reluctant during those years to prosecute people for killing Jews. Another historical investigation into the Jedwabne massacre took place in the late 1960s and early 1970s, in the aftermath of the 1968 anti-Zionist campaign. It concluded that German soldiers present in the town had killed the Jews. Later, in the early 2000s, the head of that investigative team confessed that he had received instructions from the Main Commission for the Investigation of Nazi Crimes to prosecute only German criminals.[48] The 1941 pogroms in Bessarabia and Bukovina had an even more marginal place in the collective memory of Communist-era Romania. After 1945 those two regions were occupied by the Soviet Union and divided between the Moldavian and Ukrainian Soviet Socialist Republics. Soviet courts conducted war crimes trials immediately after the war and collected extensive evidence of popular participation in the killings of Jews in 1941. However, their work remained utterly unknown in Romania. The massive pogrom in Iaşi, which did remain part of Romania after 1945, was commemorated by the Romanian Jewish community, but it was rarely mentioned in wider circles.[49]

In Poland, Hungary, and Romania, Communist regimes manipulated antifascism to rewrite a more usable history of World War II and the years that preceded it. Party ideologues silenced public memory of the Holocaust. They also endorsed and promoted a vision of the people, often implicitly or explicitly ethnicized, who were the victims of fascist exploitation, repression, and duplicity. Official histories of their tragic suffering and heroic resistance might in theory include Jews, but they could never clearly discuss how war and genocide had affected Jews and non-Jews differently. Nationalist narratives of the war that ignored the Jewish experience, or bracketed it as something unrelated to the main story, flourished in this intellectual context. Moreover, the official use of antifascist ideology to shape the history of the recent past prevented any critical examination of how the Judeo-Bolshevik myth had functioned during the war, let alone how that myth had been manipulated afterward. The result of all these distortions would be keenly felt after 1989, when calls for a more accurate history of the Holocaust collided with widespread demands to remember the victims of Communism.

Linking Jews to Communism in public discourse predated the arrival of the Red Army in Eastern Europe at the end of World War II. As Communist leaders across the region established power and then struggled to legitimize their rule in the eyes of the people they governed, they were forced to confront the legacy left by several decades of political mobilization around the idea that Judeo-Bolshevism was an antinational threat. Their responses to this challenge—choosing whom to prosecute for war crimes, whom to treat as victims of fascism, whom to label "cosmopolitan," and what aspects of the past to remember or forget—had profound consequences for the collective memory of World War II and the Holocaust before and after 1989. But the regimes inside the Soviet bloc were not the only ones grappling with the challenges posed to their authority by the entrenched association of Jews with Communism. In the West, and especially in West Germany, the idea of Judeo-Bolshevism also cast a long shadow over postwar political and social reconstruction. There, the question was not how to make Communism seem national, but how to imagine anti-Communism after Hitler.

6

From Judeo-Bolshevism to Judeo-Christian Civilization

Matthes Ziegler was reborn for the second time after the war.[1] Born in 1911 into a conservative Protestant family, his parents gave Ziegler the name Matthäus at birth. He was a nationalistic young man studying theology when the Nazi Party came to power. Matthäus abandoned his studies at once, changed his first name to the more Germanic-sounding Matthes, and soon became a prominent figure in Alfred Rosenberg's office for Nazi cultural policy. Now a "post-Protestant," Ziegler put his theological training to use as head of the department for religious-political affairs, promoting Rosenberg's dream of a Germanic religion and criticizing mainstream Christian churches around the world as historical relics compromised by their relations with Jews and Judaism. "The key to understanding the relationship between world Protestantism and Bolshevism," he wrote in those years, "lies in its warm acknowledgement of world Jewry."[2] The war offered additional opportunities for a man with his gifts and experience. In 1940 he joined the Waffen-SS and worked as a war propagandist with the SS, first during the French campaign and then on the Eastern Front.

After 1945, Ziegler's brilliant career became a liability. In American custody and facing denazification proceedings, Ziegler (re)wrote his biography. Now he claimed that his enthusiasm for Nazism had been motivated solely by his love of country. The Nazi Party, he had then believed, was the only force able to rescue Germany from post-1918 ruin and forestall its bolshevization. His work for Alfred Rosenberg notwithstanding, he declared himself to have always been a conservative Christian (*christgläubiger Mensch*). In the new postwar age, he was ready to do whatever he could to secure European life and values against "nihilism and Bolshevism."

The tribunal that heard his case was not persuaded, and Ziegler landed in prison. Others listened with more sympathy, however. Ziegler still had good contacts among Germany's conservative nationalist Protestants. They were willing to speak on his behalf, and their voices carried weight. As the Cold War heated up, the United States and Great Britain increasingly turned to Germany's Christian churches in their effort to rebuild a democratic and anti-Communist Germany. By early 1948 Ziegler was a free man. He changed his name yet again, back to Matthäus, finished his theology degree, and became a Lutheran pastor and religious instructor in the new West Germany. Matthäus Ziegler died in 1992 at the age of eighty-one.

Matthes Ziegler's political transformation was more brazen than some. It was also emblematic of the way many Europeans adapted their biographies to the realities of the new Cold War. Ziegler said he had always been an anti-Communist. Before 1933 he had feared his country's bolshevization; now he worried about Soviet expansion. No doubt he was sincere about this. He reproduced this argument in his memoirs and reflections throughout the rest of his life. However, anti-Communism allowed him to transform his Nazi past into an episode in his life that began with patriotism and ended (in hindsight) with the disappointing realization that the Nazi state had not been the savior he had hoped for. Nazism had not (he said after the war been able to protect Germany and Europe from nihilism, materialism, and Bolshevism. Instead, the Red Army had defeated Germany in on the Eastern Front, the Communist Party was consolidating power in East Germany, and Stalin in Moscow was overseeing the expansion of a totalitarian empire. The imminence of this danger, and the presence of American forces increasingly ready to defend Western Europe against it, gave Ziegler an opportunity to change the way he talked about Communism. Before 1945, Ziegler had insisted in everything he wrote that Communism was a Jewish plot. After 1945 he never mentioned the connection between Jews and Communism again. Where had it gone so suddenly? Had Ziegler and so many like him really changed their minds about Communism overnight?

The last installment of the *Deutsche Wochenschau*, the weekly news-reel produced by Joseph Goebbels's Ministry of Propaganda, was shot in late March 1945. The ten-and-a-half-minute film features Adolf Hitler awarding the Iron Cross to Hitler Youth volunteers in the garden of the Reich Chancellery in Berlin, his last public appearance before the Battle of Berlin and then his suicide. Other segments show civilians learning with grim determination how to use antitank weapons to repel the advancing Red Army. Utterly divorced from the reality that the war had long been lost, the narrator recounts acts of heroic resistance in Breslau (today: Wrocław in Poland) and other German cities and brave exploits by soldiers in the field, all signs of a people united in their will to hold out until their final victory.

The film also describes the enemy in the East. The Soviet army was descending on Germany with a "bestiality, for which there is no example in the history of mankind." As the narrator intones these words, the camera lingers on a fence painted with the plea, "Protect our women and children from the red beast." A sequence of corpses follows this shot, stills of women, children, and old people mutilated and murdered in their homes. Footage of a radio reporter interviewing

German women alternates with these scenes. "How did the soldiers and officers treat the women where you live?" the reporter asks. The "bestial hordes" had raped old and young women alike, they replied.[3]

Previous newsreels had told the same story, as did refugees from eastern Germany, who described widespread plundering, killing, and the raping of German women, when reporting what happened when Soviet forces arrived in their towns and villages. As the Red Army stormed across the borders of the German Reich and drove toward Berlin in the winter of 1944–45, Nazi media repackaged these accounts into graphic newsreels and radio broadcasts, to prove that "Asiatic" and "subhuman" Soviet "beasts" were the enemies of Western civilization and to terrorize the population into holding out for a miraculous and utterly fictional "final victory." In this climate of hysteria and fear, rumors spread that a Soviet journalist was consciously provoking men in the Red Army to rape German women as punishment for the devastation wrought on the Eastern Front by the German army. According to the story, a flyer written by the writer and Soviet war correspondent Ilya Ehrenburg was circulating among Red Army units. It read: "Kill! Kill! There is no German who is not guilty. . . . Break the racial arrogance of German women with violence! Take her as a rightful prize!"[4]

In the years that followed, various people claimed to have seen the flyer, and some works even cite it. Teams of professional historians have been charged with looking for a physical copy. None has found evidence that it ever existed. Most probably the rumor began in the German army fighting in the Baltics in the winter of 1944–45.[5] However, the virulence of the rumor reveals how powerfully Nazi propaganda shaped expectations and then perceptions of Soviet occupation. Throughout the war, newsreels and broadsheets had echoed such warnings and recounted instances of "Asiatic" atrocities—from corpses found in the jails of L'viv in 1941 to exhumed bodies in the forests at Katyn in 1943—as proof of the "bestial" horrors that awaited Germans if they lost. This rhetoric remained popular long after most

Germans had stopped believing in the promises of miracle weapons, Wehrmacht counterstrikes, and final victory. The images and fears spread by propaganda films also shaped the way German women described their experiences of being raped by Soviet soldiers. Many ascribed a "Mongol" face to their attackers. Others described feeling as if they had reenacted a scene in a horrible film they had already seen.[6]

The fictive flyer was also significant because of its supposed author. Born in 1891 in Kiev to a Jewish family, Ilya Ehrenburg was the most internationally prominent voice of the Soviet war against Nazi Germany. As a correspondent embedded in the Red Army he wrote hundreds of newspaper columns, radio addresses, and leaflets exhorting the peoples of the Soviet Union to fight back against the Nazi invaders with the same murderous hatred that the enemy had unleashed on them. "Kill!," written in 1942, was the title of Ehrenburg's best-known article. ("The old mother begs you, kill the German! Your child pleads, kill the German! The maternal earth cries out, kill the German! . . . [L]eave no one out. Kill!") Writing like this earned Ehrenburg a reputation as a "German hater." He was also perfectly cast for a role central to Nazi anti-Soviet propaganda: the ideological Jew who directed Russia's vast hordes of Asiatic barbarians to commit acts of unspeakable brutality against European civilization and culture. To Hitler, Ehrenburg was "Stalin's house Jew," the very image of the Jewish commissar the dictator had invoked to justify launching a war of annihilation in 1941. At the war's end, Ilya Ehrenburg became the perfect symbol of the vengeful Jewish Bolshevik.[7]

Fears of Soviet bestiality and Jewish revenge returned again and again as potent images in postwar West German political life. They crystallized around the figure of the Jewish displaced person (DP), widely perceived as a rootless criminal, and in anxieties about the treatment of German prisoners of war held in Soviet gulags.[8] Vengeful Jews recur in the stories German expellees from across Eastern Europe told of their experiences at the end of the war. Some said that they remembered how quickly Jews had come to dominate the black market in towns that would soon be cleansed of Germans. Others described the zeal with which Jews volunteered to serve the new Communist authorities as translators or as guards in detention camps set up for Germans. These memories, collected in massive volumes by leading historians working for the Ministry for Expellees, Refugees, and War Victims, displaced the memory of crimes that Germans had committed against Jews and Slavs on the Eastern Front during the war. Many expellees told stories of their own travails in terms that unconsciously mimicked imagery of Nazi concentration camps. They told horrible stories of rapes by Soviet soldiers, in a format devoid of any critical perspective on the typical descriptions of "Mongol" rapists driven by an "Asiatic furor." All this established a powerful moral equivalence. One expellee from Bohemia put it bluntly: "What a bad comedy all this is: nothing is original, a copy of the Hitler regime, again and again we have to hear: 'Just as you have treated the Jews.'"[9]

Even in defeat, the associations conjured by the idea of Judeo-Bolshevism remained powerful. Amid the ruins, many in occupied Germany gave credence to accounts of Jews profiting from German misery and helping Soviet occupiers expel Germans from their ancestral homes. The conviction that the Soviet soldiers who conquered Berlin and now held sway over half of Germany were like a furious Mongol or Asiatic horde was even more widespread. Yet the idea of Judeo-Bolshevism was transformed by Nazi defeat, its constitutive parts rearranged by the dramatically changed political circumstances. In the process, the overt link between Jews and Asiatic Bolshevism, so tightly coiled in Nazi propaganda, began to loosen.

In the last desperate months of the war, the character of Nazi anti-Soviet rhetoric had already changed. As the Red Army advanced relentlessly toward Berlin, Nazi propagandists often depicted the Soviet enemy as Asiatic invaders or attacking barbarians who resembled the Huns or the Mongols, without any specific mention of the Jewish plot that the Nazi regime had long insisted lay behind them. References to Judeo-Bolshevik perfidy receded from prominence in the pages of Nazi newspapers and the proclamations of the weekly newsreels.[10] What remained was the devastating barbarism of a subhuman enemy. The ideological shift was subtle but significant. The Nazi regime had justified the invasion of the Soviet Union in 1941 by calling it a preventive war that would destroy the Judeo-Bolshevik system before the enemy—a racial-ideological composite of Jews, Communists, and subhuman Slavs always labeled Asiatic and un-European—could impose a cruel reign of terror on Germany and all of Europe. After Stalingrad, Joseph Goebbels had used the idea of Jewish Bolshevik slavery to whip up support for total war. As the Third Reich collapsed, however, this ideological image of the enemy began to dissolve into discrete parts. To the end, Hitler raged in his bunker against the Jews and belief in an international Jewish conspiracy bent on Germany's destruction remained a core principle of Nazi ideology.[11] But when it looked East in the last phase of the war, Nazi propaganda focused ever more single-mindedly on the so-called Asiatic hordes who had come from the "steppes" to rape, pillage, and plunder in the heart of Germany.

American Cold War policy propelled this realignment of anti-Communist ideology. After 1945, U.S. occupation officials declared their desire to denazify Germany by putting war criminals on trial, establishing a massive bureaucracy to review the personal histories of hundreds of thousands of Germans, and suppressing groups and organizations that openly promoted Nazi ideas. Between 1945 and 1949, U.S. authorities conducted twelve large trials of leading figures in Nazi society, ranging from doctors and industrialists to security officers and military generals, in addition to taking part in the international military tribunal that prosecuted major war criminals. But American policy makers soon shifted course to rebuild western Germany into an ally, as tensions between the United States and the Soviet Union escalated. The Federal Republic of Germany became a junior partner in a new struggle against Soviet power. This time, however, the ideological tenor was set in Washington, D.C., not in Bonn. Ideals like "freedom," "truth," the "West," and "Western civilization" justified Cold War anti-Communism in Europe. The threat of Judeo-Bolshevism was absent from the new rhetoric. The combination of consequential but faltering attempts at denazification and the strategic realities of Cold War politics offered the chance of a new life to many ex-Nazis, who moved back into positions in the military, the civil service, and the diplomatic corps. As they returned to power and rebooted their careers, they loudly proclaimed their anti-Communist credentials while suppressing memories of their earlier loyalty to Nazi racial ideology. While changed political circumstances imposed serious professional consequences on those who openly called the Soviet enemy a Jewish power, the U.S.-led "crusade" to defend Western civilization aligned easily with other aspects of Nazi anti-Soviet ideology. The idea of Judeo-Bolshevism had become taboo, but "Asiatic Bolshevism" most certainly had not.[12]

This ideological blend of rupture and continuity can be seen in sanitized versions of the war on the Eastern Front, written by German generals trying to recast themselves as good anti-Communists in Cold War Europe.[13] (For example, Heinz Guderian, the famous tank expert, wrote in 1951 that Russia had become an "Asiatic" power when Lenin became its ruler.[14]) But it emerges perhaps most clearly in the work done by the propagandists who worked for a semiofficial West German anti-Communist organization called the Peoples' Alliance for Peace and Freedom (Volksbund for Friede und Freiheit, or VFF). Created in 1950, the VFF was ostensibly a civic organization made up of anti-Communists with close ties to West German government and intelligence circles. It quickly became an instrument of the Federal Republic's Ministry for All-German Affairs, which was responsible for creating and distributing information about conditions in East Germany and exhorting West Germans to remain vigilant against Communist sabotage.[15] The VFF also received funding from the CIA for its participation in what American intelligence officers called psychological warfare.

Some of the material created by the VFF—such as posters of gulag prisons disdainfully labeled as a "Soviet vacation paradise"—reflected strategies shared with other groups in a network of anti-Communist organizations that stretched across Western Europe.[16] But much of the VFF's material had a particularly German inflection: dire images of East German agents plotting subversion in all aspects of West German life; dramatizations of the plight of German POWs in Soviet prison camps that deliberately downplayed crimes that were committed in German camps. A variety of images explicitly described Soviet prisons as "Bolshevik KZs," using the Nazi-era abbreviation for "concentration camp." Other materials fused the two regimes in different but equally deceptive ways, as, for example, in the 1950 book *Heil Stalin!* (The book's author, Kurt Zentner, had enjoyed a first career as an ideologically engaged editor and publicist during the Nazi era.) The VFF drew heavily on themes widely circulated during the Nazi era, including representations of "enemies of the people" as animals or insects. One of the first stamps the organization issued was of a Communist transformed into a rat, with the slogan "Combating rats is a national duty."[17]

The founder and head of the VFF, Eberhard Taubert, embodied this ideological continuity. During the Nazi regime Taubert had been a high-ranking official responsible for anti-Communist work in Joseph Goebbels's Ministry of Propaganda. He created the Anti-Comintern, a kind of forerunner to the VFF that created and distributed "information" about Bolshevism in Germany and across Europe. In those years, Taubert attached special importance to explaining Communism as a Jewish plot extending from the Jewish commissars who ruled the Soviet Union to their agents who were active in the Spanish Civil War and elsewhere in Europe. Taubert was responsible for other pieces of Nazi anti-Semitic propaganda, as well; most notably he was the script writer for the notorious film, *The Eternal Jew* (1940). (In one of its most despicable scenes, the film visually compares Jews to rats; Taubert often used rats to symbolize Germany's enemies.) After the war, Taubert transformed himself into a Cold War anti-Communist, secure in his belief that, as he explained in a written statement for the U.S. Counterintelligence Corps, "The anti-Soviet propaganda apparatus of the German Ministry of Propaganda was the largest and most successful of its kind and thus a model for equivalent successor organizations." By 1950 he was once again directing important anti-Communist propaganda work.[18]

After 1945 Taubert dropped all references to Judeo-Bolshevism, but he retained every other ideological and symbolic feature of his earlier work. That superficial transformation is the context for one of the VFF's most blatantly racist images, a 1951 poster depicting a Soviet soldier, with Orientalized facial features and a red star on his cap, assaulting a terrified German woman. The VFF designed the poster as a response to critics in West Germany who opposed the Adenauer government's plans to rearm the country and contribute to the military defense of Western Europe. The poster reproduces the slogan of anti-rearmament critics at the top: " . . . *Ohne mich*" (Without me). But next to the woman in smaller characters is a phrase that reinforces the visual threat: "*Frau, komm . . .*" (Come, woman), words widely associated in Germany with rapes by Soviet soldiers. At the bottom, a final warning draws out the political implications of opposing West German rearmament: "This is the end of the song if you follow [Wilhelm] Pieck, [Otto] Grotewohl," and other leading East German Communists. In the VFF's own estimation, the poster was one of the most successful it ever produced.[19] With its graphic image of "Asiatic bestiality," it could easily have been produced before the fall of the Third Reich.

In time, Taubert's past was exposed and he was forced to step down. Scandal exploded around him in 1955 when samples of his 1930s-era work for the Nazi Anti-Comintern came into the hands of the editor of the general weekly newspaper of the German Jewish community, who gave the material to the national magazine *Der Spiegel*. An article about Taubert with the title "Es hat sich nichts geändert" (Nothing has changed) made the ex-Nazi propagandist a liability to the West German government.[20] Taubert continued to be paid by the VFF for several years, but by 1959 he had begun a new career, advising the secret services of South Africa and Iran about how to fight Communism.[21]

Taubert's postwar rise and fall illuminates the transformation that took place in anti-Communist politics from one perspective. But the strange erasure of Judeo-Bolshevism from the vocabulary of anti-Communist politics after 1945 can be seen in other arenas as well. Before the end of the war, a small but influential group of Christian conservatives had marked their distance from Nazi Germany's ideological crusade against Judeo-Bolshevism when they began to imagine Nazism and Communism as equivalent, and similar, totalitarian systems. Western civilization, or Christian civilization, they had insisted, was under attack from both. After Hitler's defeat, their ideas moved into the political mainstream and infused the "defense of the West" against Soviet barbarism with a new layer of meaning.

In the last days of April 1945, a group of Catholic intellectuals gathered in a small apartment in the city center in Vienna, on the narrow Annagasse. The Red Army had just conquered Vienna. A new provisional government, formed with Soviet approval, had declared Austria's secession from Hitler's Reich. In the city, the Viennese faced the fear of interrogation and arrest by Soviet authorities, mistreatment at the hands of undisciplined troops, and miserable shortages of food and habitable housing. Despite these challenges, the Catholics meeting in that Annagasse apartment were eager to begin new work. Some had fought on the front; others had been locked up in Gestapo prisons. All of them shared the same goal: to build an Austria "in which there would be no more totality, no tyrants, no idols; in which . . . human dignity, law, social community, and the culture of our homeland would be restored." Fired by this vision, they decided to create a new publication. The first issue appeared half a year later.[22]

To capture the spirit of new beginnings and new growth, they called their weekly journal *Die Furche* (The furrow). Many of the essays they published focused on Catholic social theory and its relevance for the postwar age. When it became possible, contributors also wrote critical appraisals of socialism and the efforts by Europe's socialists to adapt to the times. The journal offered readers reports on the persecution of the Catholic Church behind the so-called Iron Curtain. However, continuities with the distant past were just as important to the journal's ethos. Pictures of cultural monuments dotting Austria's landscape—a pillar in the city of Linz depicting the flagellation of Christ one week; the bust of a monk in the choir of a church in Heiligenkreuz near Vienna in another—marked Austria as a Christian land.

Ongoing debate about Austria's place in the Christian West, or the Occident (the Abendland), elaborated on this idea. An early contribution to *Die Furche* conveys the tone of the arguments, which typically combined philosophizing about the nature of the human person with speculation about the origins and essence of European culture and identity. The author praises the Western church for breaking with the Byzantine East, an action that confirmed an essential feature of Western civilization: namely, the inviolability of the human person in the face of arrogant state authority. His point recalls the interwar thought of Christian critics of totalitarianism, who typically used these ideas to criticize modern individualism, repudiate materialist ideologies like liberalism, Communism (and later, Nazism), and affirm the notion of human dignity in the face of secular state power.[23] Contributors to *Die Furche* eagerly took up these concepts after the war to underscore their political distance from Hitler's Austria. As they did, they embedded the basic features of antitotalitarian thought in a distinctly Austrian cultural landscape, complete with references to the principled conservatism of the historical Catholic Habsburg dynasty and to the many artistic and architectural treasures that Catholicism had given to the former Habsburg lands. Austria, this contributor concluded, played a central role in Christian Europe. Passing lightly over recent events—the author gestured toward ideas of a Reich and "new Europe" that were a "diabolical distortion of what the Occident ought to be"—he assigned Austria a role in offering Eastern and Western Europe a vision of human freedom that could protect society against rigid ideology as well as the chaos of rampant individualism. "From this consciousness of freedom, the new order for the Occident must arise as a free and spiritual order."[24]

The editor of *Die Furche*, Friedrich Funder, intended the journal to represent both a rupture and a renewal. In his memoirs of those years, published in 1957, Funder situated *Die Furche*'s origins in the history of Austria's struggle to defend and regain its independence as a state. Funder's experiences during the war enabled him to cast this story in personal terms as well. After Austria was annexed by Nazi Germany in 1938, Funder was arrested and imprisoned for nearly a year in concentration camps at Dachau and Flossenbürg. On his release, he was forbidden from working for the remainder of the war. These experiences marked him, as similar experiences did other leading figures in Austria's postwar Second Republic, confirming his belief that Nazi Germany had waged war against European civilization and that Austria had been its first victim. He and the others maintained that Hitler's appeals to European civilization had cruelly distorted an essential and venerable tradition. *Die Furche* would revive it, clarify its meaning, and show that Nazism had always been alien to Austrian values. The Occident would resurrect one history and bury another.

Funder's editorial enthusiasm for the new antitotalitarian tropes made him feel free to obscure the prewar past. Before the war, Funder had published the major daily newspaper of Austria's Christian

Socialist Party, the *Reichspost*, which he founded in 1894. During the interwar decades, anti-Semitism in the *Reichspost* was, in the words of one historian, both "a way to support its arguments and a flavor to spice up its rhetoric."[25] Expansive coverage of the Jewish question in all its forms—from the role of Jews in the press and in theater, to Jewish economic power, to the nature of liberalism and socialism as Jewish ideologies—was a regular feature of its journalism. Marxism was a particular enemy, since the Social Democrats, who had dominated politics in Vienna until their party was banned in 1934, were the Christian Socialists' main rivals. Articles in the *Reichspost* routinely contrasted Austria's German and Christian culture to the socialist world of Red Vienna, which they apostrophized explicitly or implicitly as "Jewish." The newspaper was also known for its pan-German orientation, promoting Austrian particularity within the wider world of German national culture. After 1933 this position made the editors of the *Reichspost* sympathetic toward "bridge-builders" between the alpine republic and the Reich to the north. As Funder's coeditor declared in 1934: "We shall promote and support whatever is good and noble and pan-German in National Socialism."[26] As German influence in Austrian politics grew, Funder also used the paper to attack more intransigent Catholic critics of Nazism, such as the center-left sociologist Ernst Karl Winter (whose calls for a common front against Nazism Funder denounced as "idiotic" and a "dance around the Kremlin") and the ultraconservative Dietrich von Hildebrand (whom Funder simply dismissed as a Jew after it was revealed that Hildebrand had a Jewish grandmother).[27]

None of this protected Funder from prison after the Germans took over, however. As the editor of an independent newspaper, he was an inevitable target. Nor did it mean that Funder would remain enthusiastic about cultural or political union with Germany. His time in a concentration camp disabused him of that idea. Like many Austrians, Funder found that Austria's transformation into a region of the German Reich called the Ostmark did not happen exactly as he had imagined it would. After the war, Funder was not the only one who chose to remember his disillusionment while forgetting his earlier views. At the same time, Funder's reemergence after 1945 as the grand old man of the Catholic press reveals how malleable the Christian West (the Occident) was as a cultural vision. Before 1945, it had been entirely consonant with German nationalism, an imagined affinity that allowed many Austrian Catholics to think of Nazism in spiritual terms, as a force that could vanquish materialist ideologies like liberalism and Communism. After the war, Funder and his fellow Catholics reshaped the idea of Occident, making it European rather than German and adding National Socialism to the list of materialisms that threatened it. Christian Europe, they declared, was the ground from which the idea of human dignity had sprung, and with it, a set of values that would protect the human person against totalitarian tyranny from the right (Nazism) and the left (Communism). This belief would prove equally attractive elsewhere as well.

Across Europe, Christians pronounced themselves changed by the war. Some, like Friedrich Funder, had been prisoners in Nazi concentration camps. Others, like Robert Schuman, who would become one of the early architects of the European Union, had joined the anti-Nazi resistance. Still others, like Konrad Adenauer, chancellor after 1949 of the new West German republic, had been forced out of Weimar-era political positions and into private life. Many more had adapted to the political realities of Nazi rule. Some had even found ways to reconcile their faith with Nazi ideology. Despite their different political choices and the variety of their wartime experiences, all of them saw 1945 as a moment of hope and rebirth and believed that Christianity was a moral and a political force that would guide Europe out of the darkness. Christian Democratic parties, built on the bones of prewar Catholic politics, were transformed into ecumenical bodies open to Catholics and Protestants alike. They soon became powerful (in some places dominant) forces in the political landscape of 1950s

Western and Central Europe. Legislators turned to Catholic social theory and found blueprints for new welfare states. Christian theories of human rights and limited state power were enshrined in foundational documents of the new postwar order, nowhere more prominently than in West Germany's 1949 Basic Law.

The postwar turn to religion brought ideas of Christian Europe, the Occident, and Christian civilization into the center of public discourse. What these terms meant was the subject of intense debate. Each of them had a long history. During the interwar decades, paeans to the Occident (Abendland), or Christian Europe, had often been shorthand for cultural conservativism. Europe, in this view, was an antimodernist community based on spiritual ideals, in a stark contrast to the vulgar materialism that defined both America, home of sordid consumerism and unchecked individualism, and the Soviet Union, where an all-powerful state brutalized human beings into objects. After 1945, conservative intellectuals revived these positions in journals and in cultural societies like the German Abendländische Akademie, which gathered together luminaries in the right wing of the Christian Democratic Party.[28] But antimaterialism and faith in Christian civilization, or the Christian West, made it possible for Christian leaders to imagine new possibilities as well—above all, a new European community that would transcend divisive national borders. Fear for the survival of the West also moved Christian politicians to change their minds about America, seeing it as a necessary security partner rather than simply a materialist plague. For Christian politicians in Western Europe, the community championed by Robert Schuman in France, Alcide de Gaspari in Italy, and Konrad Adenauer in West Germany promised a safe, peaceful, and prosperous Europe. In Germany and Austria, where the Nazi regime had so recently promised a very different European order, it held an additional meaning. Embracing Christian Europe was a way of containing and transfiguring the past.[29]

Konrad Adenauer's career as chancellor of the Federal Republic of Germany and head of that country's Christian Democratic Union (CDU) is perhaps the best testimony to the symbolic power of

Christian Europe to reconcile political innovation with the weight
of history. During his tenure in power, the new West German state
was anchored in a transatlantic alliance directed against the Communist threat in the East. At the same time, a complicated politics of
memory encouraged Germans to feel that they, too, had been Hitler's victims, seduced by him into waging an unnecessary and self-
destructive war. Adenauer sounded all these themes even before
there was a West German state to govern. In 1946 Adenauer was
elected head of the new CDU. To mark the occasion, he addressed
fellow members of his fledgling party amid the ruins of Cologne, the
town where he was born. Adenauer explained the party's identity:
"We call ourselves Christian Democrats, because we are convinced
that only a democracy rooted in the Christian-Western [*christlich-
abendländische*] worldview, in Christian natural law, and in the fun-
damentals of Christian ethics" can bring about the rebirth of Germany. He also reflected on the past. Where had National Socialism
come from, he asked? It could not have come to power if "the ground
had not been prepared for its poisonous seed." For years, Germany
had suffered under false ideas about the state, power, and the individual person. It had sacrificed the human person on the altar of the
state. All this was the fateful result of a materialist worldview that had
seeped across Germany and turned minds against the abiding truths
of ethical values and human dignity.[30]

Locating the root cause of Germany's catastrophe outside Nazism,
in a time prior to Hitler's seizure of power, allowed Adenauer to
introduce the old specter of Communism in a new way. "The materialist view of Marxism," he declared, had contributed to this development. "Those who want to centralize political and economic
power in a state or a class" had paved the way to dictatorship. They
were the enemies of human freedom. "National Socialism was
nothing other than the consequence, driven to criminal lengths,
of . . . the contempt for the value of the human person that arose from
the materialist worldview." There could be only one remedy for a so-

ciety so ravaged by the evils of materialism: Christianity. The anti-
dote to totalitarianism was to be found in the Christian-Western
worldview. To drive this point home, Adenauer hammered out a
clear moral equivalence between Nazism and Communism. "National Socialism found the strongest spiritual resistance in those
Catholic and Protestant parts of Germany that were least contami-
nated by the teachings of Karl Marx and socialism!!! That is absolutely clear!"[31]

Adenauer's speech recalled earlier anti-Communist language in
certain subtle but crucial ways. For example, his insistence that materialist Marxism had paved the way for National Socialism suggested
that Nazism might have been a reaction to the Communist threat, a
notion that the Nazi Party itself had done much to promote and that
Hitler had made the official rationale for invading the Soviet Union.
Adenauer noted in passing that he had often felt as a young man that
Berlin was a godless and heathen city that bred political parties opposed to Christianity. He quickly added that the Nazi Party had been
among one of those parties.[32] However, this sentiment was an old one
that had often been a feature of hostile critiques of "Jewish modernity" and the creatures, such as militant socialist parties, that it
spawned. Of course, Adenauer never drew these connections himself,
neither in his 1946 speech in Cologne nor in later ones. His own anti-
Nazi credentials were impeccable. They were the reason that he had
emerged as the logical leader of West Germany's Christian Democrats, in spite of the fact that he was sixty-nine years old in 1945. Even
so, postwar West German anti-Communism contained echoes of interwar anti-Bolshevism, for those with ears to hear them.

Those echoes were loudest in debates about what lay beyond the
border of the Christian West. "Asia," Adenauer once declared, "stands
on the Elbe."[33] This was no doubt an expression of the chancellor's
deeply Rhenish turn of mind, which nursed both a robust anti-
Communism and a life-long distrust of all things Prussian. But he
was by no means the only one to decry the incursion of "Asia" into

Europe. Fears of Asiatic Bolshevism were widespread in 1950s West Germany. One CDU campaign poster put this view iconographically, setting Christian maternalism against a symbol of Soviet threat and terror easily interpreted in a society in which memories of sexual violence committed by occupying Red Army soldiers were still fresh. It features a giant red hand that looms menacingly over a mother and child. As the mother casts a worried look at the hand above her, the child in her arms looks directly at the viewer with a pleading expression. The caption reads: "Protect Us, Be Ready for Defense, Vote for the CDU." The message for voters was clear. Only the Christian Right offered a strong defense of family values against the Communist threat. The poster was aimed at the rival Social Democrats, but it derived its emotional punch from a rhetoric that had deep roots: that of the Bolshevik threat to German women and children.[34]

Postwar antitotalitarianism breathed new life into the idea of a Christian Europe. It allowed West Germans (and Austrians) to obscure the recent past, and to identify with a set of values that placed faith and related notions like human dignity against the secularizing and totalizing power of the Communist bloc to the East (and—conveniently—the Nazi regime in the past). It also created a way to transform older racial fears of Soviet Asiatic barbarism into a more palatable cultural allegiance to Western civilization or the Christian West. But this was not the only variation of antitotalitarian politics in play after 1945. It existed alongside and in dialogue with Cold War anti-Communism in the United States. There, too, the idea of totalitarianism was central to assessments of the Soviet danger. And American observers closely followed events in Europe for evidence that confirmed their views.

The editors of *Time* magazine put one of West Germany's foremost Christian leaders on the cover of their April 6, 1953, issue. Otto Dibelius was the head of Germany's Lutherans in a country recently divided by the Cold War. In East Germany, where the great majority of Germany's Lutherans lived, the new Communist regime had begun to arrest pastors and disrupt church services. Dibelius, the readers of *Time* learned, firmly opposed these encroachments on the rights of the church and of believers. The magazine made this argument in striking visual terms. Dibelius, his face the picture of resolution, dominated the cover image. To his right and behind him, a yellow cross towered above the rubble of broken swastikas. Behind the cross lurked a giant red octopus, its searching tentacles an obvious symbol for the sinister designs of the Communist state. Inside, the accompanying article told the story of Dibelius's life and work and of the history of the church that he served. It emphasized that Dibelius had opposed the Nazi regime for reasons that also drove his resistance to Communist tyranny. "Jailed by the Nazis and now denounced and threatened by the Communists, Bishop Dibelius is the foremost Protestant champion of the rights of the church against an aggressive secular state." His "iron spirit" had breathed new life into Germany's Lutheran churches. But the article also described the pressures that churchgoers faced in Communist East Germany. Dibelius reflected on these with a thought that *Time*'s editors printed as the caption on the cover: "It is not easy to live as a Christian."[35]

Time's coverage of Bishop Dibelius's struggles reflected a broad consensus in the United States during the early Cold War that Communism in the Soviet bloc was not only a hostile political and economic system. It was also a menacing and destructive form of religion. During these years, U.S. politicians consistently described the struggle between East and West in religious terms, as a battle to defend freedom and civilization against "atheistic Communism." The American media followed their lead with detailed coverage of the persecution of the Christian churches in Eastern Europe. The July 18, 1949, issue of *Life* magazine ran a long story about the beleaguered Czechoslovak cardinal Josef Beran ("Beran Stands Fast for Christ and Freedom"). The show trial of the Hungarian cardinal József

Mindszenty that same year received even greater public attention. In response, American policy makers looked to the Christian churches as political allies in the fight to contain Soviet power. At home, they were joined by religious leaders, businessmen, and editors, all of whom wove faith and worship into their vision of the American way of life. Both *Time* and *Life*, for example, were owned by Henry R. Luce, whose editorial direction reflected his belief that Communism was the single greatest ideological threat to American political and moral power. Luce sat on numerous civic organization boards and was also well connected politically. Educators embraced the civic power of religion as well. After 1954, children across the United States pledged their allegiance to one nation "under God" at the beginning of every day. Not to be outdone, the U.S. Congress opened its own Congressional Prayer Room one year later, where representatives could pray before making important decisions.[36]

The praise that the editors of *Time* magazine conveyed for Otto Dibelius did not blind them to his many contradictions. A product of Germany's conservative and monarchist Protestant tradition, Dibelius had opposed Hitler but was skeptical about democracy as a form of government. In 1945 he signed a confession of guilt that chastised his own church for not having stood against Nazism more steadfastly. but he also believed that the war-crimes trials taking place in Nuremberg were unfair and unjust. Finally, he was a member of the new Christian Democratic Union in West Germany, whose leader (Konrad Adenauer) championed a strong transatlantic alliance with the United States. Yet Dibelius did not call openly for a crusade against Communism, in part because most of his fellow Lutherans lived in the East and he did not want to break ties with them. In short, Otto Dibelius, as *Time* portrayed him, was no honorary American. Still his warnings about "the dangers of the secular state" were "sound and sober." The modern secular state held total power over the individual, he said. Nothing prevented this state from becoming a totalitarian monster except the churches, which gave the state a "soul" by "by projecting its influence into the schools, the factories, every walk of life." To the readers of *Time*, Otto Dibelius stood as a witness to totalitarian tyranny. The story he told contained a powerful message for all Americans.

American officials were especially impressed. In 1947 Dibelius had already warned Myron C. Taylor, President Truman's personal envoy in Europe for religious affairs, that Soviet officials were abducting tens of thousands of German children, to indoctrinate them with Communist ideology. This news spoke directly to American fears about the tactics used by Communist regimes in the early years of the Cold War to "imprison" the "captive" nations of the East.[37] Impressed as well by Dibelius's anti-Nazi credentials, Taylor quickly became an advocate for the bishop both in the American zone of Germany and in Washington, D.C., brokering several White House visits over the following few years. At the time of their first meeting, in 1947, aides pronounced President Truman "captivated" by the moral passion of his German guest. At the second, three years later, Truman authorized funds to support Dibelius's anti-Communist educational programs, which were directed both at Germans in the western zones and German children in the Soviet zone. Dibelius continued to receive CIA funding to support his pastoral activities, allowing for the widespread printing and distribution of his sermons. Throughout these years, his unwavering anti-Communism made Bishop Otto Dibelius an important ally in America's struggle against Soviet totalitarianism.[38]

Still, *Time* might have made more of the contrast between Dibelius's anti-Communism and the American version better known to its readers. Both equated Nazism and Communism as twin forms of totalitarianism. However, the exact terms of the equation varied considerably. Under Nazi rule, Dibelius had been a leading figure in the Confessing Church, a movement of German Protestants who opposed efforts by the Nazi state to control their church and influence its teachings. Like so many others in the Confessing Church movement, he became a critic of Nazi racism sometime after 1933 because he believed it to be a godless threat to the truths of Scripture. He forcefully opposed moves by Protestants in the German Christian movement to "nazify" Christianity. For all this, he had been arrested more than once and had also been forbidden to preach. But he had supported the Nazis' first antisemitic actions, like the 1933 boycott of Jewish businesses, as a natural response to what he believed was disproportionate Jewish influence in German public life. "Public sentiment," he wrote, "turns against this." And he had written at length about the forces threatening European civilization and the church. He had come to prominence in 1926 with a programmatic book called *The Century of the Church*, in which he described the tasks awaiting the church in an age when secular forces—above all, Bolshevism—stood arrayed against the values of Christian European culture. If he did not name those forces in his 1926 book, he did later, writing in 1933: "One cannot ignore the fact that Jews have played a leading role in all the destructive manifestations of modern civilization."[39]

Dibelius did not write or speak about Jews and Communism in this way after 1945. Nevertheless, he arrived at his critique of totalitarianism through committed and deep reflection on the values that defined a moral community that he called the Christian West (in German, the Abendland) or Christian Europe. His personal experience with Nazism, and his sense of what exactly had constituted the Nazi state's greatest threat to Christianity and its churches, strengthened his resolve to oppose Communism after the war. *Time* magazine suggested that Dibelius's journey to these insights could not be replicated by an American. It might have spoken more plainly. Across the Atlantic, the moral challenge posed by Nazism had been defined somewhat differently. There, the war in Europe was also cast as a moral struggle for the survival of a community of values. In the United States, however, that community was frequently called Judeo-Christian civilization.

After World War I, the most prominent champion of Judeo-Christianity in the United States had been the National Conference of Christians and Jews (NCCJ). Founded in 1928 to combat postwar nativist attacks against Catholics and Jews, the conference was dedicated to promoting religious tolerance in American life. The organization devoted many of its efforts in the 1920s and 1930s to seminars and assemblies that promoted harmony between social groups, drawing attention to cases of ethnic and religious discrimination in America and imagining their resolution through interfaith dialogue between Protestants, Catholics, and Jews. During the war, it named Nazism as a threat to what it called the Judeo-Christian tradition. The NCCJ explained this idea in a series of pamphlets entitled *Why We Fight*, which were meant, no doubt, to expand on the messages in the famous wartime film series of the same name. These were collections of statements by Protestant, Catholic, and Jewish leaders on the meaning of the war and the challenge of building a just and lasting peace. Christians and Jews, their authors declared, had an opportunity to change the world for the better because they shared common values that derived from a shared biblical tradition. Those values held society together; they made meaningful civic participation possible. To attack them, as the Nazi regime had done, was to attack the principle of freedom itself. Reverend Everett R. Clinchy, president of the NCCJ, explained this point in a 1942 radio interview: "When society fails religiously and morally, it will fall to pieces politically. . . . When Hitler solved his economic problem by enslavement and war, he created . . . a more profound religious problem."[40]

At the same time, Clinchy insisted that the Judeo-Christian idea was not simply antifascist. It was antitotalitarian, aimed at "political party machines, led by Nazi Hitler, Communist Stalin, and Fascist Mussolini," all of whom denied the sovereignty of God and condemned the "Judeo-Christian tradition."[41] Hitler could be defeated, and still the religious problem would remain. Clinchy's conviction reflected a broad consensus on the centrality of religion to liberal democracy that took shape in late-1930s America against the backdrop of the looming international crisis. In a world beset by ideological extremism from the Left and the Right, a new generation of religious leaders adapted the idea of totalitarianism to the American context. They condemned unchecked state power and blamed the rise of illiberal ideologies in the Soviet Union, Germany, and Italy on the pernicious influence of secularism and materialism in the modern world. A robust defense of liberal democracy at home and abroad depended on clear moral values shared by society as a whole. The Judeo-Christian tradition was the source of those values. These ideas percolated into American debates about the purpose of the war and the nature of the postwar world to come, tying what was often called the "democratic way of life" to "Judeo-Christian civilization."[42]

Among those rooting the future of liberal democracy in the soil of Judeo-Christian civilization was the American theologian Reinhold Niebuhr. Identifying himself as a "Christian Realist," Niebuhr believed that liberal democracies had a moral obligation to defend and promote their beliefs around the world. After World War II began, he called for military intervention, arguing that American Christians must abandon their morally "confused" pacifism and accept the responsibility of acting as Christians in the world of power politics. He was also an advocate for increased Jewish immigration, seeing aid for Jewish refugees as a practical consequence of the prophetic spirit that Judaism had bequeathed to Christianity.[43]

Émigrés from Europe also embraced the idea of Judeo-Christianity. The Catholic theologian Jacques Maritain, a critic of the Vichy regime in his native France, spent the wartime years in exile in the United States. There, he embraced the American discourse on Judeo-Christian civilization and the threat posed to it by totalitarianism, both Communist and National Socialist.[44] In a 1942 essay in the American Catholic journal *Commonweal*, Maritain wrote that "in the face of pagan blood surging up today, our civilization is revealed as a Judaeo-Christian civilization, and . . . this civilization will perish unless both Christian and Jew come better to perceive the vital part each one plays in its total pattern."[45] Protestant theologian Paul Tillich also became a champion for Judeo-Christianity. Tillich had left

Germany in 1933 because his belief in Christian socialism made him unwelcome in the new German state and among the conservative nationalists who dominated his church. In the United States he became a colleague of Reinhold Niebuhr's at the Union Theological Seminary in New York. During the war, Tillich made a series of radio broadcasts for Voice of America between 1942 and 1944.[46] In several of them he insisted to his overseas German audience that attacks on Judaism were ultimately attacks on Christianity and thus on the moral foundations of democratic order. (Tillich's Christian socialist convictions caused him trouble in the United States after 1945. He was blacklisted by the U.S. Army as a suspected Communist sympathizer, and he suppressed references to Marx and Marxism in his own writings throughout the 1950s.[47])

Judeo-Christianity did not eliminate antisemitism from American politics and society. The National Conference of Christians and Jews had formed in part as a response to Ku Klux Klan racism directed against African Americans and Jews. During the 1930s, the concept of Judeo-Christianity was an important response to the demagoguery of racists like Father Charles Coughlin, who used his radio broadcast to air a stream of invective against Jews, calling them the puppet masters controlling Communist revolutions and predatory capitalism. Anti-Jewish prejudice remained a powerful force during the war as well.[48]

In the face of this prejudice, the concept of Judeo-Christianity made World War II into a struggle for the future of civilization that American Jews could also embrace. During the war the American military translated the associations between Judeo-Christian civilization and liberal democracy, already made by religious leaders and civic organizations, into an organizational ethos. Across the service branches, efforts were made to install and support chaplains from the three faiths fighting for democracy: Protestantism, Catholicism, and Judaism. The military also supported efforts by the NCCJ to distribute pamphlets about religious toleration to both the military clergy and the men in uniform. In turn, American Jews broadly embraced this vision of religious unity in the face of fascism, for several reasons. War against Nazi Germany was a war against an antisemitic foe. It delegitimized antisemitism in the United States as a tactic of the enemy. But the wartime Judeo-Christian consensus also offered American Jews a place within a "universalist rubric." As Reformed Jewish leader Julian Morgenstern declared in his presidential address opening the 1942–43 academic year at Hebrew Union College, Christianity and Judaism, had a "common descent, a common vision, hope, mission, [and to] face a common foe and a common fate, must achieve a common victory or share a common death." Memories of this shared struggle would propel Jewish integration after 1945.[49]

After the war Everett Clinchy and his fellow champions of Judeo-Christian civilization set their sights on the Soviet Union as the other godless threat to liberal democracy.[50] In 1948 Reinhold Niebuhr's portrait graced the cover of *Time* magazine, and the theologian was the subject of an article ("Faith for a Lenten Age") written by the former Communist turned zealous anti-Communist, Whittaker Chambers. Four years later President Eisenhower declared: "Our form of government has no sense unless it is founded on a deeply felt religious faith, and I don't care what it is. With us of course it is the Judeo-Christian concept but it must be a religion that all men are created equal."[51] In this climate the National Conference of Christians and Jews declared in its annual report for 1954, "We are engaged in a deadly world struggle between the forces of atheistic Communism and the forces for good."[52]

American Jews adapted to the transposition of Judeo-Christianity from an antifascist consensus to a pillar of anti-Communist ideology in a variety of ways. Wartime military service had offered many, especially nonreligious Jews, an "identity not rooted in historical oppression" that also promised new social opportunities in postwar America. At the same time, the realities of Cold War politics, which drove the United States to find allies among its former enemies, forced

American Jews to avoid open discussion of the Holocaust and to silence public expressions of anger and grief over the horrific slaughter in order to show support for American interests abroad. Even more important, it compelled American Jewish organizations to respond to the public prominence of Jews in the American Communist Party.[53]

During the early Cold War, anti-Communism became a "criterion of Jewish communal membership" as Jewish organizations in the United States adopted a variety of strategies to combat the association of Judaism with Communism. Some lobbied film producers in Hollywood to avoid representing Communists as Jews in such films as *I Married a Communist* (later retitled *The Woman on Pier 13*) and *The Red Menace*. Both the Anti-Defamation League and the American Jewish Committee offered to share their personnel files with the House Un-American Activities Committee.[54] When Julius and Ethel Rosenberg were tried and convicted of passing atomic secrets to the Soviet Union in 1951, American Jewish organizations forcefully distanced themselves from the couple. The American Jewish Committee (AJC) expelled the Yiddish branch of the Communist International Workers Order in 1949. In 1953, its representatives told a congressional committee that "Judaism and communism are utterly incompatible."[55] Meanwhile, important Jewish intellectuals emerged among the most ardent anti-Communists. The historian Lucy Dawidowicz argued that Jews should not support clemency pleas on behalf of the Rosenbergs and dismissed accusations that convicting the couple was anti-semitic, saying such claims were a demonstration of Communism's "Big Lie."[56]

Others elaborated the role that Judaism could play in America's Cold War struggle against totalitarian godlessness. In 1950, Will Herberg cheered the signs of a growing "reaction against the pervasive secularism of the past century." Five years later he published his classic *Protestant, Catholic, Jew: An Essay in American Religious Sociology*, in which he argued that Jews could integrate into American life by defining Jewishness as a religious identity.[57] In the 1950s in America, "religion became the major vehicle for Jewish identity, while secular Judaism as an ideology largely collapsed."[58] Symbolic of this shift was the U.S. military's decision in 1954 to replace the "H" for "Hebrew," which had come to have an ethnic or racial connotation, with a "J" for "Jewish," as a religious affiliation, on all Jewish soldiers' dog tags.[59] Whether this Jewish religious revival was more show than substance remains a matter for historical debate. Herberg's critics wondered if Judeo-Christian culture could ever be more than a slogan for pieties about toleration devoid of any theological specifics. However, a nationwide construction boom in synagogues and a renewed interest in Jewish education provide further evidence that American Judaism secured a place in Cold War America by embracing the Judeo-Christian idea.

The Judeo-Christian consensus had united America's three major religious faiths (Protestantism, Catholicism, and Judaism) in the wartime struggle against fascism. After 1945, it gave substance to the ideological oppositions distinguishing the U.S.-led West from the Soviet East. Judeo-Christianity made possible a vision of American society in which Jews could find an equal place alongside their Christian neighbors. It also served as a lens through which Americans of all faiths could examine and understand how Communist rule was remaking the Soviet bloc.

Once again, *Time* magazine serves as a useful barometer of American anti-Communist rhetoric. The September 20, 1948, issue featured a cover story about Romanian Communist Party leader Ana Pauker. On the cover, a profile drawing depicts Pauker as a stern and angry woman, her mouth open as if she is lecturing or haranguing an audience. She is dressed in red; a yellow sickle perfectly traces the outline of her head. The caption below reads: "For an old battle-ax, a new edge." The accompanying article continued in this spirit. *Time* said Pauker was the "most powerful woman alive," and—to the editors of the magazine—a living embodiment of Communism's unnatural cruelty. Pauker's physical appearance and manner suggested this: "Now she is fat and ugly; but once she was slim and (her friends remember) beautiful. Once she was warm-hearted, shy and full of pity for the oppressed, of whom she was one. Now she is cold as the frozen Danube, bold as a boyar on his own rich land and pitiless as a scythe in the Moldavian grain." The description of her personal qualities led naturally into a discussion of Communist tyranny in Romania: the Russian occupation of the country; the impoverishment of the Romanian middle class; the confiscation of crops from Romania's peasants. But the article also dwelt at length on Pauker's Jewish identity. It began and ended with scenes of Pauker's father (Zvi Rabinsohn), an elderly and pious Jew who had emigrated to Israel, where he studied Torah and preferred to remember his daughter as she had been when she was a young girl. Pauker, the article explained, "had moved a long way from the grimy Bucharest street where her father had first taught her the stern Old Testament notions of good & evil; she had abandoned the jealous God of her fathers for another faith." She had become "Ana Rabinsohn Pauker, a Communist and a key figure in the struggle for the world."[60]

Time's profile of Pauker was telling. Throughout the Cold War, American media used accounts of figures and events in Eastern Europe to construct the "truth" about Communism in the East.[61] These accounts invariably depicted a society and a political system diametrically opposed to the American "way of life." Behind the Iron Curtain, lies and propaganda dominated discourse. Poverty prevailed. Totalitarian oppression destroyed all social ties. The entire region was frequently portrayed as a vast prison camp. *Time*'s account of Pauker as a mannish harridan reflected this approach by setting up an implicit contrast between Pauker, so unlike a "normal" woman, and the more (putatively) natural division of social roles between men and women that obtained in the West. So too did its treatment of Pauker's religious upbringing. American media, *Time* magazine prominent among them, devoted considerable attention to the suppression of religion in the Communist East. The imprisonment of Hungarian cardinal József Mindszenty (himself the subject of a *Time* cover story, in 1949) and Czech cardinal Josef Beran became opportunities for the press to distinguish the religious freedom and moral order in the West from the anarchic and secular godlessness that prevailed behind the Iron Curtain. Pauker's apostasy served the same rhetorical function. In these years, Judeo-Christian civilization, symbolized in the *Time* article by Pauker's father, safe in Israel and consumed with religious study, was a central pillar of the Western image promoted by U.S. diplomats, politicians, and media outlets. Pauker herself, in contrast, had abandoned her faith, lost the moral compass that it provided, and devoted herself to a cruel new religion. As a "non-Jewish" Jewish Communist, Pauker was doubly abnormal.[62]

Communist persecution of Jews also supported the totalitarianism paradigm that shaped Cold War liberal understandings of the dangers posed to Western democracy by the Soviet Union. Into the early 1960s, politicians and public figures in the U.S. routinely compared Soviet tyranny to Nazi crimes, drawing on analyses of the totalitarian state that had been carried out on both sides of the Atlantic before World War II and that gained in intellectual prestige after the defeat of Nazi Germany and the intensification of the Cold War. Anti-Communist émigrés from Eastern Europe contributed actively to this practice and also validated it, not least because it allowed them to situate the political upheavals that had forced them to flee to the West within the widest geopolitical frame. Referring to Nazi war crimes, so fresh in the public mind after intensive coverage of the Nuremberg trials, gave moral weight to their accounts of persecution and injustice in the new Soviet bloc—accounts they hoped would strengthen Western resolve to oppose and perhaps even topple Eastern Europe's Communist regimes.

For entirely different reasons, liberal Jewish groups in the United States, led by the American Jewish Committee, also found the comparative framework of totalitarianism useful for understanding the existential perils faced by the remnant of Eastern European Jewry that still lived behind the Iron Curtain. Memory of the Holocaust gave urgency to their conviction that something must be done, in the present, to protect those Jews who remained in Eastern Europe and to assuage their grief over the fact that so little had been done to protect them against Nazi genocide. As they debated the future of Jewish identity and politics in a postwar world marked by the catastrophic loss of the once-great Jewish communities of Eastern Europe and the triumphant birth of the Jewish state of Israel, many turned to comparisons of Hitler and Stalin, or Nazism and Communism, to underscore the rightness of their own approach to these complex questions. They also highlighted evidence of Communist antisemitism in Eastern Europe, arguing that campaigns against Jewish Communists who were no longer Jews in any meaningful way demonstrated that Communist anti-Jewish policy was motivated by the same paranoid racism that had fueled Nazi genocide. With these comparisons, they hoped to demonstrate their commitment to liberal anti-Communism (and disavow any special affinity of Jews for Communism) and to assert their equal place in Judeo-Christian America.[63]

Two examples demonstrate how the totalitarian paradigm shaped perceptions of Communist antisemitism for Western audiences. The first was when, at their February 1951 Party Congress, Hungary's Communist leaders declared their intention to resettle members of the "former ruling class" from Budapest and other large cities to the countryside, where they would be compelled at last to do "useful" labor for the people's democracy. The decree was meant to target members of the former bourgeoisie as well as one-time landholders and higher-ranking members of the interwar-era civil service. In practice, however, the decree was interpreted far more broadly and

used to target a wide variety of people accused of "bourgeois tenden-
cies." (It also sparked another massive free-for-all over property, as
party functionaries and privileged industrial workers gladly took over
the properties and apartments that their former owners had been
forced to abandon.) Given the social profile of those targeted, the
decree fell heavily on the community of Jewish Holocaust survivors
in Budapest, who understandably panicked when they learned of
orders that they had to pack their belongings into a few suitcases and
report for deportation within twenty-four hours, and then be loaded
onto train cars bound for somewhere unknown. Leaders of Hungary's Jewish community tried faithfully to explain the party line, even
as complaints from Hungarian Auschwitz survivors flooded into
their offices. In a formal statement, they declared that "no individual
of the Jewish faith is among those deported because they are a member
of our confession. Rumors to the contrary, the deportees are rich
traders, factory owners, and landholders, as well as collaborators and
beneficiaries of the Horthy regime."[64] Despite these protestations,
the policy was disastrously cruel to Jews in postwar Hungary, nearly
all of whom had family members touched by the resettlement order.
Precise figures are difficult to come by, but reasonable estimates suggest that 15 to 20 percent, and perhaps as many as 30 percent, of the
forty to sixty thousand deportees to the countryside were Jewish.[65]

As news of the policy crossed the Iron Curtain and reached the
United States, it was immediately understood as an antisemitic policy
devised by a totalitarian regime. Liberal Jewish groups denounced the
action as a violation of the fundamental human rights proclaimed in
the 1948 Universal Declaration of Human Rights. They also warned
openly that the Holocaust showed where policies like these could
lead. "Under Nazism, the first yellow badges and ghettos foreshadowed the gas chambers. Under communism, mass evictions mean just
as certain, although slower and perhaps more painful, extinction. . . .
The difference between genocide and mass extinction of certain
classes is merely formal."[66] Anti-Communist émigrés on the Hun-

garian National Council in the United States, a Hungarian-émigré political group, made similar arguments, sending letters of protest to the U.S. State Department and the United Nations invoking the "horrors of Nazi deportations" and calling for action in defense of freedom and dignity in Central and Eastern Europe. Even Eleanor Roosevelt joined the chorus of criticism: "The free world thought that when the Nazis were finally defeated . . . that that would end the kind of thing done by Hitler to the Jews. . . . And unfortunately now behind the Iron Curtain . . . the mass deportations are beginning again." In this way, Communist antisemitism became a sign of the type of totalitarian assault on individual human rights waged by the Nazi and Soviet regimes alike.[67]

Then, one year later, Jewish organizations in the United States and around the world mobilized to protest the show trial in Czechoslovakia of Rudolf Slánský and his twelve codefendants.[68] There was broad agreement that the motives behind the trial were racist. Because Jewish Communists like Slánský had abandoned Judaism, the campaign against them could only be understood as a blatant case of racialized scapegoating, similar to Nazi propaganda against the Jews. As the Jewish Community Council of Greater Washington declared in an open letter to the *Washington Post* after Slánský and the others had been executed: "Jews in the free world will feel no special urge to mourn for them. They were not Jews at all. Indeed, they were traitors to Judaism. Only through the disavowal of all the principles of Judaism could they have been led to the service of Communist totalitarianism."[69] Nevertheless, their calculated scapegoating as Jews and "Zionists" raised fears that "being a Jew is in itself looked upon as a crime by the Kremlin and its henchmen" in a way that recalled Hitler's rise to power in 1933. The Anti-Defamation League described the Slánský trial similarly, as the "most vicious anti-Semitic attack by a major power since Nazi Germany."[70] Within the Jewish community, a vigorous debate unfolded about how best to take the measure of Communist antisemitism.

234 A SPECTER HAUNTING EUROPE

Many were struck by the sheer hypocrisy of Communist ideology. Whereas Hitler had been open about his hatred of Jews, the Communist regimes in Eastern Europe declared their commitment to internationalism, even as they targeted Jews simply as Jews. The shock of this betrayal led many to abandon their socialist commitments and put themselves squarely in the camp of Cold War liberalism. Fears within the Jewish community that the Slánský trial would inevitably lead to new mass deportations and mass executions, less than a decade after the Holocaust, were also expressed by organizations like the American Jewish Committee. "The Prague trial might be a prelude to a pogrom of genocidal proportions," proclaimed the AJC in its own publication on the Slánský trial.[71] The resurgence of antisemitism behind the Iron Curtain fueled comparisons of Nazism and Communism as dual totalitarian systems and offered further evidence of the Soviet bloc's hostility towards Judeo-Christian civilization.

The AJC's statement was part of a larger debate about Jewish identity in the postwar world. But it drew the support of prominent voices outside the American Jewish community. U.S. labor leader James Carey took up the theme of Communist hypocrisy at a December 1952 rally organized by the Jewish Labor Committee, relating Communist antisemitism to Communism's assault on Western values: "In a strict sense, Stalin's crime against humanity is even more monstrous than Hitler's—because it is hypocritical. . . . While mouthing the word 'democracy,' Communism directs the full fury of its anti-democratic despotism against the Jewish minority."[72] Carey was not alone. The Slánský trial had taken place in a season of political transition in Washington, D.C. Both the outgoing president, Harry Truman, and his successor, Dwight Eisenhower, made statements about the totalitarian tyranny on display in Prague that they sent to a Jewish labor rally organized to protest Soviet antisemitism. "The tragic fate of six million Jews at the hands of other totalitarian regimes does not permit us to witness the use of antisemitism without protest," wrote Truman.

To this, Eisenhower added, "The trial in Prague of Rudolf Slansky and his associates was the mockery of civilized and humanitarian values. . . . The Communists, like the Russian czars and the German Nazis, are using the Jews as scapegoats for the failure of their regime."[73] Meanwhile, the anti-Communist émigrés at Radio Free Europe were broadcasting material to Czech audiences that put the entirety of the blame for the antisemitic character of the trial on Moscow, and disregarding evidence of a popular willingness to accept the accusations of "Jewish conspiracy" as true. As they explained in their broadcasts, the trial, and the Communist regime itself, were Soviet tools used to enslave the peoples of Eastern Europe. The Czech people, democratic in spirit just like the Americans, had nothing to do with the anti-Jewish "barbarism" on display in Communist courtrooms, they declared. Communists manipulated antisemitism in order to carry on their attacks against the "free world" in the West.[74]

A theory of totalitarianism was essential to the rise of Judeo-Christian civilization as an ideological concept. Equating Nazism and Communism as similar threats to human dignity and the human person transformed the place of Jews in anti-Communist politics. No longer an instigator of Communist revolution, Judaism could now be theorized as a set of values bound to Christianity in their common opposition to materialism, secularism, and neo-paganism. In this form, Judeo-Christian civilization was a central feature of Cold War liberal rhetoric. It suggested a democratic polity in which an active civil society, best demonstrated by free religious organization, worked to defend individual freedom and social order against the predations of an all-powerful modern state. This idea unified opposition to Communism on both sides of the Atlantic, and also allowed ex-Nazis like Matthes Ziegler to reinvent themselves as Cold Warriors. In the 1960s, however, the idea of totalitarianism fell out of favor. In a time of student protest and antiwar demonstrations, the concept would seem to many like a dusty relic of a more repressed age. The rise of Holocaust memory, which cast Nazi genocide as an incomparably greater evil than Soviet repression, also cast suspicion on the political motives of anti-Communists who wanted to compare Nazism and Communism, especially in West Germany. When totalitarianism was later revived in the 1980s as a way of comparing Nazi and Soviet crimes, champions of the idea were forced to confront the legacy of the Holocaust as well. Their efforts to combine the two would place the idea of Judeo-Bolshevism at the center of debates about how to remember the twentieth century.

7

Between History and Memory

In 1998, Romanian president Emil Constantinescu visited the United States Holocaust Memorial Museum in Washington, D.C., where he made an official statement about Romania and the Holocaust. He praised Romanians who had helped Jews during that horrible time, but he also declared that "no one has the right to ignore [Romanian] responsibility for those Romanian citizens who were persecuted rather than protected by the Romanian state, [a fact that] cannot and must not be eluded."[1] These words were well received in the American capital. At home, however, they caused controversy. Why, some asked, had no Jews apologized to Romania for the crimes of Communism? One historian explained why that would have been a far more significant gesture: "Proportionally speaking, Romanians and Romania suffered more at the hands of the Communist regime, whose coming the Jews had made an important contribution to, than the Jews themselves had suffered from the Romanian state." "The Red Holocaust," he reasoned, "was incomparably more grave than Nazism."[2]

This assertion was so controversial because it contradicted the way that the Holocaust has come to be remembered and talked about. Today, Holocaust memory is widely associated with a broader set of political and moral values that include an appreciation for the norms of liberal democracy; respect for racial, ethnic, and religious differences; and a commitment to human rights. The international reach of Holocaust-memory culture in North America, Europe, and beyond has elevated Holocaust commemoration into a kind of litmus test for the presence or absence of a robust and self-critical civil society. After 1989, Holocaust recognition became a "contemporary European entry ticket" for societies newly freed from Communist rule, a shorthand in debates about the readiness of post-Communist Eastern Europe to join the wider European Union.[3] The powerful symbolism that surrounds Holocaust memory makes arguments that a "Red Holocaust" was worse than Nazism, or that Jewish-Communist perpetrators committed crimes equal to the Holocaust, into something more than failed attempts at historical comparison. Instead, they are perceived as provocations that suggest those who make them are trivializing or relativizing the Holocaust because they are opposed to the broader set of values that Holocaust memory has come to stand for.

The episode arising from President Constantinescu's visit to Washington was only one of many Holocaust controversies that have erupted since the last years of the Cold War around attempts to compare Communism and Nazism. In every case, the problem of Judeo-Bolshevism has been at the center of the furor, embedded in heated debates about who committed the crimes of Europe's Communist regimes, what bearing those crimes have on the genocide of European Jews in the Holocaust, and whether the collective memories of suffering and victimization experienced by other national groups during World War II or afterward could or should be set alongside public memory of the Holocaust. In the 1980s, these questions roiled West German society. After 1989, they cut to the heart of debates about Eastern Europe's place in the new liberal order so many hoped would unite the Continent. The idea of Judeo-Bolshevism did not die with

Communism. It outlived the Soviet Union because it became entangled in the politics of Holocaust memory.

Remembering the Holocaust is a political and moral project of recent origin. The Nuremberg trials, which gave to international law
the notion of "crimes against humanity," are often understood as a
response to the Holocaust. In fact, they were primarily motivated by
the Allied powers' desire to prosecute Germany for waging aggressive and destructive war. Similarly, the contemporaneous Conven-
tion on the Prevention and Punishment of the Crime of Genocide
and the Universal Declaration of Human Rights, both now closely
associated with Holocaust memory, were born of contested negotia-
tions between Western powers and the Soviet Union, and were initially understood as responses to a wide range of wartime atrocities
committed against many categories of victims.[4] Indeed, to achieve
consensus on general principles the framers of these documents
rarely mentioned the Jewish identity of the victims of Nazi genocide.
Only slowly, beginning in the 1960s, did widespread consciousness
of the German genocide of the Jews as something distinct from the
other horrors of World War II begin to take shape. This cultural and
moral shift had many causes, including the global impact of the 1961
trial of Adolf Eichmann in Jerusalem, the disaffection with radical
politics on the part of a new generation of humanitarian activists
working in places like Biafra, and the rise of the Holocaust witness as
a figure whose testimony was widely understood to afford unique
insights into the nature of radical evil.[5] These developments, inter-
linked in a historical conjuncture that is still being studied and assessed, connected Holocaust memory to a new human rights consciousness and made the act of remembering Nazi genocide central
to public conduct in a liberal society. The shift found perfect symbolic expression in 1978, when U.S. president Jimmy Carter, a champion of putting human rights ideals into foreign policy, asked the

well-known Auschwitz survivor and activist Elie Wiesel to chair his Presidential Commission on the Holocaust, which he charged with exploring possibilities for a national memorial to the victims of Nazi genocide. The result was the United States Holocaust Memorial Museum, which opened in 1993.

The emergence of Holocaust memory went hand in hand with understanding it as a discrete historical event. Pioneering histories of the Holocaust, above all Raul Hilberg's monumental multivolume *The Destruction of the European Jews*, traced the step-by-step emergence of Nazi genocide, from the first attacks on Germany's Jews in 1933 (and the deeper currents of European and German antisemitism that inspired them) to the ultimate horrors of Auschwitz.[6] The history they told intersected with the war against the Soviet Union at certain points but remained conceptually distinct from it. Most important, the new histories of the Holocaust assessed the behavior of Europeans during World War II as—following the title of another of Hilberg's important books—perpetrators, victims, or bystanders, according to their responses to the genocide unfolding around them.[7] The moral clarity inherent in these separate categories flattened the complex reality of life in wartime Europe, especially in Eastern Europe.[8] However, they also helped make the Holocaust a touchstone for understanding other cases of genocide and suggested criteria for differentiating genocide from the other horrors of war and ethnic conflict. According to this interpretation, the latter were driven by material interests (power, security, resources, territory) that made violence between opposing groups politically rational and also interactive— each side commits violence against the other, even if the scale is not equal. Genocide was different. It might take place "under the cover" of war, but it was driven by irrational hatreds, usually racial or ethnic, that victim groups did nothing to provoke. The victims of genocide were blameless, targeted only because of who they were, and not for what they might have done. This moral distinction made the Holocaust a paradigmatic case of evil, and charged Holocaust memory with implications for the teaching of toleration in a modern multicultural and liberal society.[9]

In this form, Holocaust memory inspired debates in Western Europe and North America about the moral imperative to intervene in contemporary humanitarian disasters, especially those taking place in the postcolonial world.[10] But this in turn raised questions about how crimes committed by Communist regimes should be acknowledged and discussed. The reconstruction of Western Europe in the 1950s had rested on a comparison of Nazi Germany and the Soviet Union as twin totalitarian evils. Antitotalitarianism had given birth to the idea of a Judeo-Christian civilization united in an interfaith defense against the godless East. It had also enabled West Germans to condemn Hitler's war (without closely examining their own complicity in it) and to rejoin the liberal West as a partner in the fight against Communism. The rise of Holocaust memory scrambled these powerful political investments. For many, totalitarianism was a slogan that legitimized the massacre of innocents in places like Southeast Asia in the name of defending the anti-Communist "free world." Young West German critics in particular saw it as an ideological device that allowed old Nazis to remain in positions of authority and to go unpunished for their genocidal crimes. But others reimagined totalitarianism in the post-1968 world because they had once been Communists and had grown disillusioned by the failures and bloody excesses of revolutionary activism. They began to ask why the crimes of the gulag as chronicled by writers like Alexander Solzhenitsyn did not enjoy the same public prominence as the Holocaust.[11]

As historian Carolyn Dean has shown, debates about totalitarianism were especially intense in France, because they emerged at a moment when the persecution of Jews during the Vichy years was receiving belated public recognition, and when Marxism and the French Communist Party were losing the prestige both had enjoyed for so long in

French intellectual and political life.[12] In this climate, a broad spectrum of intellectuals declared that the crimes of Communism ought to be remembered alongside those of Nazism. A variety of motives inspired this impulse. Some simply wanted a more rigorous empirical comparison; others found rhetorical power in the metaphorical comparison of the two systems; still others were ideologically invested in exposing Communist crimes; and, finally, some were moralists who insisted on publicizing every atrocity because all lives mattered. But one theme ran through their arguments: the Holocaust took up "too much space" in public conversation, allowing the claims of Jewish victims of Nazi crimes to drown out the voices of others who had suffered under other regimes. Many of the participants in these debates argued that Holocaust memory was ultimately a particularistic (Jewish) memory, reflecting the fact that Nazism had targeted one specific racial group for destruction. Communism, by contrast, was a universalistic ideology and its victims had come from all humanity.

This line of thinking reached its apex with the 1997 publication in France of *The Black Book of Communism*, a massive anthology of essays that aimed to catalog the crimes, terror, and repression of Communism on a global scale. In the introduction to that book, the lead editor, Stéphane Courtois, observed that Communism had claimed "100,000,000" lives around the globe, a number far in excess of Nazism's victims. "A single-minded focus on the Jewish genocide," Courtois wrote, "in an attempt to characterize the Holocaust as a unique atrocity[,] has . . . prevented an assessment of other episodes of comparable magnitude in the Communist world."[13] In response, furious critics denounced the *Black Book* as a transparent effort to canonize Communism as the "worst" evil, to minimize the atrocities of the Holocaust, and to derail public reflection on French involvement in Nazi crimes. These arguments fueled debates about the persistence of antisemitism in contemporary France. They also highlighted how the status of victims and victimhood had become central to discussions about terror and genocide in twentieth-century Europe.[14]

The idea of Judeo-Bolshevism occupied an extremely sensitive place in these debates about historical memory. The fear of Jewish Bolshevik power, and the close association of Jews with Communism on which that fear rested, had inspired and justified violence against Jews when the great empires in Eastern Europe collapsed at the end of World War I and then again, on an even more horrific scale, amid Germany's war against the Soviet Union. Time and again, historians had disproved the myth of Judeo-Bolshevism by showing that only some Jews had ever been Communists. And meticulous research by a young generation of West German military historians had proved that the claim by Nazi Germany that it was fighting a war of "preventive defense" had been a lie to mask the aggressive drive and paranoid racism of the Nazi regime and its leaders.[15] Even so, fear and anxiety about the Communist (or "Asiatic Bolshevik") threat had played an undeniable role in the entangled history of war and genocide in twentieth-century Europe in ways that histories of the Holocaust as a distinct event did not fully capture. Taking the fear and anxiety about Communism seriously blurred the line between rational threat assessment and irrational paranoia that was at the heart of what made genocide a genocide in popular understandings. They also raised questions about how to balance divided memories of different ethnic and national groups who experienced the brutality of the Nazi-Soviet war and its aftermath in very different ways.[16]

Should collective memories of anti-Communist fears or Soviet terror enjoy the same status in a liberal democratic society as Holocaust memory? Or were those memories irredeemably tainted by the way anti-Communism, antisemitism, and racism were so often fused throughout the twentieth century? Did highlighting those memories risk eroding the democratic and humanitarian norms so closely associated with public commemorations of the Holocaust? These questions loomed over arguments that exploded in the last years of the Cold War about how (and whether) to historicize the Holocaust. After 1989, they dominated public discussions across Eastern Eu-

rope as societies emerging from Communist rule struggled to decide how they should remember the twentieth century.

Two historical controversies in the 1980s demonstrate the challenge
that the idea of Judeo-Bolshevism posed to the public pedagogical
function of Holocaust memory. The first became known as the *Historikerstreit*, or "historians' debate," a contentious discussion among historians in the last years of the Federal Republic of Germany, touched
off by an essay by the conservative German historian Ernst Nolte. The
second and much smaller controversy involved a synthetic study of
Nazi war and genocide written in the United States by historian Arno
Mayer, titled *Why Did the Heavens Not Darken?* The two cases were
vastly different in scale. The West German *Historikerstreit* has itself
become the subject of scholarly analysis.[17] Arno Mayer's book is now
largely forgotten. In both cases, however, the historical works that
caused the scandals eventually became reference points for debates
that went beyond any claims in the writings themselves. And in each,
the problem of Judeo-Bolshevism played a crucial and telling role.

The West German historians' debate began with an article in
Frankfurter Allgemeine Zeitung by Ernst Nolte, entitled "The Past
That Will Not Pass." In it, Nolte argued that it was legitimate to
compare Nazi and Soviet crimes. The Holocaust, he claimed, was the
product of a "causal nexus" that bound Nazism to Communism in a
ferocious web. Hitler could imagine the horror of Auschwitz only
because Soviet rulers had preceded him with heinous crimes of their
own. "Wasn't the gulag archipelago more original than Auschwitz?"
Nolte asked. "Wasn't Bolshevik 'class murder' the logical and actual
predecessor to Nazi 'race murder?'" The essay was also remarkable
because Nolte chose not to write about Nazism or the Holocaust in
ways that identified first and foremost with the Jewish victims of National Socialism. Instead, he invited his readers to historicize the war
on the Eastern Front in ways that legitimized German fears. The war,

he argued, had been the result of the ideological clash between Bolshevism and National Socialism—he later called that clash the "European civil war." Perhaps the war had been a "preventive war" to defend Germany against Bolshevism (or "Asiatic terror") after all. "Did the National Socialists or Hitler perhaps commit an 'Asiatic' deed merely because they and their ilk considered themselves to be potential victims of an 'Asiatic' deed?"[18]

In later writings Nolte went even further, suggesting that Jews had not been passive victims. Their actions had made an impression in Hitler's mind, he said, and caused his destructive and murderous response. During the *Historikerstreit*, this perspective found its most scandalous expression at a dinner party, when Nolte suggested to historian Saul Friedländer that Chaim Weizmann's 1939 statement that Jews would side with Great Britain against Nazi Germany was a "Jewish declaration of war" that justified a German response. (Friedländer left the party.)[19] However, the most complex example of Nolte's assertions about Jewish responsibility involved Jews and Bolshevism. According to Nolte, the role that Jews had played in the Bolshevik party in Russia and elsewhere in Europe had decisively shaped Hitler's worldview. In *The European Civil War*, his 1987 book that fully develops the ideas of his 1986 essay, Nolte argued that fear of Bolshevism gave Hitler's antisemitism its "most powerful impulse" (*bewegendster Impuls*). He argued that Jewish Bolsheviks in Russia and elsewhere became the "rational core" around which National Socialist fears of Judeo-Bolshevism grew. Simultaneously, the reality of Bolshevik atrocities in Russia provoked Hitler to connect antisemitism to anti-Communism. National Socialism was transformed into a violent and apocalyptic ideology: a "counterbelief" driven by an "excessive counterpassion" (*überschiessende Gegen-Leidenschaft*). Judeo-Bolshevism made Nazism the response to the Bolshevik threat.[20]

All of this ran against the commonly accepted public discourse in West Germany about the war and the Holocaust. During the 1960s and 1970s a new culture of memory had displaced the antitotalitarian consensus that dominated in the first years of the Cold War. No longer were Nazism and Communism equivalent threats to the West. Instead, Germany's national history was understood as a unique and "special road" that led away from liberalism and toward catastrophe. The Holocaust was not just another war crime. It was unique, the singular product of German history and an enduring reminder to all Germans of the moral obligations borne by engaged citizens in a democratic society. The duty to remember Auschwitz had become the crucial marker of postnational German identity. As Jürgen Habermas wrote in one of his lengthy rejoinders to Ernst Nolte, "Our own life is connected with the context of life in which Auschwitz was possible, not through contingent circumstances, but internally. . . . Not one of us can sneak out of this milieu because our identity, both as individuals and as Germans, is permanently interwoven with it." The "collective mutual liability" for these crimes, he said, carried over into later generations.[21]

Leading historians and liberal intellectuals who shared Habermas's view of German identity denounced Ernst Nolte. They accused him of distorting the German past to escape the particular moral obligations that all Germans bore because of the Holocaust. Nolte's calls for comparative historical analysis were disingenuous, they said, a transparent ruse to divert attention from German crimes and to normalize the German past by raising examples of Soviet atrocities. They insisted that his approach reduced the Holocaust to just another (unoriginal) horror of war. It also vitiated the civic function of Holocaust memory—the idea that reflection on the crimes of the Nazi past would inspire renewed commitment to liberal democratic values in the present—by encouraging Germans to dwell on their own wartime suffering at the hands of the Soviet army and to see themselves as victims rather than as perpetrators. This criticism carried the day. In the end, Nolte found himself isolated and discredited by the mainstream of West German academia.

Around this time, the historian Arno Mayer, a professor at Princeton, made a different attempt to historicize the Holocaust in his 1988 book *Why Did the Heavens Not Darken?* Mayer's personal and intellectual background separated him from the conservative Catholic Nolte in every way. (Mayer is a Jewish Marxist from Luxembourg who escaped Hitler's Europe in 1940; his grandfather died at Theresienstadt.) Nevertheless, he also situated the destruction of Europe's Jews in a broad historical context defined by the clash between revolutionary and counterrevolutionary ideology. By doing so, Mayer hoped to restore the "centrality of ideology, politics, and war" to study of the Holocaust and to illuminate the dynamic interplay between anti-Communism and antisemitism that had long been obscured by what he called "residual Cold War blinders." In a later essay, he explained that he also hoped to desacralize the Holocaust. In Mayer's view, Holocaust memory had become "overly sectarian," "inflexible," and "undialectical, with the accent almost exclusively on the unfathomable barbarity of the Nazis and the monstrous degradation and suffering of the victims." In short, it had become a "withdrawal from history rather than a commitment to it." By situating the Holocaust within a dynamic political context of war and ideological conflict, Mayer hoped to "re-universalize" the memory of the Nazi genocide of European Jews so that it could illuminate other instances of barbarism in history.[22]

Mayer interpreted the German invasion of the Soviet Union as a fusion of total war and ideological crusade directed against a common enemy that the Nazi regime called "Judeobolshevism." Obviously, Jews were an important part of this amalgam. But Mayer located the most important roots of the Nazis' intense ideological hatred not in antisemitism but in anti-Communism and, more generally, antimodernism. Adolf Hitler grafted antisemitism onto anti-Communist zeal. "The Nazi drive against the Jews was embedded in this war-cum-crusade." When the Germans invaded the Soviet Union in June 1941, they immediately began to inflict horrible suffering on the Jews they

encountered there. But Mayer insisted that the Holocaust—he preferred to call it the "Judeocide"—began only after Germany's anti-
Soviet war began to falter in the autumn and winter of 1941.
Having failed to defeat Stalin, a frustrated Hitler opened a second
front against the Jews. The Holocaust was born, he said, of a failed
anti-Bolshevik crusade.[23]

The book ignited a firestorm of controversy. Idiosyncratically,
Mayer had given his readers no footnotes, for which he was roundly
condemned. (Mayer claimed they would have distracted readers and
inhibited serious reflection.) But the most substantial criticism of the
book centered on his argument about Judeo-Bolshevism and the
origins of the Holocaust. One of his most prominent opponents was
historian Lucy Dawidowicz, who published a scathing review in
Commentary. In her view, *Why Did the Heavens Not Darken?* was
"perverse." Mayer, she insisted, had simply gotten Hitler wrong.
Looking for context in the Führer's anti-Communism or in the course
of the war against the Soviet Union, Dawidowicz said, drew attention
away from the real cause of the Final Solution: "the unique complex
of racial ideas that fueled Hitler and his Germany." This terrible mis-
interpretation had profound moral consequences, she argued. *Why
Did the Heavens Not Darken?* "dedemonize[d] Hitler, normalize[d]
his dictatorship and substitute[d] rational political goals for the Nazis'
fanatically racist agenda." Mayer's view was more than the result of
an error in source interpretation. It was a denial of the Holocaust's
status as radical evil.[24]

A young Daniel Goldhagen echoed Dawidowicz's acid critique.
Best known today as the author of the 1996 book *Hitler's Willing
Executioners*, Goldhagen was a doctoral candidate at Harvard Uni-
versity at the time. His own review of *Why Did the Heavens Not
Darken?* was his first important published essay. In it, Goldhagen
also insisted that Mayer had fundamentally misunderstood the essence
of Nazi ideology. Antisemitism was not grafted onto anti-Communism.
It was the center of Adolf Hitler's worldview. "The Jews were a trans-

historical, demoniacal evil; and Bolshevism was but one manifestation of it," Goldhagen wrote. The Holocaust was not sublimated anti-Bolshevism triggered by the prospect of defeat. It was genocide motivated by anti-Jewish hate. According to Goldhagen, Mayer had made the same mistake as Ernst Nolte. Both had "misconstrued the relationship between the Nazis' anti-Bolshevism and their slaughter of Jews." Despite the differences between the two—"Nolte really does want to exculpate the Nazis[;] Mayer does not," he wrote—their work "issues in the same result": to "dedemonize Nazism" and "transform the Nazis into just another brutal regime: different in degree, but not in kind." In this way, the Holocaust became "just another horrible event in this century's flow of misery."[25]

More devastating criticism came from historian Christopher Browning. In many ways, Browning had little in common with Dawidowicz and Goldhagen. His research on the origins of the Final Solution had helped to refute many of the claims that Lucy Dawidowicz had made about it over the course of her career. A few years later he would become Goldhagen's rival in a debate that played out in North America and Europe about the motives of the German killers. But Browning's 1989 assessment of Mayer's book mirrored the other two critiques in revealing ways. He, too, felt that Mayer had gone wrong because he "did not take Hitler's racism seriously." He said Mayer had found any number of reasons to explain why Jews were killed except "the most simple and obvious: They were killed because they were Jews." This error led Mayer to the wrong conclusions about when and how the Holocaust began. He did not see that the mass murders of Jews committed earlier, "at the height of victory euphoria," already fit into a pattern of genocide. But there was also a larger issue. "Ultimately," Browning wrote, "Mayer does not believe there was a Final Solution, if one understands that Nazi euphemism to mean a conscious Nazi policy aimed at the systematic extermination of every last Jew in Europe." Browning said Mayer had wanted to put the Holocaust in a wider historical context. In reality, he wrote, he redefined it.[26]

Ernst Nolte and Arno Mayer took up the theme of Judeo-Bolshevism for different reasons. Nolte wanted to change the way that (West) Germans remembered the war. He viewed the idea of Judeo-Bolshevism as a device to reestablish fear of Soviet tyranny as a historical force that helped to explain what the Germans had done. Nazi propaganda may have incessantly stoked anti-Soviet fears, but Nolte insisted that those fears had been sincerely felt by Germans, nonetheless. With his interventions in the *Historikerstreit* and afterward, Nolte aimed to validate that terror and make it a topic that West Germans could discuss openly once more. In this way, he hoped to inspire a historical memory of the war based on the national experience of Germans rather than on a transatlantic consensus about the moral significance of the Holocaust. (It should be noted that German ideas of national belonging were themselves remade in the Nazi era through the violent exclusion of Jews.[27] Ernst Nolte devoted little space to this issue in his writings.)

Arno Mayer, by contrast, wanted to change the way people remembered the Holocaust. In a later essay, he wrote that "the exaggerated self-centeredness, if not entrenchment, of the Jewish memory of the Judeocide" had made Holocaust memory static and "inflexible."[28] Echoing French debates about the uniqueness of the Holocaust, Mayer argued that an exclusive focus on the "unfathomable barbarity of the Nazis and the monstrous degradation and suffering of the victims" had prevented public acknowledgment of the memories of others who had suffered under Nazi rule, as well as those who suffered from terror and violence in other times and other places.[29] In short, the ritualistic invocations of Holocaust commemoration had become a "withdrawal from history rather than a commitment to it." Mayer stated emphatically that he did not want to betray the memory of the Jewish victims. By arguing that the Holocaust had emerged from the push and pull of different political and ideological factors, ultimately crystallizing in a crusade against "Judeobolshevism," he wanted instead to "desacralize" it. Historicizing the Holocaust would, he believed, "re-universalize" Holocaust memory and empower it to illuminate other instances of barbarism in history.

Ernst Nolte and Arno Mayer were motivated by diametrically opposed political commitments. But the controversies that exploded around their analyses of the idea of Judeo-Bolshevism and its role in the Nazi war against the Soviet Union reflected the shared context of global Holocaust memory in which both took place. In the twilight of the Cold War, comparing Nazi and Soviet violence, or imagining an interaction between them, was a perilous undertaking, one that raised immediate suspicions (entirely justified, in Ernst Nolte's case) that a desire to marginalize or minimize the Holocaust lay behind the comparison. Examining the entanglement of Nazi and Soviet violence during wartime also made it increasingly difficult to conceptualize the Holocaust as a distinct historical event, upending arguments on which its status as the paradigmatic genocide rested. The similarity of the criticisms leveled at Nolte and Mayer also reflected the power of Holocaust memory as civic pedagogy, both in the United States and, even more so, in the Federal Republic of Germany.[30] Proper understanding of the Holocaust had a pedagogical function. It taught liberal democrats how to act in the world. West Germany was the model pupil. The struggle to "master the past" there had shaped a vibrant democratic culture that made it an example to the rest of Europe.

After 1989 these lessons were extended to the newly independent states of Eastern Europe. There, however, they collided with other memories and a radically different political landscape. The spread of Holocaust memory to Europe's post-Communist societies propelled the idea of Judeo-Bolshevism to the center of a politically charged debate about the twentieth century and its legacy for the future.

The fall of the Iron Curtain made it possible at last to speak openly about injustices committed by Communist regimes across Eastern Europe. New revelations about secret police forces and their extensive networks of spies and informers, the treatment of prisoners in Communist jails, and the horrors of Stalin-era labor camps and detention centers riveted the public's attention. So did fresh accounts of the duplicity and force that Communist parties across the region had used to eliminate their rivals, strangle civil society, and take power in the late 1940s. The fact that prominent figures among the new post-Communist media, business, and even political elites had enjoyed advantages under the old regime also raised concerns that the revolutions of 1989 had been incomplete. The legacy of Communism continued to exert a powerful influence. Many political leaders and civic activists insisted that confronting the history of the Communist period was the most important civic and moral challenge facing the newly independent societies in the former Eastern bloc.

But the end of Communist rule empowered other kinds of historical memory as well. For decades the murders of Eastern European Jews had been either suppressed or distorted by official ideology into crimes committed by nameless (or foreign) fascists. Calls for a more honest reflection on the force of antisemitic politics in the region, the historical richness of Eastern European Jewish life, and its violent erasure in the Holocaust had been heard only rarely.[31] After 1989 Eastern European liberals welcomed the opportunity to expand on earlier efforts and to promote public commemorations of the Holocaust. At the same time, researchers in Western Europe and North America eagerly visited newly opened archives in Eastern Europe and the former Soviet Union in search of unexamined sources on the genocide, in the process shifting the focus away from Berlin and the centers of Nazi decision making to the regional theaters of the Holocaust where most of the Jewish victims lived and were killed, and shedding new light on the complex interactions between Nazi occupiers and local people across Eastern Europe.[32] Together, these developments raised hopes on both sides of the Atlantic that a shared confrontation with the history of the destruction of European Jews could help to forge a new European identity grounded in a shared respect for toleration, multicultural diversity, and human rights.[33]

The collision of these two historical and moral agendas produced furious debates. Although specific arguments varied from one national context to another, the explosive dynamic that sparked them reflected the transnational force of Holocaust-memory politics in post-1989 Europe. And in many places—including Hungary, Romania, and Poland—the idea of Judeo-Bolshevism, transformed for a world after Communism, emerged at the center.

The controversy surrounding a visit by Elie Wiesel to Romania in 1991 revealed the international dimensions of these arguments in an especially striking way. In Europe and North America, Wiesel, an Auschwitz survivor, was the best-known champion for the moral power of Holocaust memory. The Norwegian Nobel Committee, in awarding him the Nobel Peace Prize in 1986, had declared Wiesel a "messenger to mankind," citing the moral strength that his experience gave to his writings and to his humanitarian work. The committee's laudations echoed Wiesel's own belief that the lessons of the Holocaust transcended the boundaries of nation-states and spoke to all humanity. "When human lives are endangered," Wiesel said when he accepted the prize in Oslo, "when human dignity is in jeopardy, national borders and sensitivities become irrelevant."[34] Wiesel took this message with him to Romania, where he spoke in July 1991 at the commemoration of the fiftieth anniversary of the Iași pogrom. The brutal slaughter that had taken place there in 1941 had been the first act in the Holocaust in Romania. Wiesel, who was born in the Romanian city of Sighet in 1928, went there to remember the suffering of the victims. He also went to call on Romanians to face their dark history.

Wiesel's somber reflections in Iași about the burden of memory were rudely interrupted. In the middle of his address, a woman rose in the audience to tell him that he lied. The Jews, she shouted, "did not die!" Then she attacked the purpose for Wiesel's presence. "We will not allow ourselves to be insulted by foreigners in our country!" The outburst caused pandemonium in the hall. Some members of the audience tried to shout her down. Others demanded that she be heard. After the talk was over, the mayor of Iaşi apologized to Wiesel and tried to reassure him that the woman did not express the "real sentiments of Romanians." The chief rabbi of Romania, Moses Rosen, who had organized the commemoration, furiously denounced her as a "fascist provocateur." Nationalists responded by attacking the rabbi for slandering the Romanian people, provoking the very anti-semitism that he complained of, and collaborating with the former Communist regime. They also denied that Romanians were responsible for the Iaşi pogrom and insinuated that the rabbi was involved in an international anti-Romanian plot. Romania's president, Ion Iliescu, who had sent an anodyne statement of welcome to the Iaşi commemoration, tried to calm the waters by touting his own antifascist convictions. But he also put some of the blame for the furor on Rabbi Rosen, criticizing him for saying that the "Holocaust had started in Romania," which Iliescu believed was an error that antisemites had easily exploited.[35]

The incident portended the explosion of antisemitism in the public discourse of post-Communist Romania. Like their counterparts in other post-Communist societies in Eastern Europe, nationalist politicians in Romania maneuvered to distinguish themselves from their rivals and to obscure their own personal histories during the previous decades of Communist rule. As they did so, many found that employing anti-Jewish language and symbols was a useful way to separate themselves from the Communist past and to establish their credentials as defenders of national sovereignty in the face of international critics urging Romania's new leaders to undertake political, social, and economic reforms to bring the country into line with the expectations of Western-style liberalism. The fact that leaders of the hated regime of Nicolae Ceauşescu had used antisemitism in the very same instrumental way—to distance themselves from the errors of their (Stalinist) predecessors and to establish their identity as national Communists rather than cosmopolitan outsiders—was an irony that few of them acknowledged.

A striking example of the cynical manipulation of anti-Jewish rhetoric comes from Corneliu Vadim Tudor's Greater Romania Party, one of the most prominent extreme Right parties in early 1990s Romania. Tudor, who also helped to found a newspaper of the same name, *Greater Romania,* had been a prominent intellectual with close ties to the Communist dictator Ceauşescu. Both the party and the newspaper mixed antisemitism and anti-Hungarian racism with nostalgia for the intensely nationalistic line that the Romanian Communist Party had taken in the 1970s and 1980s. Tudor and his party positioned themselves after 1989 as a leading voice of the far-right opposition by denouncing the disruptions of the transition as a "Jewish plot" and distinguishing between the positive (patriotic) and negative ("Jewish") aspects of the old regime. Meanwhile, *Greater Romania* and publications like it spun a toxic web of articles purporting to reveal the guiding hand of Jews in Romania's political fortunes, none of them more ludicrous than the story of "evidence" revealing that Ceauşescu's wife, Elena, who had also been deputy prime minister, was a Jew whose "real" maiden name was Kohn. According to *Greater Romania,* Elena Ceauşescu had been an instrument of a Jewish conspiracy that had brought Communism to power and then weakened her husband when he tried to strengthen national pride, tame the Hungarian minority, and eliminate cosmopolitanism. At the end, the paper claimed, she had served the Jewish conspiracy again by helping to engineer the collapse of Communism. Based on this nonsensical story, the newspaper concluded that it had been "Jews who brought Ceauşescu to power and Jews who liquidated him."[36]

The outburst that disrupted Elie Wiesel's speech in Iaşi also reflected efforts to revive older forms of anti-Communism, once dominant in the first half of the twentieth century, and rehabilitate them for the new environment. The woman who heckled Elie Wiesel was later identified as the daughter of Colonel Dumitru Captaru, who had been prefect in Iaşi in 1941 and an actor in the pogrom. Now the nationalism of her father's day was in favor again. Post-Communist nationalists had turned back to the years when Captaru was prefect, in their search for new national heroes and a more usable past. The centerpiece of their efforts was the public rehabilitation of Marshal Ion Antonescu, Romania's dictator during World War II, whom post-Communist nationalists recast as a great patriot, a brave anti-Communist, and an icon of national strength. In this spirit, civic organizations formed to preserve and promote Antonescu's memory by erecting statues of him and by organizing public events to discuss his achievements.

However, rehabilitating Antonescu gave new legitimacy to the threat of Judeo-Bolshevism that the marshal had feared so greatly in his lifetime. In the last years of the Communist regime, nationalistic party ideologues had already begun to advance a historical agenda that openly revived the antisemitic views of the 1930s.[37] The new Antonescu cult rested on this foundation, even as it was used to put distance between its champions and the Communist past. But it went further. As enthusiasts for Antonescu's memory began to redefine his political career, they also validated the racialized security fears that had inspired or inflected so many of his policies. Antonescu's order to identify all "Yids and Communist agents or sympathizers" on the Romanian-Soviet border had been a crucial prelude to the 1941 Iaşi pogrom.[38] Similarly, ethnonationalist security concerns about Jewish Bolshevik agents had been a major justification for the deportation or execution of Jews in Bessarabia and Bukovina when Romanian forces reoccupied those regions in the months after the pogrom. Antonescu's defenders now sought to explain all this away, even as they intimated that his fears about Jews and Bolshevism might have been rational and possibly prudent. Through their efforts, Antonescu's memory was transformed. In 1946 the marshal had been executed as a war criminal. In 1991, the Romanian parliament observed a minute of silence in his honor.[39]

In his address in Iaşi, Elie Wiesel addressed these developments. He spoke about the resurgence of antisemitism in the new Romania and addressed the new Antonescu cult specifically, deploring the country's official gesture of respect for a war criminal. Even more important, he warned his audience in Iaşi about the power of world opinion and the negative impression that such public expressions of antisemitism by politicians and public figures were making on it. "Your image is not the best. You must know that. You must know that unless these anti-Semites are shamed in society, you will suffer. You will be isolated. The world is following with astonishment, dismay, and outrage."[40] Reviving old fears of an alien Jewish threat and reconfiguring the idea of Judeo-Bolshevism as a new cosmopolitan threat to Romanian national sovereignty, Wiesel suggested, cast doubt on the prospects for the country's post-Communist transition to democracy.

Wiesel's words echoed across the Atlantic. In a letter to the *New York Times*, Harvey Meyerhoff, chairman of the United States Holocaust Memorial Council that was charged by Congress with raising funds for the construction of a Holocaust museum on the National Mall in Washington, D.C., declared that "the confusion of anti-Communism with the veneration of anti-Semitic, xenophobic and fascist regimes" served only to erect a new barrier around Romania—a barrier "of lies"—in place of the old Iron Curtain.[41] After Wiesel returned to the United States, he repeated his criticism that the revival of antisemitism stained Romania's reputation around the world. His words were heeded on Capitol Hill. Within a month the U.S. Congress produced a joint resolution condemning the antisemitism in Romania and the treatment that Wiesel had received. The resolution called on the Romanian government to respect "internationally recognized human rights," promote pluralism, and curb organizations that spread ethnic and religious intolerance.[42] The following year, congressional representatives cited the strength of antisemitism in

Romania when the U.S. House of Representatives voted not to extend most-favored-nation status to the country.

In the years that followed, Romanian officials continued to fend off criticism that their reluctance to acknowledge the painful truths about the Holocaust kept the country unfit to join the community of Western liberal societies.[43] The actions taken by the U.S. Congress in response to the 1991 Wiesel affair in Iaşi reflected the widespread belief that countries like Romania, once part of the Soviet bloc, now stood at a crossroads. Eastern and Western Europe, it was widely assumed, were inexorably converging toward a liberal world order made possible by the fall of the Berlin Wall.[44] Romania, like its neighbors, could either move forward and "catch up" to the liberal West, or it could turn back and embrace the past. In this climate, acknowledging historical truths about the Holocaust and finding adequate ways to remember them were taken as representing the region's more fundamental choice between two opposed forms of political order: civic nationalism and ethnic nationalism—the former, a pluralist vision of patriotic citizenship inspired by optimistic readings of Anglo-American political theory; the latter, a fantasy of racial communitarianism that had fueled the Holocaust at midcentury and was erupting again in the brutal civil war raging in the former Yugoslavia.[45]

In the new liberal order, history, told responsibly by scholars inside and outside of the region and validated by the sober pronouncements of political leaders, was assumed to have the power to free societies from the ghosts of the past and from xenophobic fantasies of lost national greatness. A pathbreaking 2004 document titled *Final Report of the International Commission on the Holocaust in Romania* was designed to do exactly that—establish the facts about the Holocaust in Romania and signal the country's commitment to democratic values.[46] It incorporated the most up-to-date research at the time, by internationally respected scholars. And it debunked a number of persistent and pernicious slanders that were common currency on the antiliberal nationalist Right, including the accusation that all Romanian Jews had supported Communism. But even this report, as comprehensive and well-researched as it was, was itself a product of the politics of Holocaust memory. The year before, Iliescu, back in power, had declared that there had been no Holocaust in Romania. Afterward, needing to make amends with diplomatic partners in Western Europe and the United States, he readily agreed to form the International Commission on the Holocaust in Romania, and charged it with telling the truth about the past. (Fittingly, Iliescu named Elie Wiesel to head the commission.)[47]

By the 1990s, the public forms and political expectations of Holocaust commemoration had become an international regime of remembrance that spanned the Atlantic Ocean. In the aftermath of the 1989 revolutions in Eastern Europe, they also become powerful signs of the political transition from Communist rule, representing moral values symbolically linked to the spread of liberal democracy, the extension of market capitalism, and European integration. But this same correlation between Holocaust commemoration and neoliberal expansion gave memory politics across the region an intensity it did not have in the West. Amid debates about how to strike the right balance between acknowledging the genocide of Europe's Jews and recalling other kinds of suffering—above all, suffering caused by the crimes of Communist regimes—the demands of Holocaust memory were frequently juxtaposed with another form of collective memory: national memory. The spread of Holocaust memory to a region newly freed from Communist rule sparked intense competition over what to remember as a nation and a people and who had the authority to decide. At the end of the twentieth century, having the power to define a nation's memory of its past had become a question of sovereignty. It was a question in which the problem of Judeo-Bolshevism loomed large.

An example from Hungary illustrates this dynamic. In September 1990, a prominent writer named Sándor Csoóri published excerpts from his diary in a journal linked to the nationalist party that headed Hungary's first post-Communist government. In the most explosive and widely quoted passage, Csoóri claimed that "today we are experiencing a reverse assimilationist trend. It is no longer the Hungarian nation that wishes to assimilate the Jews, but liberal Jewry that wishes to assimilate the Hungarian nation. For that purpose it possesses a more powerful weapon than it has ever possessed, namely, the parliamentary system."[48]

Csoóri arrived at this startling conclusion by arguing that history had driven Hungarians and Jews apart. But Csoóri did not lay the blame for this turn of events on the Holocaust alone. Instead, he placed the Holocaust, in which more than 500,000 Jewish Hungarians died, within a longer process of separation that had begun with the Hungarian Soviet Republic in 1919. According to Csoóri, Béla Kun and his fellow Jewish commissars poisoned relations between the two groups when they took power. Their misdeeds began a cycle of recrimination that destroyed the "spiritual and emotional bonds" between Hungarians and Jews and made it impossible for Jews to truly feel Hungarian suffering. This fateful severing had historic consequences in the present. Writing in 1990, Sándor Csoóri said he believed that liberal Jews now promoted a "style and thinking" that were critically opposed to a strong and proud national consciousness.[49]

Highly regarded in literary circles as a poet, an essayist, and the greatest living successor to an earlier generation of "populist" (or ethnonationalist) writers, Sándor Csoóri was a founding member in 1987 of the Hungarian Democratic Forum, a group of mostly nationalist intellectuals that became a political party and formed Hungary's first post-Communist government in 1990.[50] On one level, Csoóri's views on liberal Jewish power were taken as criticism of a political rival, the liberal Free Democrats. Like Csoóri's Hungarian Democratic Forum, the Free Democrats were born in the dissident intellectual circles of late Communist Hungary. In those years, all opponents of the Communist regime shared a common demand for political pluralism. But even then it was possible to discern among them subtle distinctions in orientation.[51] Where writers like Csoóri tended to imagine freedom in collective and ethnonational terms, the dissidents who gravitated toward the Free Democrats talked about it as a set of individual rights and civic values that Hungarians shared with liberal democrats in "Europe" or the "West."[52] It was also known that some of the prominent figures associated with the Free Democrats were Jewish. As the Communist state withered away, the intellectual differences among Hungary's dissidents found party-political expression in the Hungarian Democratic Forum and the rival Free Democrats. These two products of the same late-Communist dissident milieu vied to chart Hungary's post-Communist future. As the lines between the two camps hardened, Csoóri was not alone in alluding to the Jewish identity of some of his liberal opponents, in an effort to discredit liberalism as antinational.

But Csoóri's fear of "reverse assimilation" was not simply a shot across the political aisle. It was, more important, a commentary on the content of collective memory in post-Communist Hungary. Hungarians and Jews, Csoóri suggested, remembered different things about the twentieth century because they had experienced different (but—in his view—equivalent) tragedies. The Holocaust, he implied, was a Jewish catastrophe, and the scars that it left marked Jewish memory. According to Csoóri, Hungarians had suffered collective traumas of their own. Foremost in his mind was the 1920 Treaty of Trianon that had partitioned the former Kingdom of Hungary, forcibly divided the Hungarian people, and made Hungarians living outside the borders into ethnic minorities in their new countries. A passionate advocate for Hungarian minority rights, Csoóri had been at the forefront of efforts to publicize the persecution that ethnic Hungarians in Romania experienced in the 1980s at the hands of the repressive and nationalistic Communist regime of Nicolae Ceauşescu. Csoóri claimed that Hungary's Jews simply could not feel this pain, because Hungary's Jewish Bolsheviks had fatefully launched a cycle of violence that had separated Hungarians and Jews into different communities with different experiences and fates. When Csoóri said that "liberal Jewry" wanted to "assimilate" the Hungarian nation, he meant in part that liberals wanted to treat the particularistic memory of Jewish suffering as a universal norm.

Csoóri's defenders expanded on this idea. They insisted that excessive focus on the suffering of Jews in the Holocaust had created a hierarchy of victims that silenced the public memory of Hungarian trauma. Some of them focused their attention, as Csoóri had, on the plight of ethnic Hungarian minorities, and imagined that the suppression of Hungarian culture in Transylvania under Communist rule amounted to a genocide worthy of the same attention as the Holocaust. As one put it: "To us, who live in this country, the Holocaust of 6–700,000 Jews is also painful, but so is the planned genocide of 3 million Hungarians. The fact is that the Jewish Holocaust has been repeatedly mentioned since the 1970s. But the fact that for decades there has been a constant elimination of Magyardom—not just 50 years ago, but today, as well!—has received not a word in the mass media."[53]

Others expanded the argument to encompass the memory of Communist crimes more explicitly, agreeing with Csoóri that Jewish support for Communism had been the fateful act that now prevented Hungarians and Jews from understanding the history of the twentieth century in the same way. One wrote, "Hungarian-Jewish relations were poisoned not by Nazism, but by Bolshevism." He then went on to explain that although he did truly "understand" and "regret" the suffering that Jews had experienced during the Holocaust, he was also appalled by the cruelty of Jewish revenge after 1945. After joining the Communist Party following the war, Jews became "just as vile as the fascists and became so accustomed to depredation that they could not stop."[54]

Csoóri's words, as well as the endorsement they received from his supporters, ignited a storm of outrage. Critics condemned Csoóri's nightmarish vision of "reverse assimilation" as blatantly racist, an insulting view that revived toxic, xenophobic stereotypes—familiar from the years between the world wars—of Jews as aliens and outsiders whose rise to power spelled the demise of a traditional Hungarian way of life. They also rejected Csoóri's position as undemocratic because it slandered liberal democracy as a "Jewish" (and thus foreign) form of government. Imre Kertész, author of the Holocaust novel *Fatelessness* and winner of the Nobel Prize for Literature in 2002, warned that acts of discrimination were the logical consequence of this type of language. Another writer, Ottó Orbán, also deplored Csoóri's decision to label his opponents as Jews and said it put him on the same side of history as Josef Mengele. The leading historian of the Holocaust in Hungary included an excerpt of Csoóri's text in a collection of antisemitic writings on Hungarian history that he titled *Kirekesztők* (Excluders). Yet another writer, Péter Esterházy, wrote of the serious consequences that Csoóri's words might have for both the moral fabric of Hungary's young democracy and its place and reputation in the wider world. If they were not rejected and declared outside the bounds of acceptable public discourse, then Hungary would not only "fail to have Europe," he wrote, but "fail to have Christianity as well."[55]

In many ways, the Hungarian debate mirrored the intense contemporaneous discussion among French intellectuals about the power of Holocaust memory. In both places, critics like those who rose to defend Csoóri maintained that the memory of Jewish suffering enjoyed an unquestioned moral authority that drowned out the voices of those who had experienced traumas at the hands of ideologies other than Nazism. Their opponents worried that this stance would ultimately diminish the importance of Nazi crimes and stifle efforts to understand how they happened and who was responsible for them. But there were important differences amid the basic rhetorical similarity of the French and Hungarian controversies. French skeptics of Holocaust memory arrived at their views through reflection on the idea of humanity, and concluded that Communism deserved opprobrium because it, at least potentially, targeted all humankind.[56] Hungarian intellectuals, such as Sándor Csoóri, were motivated primarily by national considerations, taking issue with the hegemony of Holocaust memory because it allowed the trauma of one people (Jews) to drown out the cries of another (Hungarians). And the legacy of local Communist rule in countries like Hungary gave reflections about Jewish memory and the Holocaust a more explosive partisan potential than they had in the West. When critics like Csoóri wrote of "liberal Jews" who wanted to assimilate Hungarians into their style and way of thinking, they were speaking about the political future as much as the past. In Hungary and outside of it, liberals tied Holocaust memory to the promise of "Europeanization," which meant a sweeping array of political, economic, and sociocultural changes. Rejecting calls to acknowledge the Holocaust as a defining event in Hungary's national history (rather than a tragedy that had befallen others—Jews) was also a way to oppose that liberal vision. Jews and Jewish memory were thus easily associated with Communism in the past and liberalism in the present.

One final and much more recent example from Hungary demonstrates this point clearly. In 2014 Hungary's nationalist Fidesz (Fiatal Demokraták Szövetsége, or Alliance of Young Democrats) government erected a monument "to the victims of German occupation" in the country. (Nazi Germany occupied Hungary in 1944.) The sculpture—of an eagle, representing Germany, attacking the archangel Gabriel, who symbolizes Hungary—immediately came under fire for obscuring the particular fate that Hungary's Jews had experienced under Nazi occupation, and for suppressing the role that Hungarians played in the persecution, looting, and ghettoization of their Jewish fellow citizens. Outside Hungary, the monument drew critical attention in the United States, Israel, and among the member states of the European Union. In response, progovernment intellectuals defended the monument as a sincere expression of national feeling. One such figure was historian Mária Schmidt. The twentieth century, Schmidt declared, was "rich in tragedies," but Hungary's liberal critics had sympathy for only one of them: the Holocaust. She noted that in the very same square where the new monument stands, a 1946 memorial to the Red Army commemorates "invading Soviet soldiers who raped more than a hundred thousand Hungarian women while pillaging and terrorizing the country." Why were liberal champions of democracy and Holocaust memory not protesting that memorial, she asked. Part of the answer, Schmidt insinuated, had to do with the identity of the government's critics. "We are at a point," she wrote, "where some groups would like to consider their ancestors' tragic fate an inheritable and advantageous privilege. . . . They prescribe empathy, then close their hearts, remaining deaf and blind to the pain of others. And so, because they act as if our national mourning can have no palliative effect on tragedies past, they exclude themselves from our national community." Schmidt named no names but went on to describe the attitude of liberal critics as "cosmopolitan," "internationalist" and "flat-out anti-nation."[57]

Years after Sándor Csoóri's 1990 article, the battle lines around history and national memory remained much as he had sketched them. The controversy around the Budapest occupation memorial demonstrates how powerful the memory of Communism was in shaping debates about the history of Nazi brutality. In this context, the theory of totalitarianism seemed to offer a persuasive way to compare the impacts of Nazism and Communism. But research into the totalitarian past invariably sparked political controversies, in Hungary and elsewhere, that tied questions of empirical fact (who did what to whom, and when) to larger disagreements about the status (and sovereignty, both cultural and political) of Eastern Europe's nations within the transatlantic liberal order. At these moments, the matter of Jews and Communism played an outsize role.

Since 1989 totalitarianism has served as a powerful framing device for discussions of the historical memory of the twentieth century in

Eastern Europe.[58] In many ways, the occupation memorial in Budapest is a thoroughly antitotalitarian site of memory, since it claims to capture the moment when—according to the country's 2011 constitution—foreign occupiers robbed Hungary of its sovereignty, which the country did not regain until after the collapse of Communism. Similarly, the House of Terror museum in Budapest, headed by historian Mária Schmidt, intentionally juxtaposes Hungarian fascism and Communism in its permanent exhibition to present both as cruel systems of terror. In Romania, debates about Communist crimes were an important part of the context behind the creation of the International Commission on the Holocaust in Romania in 2003.[59] (Three years later, a Presidential Commission for the Analysis of the Communist Dictatorship in Romania was created, to produce a similar analysis of the Communist regime.) Of course, little explicit mention was made of Communism in the Wiesel Commission's *Final Report on the Holocaust*. But when President Iliescu introduced that report on Romania's first-ever Holocaust Remembrance Day, he declared that Romania had emerged from the "darkness of totalitarianism" and that the country was now embarked "on a long and not so easy road to the recovery of memory and the assumption of responsibility, in keeping with the moral and political values grounding its new status as a democratic country, a dignified member of the Euro-Atlantic community." Remembering the Holocaust, he said, gave Romanians "occasion to meditate on totalitarianism and its tragic consequences, on community relations and values of human solidarity, on the perenniality of democracy, legality, and the respect of fundamental citizen rights and liberties."[60]

In both Romania and Hungary, the theory of totalitarianism only partly fit the historical record. Nazi Germany never occupied Romania, which remained an independent state throughout the war. Its government was xenophobic and antisemitic, but nothing like the Nazi state in form and organization. (For this reason, the authors of the Wiesel commission's report had used the word "totalitarian" more cautiously than President Iliescu did, reserving it mainly for describing genocidal antisemitism as "totalitarian" propaganda.) Hungary was occupied by Nazi Germany in 1944. But the government that was formed after the Germans arrived and ruled between March and October of that year could hardly be described as a puppet regime. Considered legitimate by the vast majority of Hungary's social elite, it retained considerable power to shape many aspects of domestic policy—including, especially, Jewish policy. In July 1944 the Hungarian regent decided to halt the deportations of Hungarian Jews to Auschwitz. The SS in Hungary was too weak to overrule him. Only in October 1944, when deportations to Auschwitz were long over, did German occupiers depose the government and install a slavishly loyal fascist government that ruled with anarchic brutality during the very last months of the war.

In Poland, as in the rest of what historian Timothy Snyder has named Europe's "bloodlands," the situation was very different.[61] Caught between the Soviet Union and Nazi Germany, Poland was divided between the two in 1939 and then occupied by Germany alone after 1941. Soviet and Nazi occupation regimes destroyed the Polish state and devastated Polish society, albeit in different ways and according to different ideological prescriptions. A similar fate befell Lithuania and the other Baltic states, occupied by the Soviet Union in 1940, then by Nazi Germany in 1941, and again by Soviet forces at the end of World War II. In this part of Europe, the relationship between Nazism and Communism was not simply diachronic, it was interactive. Nazi occupiers took power in societies that had already been radically remade by Soviet authorities. In turn, Soviet forces returned a few years later to reassert authority over regions that had been under the brutal thumb of Nazi violence. Traumatic memories of life under both occupation regimes made comparisons of the two systems inevitable and also more politically charged than elsewhere.

The furor surrounding the publication, in 2000, of historian Jan Tomasz Gross's book *Neighbors* brought this issue to the fore, producing what is to date the most significant debate about Holocaust memory in post-Communist Eastern Europe.[62] The book recounts the vicious murder of Jews by Poles in the eastern Polish town of Jedwabne in the first days after the Germans drove Soviet occupiers from the region and established their own occupation regime in their place. The story that Gross told was graphic. He described how the townspeople taunted and humiliated the town's Jews, forced them into the barn of a local farmer, and then set it aflame. Then, Gross wrote, after they had burned alive everyone inside, they plundered their Jewish neighbors' homes for valuables. Gross based his work on a variety of sources, including interrogation records from a 1949 trial and the 1945 testimony from one of the only seven Jewish survivors of the massacre. The accounts he found starkly contradicted the findings of the investigation done in the early 1970s that concluded the Germans had been solely responsible.[63] They also ran counter to the narrative of events publicly asserted by many in Jedwabne and the surrounding area, both those old enough to have been eyewitnesses and their children, which tended to suppress the involvement of locals in the killing, throw blame on German occupiers, and highlight the role that the perceived sympathy of local Jews for Soviet occupation between 1939 and 1941 had played in stirring up anti-Jewish sentiment in the region. Most important, Gross's reconstruction of events exploded the widely held myth that Poles had been only victims during the German wartime occupation and ignited a furious debate about the responsibility of Poles for the murders of Jews during the Holocaust. In time, the book provoked an official investigation, led to government commemorations of the victims, and inspired important historical research into violence committed by Poles against Jews during the war. The book also energized what are ongoing efforts to remember and reaffirm the central place that Jews have played in Polish history.[64]

Neighbors was a work of historical research, but it was immediately read in civic and moral terms as well. Gross's supporters welcomed the book for starting a painful conversation about a dark chapter in the national past that they believed—much in the way that Jürgen Habermas had during the West German *Historikerstreit* nearly fifteen years earlier—would contribute to building a more democratic and pluralist national society. Speaking for many, Hanna Świeda-Ziemba, a professor at the University of Warsaw, wrote that Poles had a "moral obligation not just to accept the truth about Jedwabne into our consciousness and make a series of symbolic gestures." She also declared that public remembrance of Jedwabne should become a "source for reflection" that opened a "new chapter in our self-knowledge." The Jedwabne massacre showed the violent potential that lurked within even the most innocuous forms of anti-Jewish prejudice. "Jedwabne serves as a warning for the people of today," Świeda-Ziemba wrote.[65] In this spirit, Polish president Aleksander Kwaśniewski commemorated the sixtieth anniversary of the massacre at a public ceremony in Jedwabne. "We have come to realize," he stated, "that we are responsible for our attitude toward the black pages of history. We have understood that those who counsel the nation to deny this past serve the nation ill. Such an attitude leads to moral self-destruction."[66]

Not everyone shared this vision.[67] Critics raised historical or methodological objections, accusing Gross of misreading sources, giving too much credence to the voices of lone Jewish survivors instead of the chorus of Polish testimonies that offered a different story, and underestimating the role that the Germans played on that horrible day. For many of them, Gross's approach to the problem of Judeo-Bolshevism was especially problematic. In *Neighbors*, Gross argued that there was no empirical evidence of widespread Jewish euphoria when Soviet forces occupied eastern Poland in 1939. And he concluded that sources to the contrary were, on closer analysis, typically little more than clichéd stereotypes and observations that could be used to confirm anything at all, such as a "group of Jewish children marching down the street," a "Jew who worked in the post office," or a Jew who "spoke arrogantly to a passerby in the street."[68] But Gross's critics insisted that collective Polish memories of Jewish collaboration with Soviet occupiers reflected reality, and were decisive for understanding anti-Jewish violence in 1941 eastern Poland. Antoni Macierewicz, a historian and former opposition activist who became a prominent figure on the new Polish Right after 1989, derided Gross's preference for the voices of the few Jewish survivors over the numerous accounts, given by Poles in written testimony from the period and in present-day oral histories, that testified to Jewish support for the Soviet occupation. According to Macierewicz, those sources showed that "Jews played the role of a 'fifth column'" when Soviet forces occupied eastern Poland in 1939, and that they were driven by a "terrible hatred toward Poland" and a thirst for "cruel revenge on Poles."[69] Tomasz Strzembosz, one of Gross's chief critics among historians, made a similar argument. He asserted that an unspecified number of Jewish revolts against Polish authorities in the days before the Soviet takeover in 1939 had been tantamount to "armed collaboration" and "treason" against the Polish state "during the days of defeat."[70] Historian Bogdan Musiał agreed, and insisted that Gross had "glossed over" the fact that the presence of Jews in the Soviet occupation apparatus caused a "distinct rise" in the popular fear and loathing of Jews in Poland.[71]

But opposition to the book extended well beyond questions of source criticism or historiographic practice. Some of Gross's opponents saw *Neighbors* as part of a broader international assault on the nation, its memory, and its identity. Since 1989 right-wing nationalist and Catholic circles had cast "Jewish liberalism" as a menace to Poland's successful post-Communist transition and used it to tarnish their opponents on the left as antinational, cosmopolitan agents of neoliberal social and cultural restructuring.[72] Polish populists understood transnational Holocaust memory in this light, rejecting its moral authority—and the liberal civic pedagogical project so closely associated with it—as an infringement on the nation's cultural sovereignty. They insinuated that calls for deeper public reflection on Polish complicity were simply part of an international (or Jewish, or liberal) agenda to discredit central elements of national culture (such as religion) and erode vital feelings of national honor and esteem.[73] Antoni Macierewicz's critique of *Neighbors* offers one example of this reaction. In his response to the book, Macierewicz did more than take issue with Gross's approach to the problem of Jews and Communism during the Soviet occupation of eastern Poland between 1939 and 1941. He also associated the book with those in "Jewish and liberal circles" who wanted "to prove that the Poles were responsible for the crime of genocide committed against the Jews by the Germans—for the Holocaust." In writing *Neighbors*, Gross had undertaken "a campaign of hatred directed at Poles and Poland," according to Macierewicz, one that abetted the (unnamed) Jewish and liberal voices "calling loudly for the punishment of the Polish nation for its crimes against the Jews."[74]

The hostile responses to *Neighbors* revealed how easily historical debate about Jews and Communism in 1941 eastern Poland could be made into a metonym for current contests over the future of liberalism in post-Communist Eastern Europe. Critics like Macierewicz insisted that sources and memories telling of widespread Jewish support for Communism were true, to discount the authority of Holocaust memory as a universal moral project. They cast it instead as a particularistic Jewish (liberal) memory that sucked attention away from what the Polish nation had endured. The unwillingness to recognize Jewish complicity in Communist crimes, they suggested, was proof that liberals who declared Jews to be victims of genocide without also acknowledging that they were perpetrators of a different great crime were simply hypocrites. The moral authority of Holocaust memory had empowered a liberal political vision that tied Poland and the rest of post-Communist Europe to the West through shared moral values. But even as some in Poland welcomed the publication of *Neighbors* and the ensuing debate about it as a sign of the health and vitality of that liberal civic culture, their opponents took it as a sign that a kind of international "political correctness" had descended on Poland that would strip the nation of its honor and its identity.[75]

After the Cold War and the fall of Communism in Eastern Europe, the myth of Judeo-Bolshevism was translated into memory. No longer a rhetorical tool to discredit or demonize an actual, existing government or political movement, the figure of the Jewish Bolshevik became instead a symbol embedded in debates about how to compare Nazism and Communism, in a region that had experienced both. New research into the Holocaust in Eastern Europe and the Nazi war against the Soviet Union demonstrated the essential entanglement of war and genocide, revealed how the persecution and mass murder of so many different victim groups, including Eastern European Jews, were linked in various ways by the same Nazi racist imperialism, and uncovered the importance of local history, including the history of Soviet occupation, for the course of genocide in specific places in Eastern Europe. These findings inspired empirical research and promised to transform, expand, and enrich histories of the Holocaust and Europe's twentieth century.

However, right-wing populists and nationalist intellectuals across Eastern Europe saw an opportunity in these intellectual developments, recognizing that they necessarily rendered problematic, if not untenable, the conceptual distinction between the Holocaust and the wider war that had been so crucial to the emergence of transnational Holocaust memory in previous decades. The belief that Jews had collaborated with Soviet power had carried ideological and emotional force at crucial moments during World War II and afterward, even when careful historical investigation of specific sources and particular contexts proved that belief to be facile and often false. Voices on the Right ignored this crucial but subtle distinction and insisted that collective memories of Jewish-Soviet collaboration amounted to evidence that the myth of Judeo-Bolshevism had a kernel of truth after all. They used this conclusion to cast the anti-Jewish violence that followed the defeat of Soviet occupiers—in places like Jedwabne in 1941, or Iaşi—as vengeance, and the Jews who were killed in those attacks as implicated participants in a clash of totalitarian systems, rather than blameless victims of paranoid racial hatred that victims of genocide were generally understood to be. And they mobilized the association of Jews and Communism to downplay the importance of the Holocaust for national history and to focus public attention instead on other victims.

In this way, right-wing and populist calls to acknowledge Jews' support for the Communist occupiers, to describe international Holocaust memory culture as a particularistic Jewish memory that silenced other ethnic memories, or even to recognize the victims of a so-called Red Holocaust, functioned much as Ernst Nolte's arguments about a "causal nexus" between Communism and Nazism had worked a generation earlier—as a strategy, using the authority of historical comparison, to minimize, relativize, or deflect attention from the Holocaust and to undermine the kind of national self-reflection its memory was meant to inspire. The Judeo-Bolshevik myth was reborn in post-Communist Europe as a tool for challenging the premises on which transnational memory of the Holocaust rested— and with those premises, the liberal civic ideals of multicultural toleration, human rights, and European integration that Holocaust memory culture had come to symbolize so powerfully.

Epilogue

Jérôme and Jean Tharaud described their departure from Budapest in 1920 in vivid terms. The two authors had gone to Hungary for a few weeks to gather material for what would become *When Israel Is King*, their antisemitic account of the Hungarian Bolshevik revolution and the role that Jews played in it. In the book, as the narrator boards the train to return to France he looks around the Budapest train station one last time and describes seeing crowds of people living in railway cars that had been shunted onto sidetracks overgrown with grass and weeds. In truth, Budapest's train stations were filled with refugees after 1918, many of whom were Hungarian civil servants from the provinces who had fled to the capital when the homes where they lived and the offices where they worked were suddenly in a different country after the former Kingdom of Hungary was divided at the end of World War I.[1] But the Tharauds wanted to write about only one group—Jews from the East. According to the Tharauds, the station was teeming with them. The men, women, and children lived in crowded and fetid train compartments and slept in wagon corridors, always "talking, gesticulating, and shouting." The authors explained that these Jews could not cross the border because no European countries wanted to accept them—so they had formed "a ghetto in the wagons." The Tharauds used this scene to offer some final pathos-laden thoughts about "the eternal wandering Jew." But they gave the last word to a nameless and imaginary Christian Hungarian, who summarizes the argument of the book with a telling comparison. The Muslim Turks who had invaded Hungary in the 1500s, he declares, had been far less dangerous than "the disheveled Jew, who sits there on his dirty traveling sack." In the final sentence, this fictional Hungarian witness concludes with dismay: "The last onslaught of Asiatic peoples has crushed us!".[2]

Nearly a century later, Budapest's Keleti (Eastern) Railway Station was filled with migrants once again. Throughout the summer of 2015, tens of thousands of people fleeing civil war and state collapse in Syria, Iraq, and Afghanistan had journeyed north through the Balkans. They traveled on trains, were smuggled through in the suffocating cargo holds of trucks, or walked slowly northward on foot. Those who reached Budapest's Eastern Station intended to take trains west and north to countries like Germany or Sweden, where they hoped to find refuge, apply for asylum, and build new lives. But Europe's governments refused to admit them, fearing that it would only encourage even more to come. In response, Hungarian officials closed the train station and turned its courtyard into a makeshift camp where the migrants were forced to wait, with their few belongings, amid rapidly deteriorating conditions. The unfolding humanitarian crisis soon forced German authorities to relent, and the migrants were allowed to leave the station and continue their journey. But Germany and other European Union member states immediately began to take measures to halt future waves of migrants who want to enter the European Union. Meanwhile, the Hungarian government blamed the European Union for stoking the crisis through its overly welcoming attitude toward immigrants. It warned that Europe would soon be flooded with millions more immigrants from the Middle East if harsh policing measures were not implemented As proof of their resolve,

Hungarian officials began to build a fence on their southern border to physically prevent people from crossing into their country.

These two scenes are different in many ways. The first comes from a highly problematic travelogue written by two authors who spent their lives writing semifictional accounts of Europe's encounters with dangerous ethnoreligious outsiders. The second was covered by reputable media outlets around the world in the summer and autumn of 2015. When the Tharauds went to Budapest in 1920, Europe's governments were obsessed with the threat of Communist revolution. By 2015, Communist regimes had been gone from the political landscape of Europe for more than twenty-five years. In 1920 the Tharauds and many other Europeans were fearful of the mass influx of Jewish refugees who were fleeing the bloodshed and upheaval of war, civil war, and imperial collapse in Europe's eastern borderlands. The migrants who were desperately trying to reach northern Europe in 2015 were primarily Muslims, escaping civil war and state breakdown in another part of the world. Most important, the Tharauds captured the prevailing sense of political and cultural crisis in post–World War I Europe by describing events in Hungary as the triumph of "Judeo-Bolshevism." That term had no place in debates about Muslim migration to post–Cold War Europe.

Yet eerie similarities connect the two episodes, despite their significant differences. In their book, the Tharauds wrote in glowing phrases about Hungary's traditional national culture as an organic expression of Western civilization. *When Israel Is King* was popular in France precisely because its authors cast Judeo-Bolshevism as a specter that simultaneously threatened individual nations in Europe, like Hungary and France, and Europe itself, imagined as a community of shared values they called Christian Europe, or Western Christendom, or simply the Occident. The two writers also described Judeo-Bolshevism as a powerful fusion of race, religion, and political ideology. According to the Tharauds, Hungary's Jewish revolutionaries had abandoned their ancient religious faith but transformed its messianic ideals into a new and destructive ideology, which now inspired them to transform the world through violence and terror. In the story the Tharauds told, decades of Jewish migration to Hungary had prepared the ground for the political and cultural catastrophe of Bolshevism. It had also produced the revolutionaries who brought that evil to life. These themes, so central to *When Israel Is King*, reflected wider fears that associated Jews and Communism with threats to national sovereignty, social order, and cultural tradition. Across Europe during the period between the two world wars, the figure of the Jewish Bolshevik loomed in many different national contexts as an ethno-ideological enemy who spread mayhem and terror. Nearly a hundred years later, echoes of the fears that crystallized around the Jewish Bolshevik in the first half of the last century could be heard in the first decades of the twenty-first in debates about a new ethnoreligious threat to Europe and Europe's nations: the radical Islamic terrorist.

Current anxieties about the place of Islam in Europe have many sources. These range from the end of Europe's global empires and the upheavals of decolonization, to the post-1945 migration to Europe of laborers and their families from Turkey, South and Southeast Asia, North Africa, and elsewhere, to the debates—raised by the presence in Europe of large Muslim communities (now generations old)—about social and cultural integration, public displays of non-Christian religiosity, and differences in sexual mores.[3] But the language that many Europeans, and not only those on the far right, use to debate the "Muslim question" and the challenges they believe it poses to ideas of national and European identity has roots in older moments of cultural crisis. Examining the ideological function that the idea of Judeo-Bolshevism has played in European politics since the end of World War I reveals that this myth—a potent fusion of racism and ideological defensiveness—is one of the most fertile sources for anti-Muslim and anti-Islamic sentiment today.

The Judeo-Bolshevik myth resonates in contemporary debates about Islam, Muslims, and Europe in several different ways. Most significantly, echoes of earlier panics over the Judeo-Bolshevik menace can be heard in current anxieties about the fragile sovereignty of European nations. In the decades after the Bolshevik revolution in Russia, the Judeo-Bolshevik idea framed these same fears throughout the Continent. The figure of the Jewish Bolshevik was imagined as a cunning border crosser who brought a dangerous and foreign ideology to a disloyal and discontented minority. The Judeo-Bolshevik menace became a rationale in certain places in Eastern Europe for intensified border surveillance, official discrimination against Jews (especially in border regions), and ultimately, expulsion and murder. Throughout the years between World War I and the end of World War II, Judeo-Bolshevism was condemned as an enemy of civilization, hostile to the idea of Europe as a community of nations and a supranational culture. Some described Europe under siege in religious terms, setting the threat of Judeo-Bolshevism against notions of a Christian Europe, Christian civilization, or Christian nation. Nazi Germany and its fascist supporters across the Continent conceived of their crusade against Judeo-Bolshevism differently and in purely racist terms, as a preventive war against a barbaric Asiatic enemy. The collision, intersection, and competition between these two varieties of anti-Communism left a powerful legacy for post–World War II Europe, for the memory of war and genocide, and for contemporary European political discourse about new civilizational threats from other sources, such as Muslim migrants and the specter of Islamic radicalism in Europe.

The Judeo-Bolshevik myth resonates in a second way. As we have seen, the moral power of global Holocaust memory, signifying broader commitments to liberal politics, multicultural toleration, and human rights, has infused arguments about Jews' affinity for Communism and the responsibility of Jewish Communists for provoking antisemitic violence with a power that right-wing intellectuals and politicians have used to oppose and stigmatize liberalism more broadly. In this context, identifying notorious Communists as Jews and explicitly associating Jews with crimes committed by Communist regimes has become, in the world of the European Right, an act of intellectual courage—a right-wing fable of speaking inconvenient and politically incorrect truths to liberal power. It is revealing that Götz Kubitschek, for example, a far-right activist in Germany known for his anti-immigrant views, was deeply impressed as a young man by the writings of Ernst Nolte during West Germany's historians' debate of the late 1980s.[4] Kubitschek found special significance in the ideas that Germans paid excessive attention to the Holocaust and that Nazism had been, in any case, a response to the threat of Bolshevism. Precisely because these views caused (and continue to cause) such outrage, they seemed to him to be contrarian and brave. Today Kubitschek, like many rightist intellectuals across the Continent, casts himself in that role, as someone unafraid to speak about problems that Europe's liberal elites would rather shroud in silence, publishing books about the immigrant peril with titles like *German Victims, Alien Perpetrators: Violence by Foreigners in Germany.*[5]

Traces of earlier panics over the Judeo-Bolshevik threat can be found in immigration debates about Europe's ability to "absorb" large numbers of Muslim immigrants, how Islam fits into European society, and the links between Islam and terrorist violence in many places. In the weeks following the migrant crisis in Budapest's Eastern Station, Hungary's prime minister, Viktor Orbán, speculated that the uproar over mass migration had both awakened the European community to the existential threat that migrants from the Muslim world posed to its values and created an opportunity to retire liberal pieties about European multiculturalism, saying: "The national-Christian order of ideas—this way of thinking, this approach—might regain its dominance not only in Hungary, but in all of Europe."[6] A leading figure in Orbán's Fidesz party echoed these sentiments in an interview: "We have to ask ourselves," he said, "whether we want our grandchildren to live in the United Caliphates of Europe."[7] Elsewhere, far-right People's Parties in Switzerland, Denmark, and other Scandinavian countries have made fears about the creeping "Islamization" of Europe central to their political platforms. In Germany, members of Pegida, a political movement whose name is an acronym for the much longer Patriotic Europeans against the Islamization of the West, hold weekly rallies to demonstrate against what they perceive as the rising power of Islam in Germany and the inability of "ordinary" Germans to speak out against it.[8] In France, the right-wing National Front candidate Marine Le Pen launched her 2017 presidential campaign with the declaration, "We do not want to live under the yoke of the threat of Islamic fundamentalism."[9] In the Netherlands, the far-right Party for Freedom politician Geert Wilders has made a career out of calling to "de-Islamize" Dutch and European society.

Some of these groups have faced setbacks. The parties of both Marine Le Pen and Geert Wilders performed much worse than expected in 2017 elections, and the Pegida movement has splintered since its rise to prominence in 2014. Even so, the issues that they champion remain at the center of political life across the Continent. British voters opted to leave the European Union in large measure because they believed that a "Brexit" would give their government more power to expel unwelcome immigrants. In Poland, the ruling Law and Justice Party has emerged as a leading voice opposing European Union plans to resettle refugees from the Middle East in every member country, including those in Eastern Europe. And nationalist conservatives in the United States write about the "Islamization of Europe" in much the same way that the Tharauds used the Hungarian Bolshevik revolution—as a dystopian future that could threaten the United States as well, fanning Americans' fears about the demise of national culture and the spread of internationalist ideas.[10] As was the case with Judeo-Bolshevism in the twentieth century, these fears have also fueled related debates on both sides of the Atlantic about how and where to distinguish between the myth and the reality of "Islamic terrorism."

The history of the idea of Judeo-Bolshevism casts one other shadow as well. After 1945, the ideological position of "Jews" as a symbolic reference in anti-Communist thought shifted in dramatic ways. Once associated with Communist conspiracy, Judaism was reimagined during the Cold War as an ideological ally of Christianity in the West's struggle against the secular totalitarian evil of Communism. Though it never completely replaced notions of a Christian Europe or the Christian West in the European imagination, the idea of Judeo-Christian civilization became a powerful image of a transatlantic community of values united against Communism. The Soviet Union dissolved in 1991, but the complex interplay between notions of Judeo-Christian civilization and Christian Europe survived in debates about the Islamic menace in Europe. Geert Wilders, among others, explicitly calls for Europe to defend its Western "Judeo-Christian culture" from the onslaught of an invading "Islamic culture." Europe's courts have reimagined the right to religious freedom, once understood as an essential element of Western resistance to Communist indoctrination, as a way to defend secularism against attacks from repressive and fanatical Muslim immigrants.[11] Collective national and regional memories of historic battles against the Ottoman Empire, repurposed during the interwar years of the twentieth century as symbols of anti-Communist resolve, are once again being invoked to signal resistance to the new (and ancient) threat from the East.[12]

Most significantly, debates about totalitarianism have expanded to include the Muslim alongside the Communist. As scholars consider whether "Islamism" should be understood as a form of totalitarian ideology, political leaders contrast the present danger of radical Islam with the past danger of Communism, much as an earlier generation of anti-Communists at the dawn of the Cold War imagined Soviet expansionism as the enduring menace in their own time and Nazism as the recently vanquished evil. This was the message that U.S. president Donald Trump took to Warsaw in 2017, when he addressed a large crowd before the monument to the 1944 Warsaw Uprising against Nazi occupation. "This continent no longer confronts the specter of Communism," he said. But, he stated, "we are confronted by another oppressive ideology—one that seeks to export terrorism and

extremism around the globe." He praised Poles for their historic resolve in resisting Nazi and Soviet occupation and held it up as a model
for Western civilization, under threat once more from forces coming
from "the inside or out, from the South or the East." "The fundamental question of our time," he declared, "is whether the West has
the will to survive."[13]

Jérôme and Jean Tharaud would have understood that question. It
animated them as they began to write their account of the Hungarian Bolshevik revolution on their return to Paris in 1920. For
them, as for so many others in this book, the idea of Judeo-Bolshevism
represented fears of ideological forces that transected borders from
inside and out, imperiling national sovereignty and eroding deeper
certainties about the future of European civilization. The political
context that gave meaning to this work of ideological imagination
was transformed utterly in 1989. When the Cold War ended, the
threat of Communism evaporated and panic about the influence of
"Jewish Bolsheviks" was translated into the politics of contested
memory But the fears that the idea of Judeo-Bolshevism expressed
and the figure of the Jewish Bolshevik embodied still persist. They
have been transposed into new debates about national and European identities and transfigured in a new avatar: the Islamic funda-
mentalist in Europe. Today, Europe's nationalists imagine defending
national sovereignty as part of a broader European effort to prevent
the "Islamization of the West." In rhetoric and intensity, their efforts
recall chapters in the older history of the idea of Judeo-Bolshevism.
Long after the demise of Communism, the figure of the Jewish Bolshevik continues to flicker around the issue of European identity.

Notes

Acknowledgments

Index

Notes

Introduction

1. Thomas Chatterton Williams, "The French Origins of 'You Will Not Replace Us,'" *New Yorker*, December 4, 2017, accessed January 12, 2018, www.newyorker.com/magazine/2017/12/04/the-french-origins-of-you-will-not-replace-us.

2. Paul Hockenos, "Poland and the Uncontrollable Fury of the Far Right," *Atlantic*, November 15, 2017, accessed January 12, 2018, www.theatlantic.com/international/archive/2017/11/europe-far-right-populist-nazi-poland/524559/.

3. Matthew Taylor, "'White Europe': 60,000 Nationalists March on Poland's Independence Day," *Guardian*, November 12, 2017, accessed January 12, 2018, www.theguardian.com/world/2017/nov/12/white-europe-60000-nationalists-march-on-polands-independence-day.

4. Megan Specia, "Nationalist March Dominates Poland's Independence Day," *New York Times*, November 11, 2017, accessed January 12, 2018, www.nytimes.com/2017/11/11/world/europe/poland-nationalist-march.html.

5. Emma Green, "Why the Charlottesville Marchers Were Obsessed with Jews," *Atlantic*, August 15, 2017, accessed August 28, 2017, www.theatlantic.com/politics/archive/2017/08/nazis-racism-charlottesville/536928/.

See also the HBO Vice News documentary *Charlottesville: Race and Terror,* accessed August 28, 2017, https://news.vice.com/story/vice-news-tonight-full -episode-charlottesville-race-and-terror.

6. "Jobbik Rally against World Jewish Congress in Budapest," BBC News, accessed August 28, 2017, www.bbc.com/news/world-europe-22413301.

7. See, e.g., Rafał Pankowski, *The Populist Radical Right in Poland: The Patriots* (London, 2010).

8. Sofia Vasilopoulou and Daphne Halikiopoulou, *The Golden Dawn's Nationalist Solution: Explaining the Rise of the Far Right in Greece* (New York, 2015). More generally, see Jean-Yves Camus and Nicolas Lebourg, *Far-Right Politics in Europe,* trans. Jane Marie Todd (Cambridge, MA, 2017), and Andrea Mammone et al., *Mapping the Extreme Right in Contemporary Europe: From Local to Transnational* (London, 2012).

9. I am grateful to Agnieszka Pasieka for bringing this to my attention. See Agnieszka Pasieka, "Taking Far-Right Claims Seriously and Literally: Anthropology and the Study of Right-Wing Radicalism," *Slavic Review* 76, no. 1 (August 2017): 19–29.

10. Excellent studies include André Gerrits, *The Myth of Jewish Communism: A Historical Interpretation* (New York, 2009); Jaff Schatz, *The Generation: The Rise and Fall of the Jewish Communists of Poland* (Berkeley, CA, 1991); Yuri Slezkine, *The Jewish Century* (Princeton, NJ, 2004).

11. Two examples: Jeffrey Herf, *The Jewish Enemy: Nazi Propaganda during World War II and the Holocaust* (Cambridge, MA, 2006); Jacob Katz, *From Prejudice to Destruction: Anti-Semitism, 1700–1933* (Cambridge, MA, 1980).

12. Andrei Oişteanu, *Inventing the Jew: Antisemitic Stereotypes in Romanian and Other Central East-European Cultures* (Lincoln, NE, 2009); Gavin I. Langmuir, *History, Religion, and Antisemitism* (Berkeley, CA, 1990).

13. Shulamit Volkov, "Antisemitism as a Cultural Code: Reflections on the History and Historiography of Antisemitism in Imperial Germany," *Leo Baeck Institute Year Book* 23 (1978): 25–46, citation on 35. See also the remarks in Samuel Moyn, "Antisemitism, Philosemitism and the Rise of Holocaust Memory," *Patterns of Prejudice* 43, no. 1 (2009): 1–16, here 2–3.

1. The Idea of Judeo-Bolshevism

1. John Cornwell, *Hitler's Pope: The Secret History of Pius XII* (New York, 1999), citation on 74–75. Pacelli would become Pope Pius XII in 1939.

2. On the controversy surrounding this episode, see Joseph Bottum and David G. Dalin, eds., *The Pius War: Responses to the Critics of Pius XII* (Lanham, MD, 2004).

3. Winston S. Churchill, "Zionism versus Bolshevism: A Struggle for the Soul of the Jewish People," *Illustrated Sunday Herald*, February 8, 1920.

4. Thomas Mann, *Tagebücher 1918–1921*, ed. Peter de Mendelsohn (Frankfurt am Main: S. Fischer, 1979), 223. For a thoughtful discussion of this passage in context, see Gerd Koenen, "Betrachtungen eines Unpolitischen: Thomas Mann über Russland und den Bolschewismus," in *Deutschland und die Russische Revolution, 1917–1924*, ed. Gerd Koenen and Lew Kopelew (Munich, 1998), 313–379, esp. 331–334.

5. Miklós Kozma, *Az összeomlás, 1918–19* (Budapest, 1933), 52.

6. *Totengräber Russlands* (Munich, 1921).

7. Allan Mitchell, *Revolution in Bavaria, 1918–1919: The Eisner Regime and the Soviet Republic* (Princeton, NJ, 1965), 195.

8. Robert Gerwarth and John Horne, "Bolshevism as Fantasy: Fear of Revolution and Counter-Revolutionary Violence, 1917–1923," in *War in Peace: Paramilitary Violence in Europe after the Great War*, ed. Gerwarth and Horne (Oxford, 2012), 40–51, esp. 41.

9. Johannes Baur, "Die Revolution und die 'Weisen von Zion': Zur Entwicklung des Russlandbildes in der frühen NSDAP," in *Deutschland und die Russische Revolution*, ed. Gerd Koenen and Lew Kopelew (Munich, 1998), 164–190, here 175. More generally, see Werner Jochmann, "Die Ausbreitung des Antisemitismus," in *Deutsches Judentum in Krieg und Revolution, 1916–1923*, ed. Werner E. Mosse and Arnold Pauker (Tübingen, 1971).

10. Oleg Budnitskii, *Russian Jews between the Reds and the Whites, 1917–1920*, trans. Timothy J. Portice (Philadelphia, 2012), 174.

11. See the essays by Werner T. Angress, "Juden im politischen Leben der Revolutionszeit," and Werner Jochmann, "Die Ausbreitung des Antisemitismus," in Mosse and Paucker, eds., *Deutsches Judentum*, 137–315 and 409–510, respectively; for "high-handed conduct," see 144–146.

12. "A pesti zsidó hitközség nyilatkozata," *Egyenlőség* 38, no. 17 (November 11, 1919): 1. The Pest Israelite Community issued this statement on August 28, 1919. On Jews in the Hungarian Soviet leadership, see William O. McCagg, "Jews in Revolution: The Hungarian Experience," *Journal of Social History* 6, no. 1 (Fall 1972): 78–105.

13. Sharman Kadish, *Bolsheviks and British Jews: The Anglo-Jewish Community, Britain and the Russian Revolution* (London, 1992), 120–131.

14. J. L. Talmon, "Jews between Revolution and Counter-Revolution," in *Israel among the Nations* (New York, 1971), 1–87, citations on 1 and 2.

15. Carole Fink, *Defending the Rights of Others: The Great Powers, the Jews, and International Minority Protection, 1878–1938* (Cambridge, 2004); Mark Levene, *War, Jews and the New Europe: The Diplomacy of Lucien Wolf, 1914–1919*, rev. ed. (London, 2009).

16. Figure cited in Budnitskii, *Russian Jews between the Reds and Whites*, 217.

17. Christoph Dieckmann, "'Jüdischer Bolschewismus,' 1917–1921: Überlegungen zur Verbreitung, Wirkungsweise, und jüdischen Reaktionen," in *Holocaust und Völkermorde: Die Reichweite des Vergleichs*, ed. Sybille Steinbacher (Frankfurt am Main, 2012), 55–82; David Engel, "Being Lawful in a Lawless World: The Trial of Scholem Schwarzbard and the Defense of East European Jews," *Simon Dubnow Institute Yearbook* 5 (2006): 83–97. One example from the discussion is Elias Heifetz, *The Slaughter of Jews in the Ukraine, 1919* (New York, 1921).

18. Mark Levene, "The Balfour Declaration: A Case of Mistaken Identity," *English Historical Review* 107, no. 422 (January 1992): 54–77.

19. The literature on this topic is vast. See Benjamin Nathans, *Beyond the Pale: The Jewish Encounter with Late Imperial Russia* (Berkeley, CA, 2002); Ezra Mendelsohn, *On Modern Jewish Politics* (New York, 1993); Jonathan Frankel, *Prophecy and Politics: Socialism, Nationalism, and the Russian Jews, 1862–1917* (Cambridge, 1981); and, in a more essayistic vein, Yuri Slezkine, *The Jewish Century* (Princeton, NJ, 2006), 105–204.

20. Jeffrey S. Kopstein and Jason Wittenberg, "Who Voted Communist? Reconsidering the Social Bases of Radicalism in Interwar Poland," *Slavic Review* 62, no. 1 (Spring 2003): 87–109, citation and figures on 104–105.

21. Marci Shore, *Caviar and Ashes: A Warsaw Generation's Life and Death in Marxism, 1918–1968* (New Haven, CT, 2009); Jaff Schatz, *The Generation: The Rise and Fall of the Jewish Communists in Poland* (Berkeley, CA, 1991); Ezra Mendelsohn, *The Jews of East Central Europe between the World Wars* (Bloomington, IN, 1983), 11–85.

22. Budnitskii, *Russian Jews*, 55; Jonathan Frankel, "The Dilemmas of Jewish National Autonomism: The Case of Ukraine, 1917–1920," in *Ukrainian-Jewish Relations in Historical Perspective*, ed. Peter J. Potichnyj and Howard Aster (Edmonton, AB, 1988), 263–279; Zvi Gitelman, *Jewish Nationality and Soviet Politics: The Jewish Sections of the CPSU, 1917–1930* (Princeton, NJ, 1972).

23. Anson Rabinbach, ed., *The Austrian Socialist Experiment: Social Democracy and Austromarxism, 1918–1934* (Boulder, CO, 1985); Helmut Gruber, *Red Vienna: Experiment in Working-Class Culture, 1919–1934* (New York, 1991).

24. Rosa Luxemburg, *Reform or Revolution and Other Writings* (Mineola, NY, 2006), 31.

25. Angress, "Juden im politischen Leben der Revolutionszeit," 210–212.

26. Pierre Birnbaum and Ira Katznelson, eds., *Paths of Emancipation: Jews, States, and Citizenship* (Princeton, NJ, 1995).

27. For example, on the complexities of Hungarian Jewish identity after World War I, see Guy Miron, *The Waning of Emancipation: Jewish History, Memory, and the Rise of Fascism in Germany, France, and Hungary* (Detroit, 2011), and Ilse Lazaroms, *Emigration from Paradise: Post–World War I Jewish Hungary* (Stanford, CA, forthcoming).

28. György Borsányi, *The Life of a Communist Revolutionary, Béla Kun*, trans. Mario D. Fenyo (Boulder, CO, 1993).

29. Slezkine, *The Jewish Century*.

30. Stephanie Zloch, "Nationsbildung und Feinderklärung—'Judischer Bolschewismus' und der polnisch-sowjetische Krieg 1919/1920," *Simon Dubnow Institute Yearbook* (2005): 279–303; here, 291.

31. David Nirenberg, *Anti-Judaism: The Western Tradition* (New York, 2013); Uriel Tal, *Christians and Jews in Germany. Religion, Politics, and Ideology in the Second Reich, 1870–1914* (Ithaca, NY, 1975). On misrule and

inversion, see Stuart Clark, "Inversion, Misrule, and the Meaning of Witchcraft," *Past and Present* 87 (May 1980): 98–127. Special thanks to my colleague Alastair Bellany for drawing my attention to this work and for generously discussing moral panics in early modern Europe with me.

32. Michel Leymarie, "Les frères Tharaud et la Hongrie," *Bulletin de la Société d'histoire moderne et contemporaine* 43, supplement 3/4 (1996): 40–51.

33. On Russia, see Hans Rogger, *Jewish Policies and Right-Wing Politics in Imperial Russia* (Berkeley, CA, 1986); on France, Pierre Birnbaum, *The Jews of the Republic: A Political History of State Jews in France from Gambetta to Vichy* (Stanford, CA, 1996); on Hungary, Paul Hanebrink, "Transnational Culture War: Christianity, Nation, and the Judeo-Bolshevik Myth in Hungary, 1890–1920," *Journal of Modern History* 80, no. 1 (2008): 55–80.

34. Emilio Gentile, *Contro Cesare: Cristianesimo e totalitarismo nell'epoca dei fascismi* (Milan, 2010), 75.

35. There is a huge literature on the *Protocols*. See Michael Hagemeister, "The Protocols of the Elders of Zion: Between History and Fiction," *New German Critique* 35, no. 1 (Spring 2008): 83–95, and Pierre-André Taguieff, *Les Protocoles des sages de Sion* (Paris, 1992). The little Hungarian book is *Földalatti összeesküvők: A Morning Post czikkei a forradalmak okairól* (Budapest, 1921). I am grateful to Eric Weaver for bringing this text to my attention.

36. Robert Weinberg, *Blood Libel in Late Imperial Russia: The Ritual Murder Trial of Mendel Beilis* (Bloomington, IN, 2014).

37. Cécile Tormay, *An Outlaw's Diary* (London, 1923), 98.

38. Richard Francis Crane, *Passion of Israel: Jacques Maritain, Catholic Conscience and the Holocaust* (Scranton, PA, 2010), 10–16, citation on 7.

39. On the legacy of the nineteenth-century culture wars, see Christopher Clark and Wolfram Kaiser, eds., *Secular-Catholic Conflict in Nineteenth-Century Europe* (Cambridge, 2003); on French and Italian Catholic networks, see: Nina Valbousquet, "Tradition catholique et matrice de l'antisémitisme à l'époque contemporaine," *Revue d'Histoire Moderne et Contemporaine* 62, no. 2/3 (September 2015): 63–88; articles from *Das neue Reich* include Joseph Eberle, "Zusammenhänge zwischen der 'roten' und 'goldenen' In-

ternationale," *Das neue Reich* 1, no. 19 (February 6, 1919): 331–333, and Ottokar Prohászka, "Die Judenfrage in Ungarn," *Das neue Reich* 2, no. 10 (December 7, 1919): 150–152.

40. Robert Wilton, *Russia's Agony* (London, 1918), 137–138.

41. Robert Wilton, *The Last Days of the Romanovs* (London, 1920).

42. Nesta Webster, *World Revolution: The Plot against Civilization* (London, 1921), 293. On Webster, see Markku Ruotsila, "Mrs. Webster's Religion: Conspiracist Extremism on the Christian Far Right," *Patterns of Prejudice* 38, no. 2 (2004): 109–126.

43. Winston S. Churchill, "Zionism versus Bolshevism: A Struggle for the Soul of the Jewish People," *Illustrated Sunday Herald*, February 8, 1920.

44. Kadish, *Bolsheviks and British Jews*; Alyson Pendlebury, "The Politics of the 'Last Days': Bolshevism, Zionism and 'the Jews,'" *Jewish Culture and History* 2, no. 2 (1999): 96–115; Colin Holmes, "Public Opinion in England and the Jews, 1914–1918," in *Michael: On the History of the Jews in the Diaspora*, vol. 10, ed. R. A. Rockaway and S. Simonsohn (Tel Aviv, 1986), 97–115.

45. Diana Dimitru, *The State, Antisemitism, and Collaboration in the Holocaust: The Borderlands of Romania and the Soviet Union* (New York, 2016), 62–63.

46. Robert H. Johnston, *New Mecca, New Babylon: Paris and the Russian Exiles, 1920–1945* (Kingston, ON, 1988).

47. Michael Kellogg, *The Russian Roots of Nazism: White Émigrés and the Making of National Socialism, 1917–1945* (Cambridge, 2005).

48. Alfred Rosenberg, *Die Spur des Juden im Wandel der Zeiten* (Munich, 1920), 117.

49. On entanglements between White Russian émigrés and *völkisch*, or extremist German nationalism, see Kellogg, *The Russian Roots of Nazism*, and Matthias Vetter, "Die Russische Emigration und ihre 'Judenfrage,'" in *Russische Emigration in Deutschland 1918 bis 1941*, ed. Karl Schlögel (Berlin, 1995), 109–124. On the influence of these émigrés on Hitler, see Ian Kershaw, *Hitler: 1889–1936: Hubris* (New York, 1999), 152–153.

50. On Communist mass mobilization and the fear it provoked in Germany, see Andreas Wirsching, *Vom Weltkrieg zum Bürgerkrieg? Politischer*

Extremismus in Deutschland und Frankreich 1918–1933/39: Berlin und Paris im Vergleich (Munich, 1999); Dirk Schumann, *Political Violence in the Weimar Republic, 1918–1933: Fight for the Streets and Fear of Civil War* (New York, 2009); and (with much caution) Ernst Nolte, *Der europäische Bürgerkrieg, 1917–1945: Nationalsozialismus und Bolschewismus* (Munich, 1997), 103–121.

51. One example: "An die besser zu informierende Welt," *Reichspost*, April 5, 1919.

52. Dr. P. Kr., "Eine überwundene Krise," *Reichspost*, March 29, 1919, 1.

53. Jérôme Tharaud and Jean Thaurad, *Quand Israël est roi* (Paris, 1921).

54. Citations here and in the following paragraph are taken from the German-language translation: Jérôme Tharaud and Jean Tharaud, *Die Herrschaft Israels* (Zurich, 1927), 167, 194–195, 211–212. English translations are mine.

55. Tharaud and Tharaud, *Herrschaft*, 167, 194–195, 211–212.

56. Jérôme Tharaud and Jean Thaurad, *L'ombre de la croix* (Paris, 1917).

57. On the lives and writings of the Tharaud brothers, see Michel Leymarie, *La preuve par deux: Jérôme et Jean Tharaud* (Paris, 2014).

58. Jean-Jacques Becker and Serge Berstein, *Histoire de l'anticommunisme*, vol. 1: *1917–1940* (Paris, 1987), 85.

59. Stephanie Zloch, "Nationsbildung und Feinderklärung—'Judischer Bolschewismus' und der polnisch-sowjetische Krieg 1919/1920," *Simon Dubnow Institute Yearbook* (2005): 279–303, here 292.

60. Józef Lewandowski, "History and Myth: Pińsk, April 1919," *Polin* 2 (1987): 50–71.

61. Peter Holquist, "'Information is the Alpha and Omega of Our Work': Bolshevik Surveillance in Its Pan-European Context," *Journal of Modern History* 69, no. 3 (September 1997): 433–438.

62. Budnitskii, *Russian Jews*, 184.

63. Paul A. Hanebrink, "Transnational Culture War: Christianity, Nation, and the Judeo-Bolshevik Myth in Hungary, 1890–1920," *Journal of Modern History* 80, no. 1 (March 2008): 78–80.

64. Ottokár Prohászka, "Mi, magyarság és kereszténység," *Nemzeti Újság*, November 12, 1919. Reprinted in *Összegyűjtött munkái*, vol. 22: *Iránytű*, ed. Antal Schutz (Budapest, 1927), 213–215.

65. Ottokár Prohászka, "A marxizmus csődje a tények világánál," in *A proletárdiktatúra Magyarországon*, ed. Károly Huszár (Budapest, 1920), 212, 216.

2. The Greater War

1. Henry Abramson, *A Prayer for the Government: Ukrainians and Jews in Revolutionary Times, 1917–1920* (Cambridge, MA, 1999), 122.

2. On the Proskurov pogrom, see Abramson, *Prayer for the Government*, 109–141. Numbers for the victims vary. Oleg Budnitskii counts 1,650; see Budnitskii, *Russian Jews between the Reds and the Whites, 1917–1920*, trans. Timothy J. Portice (Philadelphia, 2012), 218.

3. "30,000 Jews were killed directly." Zvi Y. Gitelman, *A Century of Ambivalence: The Jews of Russia and the Soviet Union, 1881 to the Present*, 2nd ed. (Bloomington, IN, 2001), 70–71. On the pogroms generally, see Budnitskii, *Russian Jews*, 216–275.

4. On the *landsmanshaftn*, Rebecca Kobrin, *Jewish Bialystok and Its Diaspora* (Bloomington, IN, 2010). On writing the history of the pogroms, Joshua Karlip, "Between Martryology and Historiography: Elias Tscherikower and the Making of a Pogrom Historian," *East European Jewish Affairs* 38, no. 3 (2008): 257–280, and Laura Jockusch, *Collect and Record! Jewish Holocaust Documentation in Early Postwar Europe* (New York, 2012), 18–46. On minority protection for Jews, Carole Fink, *Defending the Rights of Others: The Great Powers, the Jews, and International Minority Protection, 1878–1938* (Cambridge, 2004), and Mark Levene, *War, Jews and the New Europe: The Diplomacy of Lucien Wolf, 1914–1919*, rev. ed. (London, 2009).

5. Elias Heifetz, *The Slaughter of the Jews in the Ukraine in 1919* (New York, 1921), iii.

6. Ibid., iii, 9–10, 56.

7. On White diplomacy, see Budnitskii, *Russian Jews*, 296–334. On Ukrainian diplomacy, Thomas Chopard, "Indentifier, légitimer, stigmatiser:

Les matériaux de la Délegation ukrainienne à la Conférence de la Paix de Paris (1918–1920)," *Matériaux pour l'Histoire de Notre Temps* 113/114 (2014): 180–185. On Ukrainian-Jewish debates about the pogroms, Taras Hunczak, "A Reappraisal of Symon Petliura and Ukrainian-Jewish Relations, 1917–1921," *Jewish Social Studies* 31, no. 3 (Fall 1969): 163–183, and Zosa Szajkowski, "A Reappraisal of Symon Petliura and Ukrainian-Jewish Relations, 1917–1921: A Rebuttal," *Jewish Social Studies* 31, no. 3 (Fall 1969): 184–213. Conflict over the meaning of the pogroms resurfaced when Symon Petliura was assassinated in Paris in 1926. See *Documents sur les pogromes en Ukraine et l'assassinat de Simon Petlura à Paris (1917–1921–1926)* (Paris, 1927), and David Engel, *The Assassination of Symon Petliura and the Trial of Scholem Schwarzbard, 1926–1927: A Selection of Documents* (Göttingen, 2016).

8. On the rumors involving cow stomachs and chicken eggs, see Budnitskii, *Russian Jews*, 225 and, more generally, 225–240. See also Eric Lohr, "The Russian Army and the Jews: Mass Deportation, Hostages, and Violence during World War I," *Russian Review* 60, no. 3 (July 2001): 404–419; Peter Gatrell, *A Whole Empire Walking: Refugees in Russia during World War I* (Bloomington, IN, 1999), 145–150.

9. On the circular citing the Jewish threat to "incite discontent and protests," see Budnitskii, *Russian Jews*, 238. See also, more generally, Eric Lohr, *Nationalizing the Russian Empire: The Campaign against Enemy Aliens during World War I* (Cambridge, MA, 2003).

10. Simon Bernstein, *Die Judenpolitik der rumänischen Regierung* (Copenhagen, 1918), 127–150; Carol Iancu, *L'émancipation des juifs de Roumanie (1913–1919): De l'inégalité civique aux droits de minorité: L'originalité d'un combat à partir des guerres balkanique et jusqu'à la Conférence de paix de Paris* (Montpellier, 1992), 89–101.

11. S. Ansky, *The Enemy at His Pleasure: A Journey through the Jewish Pale of Settlement during World War I*, ed. and trans. Joachim Neugroschel (New York, 2003), 181, 197–198. See also Frank M. Schuster, *Zwischen allen Fronten: Osteuropäische Juden während des Ersten Weltkrieges (1914–1919)* (Cologne, 2004).

12. Péter Bihari, *Lövészárkok a hátországban: Középosztály, zsidókérdés, antiszemitizmus az első világháború Magyarországon* (Budapest, 2008),

118, 152, 196–223; Paul A. Hanebrink, "Transnational Culture War: Christianity, Nation, and the Judeo-Bolshevik Myth, 1890–1920," *Journal of Modern History* 80, no. 1 (March 2008): 55–80, here 66–70. On Vienna, see David Rechter, "Galicia in Vienna: Jewish Refugees in the First World War," *Austrian History Yearbook* 28 (1997): 113–130, and Beatrix Hoffmann-Holter, *"Abreisendmachung": Jüdische Kriegsflüchtlinge in Wien, 1914–1923* (Vienna, 1995).

13. "Jews are everywhere!" cited in Ulrich Herbeck, *Das Feindbild vom 'jüdischen Bolschewiken': Zur Geschichte des russischen Antisemitismus vor und während der Russischen Revolution* (Berlin, 2009), 113. See also Lohr, "Russian Army and the Jews," 418.

14. On these wars in their regional context, see Jochen Böhler, "Enduring Violence: The Postwar Struggles in East-Central Europe, 1917–1921," *Journal of Contemporary History* 50, no. 1 (2015): 58–77.

15. Jerzy Tomaszewski, "Pińsk, Saturday 5 April 1919." *Polin* 1 (1986): 227–51; also Józef Lewandowski, "History and Myth: Pińsk, April 1919," *Polin* 2 (1987): 50–71.

16. Sarunas Liekis, Lidia Miliakova, and Antony Polonsky, "Three Documents on Anti-Jewish Violence in the Eastern Kresy during the Polish-Soviet Conflict," *Polin* 14 (2001): 116–149.

17. Isabell V. Hull, *A Scrap of Paper: Breaking and Making International Law during the Great War* (Ithaca, NY, 2014), 51–95.

18. Budnitskii, *Russian Jews*, 245–254; scissors on 248.

19. For a comprehensive overview of anti-Jewish violence in Eastern Europe during these years, see Piotr Wróbel, "The Kaddish Years: Anti-Jewish Violence in East-Central Europe, 1918–1921," *Jahrbuch des Simon-Dubnow-Instituts* 4 (2005): 211–236.

20. Joanna Beata Michlic, *Poland's Threatening Other: The Image of the Jew from 1880 to the Present* (Lincoln, NE, 2006), 109–130; "hostile to us," 120. "demonstrate their antagonistic position" in Golczewski, *Polnisch-jüdische Beziehungen*, 233. On Dmowski's influence, see Grzegorz Krzywiec, "Between Realpolitik and Redemption: Roman Dmowski's Solution to the 'Jewish Question,'" in *Antisemitism in an Era of Transition: Continuities and Impact in Post-Communist Poland and Hungary*, ed. Francois Guesnet and Gwen Jones (Frankfurt am Main, 2014), 69–90.

21. On the internment camps, see Frank Golczewski, *Polnisch-jüdische Beziehungen, 1881–1922: Eine Studie zur Geschichte des Antisemitismus in Osteuropa* (Wiesbaden, 1981), 240–245; Pawel Korzec, *Juifs en Pologne: La question juive pendant l'entre-deux-guerres* (Paris, 1980), 110–113; and Norman Davies, *White Eagle, Red Star: The Polish-Soviet War, 1919–20* (New York, 1972), 162–163. On Leśniewski, see Golczewski, *Polnisch-jüdische Beziehungen*, 240.

22. Timothy Snyder, *The Reconstruction of Nations: Poland, Ukraine, Lithuania, Belarus, 1569–1999* (New Haven, CT, 2003), esp. 52–73 and 133–154.

23. On transnational Jewish politics between the two world wars, see Hasia R. Diner and Gennady Estraikh, eds., *1929: Mapping the Jewish World* (New York, 2013).

24. I take the idea of "sovereignty panics" from Michael Geyer, who has proposed it in a number of unpublished papers. More generally, see Robert Gerwarth, *The Vanquished: Why the First World War Failed to End* (New York, 2016); Jochen Böhler, Włodzimierz Borodziej, and Joachim von Puttkamer, eds., *Legacies of Violence: Eastern Europe's First World War* (Munich, 2014).

25. Here, and for much of what follows on the next pages, I refer to Irina Livezeanu, *Cultural Politics in Greater Romania: Regionalism, Nation Building and Ethnic Struggle, 1918–1930* (Ithaca, NY, 1995), 245–296.

26. Corneliu Zelea Codreanu, *For My Legionaries* (Madrid, 1976).

27. Demographic statistics taken from Livezeanu, *Cultural Politics in Greater Romania*, 8–11.

28. On Romanian youth, see Roland Clark, *Holy Legionary Youth: Fascist Activism in Interwar Romania* (Ithaca, NY, 2015), 28–63. On the image of Judeo-Bolshevism in Romanian fascist ideology, see Radu Ioanid, *The Sword of the Archangel: Fascist Ideology in Romania* (Boulder, CO, 1990).

29. Citations in Diana Dumitru, *The State, Antisemitism, and Collaboration in the Holocaust: The Borderlands of Romania and the Soviet Union* (New York, 2016), 79–80, and more generally, 53–93. On the army's promotion of cultural nationalism, see Livezeanu, *Cultural Politics in Greater Romania*, 109–112. On Bessarabian Jewish politics, see Ezra Mendelsohn,

The Jews of East Central Europe between the Two World Wars (Bloomington, IN, 1983), 189–202.

30. Glenn E. Torrey, "The Romanian Intervention in Hungary, 1919," in *Revolutions and Interventions in Hungary and Its Neighbor States, 1918–1919*, ed. Peter Pastor (Boulder, CO, 1988), 301–320, citation on 301. See also Livezeanu, *Cultural Politics in Greater Romania*, esp. 151 (Transylvanian demography) and 251 (use of Hungarian Bolshevism in Romanian propaganda).

31. On the formation after November 1918 of paramilitary groups in Hungary, see Tibor Zinner, *Az ébredők fénykora, 1919–1923* (Budapest, 1989), 13–15.

32. Citation in József Szekeres, ed., *Források Budapest történetéhez, 1919–1945* (Budapest, 1971), 21.

33. The leading historian of Hungary's White Terror is Béla Bodó. One representative essay out of many is Béla Bodó, "The White Terror in Hungary, 1919–1921: The Social Worlds of Paramilitary Groups," *Austrian History Yearbook* 42 (2011): 133–163.

34. Some examples include Albert Váry, *A vörös uralom áldozatai Magyarországon: Hivatalos jelentések és bírói ítéletek alapján* (Budapest, 1922), and Cécile Tormay, *A bujdosó könyv* (Budapest, 1920–21). For a European perspective on the phenomenon, see Robert Gerwarth and John Horne, "Bolshevism as Fantasy: Fear of Revolution and Counter-Revolutionary Violence, 1917–1923," in *War in Peace: Paramilitary Violence in Europe after the Great War*, ed. Robert Gerwarth and John Horne (Oxford, 2012).

35. These figures are taken from Bodó, "The White Terror in Hungary," 133.

36. Ottokár Prohászka, "A keresztény kurzus kisíklása," *Uj Nemzedék*, June 20, 1920.

37. Gusztáv Gratz, *A forradalmak kora: Magyarország története, 1918–1920* (Budapest, 1935), 252–253.

38. An example: Gyula Szekfű, *Három nemzedék: Egy hanyatló kor története* (Budapest, 1920).

39. Ottokár Prohászka, "A marxizmus csődje a tények világánál," in *A proletárdiktatúra Magyarországon*, ed. Károly Huszár (Budapest, 1920), 212, 216.

40. Béla Túri, "Az út a bolsevizmus felé," in Huszár, A *proletárdiktatúra Magyarországon*, 8, 10

41. Pál Prónay, A *határban a halál kaszál: Fejezetek Prónay Pál feljegyzéseiből* (Budapest, 1963), 102–103.

42. *Report on Alleged Existence of "White Terror" in Hungary* (London, 1920)

43. Harold Sidney Harmsworth (Viscount Rothermere), *My Campaign for Hungary* (London, 1939).

44. See the series of reports published in the Hungarian Jewish weekly *Egyenlőség*: "A dunántúli zsidóüldözések aktáiból," *Egyenlőség*, September 11, 18, and 25, 1919).

45. Nathaniel Katzburg, "Louis Marshall and the White Terror in Hungary, 1919–1920," *American Jewish Archives* 45, no. 1 (Spring / Summer 1993): 1–12, citation on 5.

46. On leftist émigrés, see Josef Pogány, *Der weisse Terror in Ungarn* (Vienna, 1920), and also the essays on Mihály Biró's graphic representations of the White Terror in *Mihály Biró: Pathos in rot / Pathos in red* (Vienna and Nuremburg, 2010). For an overview of international investigations in Hungary, see Emily Gioielli, "White Misrule: Terror and Political Violence during Hungary's Long World War I," Ph.D. diss, Central European University, 2015, chapters 4 and 5. On Hungarian efforts to manage the country's reputation diplomatically, see Miklós Zeidler, A *revíziós gondolat* (Budapest, 2001), and Zsolt Nagy, *Great Expectations and Interwar Realities: Cultural Diplomacy in Horthy's Hungary* (Budapest and New York, 2017).

47. Citation from Woodrow Wilson, *Woodrow Wilson: The Essential Political Writings*, ed. Ronald J. Pestritto (Lanham, MD, 2005), 261. More generally, see Arno J. Mayer, *Politics and Diplomacy of Peacemaking: Containment and Counterrevolution at Versailles, 1918–1919* (New York, 1967).

48. Mayer, *Politics and Diplomacy*, and Fink, *Defending the Rights of Others*; Susan Pedersen, *The Guardians: The League of Nations and the Crisis of Empire* (New York, 2015). See also Klaus Richter, "'Eine durch und durch demokratische Nation': Demokratie und Minderheitenschutz in der Aussendarstellung Litauens nach 1918," *Zeitschrift für Ostmitteleuropaforschung* 64, no. 2 (2015): 194–217.

49. Examples of articles from the journal of the Alliance Israélite Universelle include "Les Réfugiés d'Ukraine en Roumanie," *Paix et Droit,* November 1, 1921, 3–4, and "Désordres en Roumanie," *Paix et Droit,* December 1, 1922. On Romanian Jews and citizenship, see Carol Iancu, "L'Émancipation des Juifs de Roumanie devant la Conférence de paix de Paris (1919)," *Shvut* 16 (1993): 257–279.

50. For "best French colony" and "gendarme of the Entente" citations, see Torrey, "The Romanian Intervention in Hungary," 304, 307. On French military attitudes toward Hungary, particularly the first non-Bolshevik revolutionary regime, see Peter Pastor, *Hungary between Wilson and Lenin: The Hungarian Revolution of 1918–1919 and the Big Three* (New York, 1976), esp. 62.

51. Piotr S. Wandycz, *France and Her Eastern Allies, 1919–1925: French-Czechoslovak-Polish Relations from the Paris Peace Conference to Locarno* (Minneapolis, 1962), 122.

52. See "Fourteen Points," in Wilson, *The Essential Political Writings,* 259–265.

53. Levene, *War, Jews, and the New Europe.*

54. Israel Cohen, *A Report on the Pogroms in Poland* (London, 1919), 35.

55. Carole Fink, *Defending the Rights of Others: The Great Powers, the Jews, and International Minority Protection, 1878–1938* (Cambridge, 2004), esp. 171–209; Norman Davies, "Great Britain and the Jews, 1918–1920," *Journal of Contemporary History* 8, no. 2 (April 1973): 119–142; Neal Pease, "'This Troublesome Question': The United States and the 'Polish Pogroms' of 1918–1919," in *Ideology, Politics, and Diplomacy in East Central Europe,* ed. M. B. B. Biskupski (Rochester, NY, 2003), 58–79.

56. "36 Jewish Youths Shot," *New York Times,* May 15, 1919.

57. "Call on Nations to Protect Jews," *New York Times,* May 22, 1919.

58. "Denies That Poland Is Slaying Jews," *New York Times,* May 23, 1919.

59. "Lemberg Pogroms Were Not by Poles," *New York Times,* June 2, 1919.

60. Paderewski is quoted in Liekis, Miliakova, and Polonsky, "Three Documents," 118.

61. On Lucien Wolf, see Davies, "Great Britain and the Jews," 128.

62. Fink, *Defending the Rights of Others,* 250.

63. "Call on Nations to Protect Jews," *New York Times.*

64. The commission's 1919 "Report of the Mission of United States to Poland" is reprinted in Henry Morgenthau, *All in a Life-Time* (New York, 1922), 407–437, here 411. Generally, see also Pease, "'This Troublesome Question.'"

65. Pawel Korzec, "Polen und der Minderheitenschutzvertrag (1919–1934)," *Jahrbücher für Geschichte Osteuropas* 22, no. 4 (1974): 515–555; Mark Levene, "Britain, a British Jew, and Jewish Relations with the New Poland: The Making of the Polish Minorities Treaty of 1919," *Polin* 8 (1994): 14–41; Mark Mazower, "Minorities and the League of Nations in Interwar Europe," *Daedalus* 126, no. 2 (Spring 1997): 47–63.

3. Refashioned by Nazism

1. Ian Kershaw, *Hitler, 1889–1936: Hubris* (London, 1998), esp. 110–116. On revolution in Bavaria, see Alan F. Mitchell, *Revolution in Bavaria, 1918–1919: The Eisner Regime and the Soviet Republic* (Princeton, NJ, 1965), and Eliza Ablovatski, "The 1919 Central European Revolutions and the Judeo-Bolshevik Myth," *European Review of History* 17, no. 3 (June 2010): 473–489. One example of a contemporary assessment is Josef Karl, *Die Schreckensherrschaft in München und Spartakus im bayr: Oberland* (Munich, 1919).

2. For "funeral wreath of humanity," see Paul R. Mendes-Flohr and Jehuda Reinharz, eds., *The Jew in the Modern World: A Documentary History* (New York, 1980), 485–487, quotation on 487. On Hitler's ideological development, see Kershaw, *Hitler: Hubris*, 60–69; 149–153, and 240–250. More generally, see Claus-Ekkehard Bärsch, *Die politische Religion des Nationalsozialismus: Die religiöse Dimension der NS-Ideologie in den Schriften von Dietrich Eckart, Joseph Goebbels, Alfred Rosenberg, und Adolf Hitler* (Munich, 1998).

3. Manfred Gailus, "Vom Feldgeistlichen des Ersten Weltkriegs zum politischen Prediger des Bürgerkriegs: Kontinuitäten in der Berliner Pfarrer Familie Wessel," *Zeitschrift für Geschichtswissenschaft* 50, no. 9 (2002): 773–803.

4. Daniel Siemens, *The Making of a Nazi Hero: The Murder and Myth of Horst Wessel*, trans. David Burnett (London, 2013); Jay W. Baird, *To Die*

for Germany: *Heroes in the Nazi Pantheon* (Bloomington, IN, 1990), 73–108.

5. Baird, *To Die for Germany*, 82–83.

6. Citations and analysis in Karl-Heinz Schoeps, *Literature and Film in the Third Reich*, trans. Kathleen M. Dell'Orto (Rochester, NY, 2004), 83–87, citations on 85. Hanns Heinz Ewers, *Horst Wessel: Ein deutsches Schicksal* (Berlin, 1932).

7. On the film, see Jay W. Baird, "Goebbels, Horst Wessel, and the Myth of Resurrection and Return," *Journal of Contemporary History* 17, no. 4 (October 1982): 633–650, here 642–645.

8. On political violence in the Weimar Republic, see Dirk Schumann, *Political Violence in the Weimar Republic, 1918–1933: Fight for the Streets and Fear of Civil War*, trans. Thomas Dunlap (New York, 2009), and Andreas Wirsching, *Vom Weltkrieg zum Bürgerkrieg? Politischer Extremismus in Deutschland und Frankreich, 1918–1933/39* (Munich, 1999), esp. 299–330 and 461–467. On violence and the SA more generally, see Sven Reichardt, *Faschistische Kampfbünde: Gewalt und Gemeinschaft im italienischen Squadrismus und in der deutschen SA* (Cologne, 2002).

9. On the political unrest of this period, see Dirk Blasius, *Weimars Ende: Bürgerkrieg und Politik, 1930–1933* (Göttingen, 2005), and Heinrich August Winkler, *Weimar, 1918–1933: Die Geschichte der ersten deutschen Demokratie* (Munich, 1993), 477–521.

10. On Goebbels and Berlin, see Wirsching, *Vom Weltkrieg zum Bürgerkrieg?* 461–467; citations on 465–466. See also Joseph Goebbels, *Der Angriff. Aufsätze aus der Kampfzeit* (Munich, 1935), 308–371

11. Adolf Ehrt and Hans Roden, *Terror: Die Blutchronik des Marxismus in Deutschland: Auf Grund amtlichen Materials bearbeitet* (Berlin, 1934).

12. Joseph Goebbels, *Communism with the Mask Off: Speech Delivered in Nürnberg on September 13 1935 at the Seventh National-Socialist Party Congress* (Berlin, 1935), citations on 13, 33.

13. F. O. H. Schulz, *Jude und Arbeiter: Ein Abschnitt aus der Tragödie des deutschen Volkes* (Berlin, 1934), 7, 174.

14. Steven E. Aschheim, *Brothers and Strangers: The East European Jew in German and German Jewish Consciousness, 1800–1923* (Madison, WI, 1982), 215–246, and Dieter Gosewinkel, "'Unerwünschte Elemente:'

Einwanderung und Einbürgerung der Juden in Deutschland, 1848–1933," *Tel Aviver Jahrbuch für Deutsche Geschichte* 27 (1998): 71–106.

15. Björn Laser, *Kulturbolschewismus! Zur Diskurssemantik der "totalen Krise,"* 1929–1933 (Frankfurt am Main, 2010); Eckhard John, *Musikbolschewismus: Die Politisierung der Musik in Deutschland, 1918–1938* (Stuttgart, 1994); and Olaf Peters, ed., *Degenerate Art: The Attack on Modern Art in Nazi Germany, 1937* (Munich, 2014).

16. Citation in Richard Steigmann-Gall, *The Holy Reich: Nazi Conceptions of Christianity, 1919–1945* (Cambridge, 2003), 118.

17. Gebensleben citation in Richard J. Evans, *The Third Reich in Power, 1933–1939* (New York, 2005), 450. Victor Klemperer, *I Will Bear Witness, 1933–1941: A Diary of the Nazi Years,* trans. Martin Chalmers (New York, 1999), 45, 166–167. On Nazi "law and order" tactics, see Robert Gellately, *Backing Hitler: Coercion and Consent in Nazi Germany* (Oxford, 2001), 17–19.

18. Michael Wildt, *An Uncompromising Generation: The Nazi Leadership of the Reich Security Main Office,* trans. Tom Lampert (Madison, WI, 2009), 137. See also Peter Longerich, *Heinrich Himmler,* trans. Jeremy Noakes and Lesley Sharpe (Oxford, 2012), 193–194, 202–203.

19. All citations from Isabelle Rohr, "The Use of Antisemitism in the Spanish Civil War," *Patterns of Prejudice* 37, no. 2 (2003): 195–211, here 200. See also Paul Preston, *The Spanish Holocaust: Inquisition and Extermination in Twentieth-Century Spain* (London, 2012), esp. 34–52.

20. Figures from Rohr, "Antisemitism in the Spanish Civil War," 204–205.

21. Arno Lustiger, *Schalom Libertad! Juden im spanischen Bürgerkrieg* (Berlin, 2001).

22. Citation in Rohr, "Antisemitism in the Spanish Civil War," 202–203.

23. Vejas Liulevicius, *War Land on the Eastern Front: Culture, National Identity, and German Occupation in World War I* (Cambridge, 2000), esp. 227–246.

24. Rohr, "Antisemitism in the Spanish Civil War," 196–199.

25. Borja Villalonga, "The Theoretical Origins of Catholic Nationalism in Nineteenth Century Europe," *Modern Intellectual History* 11, no. 2 (August 2014): 307–331.

26. On Nazi attitudes toward Freemasonry: Stefan-Ludwig Hoffmann, *The Politics of Sociability: Freemasonry and German Civil Society, 1848–1918*, trans. Tom Lampert (Ann Arbor, MI, 2007), 275–295.

27. Cited in Preston, *The Spanish Holocaust*, 41.

28. Adolf Hitler, *Reden des Führers am Parteitag der Ehre 1936* (Munich, 1936), 68, 72, 73.

29. *Das Rotbuch über Spanien: Bilder, Dokumente, Zeugenaussagen* (Berlin, 1937), 11–19, here 16.

30. Maria de Smeth, *Viva España! Arriba España! Eine Frau erlebt den spanischen Krieg* (Berlin, 1937), 224. On de Smeth, see Babette Quinkert, "Propagandistin gegen den 'jüdischen Bolschewismus': Maria de Smeths Reisebericht aus Spanien 1936/37," in *Volksgenossinnen: Frauen in der NS-Volksgemeinschaft*, ed. Sybille Steinbacher (Göttingen, 2007), 173–186, esp. 177–178 and 182–183. The Nibelungen Press reprinted her book about her time in a Soviet prison as *Unfreiwillige Reise nach Moskau* (Berlin, 1939).

31. Conrad Kent, "What the Condor Saw: Nazi Propaganda Images of the Spanish Civil War," in *The Lion and the Eagle: Interdisciplinary Essays on German-Spanish Relations over the Centuries*, ed. Conrad Kent, Thomas K. Wolber, and Cameron M. K. Hewitt (New York, 2000), 325–359.

32. Lorna Waddington, *Hitler's Crusade: Bolshevism and the Myth of the Jewish Conspiracy* (London, 2007).

33. Cited in Nationalsozialistische Deutsche Arbeiter-Partei, *Der Parteitag der Arbeit vom 6. bis 13. September 1937: Offizieller Bericht über den Verlauf des Reichsparteitages mit sämtlichen Kongressreden* (Munich, 1938), 377–378.

34. Here and the next paragraphs, see Hilari Raguer, *Gunpowder and Incense: The Catholic Church and the Spanish Civil War*, trans. Gerald Howson (London, 2007).

35. For the full text of the papal allocution, see www.vatican.va/holy_father /pius_xi/speeches/documents/hf_p-xi_spe_19360914_vostra-presenza_it .html, accessed November 6, 2013.

36. Ronald Modras, *The Catholic Church and Antisemitism: Poland, 1933–1939* (Chur, Switzerland; Langhorne, PA, 1994), 166.

37. Gerhard Besier, "Anti-Bolshevism and Antisemitism: The Catholic Church in Germany and National Socialist Ideology, 1936–37," *Journal of Ecclesiastical History* 43, no. 3 (July 1992): 447–456, citations on 453 and 455. One of the best analyses of this particular moment in German church-state relations remains Klaus Scholder, "Politics and Church Politics in the Third Reich: The Shift in Church Politics in Germany, 1936–7," in A *Requiem for Hitler and Other New Perspectives on the German Church Struggle,* trans. John Bowden (London, 1989), 140–156.

38. Richard Francis Crane, *Passion of Israel: Jacques Maritain, Catholic Conscience and the Holocaust* (Scranton, PA, 2010), 10–16, citation on 7.

39. Ibid.; see also Robert Royal, ed., *Jacques Maritain and the Jews* (Mishawaka, IN, 1994). On Maritain more generally, see Samuel Moyn, "Jacques Maritain, Christian New Order, and the Birth of Human Rights," May 1, 2008, Social Science Research Network (SSRN), accessed August 28, 2017, https://ssrn.com/abstract=1134345 or http://dx.doi.org/10 .2139/ssrn.1134345.

40. Dietrich v. Hildebrand, "Falsche Fronten," *Christliche Ständestaat,* September 27, 1936. See also Hildebrand, "Warum Kampf gegen den Bolschewismus?" *Christliche Ständestaat,* November 8, 1936.

41. On Hildebrand, see James Chappel, *Catholic Modern: The Challenge of Totalitarianism and the Remaking of the Church* (Cambridge, MA, 2018), and John Connelly, *From Enemy to Brother: The Revolution in Catholic Teaching on the Jews, 1933–1965* (Cambridge, MA, 2012), 94–146. On Hildebrand's newspaper *Christliche Ständestaat,* see Rudolf Ebneth, *Die österreichische Wochenschrift "Der christliche Ständestaat": Deutsche Emigration in Österreich, 1933–1938* (Mainz, 1976).

42. Samuel Moyn, *Christian Human Rights* (Philadelphia, 2015).

43. For an overview, see Paul Hanebrink, "European Protestants between Anti-Communism and Anti-Totalitarianism," *Journal of Contemporary History,* forthcoming in print; available online at http://journals.sagepub .com/doi/abs/10.1177/0022009417704894.

44. "Judentum gegen Christentum," *Evangelium im Dritten Reich* 6, no. 13 (March 28, 1937): 4. On editor Johannes Schleuning, see Manfred

Gailus, *Protestantismus und Nationalsozialismus. Studien zur nationalsozialistischen Durchdringung des protestantischen Sozialmilieus in Berlin* (Cologne, 2001), 466–74.

45. Scholder, "Politics and Church Politics in the Third Reich," 150.

46. Wolfgang Gerlach, *And the Witnesses Were Silent: The Confessing Church and the Persecution of the Jews*, trans. Victoria J. Barnett (Lincoln, NE, 2000), citation on 105.

47. J. H. Oldham, *The Oxford Conference (Official Report)* (Chicago, 1937), 49, 85–86.

48. Jérôme Tharaud and Jean Tharaud, *Quand Israël n'est plus roi* (Paris, 1933).

49. Ibid., esp. 74–76, 166–167, 211–238.

50. Jérôme and Jean Tharaud, *Cruelle Espagne* (Paris, 1937), 253.

51. Martin Hurcombe, *France and the Spanish Civil War: Cultural Representations of the War Next Door, 1936–1945* (Farnham, Surrey; Burlington, VT, 2011), 27–28.

52. Ibid., 43. For Maurras's preface, see Maxime Real de Sarte, *Au pays de Franco: Notre frère latin* (Paris, 1937).

53. Jean-Jacques Becker and Serge Berstein, *Histoire de l'anticommunisme* (Paris, 1987), 280–299 and 320–328; citations on 321, 322.

54. Ralph Schor, *L'antisémitisme en France pendant les années trente: Prélude à Vichy* (Brussels, 1992), 117–129.

55. Mathieu Delgeilh, *Les juifs en U.R.S.S.* (Paris, 1935).

56. Pierre Birnbaum, *Anti-Semitism in France: A Political History from Léon Blum to the Present*, trans. Miriam Kochan (Oxford, 1992), 242–247; citations on 243.

57. Schor, *L'antisémitisme en France*, 175–177.

58. Louis Massoutié, *Judaïsme et Marxisme* (Paris, 1939), 120–139, citation on 138–139.

59. Henri Massis, *Defence of the West*, trans. F. S. Flint (New York, 1928), 23.

60. Paul Mazgaj, *Imagining Fascism: The Cultural Politics of the French Young Right, 1930–1945* (Newark, DE, 2007).

61. Sandrine Sanos, *The Aesthetics of Hate: Far-Right Intellectuals, Antisemitism, and Gender in 1930s France* (Stanford, CA, 2013).

62. Ibid., 158–193, citation on 175. See also Paul J. Kingston, *Anti-Semitism in France during the 1930s: Organisations, Personalities and Propaganda* (Hull, UK, 1983), 95–102.

63. Samuel Kalman, *"Le Combat par Tous les Moyens:* Colonial Violence and the Extreme Right in 1930s Oran," *French Historical Studies* 34, no. 1 (Winter 2011): 125–153, esp. 145–146.

64. Andreas Wirsching, "Auf dem Weg zur Kollaborationsideologie: Antibolschewismus, Antisemitismus und Nationalsozialismus im Denken der französischen extremen Rechten 1936 bis 1939," *Vierteljahrshefte für Zeitgeschichte* 41 (1993): 31–60.

65. Agnieszka Pufelska, *Die 'Judäo-Kommune': Ein Feindbild in Polen: Das polnische Selbstverständnis im Schatten des Antisemitismus, 1939–1948* (Paderborn, 2007), 53.

66. Modras, *The Catholic Church and Antisemitism,*112–113.

67. Quoted in Joanna B. Michlic, *Poland's Threatening Other: The Image of the Jew from 1880 to the Present* (Lincoln, NE, 2006), 90–91.

68. Timothy Snyder, *Sketches from a Secret War: A Polish Artist's Mission to Liberate Soviet Ukraine* (New Haven, CT, 2005), 28.

69. Peter Polak-Springer, *Recovered Territory: A German-Polish Conflict Over Land and Culture, 1919–89* (New York, 2015).

70. Waddington, *Hitler's Crusade,* 117–118.

71. Mikołaj Stanisław Kunicki, *Between the Brown and the Red: Nationalism, Catholicism, and Communism in Twentieth-Century Poland: The Politics of Bolesław Piasecki* (Athens, OH, 2012), 28–51.

72. Waddington, *Hitler's Crusade,* 116–117; C. A. Macartney, *October Fifteenth: A History of Modern Hungary, 1929–1945,* 2nd ed., Part 1 (Edinburgh, 207); "formal gesture": Gerhard Weinberg, *Hitler's Foreign Policy, 1933–1939: The Road to World War II* (New York, 2005), 668.

73. János Gyurgyák, *A zsidókérdés Magyarországon: Politikai eszmetörténet* (Budapest,2001), 377–430.

74. Gyula Gömbös, *Válogatott politikai beszédek és írások,* ed. József Vonyó (Budapest, 2004), 666.

75. Gyurgák, *A zsidókérdés Magyarországon,* 411–430. See also Mária M. Kovács, *Törvénytől sújtva: A numerus clausus Magyarországon, 1920–1945* (Budapest, 2012).

76. Hermann Fehst, *Bolschewismus und Judentum: Das jüdische Element in der Führerschaft des Bolschewismus* (Berlin, 1934).

77. Hermann Fehst, *Bolsevizmus és a zsidóság*, trans. Zoltán Bosnyák (Mezőberény, Hungary, 1936).

78. Valentin Săndulescu, "Sacralised Politics in Action: The February 1937 Burial of the Romanian Legionary Leaders Ion Moța and Vasile Marin," *Totalitarian Movements and Political Religions* 8, no. 2 (June 2007): 259–269.

79. For another account of the Romanian legionaries in Spain, see Judith Keene, *Fighting for Franco: International Volunteers in Nationalist Spain during the Spanish Civil War, 1936–1939* (London, 2001), 215–244; On Romanian foreign policy in this period, see Rebecca Haynes, *Romanian Policy towards Germany, 1936–40* (New York, 2000); on the history of Romanian Communism in the interwar years, see Vladimir Tismaneanu, *Stalinism for All Seasons: A Political History of Romanian Communism* (Berkeley, CA, 2003), 37–85.

80. Moța citation in Săndulescu, "Sacralised Politics in Action," 261, see also 265; Eliade citations are in Leon Volovici, *Nationalist Ideology and Antisemitism: The Case of Romanian Intellectuals in the 1930s*, trans. Charles Kormos (Oxford, 1991), 83–84; "The Bolshevik demon . . .": quoted in Radu Ioanid, *The Sword of the Archangel: Fascist Ideology in Romania*, trans. Peter Heinegg (Boulder, CO, 1990), 147.

81. Ioanid, *The Sword of the Archangel*, 102.

82. Mihail Sebastian, *Journal: 1935–1944*, trans. Patrick Camiller (Chicago, 2000), 60.

83. On the history of Jewish emancipation in Romania, see Carol Iancu, *Jews in Romania, 1866–1919: From Exclusion to Emancipation*, trans. Carvel de Bussy (Boulder, CO, 1996), and Carole Fink, *Defending the Rights of Others: The Great Powers, the Jews, and International Minority Protection, 1878–1938* (Cambridge, 2004), 3–38. On "anti-politicianism," see Roland Clark, "Anti-Masonry as Political Protest: Fascists and Freemasons in Interwar Romania," *Patterns of Prejudice* 46, no. 1 (2012): 40–57. Both Codreanu citations come from his 1936 book *Pentru legionari*, as translated in Corneliu Zelea Codreanu, *For My Legionaries* (Madrid, 1976), accessed September 9, 2013, http://ia600501.us.archive.org/10/items/ForMyLegionaries TheIronGuard/ForMyLegionaries.pdf.

4. A Barbarous Enemy

1. François Furet, *The Passing of an Illusion: The Idea of Communism in the Twentieth Century*, trans. Deborah Furet (Chicago, 1999), 315–330.

2. Cited in Richard Francis Crane, *Passion of Israel: Jacques Maritain, Catholic Conscience, and the Holocaust* (Scranton, PA, 2010), 155n67.

3. Charles F. Delzell, "Pius XII, Italy, and the Outbreak of War," *Journal of Contemporary History* 2, no. 4 (October 1967): 137–161, here 147–151.

4. Agnieszka Pufelska, *Die "Judäo-Kommune": Ein Feindbild in Polen: Das polnische Selbstverständnis im Schatten des Antisemitismus, 1939–1948* (Paderborn, 2007), 64–88 and 95–100.

5. Rudolf Paksa, "Szélsőjobboldali mozgalmak az 1930-as években," in *A magyar jobboldali hagyomány, 1900–1948*, ed. Ignác Romsics (Budapest, 2009), 275–304.

6. C. A. Macartney, *October Fifteenth: A History of Modern Hungary, 1929–1945*, 2nd ed., 2 vols.(Edinburgh, 1961), 1:365–366.

7. Lorna Waddington, *Hitler's Crusade: Bolshevism and the Myth of the Jewish Conspiracy* (London, 2007), 157 and 256n4.

8. Wolfram Wette, "Das Russlandbild in der NS-Propaganda: Ein Problemaufriss," in *Das Russlandbild im Dritten Reich*, ed. Hans-Erich Volkmann (Cologne, 1994), 63.

9. Jeffrey Herf, *The Jewish Enemy: Nazi Propaganda during World War II and the Holocaust* (Cambridge, MA, 2008), 27.

10. Lorna Waddington, "The Anti-Komintern and Nazi Anti-Bolshevik Propaganda in the 1930s," *Journal of Contemporary History* 42, no. 4 (2007): 573–594, here 592.

11. Ibid., 592.

12. Ian Kershaw, *Hitler, 1936–45: Nemesis* (New York, 2000), 12.

13. Gerhard L. Weinberg, "The Nazi-Soviet Pacts: A Half-Century Later," in *Germany, Hitler, and World War II: Essays in Modern German and World History* (Cambridge, 1995), 168–181.

14. Elke Fröhlich, ed., *Die Tagebücher von Joseph Goebbels*, Part 1, vol. 9 (Munich, 1998–2008), 400 (entry of June 24, 1941).

15. Hermann Greife, *Sowjetforschung* (Berlin, 1936), 31–36, 70. See also Andre Gerrits, *The Myth of Jewish Communism* (New York, 2008), 64.

16. Jan C. Behrends, "Back from the USSR: The Anti-Comintern's Publications on Soviet Russia in Nazi Germany (1935–1941), *Kritika* 10, no. 3 (Summer 2009): 536n45.

17. Hermann Greife, *Zwangsarbeit in der Sowjetunion* [Forced labor in the Soviet Union] (Berlin, 1936), citations on 5 and 45. For a reliable account of the White Sea Canal project with figures on numbers of workers and death rates, see Anne Applebaum, *Gulag: A History* (New York, 2003), 58–72. Recent scholarly analyses of the gulag system include Applebaum's *Gulag* and Oleg V. Khlevniuk, *The History of the Gulag: From Collectivization to the Great Terror*, trans. Vadim A. Staklo (New Haven, CT, 2004).

18. Greife, *Sowjetforschung*, 12.

19. Hermann Greife, *Ist eine Entwicklung der Sowjetunion zum nationalen Staat möglich?* (Berlin, 1939).

20. Greife, *Sowjetforschung*, 70.

21. In addition to the works by Greife, some examples include: Herman Fehst, *Bolschewismus und Judentum: Das jüdische Element in der Führerschaft des Bolschewismus* (Berlin, 1934); Adolf Ehrt, *Der Weltbolschewismus: Ein internationales Gemeinschaftswerk über die bolschewistische Wühlarbeit und die Umsturzversuche der Komintern in allen Ländern* (Berlin, 1936); and Niels Närk, *Das bringt die Rote Armee* (Berlin, 1936). On Soviet studies in Nazi Germany, see the remarks by Jan C. Behrends in Behrends, "Back from the USSR, 536n45.

22. Adolf Ehrt, *Bewaffneter Aufstand! Enthüllungen über kommunistischen Umsturzversuch am Vorabend der nationalen Revolution* (Berlin, 1933).

23. Hans-Erich Volkmann, ed., *Das Russlandbild im dritten Reich* (Cologne, 1994); Michael Burleigh, *Germany Turns Eastwards: A Study of Ostforschung in the Third Reich* (Cambridge, 1988).

24. For Hitler's appeal to soldiers on the Eastern Front (June 22, 1941) and notes from his address to military leaders (March 30, 1941), see Gerd R. Ueberschär and Wolfram Wette, eds., *"Unternehmen Barbarossa": Der deutsche Überfall auf der Sowjetunion, 1941: Berichte, Analysen, Dokumente* (Paderborn, 1984), 302–303 and 319–323.

25. Gesamtverband deutscher antikommunistischer Vereinigungen, *Warum Krieg mit Stalin? Das Rotbuch der Anti-Komintern* (Berlin, 1941).

26. Quoted in Wette, "Das Russlandbild in der NS Propaganda," 65. See also Herf, *The Jewish Enemy*, esp. 92–138. For another typical example, see Joseph Goebbels, "Mimikry" (July 20, 1941), in *Die Zeit ohne Beispiel: Reden und Aufsätze aus den Jahren 1939/40/41* (Munich, 1941), 526–531.

27. For texts of the Guidelines for the Conduct of Troops in the East, the so-called Commissar Order, and General Gerd Hoepner's order to the Fourth Tank Group, see Ueberschär and Wette, *"Unternehmen Barbarossa,"* 305, 312–315.

28. See the documents in ibid.; see also Peter Longerich, *Holocaust: The Nazi Persecution and Murder of the Jews* (Oxford, 2010), 190.

29. Quoted in Kai Struve, *Deutsche Herrschaft, ukrainischer Nationalismus, antijüdische Gewalt: Der Sommer 1941 in der Westukraine* (Berlin, 2015), 129 and, generally, 124–130.

30. Klaus-Michael Mallman, "Die Türöffner der 'Endlösung': Zur Genesis des Genozids," in *Die Gestapo im Zweiten Weltkrieg: 'Heimatfront' und besetztes Europa*, ed. Gerhard Paul and Klaus-Michael Mallmann (Darmstadt, 2000), 437–463, here 443.

31. Mark Edele and Michael Geyer, "States of Exception: The Nazi-Soviet War as a System of Violence, 1939–1945," in *Beyond Totalitarianism: Stalinism and Nazism Compared*, ed. Michael Geyer and Sheila Fitzpatrick (Cambridge, 2009), 345–395.

32. The so-called Reichenau Order is reprinted in Ueberschär and Wette, *"Unternehmen Barbarossa,"* 339–340. On Reichenau and the Sixth Army, see Bernd Boll and Hans Safrian, "On the Way to Stalingrad: The 6th Army in 1941–42," in *War of Extermination: The German Military in World War II, 1941–1944*, ed. Hannes Heer and Klaus Naumann (New York, 2000), 237–271.

33. Felix Römer, *Der Kommissarbefehl: Wehrmacht und NS-Verbrechen an der Ostfront* (Paderborn, 2008); Christian Streit, *Keine Kameraden: Die Wehrmacht und die sowjetischen Kriegsgefangenen* (Stuttgart, 1978).

34. Longerich, *Holocaust*, 196–205, citation on 202.

35. Edward B. Westermann, *Hitler's Police Battalions: Enforcing Racial War in the East* (Lawrence, KS, 2005), 163–199, citation on 175.

36. Tarik Cyril Amar, *The Paradox of Ukrainian Lviv: A Borderland City between Stalinists, Nazis, and Nationalists* (Ithaca, NY, 2015), 95n37.

37. Jutta Sywottek, *Mobilmachung für den totalen Krieg: Die propagandistische Vorbereitung der deutschen Bevölkerung auf den Zweiten Weltkrieg* (Opladen, Germany, 1976); Jay W. Baird, *The Mythical World of Nazi War Propaganda, 1939–1945* (Minneapolis, 1974).

38. Ben Shepherd, *War in the Wild East: The German Army and Soviet Partisans* (Cambridge, MA, 2004), 58–83.

39. Estimates of the number of people murdered by the NKVD in L'viv's prisons in the summer of 1941 vary. Historian Tarik Amar suggests there were about 2,500 victims. Amar, *The Paradox of Ukrainian Lviv*, 95n37.

40. "'Once again I've got to play general to the Jews': From the Diary of Blutsordenträger Felix Landau," in *"The Good Old Days": The Holocaust as Seen by Its Perpetrators and Bystanders*, ed. Ernst Klee, Willi Dressen, and Volker Riess, trans. Deborah Burnstone (New York, 1991), 89–91. On L'viv / Lwów / Lemberg during the transition from Soviet to Nazi rule, see Amar, *The Paradox of Ukrainian Lviv*, 88–142, esp. 93–101, and Christoph Mick, *Lemberg, Lwów, L'viv, 1914–1947: Violence and Ethnicity in a Contested City* (West Lafayette, IN, 2016), 259–372.

41. Jürgen Matthäus et al., eds., *Ausbildungsziel Judenmord? 'Weltanschauliche Erziehung' von SS, Polizei und Waffen-SS im Rahmen der 'Endlösung'* (Frankfurt-am-Main, 2003). The following case is cited in Struve, *Deutsche Herrschaft*, 225–229.

42. Christian Gerlach, *The Extermination of the European Jews* (Cambridge, 2016), 141–311.

43. See Mallmann, "Die Türöffner der 'Endlösung,'" and also Christian Streit, "Ostkrieg, Antibolschewismus, und 'Endlösung,'" *Geschichte und Gesellschaft* 17, no. 2 (1991): 242–255.

44. Jean Ancel, "The Iassy Syndrome (I)," *Romanian Jewish Studies* 1, no. 1 (Spring 1987): 33–49, here 43–46. See also the 2004 Final Report of the International Commission on the Holocaust in Romania, available on the United States Holocaust Memorial Museum web page "Romania: Facing Its Past," accessed January 8, 2018, www.ushmm.org/research/scholarly-presentations/symposia/holocaust-in-romania/romania-facing-its-past.

45. Dennis Deletant, *Hitler's Forgotten Ally: Ion Antonescu and His Regime, Romania 1940–1944* (Houndmills, Basingstoke, UK, 2006), 130.

46. On the Iaşi pogrom, see Radu Ioanid, "The Holocaust in Romania: The Iaşi Pogrom of 1941," *Contemporary European History* 2, no. 2 (July 1993): 119–148. "Did you think": quoted in Dennis Deletant, "Transnistria and the Romanian Solution to the 'Jewish Problem,'" in *The Shoah in Ukraine: History, Testimony, Memorialization*, ed. Ray Brandon and Wendy Lower (Bloomington, IN, 2008), 156–190, here 160. "Diabolical perseverance": Deletant, *Hitler's Forgotten Ally*, 116. On the Holocaust in Romania generally, see Radu Ioanid, *The Holocaust in Romania: The Destruction of Jews and Gypsies under the Antonescu Regime, 1940–1944* (Chicago, 2000).

47. On Poland, see Jan Tomaz Gross, *Revolution from Abroad: The Soviet Conquest of Poland's Western Ukraine and Western Belorussia* (Princeton, NJ, 1988); on Lithuania, Christoph Dieckmann, *Deutsche Besatzungspolitik in Litauen, 1941–1944* (Göttingen, 2011), 147–177.

48. Deletant, *Hitler's Forgotten Ally*, 17.

49. On Karski, see Pufelska, "*Judäo-Kommune*," 75.

50. Elazar Barkan, Elizabeth A. Cole, and Kai Struve, eds., *Shared History, Divided Memory: Jews and Others in Soviet-Occupied Poland, 1939–1941* (Leipzig, 2007).

51. Anna Bikont, *The Crime and the Silence: Confronting the Massacre of Jews in Wartime Jedwabne*, trans. Alissa Valles (New York, 2015), 105. See also Pufelska, "*Judäo-Kommune*," 64–88, and Joanna B. Michlic, "The Soviet-Occupation of Poland, 1939–1941, and the Stereotype of the Anti-Polish and Pro-Soviet Jew," *Jewish Social Studies* 13, no. 3 (Spring/Summer 2007): 135–176, here 142–146.

52. *Final Report of the International Commission*, section 3, "The June/July 1940 Romanian Withdrawal," 14–15, accessed January 6, 2018, www.ushmm.org/m/pdfs/20080226-romania-commission-bessarabia.pdf.

53. Vladimir Solonari, "Patterns of Violence: The Local Population and the Mass Murder of Jews in Bessarabia and Northern Bukovina, July–August 1941," *Kritika* 8, no. 4 (Fall 2007): 778.

54. Struve, *Deutsche Herrschaft*, 130–137, citations on 130, 132, 134.

55. On the L'viv pogrom, see ibid., 247–432; John-Paul Himka, "The Lviv Pogrom of 1941: The Germans, Ukrainian Nationalists, and the Carnival Crowd," *Canadian Slavonic Papers/Revue canadienne des slavistes* 53 (2011): 209–243.

56. On the Kaunas pogrom, see Dieckmann, *Deutsche Besatzungspolitik in Litauen*,313–337, figures on 331.

57. Jan Tomasz Gross, *Neighbors: The Destruction of the Jewish Community in Jedwabne, Poland* (New York, 2002).

58. The number of victims is taken from Longerich, *Holocaust*, 195.

59. Diana Dumitru, *The State, Antisemitism, and Collaboration in the Holocaust: The Borderlands of Romania and the Soviet Union* (New York, 2016), 139–176, incident at Pepeni on 151–153.

60. Gross, *Neighbors*, 45.

61. On L'viv, see Struve, *Deutsche Herrschaft*, here esp. 428–432, and Himka, "The Lviv Pogrom of 1941." On Kaunas, see Dieckmann, *Deutsche Besatzungspolitik in Litauen*, 317–319, citation on 317.

62. Timothy Snyder makes this point in *Black Earth: The Holocaust as History and Warning* (New York, 2015), esp. 144–178.

63. Struve, *Deutsche Herrschaft*, 247–432.

64. On Romanian-German frictions over ethnic policy, see Vladimir Solonari, *Purifying the Nation: Population Exchange and Ethnic Cleansing in Nazi-Allied Romania* (Washington, DC, and Baltimore, 2010), and Andrej Angrick, *Besatzungspolitik und Massenmord: Die Einsatzgruppe D in der südlichen Sowjetunion, 1941–1943* (Hamburg, 2003). Citation from Andrej Angrick, "Otto Ohlendorf und die Tätigkeit der Einsatzgruppe D," in *Nachrichtendienst, politische Elite, Mordeinheit: Der Sicherheitsdienst des Reichsführers SS*, ed. Michael Wildt (Hamburg, 2003), 267–302, here 274.

65. Kai Struve, "Rites of Violence? The Pogroms of Summer 1941," *Polin* 24 (2011): 257–274. On folk beliefs in Jewish otherness: Alina Cala, *The Image of the Jew in Polish Folk Culture* (Jerusalem, 1995), and Andrei Oişteanu, *Inventing the Jew: Antisemitic Stereotypes in Romanian and Other Central East-European Cultures* (Lincoln, NE, and Jerusalem, 2009). On pogroms as symbolic violence: William W. Hagen, "The Moral Economy of Ethnic Violence: The Pogrom in Lwów, November 1918," *Geschichte und Gesellschaft* 31, no. 2 (2005): 203–226.

66. Gross, *Neighbors*, 61–62.

67. Armin Heinen, *Rumänien, der Holocaust und die Logik der Gewalt* (Munich, 2007), 109–126, esp. 121–124.

68. Solonari, "Patterns of Violence," 779–780.

69. Gross, *Neighbors*, 109. The question of "double collaboration" is a major theme in Snyder, *Black Earth*. See also Marci Shore's reflections on this in "Conversing with Ghosts: Jedwabne, *Żydokomuna*, and Totalitarianism," *Kritika* 6, no. 2 (Spring 2005): 345–374.

70. Struve, *Deutsche Herrschaft*, 392–394, here 392.

71. Fröhlich, *Die Tagebücher von Joseph Goebbels*, 9:428, entry of July 6, 1941.

72. On L'viv in German newsreels, see Bianka Pietrow-Ennker, "Die Sowjetunion in der Propaganda des Dritten Reiches: Das Beispiel der *Wochenschau*," *Militärgeschichtliche Mitteilungen* 2 (1989): 79–120, here 94–95.

73. "Satanic criminals": Struve, *Deutsche Herrschaft*, 394. Joseph Goebbels, "Der Schleier fällt," *Das Reich*, July 6, 1941, reprinted in Goebbels, *Zeit ohne Beispiel*.

74. Gerhard Paul, *BilderMACHT: Studien zur Visual History des 20. und 21. Jahrhunderts* (Göttingen, 2013), 155–199.

75. Wolfgang Diewerge, *Feldpostbriefe aus dem Osten: Deutsche Soldaten sehen die Sowjetunion* (Berlin, 1941), 41–42. For a critical discussion of these letters, see Jochen Hellbeck, "'The Diaries of Fritzes and the Letters of Gretchens': Personal Writings from the German-Soviet War and Their Readers," *Kritika* 10, no. 3 (Summer 2009): 571–606, here 578–580.

76. Hellbeck, "'The Diaries of Fritzes and the Letters of Gretchens,'" 579, and Nicholas Stargardt, *The German War: A Nation under Arms, 1939–1945* (New York, 2005), 157–200, here esp. 164–166.

77. Citations in Stargardt, *The German War*, 163 ("Jewish-Asiatic hordes") and 162 (Bishop Galen).

78. Fröhlich, *Die Tagebücher von Joseph Goebbels*, 9:430, entry of July 7, 1941.

79. Instructions to the Press, June 27, 1941, reprinted in Pietrow-Ennker, "Die Sowjetunion in der Propaganda des Dritten Reiches," 109–112.

80. On Rajniss, see Péter Sipos, "Rajniss Ferenc, a publicista és a politikus," in *Szálasi minisztere voltam: Rajniss Ferenc naplója*, ed. Péter Sipos (Budapest, 2001), 7–43.

81. Brett Bowles, "German Newsreel Propaganda in France, 1940–1944," *Historical Journal of Film, Radio and Television* 24, no. 1 (2004): 45–67.

82. On the exhibition in Paris: Renée Poznanski, *Jews in France during World War II*, trans. Nathan Bracher (Hanover, NH, 2001), 212. More generally: Waddington, *Hitler's Crusade*, 187–196.

83. Maria Bucur-Deckard, *Heroes and Victims: Remembering War in Twentieth Century Romania* (Bloomington, IN, 2010), 148–154.

84. Owen Anthony Davey, "The Origins of the *Légion Volontaire Française contre le Bolchévisme*," *Journal of Contemporary History* 6, no. 4 (1971): 29–45, here 34. On crusade imagery more generally, see Arno Mayer, *Why Did the Heavens Not Darken? The "Final Solution" in History* (New York, 1990), 200–233.

85. Fröhlich, *Die Tagebücher von Joseph Goebbels*, 9:413, entry of June 30, 1941. More generally, see Mark Mazower, *Hitler's Empire: How the Nazis Ruled Europe* (New York, 2008).

86. Gerlach, *Extermination of the European Jews*, 295–296; Peter Lieb, *Konventioneller Krieg oder NS-Weltanschauungskrieg? Kriegführung und Partisanenbekämpfung in Frankreich 1943/44* (Munich, 2007), 20–31.

87. Zoltán Bosnyák, ed., *Az antibolsevista kiállítás tájékoztatója* (Budapest, 1941). See also Holly Case, *Between States: The Transylvanian Question and the European Idea during World War II* (Stanford, CA, 2013).

88. *Warum Krieg mit Stalin?* 126.

89. István Milotay, "Vihar a Kárpátok fölött," *Új Magyarság*, July 3, 1941, 1–2. On Milotay, see Péter Sipos, "Milotay István pályaképéhez," *Századok* 105, no. 3–4 (1971): 709–735; János Gyurgyák, *A zsidókérdés Magyarországon* (Budapest, 2001), 440–446.

90. Robert O. Paxton, *Vichy France: Old Guard and New Order, 1940–1944* (New York, 1972), 249.

91. Lucien Rebatet, *Le bolchevisme contre la civilisation* (Paris, 1941). On Rebatet, see Robert Belot, *Lucien Rebatet: Un itinéraire fasciste* (Paris, 1994).

92. Joseph Goebbels, "Nun, Volk steh auf, und Sturm brich los! Rede im Berliner Sportpalast," German Propaganda Archive, Calvin College, accessed July 21, 2017, http://research.calvin.edu/german-propaganda-archive /goeb36.htm.

93. Peter Longerich, *Joseph Goebbels: Biographie* (Munich, 2010), 570–572, see the diary entry of April 16, 1943, cited on 570.

94. Claudia Weber, "'Too Closely Identified with Dr. Goebbels': Die Massenerschiessungen von Katyn in der Geschichte des zweiten Weltkriegs und des kalten Kriegs," *Zeithistorische Forschungen* 8, no. 1 (2011): 37–59, here 37.

95. Longerich, *Joseph Goebbels*, 570–577.

96. Thomas W. Laqueur, "The Dead Body and Human Rights," in *The Body*, ed. Sean Sweeney and Ian Hodder (Cambridge, 2002), 75–94, citation on 83.

97. Barbara Berzel, *Die französische Literatur im Zeichen von Kollaboration und Faschismus: Alphonse de Châteaubriant, Robert Brasillach, und Jacques Chardonne* (Tübingen, 2012), 193–194.

98. I am grateful to István Deák for sharing with me his memories of wartime anti-Bolshevik discourse in Hungary.

99. László Karsai, "'Shylock Is Whetting His Blade': Fear of the Jews' Revenge in Hungary during World War II," in *The Jews Are Coming Back: The Return of the Jews to Their Countries of Origin after WWII*, ed. David Bankier (Jerusalem, 2005), 293–311, here 297.

100. Jan Grabowski, "German Anti-Jewish Propaganda in the Generalgouvernement, 1939–1945: Inciting Hate through Posters, Film, and Exhibitions," *Holocaust and Genocide Studies* 23, no. 3 (Winter 2009): 381–412, citations on 391–392.

101. "'Ghetto Resistance Seen Correctly,' from the Polish Underground Press," in *Documents on the Holocaust: Selected Sources on the Destruction of the Jews of Germany and Austria, Poland, and the Soviet Union*, ed. Yitzhak Arad et al. (Lincoln, NE, 1999), 322–323.

102. Pufelska, *"Judäo-Kommune,"* 133–141. See also Frank Golczewski, "Die Heimatarmee und die Juden," in *Die polnische Heimatarmee: Geschichte und Mythos der Armia Krajowa seit dem Zweiten Weltkrieg*, ed. Bernhard Chiari (Munich, 2003): 635–679.

103. Ian Kershaw, *The End: The Defiance and Destruction of Hitler's Germany, 1944–45* (New York, 2012), 92–128, esp. 112–114 (for a careful account of what can be known about the Nemmersdorf massacre). See also Longerich, *Joseph Goebbels*, 648.

104. Alice Kaplan, *The Collaborator: The Trial and Execution of Robert Brasillach* (Chicago, 2000), 55.

105. Pufelska, *"Judäo-Kommune,"* here 176–186.

106. Citation in Deletant, "Transnistria," 183n15.

107. "A Belügyminisztérium felhívása a bolsevizmus és a nemzetközi zsidóság elleni harcra, valamint a német biztonsági szolgálat támogatására," Nógrád Megyei Levéltár V. 83. 25 biz / 1944, 1–2. p., from an online collection of documents pertaining to the Holocaust in Nógrád County, within the digital archive of the Nógrád County Archives, accessed January 7, 2018, http://digitalisleveltar.nogradarchiv.hu/NMLFiler/DHOsearch.jsp.

108. István Milotay, "Nem volt más út . . . ," *Új Magyarság*, October 22, 1944.

109. See, e.g., István Milotay, "A megtiport Alföld," *Új Magyarság*, November 26, 1944; Milotay, "Rémtettek kisérik a bolseviták útját a Magyar Alföldön," *Összetartás*, November 5, 1944; Milotay, "Szovjet katonák rémtettei," *Összetartás*, November 29, 1944. On fascist politicization of rape before the end of the war, see James Mark, "Remembering Rape: Divided Social Memory and the Red Army in Hungary, 1944–1945," *Past and Present*, no. 188 (August 2005): 133–161, see esp. 145–154. Magdolna Gergely, "Anka naplója," *Budapesti Negyed* 10, no. 3 (Fall 2002), entry for September 1, 1944, accessed January 7, 2018, http://epa.oszk.hu/00000/00003/00028/.

110. István Milotay, "Az ember üvölt . . . ," *Új Magyarság*, December 14, 1944.

5. Under Communist Rule

1. István Deák, *Europe on Trial: The Story of Collaboration, Resistance, and Retribution during World War II* (Philadelphia, 2015), 139–164.

2. Agnieszka Pufelska, *Die "Judäo-Kommune": Ein Feindbild in Polen: Das polnische Selbstverständnis im Schatten des Antisemitismus, 1939–1948* (Paderborn, 2007), 164–202.

3. Šarūnas Liekis, "Soviet Resistance and Jewish Partisans in Lithuania," *Polin* 25 (2012): 331–356. More generally, see Christoph Dieckmann, *Deutsche Besatzungspolitik in Litauen, 1941–1944*, 2 vols. (Göttingen,

2011), 2:1400–1496; and Bogdan Musiał, *Sowjetische Partisanen, 1941–1944: Mythos und Wirklichkeit* (Paderborn, 2009), 378–406.

4. On László Németh: László Karsai, "'Shylock Is Whetting His Blade': Fear of the Jews' Revenge in Hungary during World War II," in *The Jews are Coming Back: The Return of the Jews to Their Countries of Origin after World War II*, ed. David Bankier (New York and Jerusalem, 2005), 293–311. On the populist movement, see Levente Sipos and Pál Péter Tóth, eds., *A népi mozgalom és a magyar társadalom: Tudományos tanácskozás a szárszói találkozó 50. évfordulója alkalmából* (Budapest, 1997).

5. Jean Ancel, "'The New Jewish Invasion': The Return of the Survivors from Transnistria," in Bankier, *The Jews Are Coming Back*, 231–256, here 235.

6. Andrea Pető estimates between 50,000 and 200,000 instances of rape in Budapest. See Andrea Pető, "Átvonuló hadsereg, maradandó trauma," *Történelmi Szemle* 41, no. 1–2 (1999): 85–108.

7. "Our situation" and "people blame": Peter Kenez, *Hungary from the Nazis to the Soviets: The Establishment of the Communist Regime in Hungary, 1944–1948* (Cambridge, 2006), 44–45; "the people live in fear": Krisztián Ungváry, *Battle for Budapest: One Hundred Days in World War II*, trans. Ladislaus Löb (London, 2003), 288. On Soviet violence in Eastern Europe generally, see Anne Applebaum, *Iron Curtain: The Crushing of Eastern Europe, 1944–1956* (New York, 2012), 94–123.

8. Esztergomi Prímási Levéltár (EPL) 3282/1946, letter of Magdolna Homonnay.

9. Marci Shore, "'If We're Proud of Freud . . .': The Family Romance of Judeo-Bolshevism," *East European Politics and Societies* 23, no. 3 (Summer 2009): 298–314, here 310.

10. On Poland, see Jan Tomasz Gross, *Fear: Anti-Semitism in Poland after Auschwitz: An Essay in Historical Interpretation* (New York, 2006), 227, and Jaff Schatz, *The Generation: The Rise and Fall of the Jewish Communists of Poland* (Berkeley, CA, 1991); Hungary: István Deák, "Jews and Communism: The Hungarian Case," in *Dark Times, Dire Decisions: Jews and Communism*, ed. Jonathan Frankel (Oxford, 2004), 38–62; Romania: Robert Levy, *Ana Pauker: The Rise and Fall of a Jewish Communist* (Berkeley, CA, 2001).

11. André Gerrits, *The Myth of Jewish Communism: A Historical Interpretation* (Brussels, 2009), 130–154.

12. László Karsai, "Crime and Punishment: People's Courts, Revolutionary Legality, and the Hungarian Holocaust," 1–13, citation on 7, accessed June 14, 2017, http://ece.columbia.edu/files/ece/images/karsai2.pdf. Also see Mária Palasik, *Félelembe zárt múlt: Politikai gyilkosságok Gyömrőn és környékén 1945-ben* (Budapest, 2010).

13. Gross, *Fear*, 52–57; Karsai, "Crime and Punishment," 7.

14. On the Kunmadaras pogrom, see Éva Standeisky, "Antiszemita megmozdulások Magyarországon a koaliciós időszakban," *Századok* 128, no. 2 (1992): 284–308; Péter Apor, "A népi demokrácia építése: Kunmadaras, 1946," *Századok* 132, no. 3 (1998): 601–632. There is a large literature on the Kielce pogrom. For one account, see Bożena Szaynok, "The Pogrom of Jews in Kielce, July 4, 1946," *Yad Vashem Studies* 22 (1992): 199–235. For an interpretation, see Gross, *Fear*.

15. Gross, *Fear*, 145.

16. Bożena Szaynok, "The Role of Antisemitism in Postwar Polish-Jewish Relations," in *Antisemitism and Its Opponents in Modern Poland*, ed. Robert Blobaum (Ithaca, NY, 2005), 265–284, here 277.

17. In addition to Gross, *Fear*, see Joanna Tokarska-Bakir, "Cries of the Mob in the Pogroms in Rzeszów (June 1945), Cracow (August 1945), and Kielce (July 1946) as a Source for the State of Mind of the Participants," *East European Politics and Societies* 25, no. 3 (August 2011): 553–574; Marcin Zaremba, "The Myth of Ritual Murder in Post-War Poland," *Polin* 23 (2010): 465–506; János Pelle, *Az utolsó vérvádak: Az etnikai gyűlölet és a politikai manipuláció kelet-európai történetéből* (Budapest, 1996).

18. József Darvas, "Őszinte szó a zsidókérdésben!," *Szabad Nép*, March 25, 1945.

19. Levy, *Ana Pauker*, 76.

20. Cited in Róbert Győri Szabó, *A kommunizmus és a zsidóság az 1945 utáni Magyarországon* (Budapest, 2009), 122.

21. Apor, "A népi demokrácia építése," 601–632.

22. Gross, *Fear*, 126–127.

23. Ibid., 120–128 and 153–156, citations on 124–125.

24. Éva Standeisky, "Antiszemita megmozdulások Magyarországon a koaliciós időszakban," *Századok* 128, no. 2 (1992): 284–308, here 290–291. See also Apor, "A népi demokácia építése," 605–607, citation on 607.

25. Standeisky, "Antiszemita megmozdulások," 291.

26. Andrew C. Janos, "The Agrarian Opposition at the National Congress of Councils," in *Revolution in Perspective: Essays on the Soviet Hungarian Republic of 1919*, ed. Andrew C. Janos and William B. Slottman (Berkeley, CA, 1971), 85–108.

27. T. David Curp, *A Clean Sweep? The Politics of Ethnic Cleansing in Western Poland, 1945–1960* (Rochester, NY, 2006).

28. Michal Frankl, "'Sonderweg' of Czech National Antisemitism? Nationalism, National Conflict, and Antisemitism in Czech Society in the Late 19th Century," *Bohemia* 46, no. 1 (2005): 120–134. On antisemitism in wartime Slovakia, see Ivan Kamenec, *On the Trail of Tragedy: The Holocaust in Slovakia* (Bratislava, 2007).

29. On Eastern Europe's show trials, see Melissa Feinberg, *Curtain of Lies: The Battle over Truth in Stalinist Eastern Europe* (New York, 2017), 1–30.

30. Ibid., 6.

31. On the conception of the trial, see Karel Kaplan, "Der politische Prozess gegen R. Slánský und Genossen," in *Der Spätstalinismus und die 'jüdische Frage': Zur antisemitischen Wendung des Kommunismus*, ed. Leonid Luks (Cologne, 1998), 169–188.

32. On the trial and popular antisemitism, see Melissa Feinberg, "Fantastic Truths, Compelling Lies: Radio Free Europe and the Response to the Slánský Trial in Czechoslovakia," *Contemporary European History* 22, no. 1 (2013), 107–125, and Kevin McDermott, "A 'Polyphony of Voices'? Czech Popular Opinion and the Slánský Affair," *Slavic Review* 67, no. 4 (Winter 2008), 840–865.

33. On the Czech-German ethnic dimension, see Jan Gerber, *Ein Prozess in Prag: Das Volk gegen Rudolf Slánský und Genossen* (Göttingen, 2016).

34. Amir Weiner, "When Memory Counts: War, Genocide, and Postwar Soviet Jewry," in *Landscaping the Human Garden: Twentieth Century Population Management in a Comparative Framework*, ed. Amir Weiner (Stanford, CA, 2003), 167–188; Zvi Y. Gitelman, *A Century of Ambivalence: The Jews of Russia and the Soviet Union, 1881 to the Present*, 2nd expanded ed. (Bloomington, IN, 2001), 144–173; Jeffrey Veidlinger, *The Moscow State*

Yiddish Theater: Jewish Culture on the Soviet Stage (Bloomington, IN, 2000), 252–275.

35. On the Hungarian case: Róbert Győri Szabó, A *kommunizmus és a zsidóság az 1945 utáni Magyarországon* (Budapest, 2009), 204–227. On Paul Merker: Jeffrey Herf, "East German Communists and the Jewish Question: The Case of Paul Merker," *Journal of Contemporary History* 29, no. 4 (October 1994): 627–661.

36. Raymond Taras, "Gomułka's 'Rightist-Nationalist Deviation,' the Postwar Jewish Communists, and the Stalinist Reaction in Poland," *Nationalities Papers* 22, Supplement no. 1 (1994): 111–127, citations on 113, 118. On the letter to Stalin, see Lech W. Głukowski, ed., "Gomułka Writes to Stalin in 1948," *Polin* 17 (2004): 365–384, citation on 379.

37. Audrey Kichelewski, "Imagining 'the Jews' in Stalinist Poland: Nationalists or Cosmopolites?" *European Review of History: Revue européenne l'histoire* 17, no. 3 (2010): 503–522.

38. Dariusz Stola, "The Hate Campaign of March 1968: How Did It Become Anti-Jewish?" *Polin* 21 (2009): 16–36.

39. Levy, *Ana Pauker*. See also Pavel Câmpeanu, "Aspects of Romanian Stalinism's History: Ana Pauker, a Victim of Anti-Semitism?" *East European Politics and Societies* 14, no. 2 (2000): 157–178.

40. Katherine Verdery, *National Ideology under Socialism: Identity and Cultural Politics in Ceauşescu's Romania* (Berkeley, CA, 1991), and Michael Shafir, "The Men of the Archangel Revisited: Anti-Semitic Formations among Communist Romania's Intellectuals," *Studies in Comparative Communism* 16, no. 3 (Autumn 1983): 223–243.

41. "Perpetual light of remembrance": Courtney Glore Crimmins, "Reinterpreting the Soviet War Memorial in Berlin's Treptower Park after 1990," in *Remembering the German Democratic Republic: Divided Memory in a United Germany*, ed. David Clarke and Ute Wölfel (Houndmills, Basingstoke, UK, 2011), 54–65, here 55. "In the center of Europe": Martin Gegner, "War Monuments in East and West Berlin: Cold War Symbols or Different Forms of Memorial?" in *The Heritage of War*, ed. Martin Gegner and Bart Ziino (London, 2012), 64–87, here 72. On Soviet war memorials in Berlin, see Helga Köpstein, *Die sowjetischen Ehrenmale in Berlin* (Berlin, 2006), esp. 83–170.

42. Jeffrey Herf, *Divided Memory: The Nazi Past in the Two Germanys* (Cambridge, MA, 1997); Christina Morina, *Legacies of Stalingrad: Remembering the Eastern Front in Germany since 1945* (New York, 2011).

43. Eric D. Weitz, "Rosa Luxemburg Belongs to Us! German Communism and the Luxemburg Legacy," *Central European History* 27, no. 1 (March 1994): 27–64.

44. In addition to Herf, *Divided Memory*, see Thomas Fox, *Stated Memory: East Germany and the Holocaust* (Rochester, NY, 1999), and Peter Monteath, "The German Democratic Republic and the Jews," *German History* 22, no. 3 (July 2004): 448–468.

45. Péter Apor, *Fabricating Authenticity in Soviet Hungary: The Afterlife of the First Hungarian Soviet Republic in the Age of State Socialism* (London, 2015). See also István Rév, *Retroactive Justice: Prehistory of Post-Communism* (Stanford, CA, 2005), 210–224.

46. Maria Bucur, *Heroes and Victims: Remembering War in Twentieth-Century Romania* (Bloomington, IN, 2009), 144–193, citation on 159.

47. On memory of the Holocaust in Communist Poland, see Michael C. Steinlauf, *Bondage to the Dead: Poland and the Memory of the Holocaust* (Syracuse, NY, 1997), citations on 69 and 73. On memory of the Home Army under Communism, see Andrzej Waśkiewicz, "The Polish Home Army and the Politics of Memory," *East European Politics and Societies* 24, no. 1 (Winter 2010): 44–58, and Bernhard Chiari, ed., *Die polnische Heimatarmee: Geschichte und Mythos der Armia Krajowa seit dem Zweiten Weltkrieg* (Munich, 2003), 679–864.

48. Jan Tomasz Gross, *Neighbors: The Destruction of the Jewish Community in Jedwabne, Poland* (New York, 2002), 8–14; Gross, *Fear*, 52–57; Anna Bikont, *The Crime and the Silence: Confronting the Massacre of Jews in Wartime Jedwabne*, trans. Alissa Valles (New York, 2015), 513–524, esp. 516–517.

49. Vladimir Solonari, "Public Discourses on the Holocaust in Moldova: Justification, Instrumentalization, and Mourning," in *Bringing the Dark Past to Light: The Reception of the Holocaust in Postcommunist Europe*, ed. John-Paul Himka and Joanna Beata Michlic (Lincoln, NE, 2013), 377–402. Soviet trial sources were used to write the history of the Holocaust in Romania in Vladimir Solonari, "Patterns of Violence: The Local Popu-

lation and the Mass Murder of Jews in Bessarabia and Northern Bukovina, July–August 1941," *Kritika* 8, no. 4 (Fall 2007): 749–787," and Diana Dumitru, *The State, Antisemitism, and Collaboration in the Holocaust: The Borderlands of Romania and the Soviet Union* (New York, 2016). On memory of the Iași pogrom, see Bucur, *Heroes and Victims*, 157–158.

6. From Judeo-Bolshevism to Judeo-Christian Civilization

1. On the curious biography of Matthes Ziegler, see Manfred Gailus, "Vom 'gottgläubigen' Kirchenkämpfer Rosenbergs zum 'christgläubigen' Pfarrer Niemöllers: Matthes Zieglers wunderbare Wandlungen im 20. Jahrhundert," *Zeitschrift für Geschichtswissenschaft* 54, no. 11 (2006): 937–973.

2. Matthes Ziegler, *Der Protestantismus zwischen Rom und Moskau* (Munich, 1937), 28.

3. *Deutsche Wochenschau*, no. 755/10, 1945, accessed June 2, 2016, https://archive.org/details/1945-03-22-Die-Deutsche-Wochenschau-Nr.755.

4. Carola Tischler, "Die Vereinfachungen des Genossen Erenburg: Eine Endkriegs- und eine Nachkriegskontroverse," in *Rotarmisten schreiben aus Deutschland: Breife von der Front (1945) und historische Analysen*, ed. Elke Scherstjanoi (Munich, 2004), 326–339, citation on 333.

5. Ibid.; see also Peter Jahn, ed., *Ilya Ehrenburg und die Deutschen* (Berlin, 1997), esp. 67–77.

6. Atina Grossmann, "A Question of Silence: The Rape of German Women by Occupation Soldiers," *October* 72 (Spring 1995): 42–63, here esp. 50–53; Norman M. Naimark, *The Russians in Germany: A History of the Soviet Zone of Occupation, 1945–1949* (Cambridge, MA, 1995), 69–140.

7. "Kill!": Tischler, "Die Vereinfachungen," 330; "Stalin's house Jew": Jahn, *Ilya Ehrenburg*, 71. See also Eveline Passet, "Im Zerrspiegel der Geschichte: Deutsche Bilder von Ilja Ehrenburg," *Osteuropa* 57, no. 12 (December 2007): 17–48.

8. On DPs, see Michael Berkowitz and Suzanne Brown-Fleming, "Perceptions of Jewish Displaced Persons as Criminals in Early Postwar Germany: Lingering Stereotypes and Self-fulfilling Prophecies," in *"We Are*

Here": *New Approaches to Jewish Displaced Persons in Postwar Germany*, ed. Avinoam J. Patt and Michael Berkowitz (Detroit, 2010), 167–193. On fears about POWs, see Christina Morina, *Legacies of Stalingrad: Remembering the Eastern Front in Germany since 1945* (Cambridge, 2011).

9. On the collection of expellees' memories, see Robert G. Moeller, *War Stories: The Search for a Usable Past in the Federal Republic of Germany* (Berkeley, CA, 2001), 51–87, citation on 78.

10. The argument in this paragraph follows Peter Longerich, *Davon haben wir nichts gewusst! Die Deutschen und die Judenverfolgung, 1933–1945* (Munich, 2006), 297–313, esp. 298–300.

11. Jeffrey Herf, *The Jewish Enemy: Nazi Propaganda during World War II and the Holocaust* (Cambridge, MA, 2006), 231–264.

12. Norbert Frei, *Adenauer's Germany and the Nazi Past: The Politics of Amnesty and Integration*, trans. Joel Golb (New York, 2002).

13. Wolfram Wette, *The Wehrmacht: History, Myth, Reality* (Cambridge, MA, 2006).

14. Heinz Guderian, *Kann Westeuropa verteidigt werden?* (Göttingen, 1951), 21.

15. Stefan Cruzberger, "Kampf gegen den inneren Feind: Das gesamtdeutsche Ministerium und der staatlich gelenkte Antikommunismus in der Bundesrepublik Deutschland," in *"Geistige Gefahr" und "Immunisierung der Gesellschaft": Antikommunismus und politische Kultur in der frühen Bundesrepublik*, ed. Stefan Creuzberger and Dierk Hoffmann (Munich, 2014), 87–104.

16. Bernard Ludwig has explored the intersections between the VFF and the French Paix et liberté organization in several studies; see, e.g., Ludwig, "A Transnational Anti-Communist Network," in *Transnational Anti-Communism and the Cold War: Agents, Activities, and Networks*, ed. Luc van Dongen, Stéphanie Roulin, and Giles Scott-Smith (Houndmills, Basingstoke, UK, 2014), 81–95.

17. Mathias Friedel, *Der Volksbund für Frieden und Freiheit (VFF): Eine Teiluntersuchung über westdeutsche antikommunistische Propaganda im Kalten Krieg und deren Wurzeln im Nationalsozialismus* (Sankt Augustin, Germany, 2001).

18. Klaus Körner, *"Die rote Gefahr": Antikommunistische Propaganda in der Bundesrepublik, 1950–2000* (Hamburg, 2003), 21–29, citation on 25.

19. For an image of the poster, see "Frau komm. . . . ohne mich," accessed June 6, 2016, www.deutsche-digitale-bibliothek.de.

20. "Es hat sich nichts geändert," *Der Spiegel* (August 17, 1955), 11–13.

21. Körner, *"Die rote Gefahr,"* 58–62; Friedel, *Der Volksbund*, 144–151.

22. Friedrich Funder, *Als Österreich den Sturm Bestand: Aus der Ersten in die Zweite Republik* (Vienna, 1957), 338.

23. Samuel Moyn, *Christian Human Rights* (Philadelphia, 2015), 65–100.

24. Endre von Ivanka, "Christliches Abendland," *Die Furche* 1, no. 3 (December 15, 1945): 1–2.

25. Ulrich Weinzierl, "Die Kultur der *Reichspost*," in *Aufbruch und Untergang: Österreichische Kultur zwischen 1918 und 1938*, ed. Franz Kadrnoska (Vienna, 1981), 325–344, here 330.

26. Cited in Julie Thorpe, *Pan-Germanism and the Austrofascist State, 1933–38* (Manchester, UK, 2011), 113.

27. Funder on Winter: see Thorpe, *Pan-Germanism*, 114; Funder on Hildebrand: see John Connelly, *From Enemy to Brother: The Revolution in Catholic Teaching on the Jews, 1933–1965* (Cambridge, MA, 2012), 128. On Funder generally, see Hedwig Pfarrhofer, *Friedrich Funder: Ein Mann zwischen Gestern und Morgen* (Graz, 1978).

28. Vanessa Conze, *Das Europa der Deutschen: Ideen von Europa in Deutschland zwischen Reichstradition und Westorientierung (1920–1970)* (Munich, 2005); Axel Schildt, *Zwischen Abendland und Amerika: Studien zur westdeutschen Ideenlandschaft der 50er Jahre* (Munich, 1999).

29. Wolfram Kaiser, *Christian Democracy and the Origins of the European Union* (Cambridge, 2007); Maria D. Mitchell, *The Origins of Christian Democracy: Politics and Confession in Modern Germany* (Ann Arbor, MI, 2012).

30. Konrad Adenauer, "Grundsatzrede des 1. Vorsitzenden der Christlich-Demokratischen Union für die Britische Zone in der Aula der Kölner Universität," in *Reden 1917–1967: Eine Auswahl*, ed. Hans-Peter Schwarz (Stuttgart, 1975), 82–106, here 85–87.

31. Ibid., 85–87.

32. Ibid., 88.

33. Gottfried Niedhardt and Normen Altmann, "Zwischen Beurteilung und Verurteilung: Die Sowjetunion im Urteil Konrad Adenauers,"

in *Adenauer und die deutsche Frage*, ed. Josef Foschepoth (Göttingen, 1988), 102.

34. Robert G. Moeller, *Protecting Motherhood: Women and the Family in the Politics of Postwar West Germany* (Berkeley, CA, 1993), fig. 18.

35. "Bishop in the Front Line," *Time*, April 6, 1953.

36. There is a growing literature on religion in early Cold War America. See, e.g., Jonathan P. Herzog, *The Spiritual-Industrial Complex: America's Religious Battle against Communism in the Early Cold War* (New York, 2011); Dianne Kirby, ed., *Religion and the Cold War* (New York, 2003); William Inboden, *Religion and American Foreign Policy, 1945–1960: The Soul of Containment* (Cambridge, 2008).

37. Melissa Feinberg, *Curtain of Lies: The Battle over Truth in Stalinist Eastern Europe* (New York, 2017).

38. William Inboden, *Religion and American Foreign Policy, 1945–1960: The Soul of Containment* (Cambridge, 2008), 125–126, 148, 262.

39. Hartmut Fritz, *Otto Dibelius: Ein Kirchenmann in der Zeit zwischen Monarchie und Diktatur* (Göttingen, 1998); Roland Kurz, *Nationalprotestantisches Denken in der Weimarer Republik: Voraussetzungen und Ausprägungen des Protestantismus nach dem Ersten Weltkrieg in seiner Begegnung mit Volk und Nation* (Gütersloh, 2007); on Dibelius and antisemitism, see Wolfgang Gerlach, *And the Witnesses Were Silent: The Confessing Church and the Persecution of the Jews*, trans. and ed. Victoria J. Barnett (Lincoln, NE, 2000), 13–16, citation on 14.

40. "Everett R. Clinchy: Freedom of Religion," NYPR Archive Collections, accessed March 16, 2016, www.wnyc.org/story/everett-r-clinchy -freedom-of-religion/.

41. Citation in Kevin Michael Schultz, *Tri-Faith America: How Catholics and Jews Held Postwar America to Its Protestant Promise* (New York, 2011), 58.

42. Mark Silk, "Notes on the Judeo-Christian Tradition in America," *American Quarterly* 36, no. 1 (Spring 1984): 65–85; see also Will Herberg, *Protestant, Catholic, Jew: An Essay in American Religious Sociology* (New York, 1955).

43. Richard Wrightman Fox, *Reinhold Niebuhr: A Biography* (New York, 1985), 193–224.

44. Jacques Maritain, *The Twilight of Civilization*, trans. Lionel Landry (New York, 1943), esp. 17–28. This book is a translation of a lecture that Maritain gave in Paris in 1939.

45. Jacques Maritain, "Anti-Semitism as a Problem for the Jew," *Commonweal*, September 25, 1942, reprinted in Jacques Maritain and Raïssa Maritain, *Oeuvres Complètes*, vol. 8 (Fribourg, 1989), 734–754, here 746, 748.

46. Ronald H. Stone and Matthew Lon Weaver, eds., *Against the Third Reich: Paul Tillich's Wartime Radio Broadcasts into Nazi Germany* (Louisville, KY, 1998), 13–17.

47. Francis Ching-Wah Yip, *Capitalism as Religion? A Study of Paul Tillich's Interpretation of Modernity* (Cambridge, MA, 2010), 21–22.

48. On Couglin: Donald Warren, *Radio Priest: Charles Coughlin, the Father of Hate Radio* (New York, 1996); on American antisemitism during World War II: Leonard Dinnerstein, *Antisemitism in America* (New York, 1995), 128–150.

49. Deborah Dash Moore, "Jewish GIs and the Creation of the Judeo-Christian Tradition," *Religion and American Culture* 8, no. 1 (Winter 1998): 31–53, "universalist rubric" on 47, "common descent" on 35.

50. For a review of the literature on the Judeo-Christian idea and its centrality to American Cold War–era liberalism, see K. Healan Gaston, "Interpreting Judeo-Christianity in America," *Relegere: Studies in Religion and Reception* 2, no. 2 (2012): 291–304. For the classic Cold War–era statement, see Herberg, *Protestant, Catholic, Jew*.

51. Silk, "Notes on the Judeo-Christian Tradition," 65.

52. Citation in Schultz, *Tri-Faith America*, 77.

53. Peter Novick, *The Holocaust in American Life* (Boston, 1999), 92–98. For "identity" citation, see Moore, "Jewish GIs," 47.

54. Novick, *Holocaust*, 94–98.

55. Deborah Dash Moore, "Reconsidering the Rosenbergs: Symbol and Substance in Second Generation American Jewish Consciousness," *Journal of American Ethnic History* 8, no. 1 (Fall 1988): 21–37, "criterion" and "incompatible" citations on 26.

56. Lucy S. Dawidowicz, "'Anti-Semitism' and the Rosenberg Case: The Latest Communist Propaganda Trap," *Commentary* (July 1952): 41–45. See also Nancy Sinkoff, *From Left to Right: Lucy S. Dawidowicz, the New York*

Intellectuals, and the Politics of Jewish History (Detroit, forthcoming), and Nancy Sinkoff, "*Yidishkayt* and the Making of Lucy S. Dawidowicz," introduction to *From That Time and Place: A Memoir, 1938–1947*, by Lucy Dawidowicz (New Brunswick, NJ, 2008).

57. K. Healan Gaston, "The Cold War Romance of Religious Authenticity: Will Herberg, William F. Buckley, Jr., and the Rise of the New Right," *Journal of American History* 99, no. 4 (March 2013): 1133–1158, "reaction against" on 1141.

58. Jonathan Sarna, *American Judaism: A History* (New Haven, CT, 2004), 274–282, citation on 275.

59. Moore, "Jewish GIs," 47. Moore observes that this shift also marked Jewish soldiers as "white" in a racially segregated army.

60. "The Girl Who Hated Cream Puffs," *Time*, September 20, 1948.

61. I am grateful to Melissa Feinberg for many conversations about early Cold War political culture. Here and throughout this section, see Feinberg, *Curtain of Lies*.

62. The phrase is Isaac Deutscher's; see Deutscher, *The Non-Jewish Jew and Other Essays* (New York, 1968).

63. Hasia Diner, *We Remember with Reverence and Love: American Jews and the Myth of Silence after the Holocaust, 1945–1962* (New York, 2009), 266–320, esp. 278–293; Peter Novick, *Holocaust*, 85–102, esp. 98–101. See also Marianne Rachel Sanua, *Let Us Prove Strong: The American Jewish Committee, 1945–2006* (Waltham, MA, 2007), 72–77.

64. "A magyar zsidóság képviselőnek nyilatkozata," *Új Élet*, June 19, 1951, 1.

65. Róbert Győri Szabó, *A kommunizmus és a zsidóság az 1945 utáni Magyarországon* (Budapest, 2009), 169–178.

66. "The Terror at Dawn," *Washington Post*, July 22, 1951, B5.

67. For "horrors of Nazi deportations" and "free world thought" citations, see David Frey, "Echoes of the Shoah: The 1951 Resettlement of Budapest's Jews," unpublished manuscript,8 and 10, respectively. I am grateful to David Frey for generously sharing his unpublished work with me.

68. Here and in the next paragraphs, see the excellent dissertation by Helaine D. Blumenthal, "Fourteen Convicted, Three Million Condemned:

The Slansky Affair and the Reconstitution of Jewish Identities after the Holocaust," PhD diss., University of California, Berkeley, 2012.

69. "Reds Boldly Display Nazi Anti-Semitism," *Washington Post*, December 21, 1952.

70. Allen Lesser and Anti-Defamation League of B'nai B'rith, *The Protocols and the Purge Trial: A Report of Anti-Defamation League of B'nai B'rith* (New York, 1953), 5.

71. American Jewish Committee, *The Anti-Semitic Nature of the Czechoslovak Trial (Nov.-Dec. 1952)* (New York, 1953), 2.

72. Citation in Blumenthal, "Fourteen Convicted, Three Million Condemned," 6.

73. "Truman, Eisenhower Condemn Antisemitism in Prague Trial," *Washington Post*, December 22, 1952.

74. Melissa Feinberg, "Fantastic Truths, Compelling Lies: Radio Free Europe and the Response to the Slánský Trial in Czechoslovakia," *Contemporary European History* 22, no. 1 (2013): 110–117.

7. Between History and Memory

1. Cited in Michael Shafir, "Public Discourse and Remembrance: Official and Unofficial Narratives," in *Romania and the Holocaust: Events, Contexts, Aftermath*, ed. Simon Geissbühler (Stuttgart, 2016), 203–240, here 205.

2. Cited in Michael Shafir, "Between Denial and 'Comparative Trivialization': Holocaust Negationism in Post-Communist East Central Europe," in *The Treatment of the Holocaust in Hungary and Romania during the Post-Communist Era*, ed. Randolph L. Braham (New York, 2004), 43–136, here 114.

3. Tony Judt, *Postwar: A History of Europe since 1945* (New York, 2005), 803.

4. Marco Duranti, "The Holocaust, the Legacy of 1789 and the Birth of International Human Rights Law: Revisiting the Foundation Myth," *Journal of Genocide Research* 14, no. 2 (June 2012): 159–186. See also Samuel Moyn, *The Last Utopia: Human Rights in History* (Cambridge, MA, 2010).

5. On the rise of the Holocaust witness, see Annette Wieviorka, *The Era of the Witness*, trans. Jared Stark (Ithaca, NY, 2006). On postrevolutionary humanitarian activism: Eleanor Davey, *Idealism beyond Borders: The French Revolutionary Left and the Rise of Humanitarianism, 1954–1988* (Cambridge, 2015), 144–181. On the emergence of Holocaust memory generally: Aleida Assmann, *Shadows of Trauma: Memory and the Politics of Postwar Identity*, trans. Sarah Clift (New York, 2016). On the historical intersection between Holocaust memory and human rights: Samuel Moyn, *Human Rights and the Uses of History*, expanded 2nd ed. (London, 2014), 87–99.

6. Raul Hilberg, *The Destruction of the European Jews*, rev. ed., 3 vols. (New York, 1985). Hilberg published the first version of this seminal work in 1961. Another example, once widely used as a textbook in American university courses on the Holocaust, is Yehuda Bauer, *A History of the Holocaust* (New York, 1982).

7. Raul Hilberg, *Perpetrators, Victims, Bystanders: The Jewish Catastrophe, 1933–1945* (New York, 1993).

8. István Deák, *Europe on Trial: The Story of Collaboration, Resistance, and Retribution during World War II* (Boulder, CO, 2015).

9. On the emergence of the Holocaust as narrative, see A. Dirk Moses, "The Holocaust and Genocide," in *The Historiography of the Holocaust*, ed. Dan Stone (New York, 2004), A. Dirk Moses, "Paranoia and Partisanship: Genocide Studies, Holocaust Historiography, and the 'Apocalyptic Conjuncture,'" *The Historical Journal* 54, no. 2 (June 2011): 553–583, and Dan Stone, *Constructing the Holocaust: A Study in Historiography* (London, 2003). On the Holocaust and the teaching of toleration, see Thomas D. Fallace, "The Origin of Holocaust Education in American Public Schools," *Holocaust and Genocide Studies* 20, no. 1 (2006): 80–102; Alan E. Steinweis, "Reflections on the Holocaust from Nebraska," in *The Americanization of the Holocaust*, ed. Hilene Flanzbaum (Baltimore, 1999).

10. Michael Rothberg, *Multidirectional Memory: Remembering the Holocaust in the Age of Decolonization* (Stanford, CA, 2009).

11. Michael Scott Christofferson, *French Intellectuals against the Left: The Anti-Totalitarian Moment of the 1970s* (New York, 2004); Abbot Gleason, *Totalitarianism: The Inner History of the Cold War* (New York, 1995), 143–166; Anson Rabinbach, *Begriffe aus dem Kalten Krieg: Totalita-*

rismus, Antifaschismus, Genozid (Göttingen, 2009); Mike Schmeitzner, ed., *Totalitarismuskritik von links: Deutsche Diskurse im 20. Jahrhundert* (Göttingen, 2007), esp. 247–392.

12. Carolyn J. Dean, "Recent French Discourses on Stalinism, Nazism, and 'Exorbitant' Jewish Memory," *History and Memory* 18, no. 1 (Spring/Summer 2006): 43–85.

13. Stéphane Courtois, "Introduction: The Crimes of Communism," in *The Black Book of Communism: Crimes, Terror, Repression*, ed. Stéphane Courtois et al., trans. Jonathan Murphy and Mark Kramer (Cambridge, MA, 1999), 1–32, here 23.

14. In addition to Dean, "Recent French Discourses," see also Donald Reid, "In Search of the Communist Syndrome: Opening the Black Book of the New Anti-Communism in France," *International History Review* 27, no. 2 (June 2005): 295–318.

15. Horst Boog et al., *Der Angriff auf die Sowjetunion*, vol. 4 of *Das deutsche Reich und der Zweite Weltkrieg* (Stuttgart, 1983), and Gerd Ueberschär et al., *"Unternehmen Barbarossa": Der deutsche Überfall auf die Sowjetunion, 1941: Berichte, Analysen, Dokumente* (Paderborn, 1984).

16. Kai Struve, "Eastern Experience and Western Memory: 1939–1941 as a Paradigm of European Memory Conflicts," in *Shared History, Divided Memory: Jews and Others in Soviet-Occupied Poland, 1939–1941*, ed. Elazar Barkan, Elizabeth A. Cole, and Kai Struve (Leipzig, 2007).

17. Among numerous analyses of the *Historikerstreit*, see Charles Maier, *The Unmasterable Past: History, Holocaust, and German National Identity* (Cambridge, MA, 1988); the roundtable discussion "Forum: The Historikerstreit Twenty Years On," *German History* 24, no. 4 (October 2006): 587–607; and, most recently, "Holocaust Scholarship and Politics in the Public Sphere: Reexamining the Causes, Consequences, and Controversy of the *Historikerstreit* and the Goldhagen Debate: A Forum with Gerrit Dworok, Richard J. Evans, Mary Fulbrook, Wendy Lower, A. Dirk Moses, Jeffrey K. Olick, and Timothy Snyder," *Central European History* 50, no. 3 (September 2017): 375–403.

18. Nolte's essay and other key interventions in the *Historikerstreit* are collected and translated in *Forever in the Shadow of Hitler? Original Documents of the Historikerstreit: The Controversy Concerning the Singularity of*

the Holocaust, trans. James Knowlton and Truett Cates (Atlantic Highlands, NJ, 1993), 18–23.

19. The story is recounted in Maier, *Unmasterable Past,* 179n34.

20. Citations from Ernst Nolte, *Der europäische Bürgerkrieg* [The European civil war], *1917–1945: Nationalsozialismus und Bolschewismus* (Munich, 1997), 131–133. The first edition of this book was published in 1987. Nolte articulated his argument about the "rational core" of Judeo-Bolshevism most clearly in his subsequently published exchange of letters with French historian François Furet: François Furet and Ernst Nolte, *Fascism and Communism,* trans. Katherine Golsan (Lincoln, NE, 2001), esp. 41–45.

21. Jürgen Habermas cited in, *Forever in the Shadow of Hitler?,* 162–170.

22. Arno J. Mayer, "Memory and History: On the Poverty of Remembering and Forgetting the Judeocide," *Radical History Review* 56 (Spring 1993): 5–20, here 6–8 and 17–18.

23. Arno J. Mayer, *Why Did the Heavens Not Darken? The "Final Solution" in History* (New York, 1990), citations on viii, xiii, and 31.

24. Lucy S. Dawidowicz, "Perversions of the Holocaust," *Commentary* 88, no. 4 (October 1989): 56–60. On Dawidowicz generally, see the forthcoming Sinkoff, *From Left to Right.*

25. Daniel Jonah Goldhagen, "False Witness," *New Republic,* April 17, 1989, 39–44.

26. Christopher R. Browning, "The Holocaust Distorted," *Dissent* (Summer 1989): 397–400. See also Christopher R. Browning, "The Holocaust as By-product? A Critique of Arno Mayer," in *The Path to Genocide: Essays on Launching the Final Solution* (Cambridge: Cambridge University Press, 1992), 77–86.

27. See, e.g., Michael Wildt, *Hitler's Volksgemeinschaft and the Dynamics of Racial Exclusion: Violence against Jews in Provincial Germany, 1919–1939* (New York, 2011).

28. Arno J. Mayer, "Memory and History: On the Poverty of Remembering and Forgetting the Judeocide," *Radical History Review* 56 (Spring 1993): 5–20, citations in this paragraph from 6–8 and 17–18.

29. In addition to Dean, "Recent French Discourses," see Tzvetan Todorov, *Hope and Memory: Lessons from the Twentieth Century,* trans. David Bellos (Princeton, NJ, 2016).

30. Jacob Eder, *Holocaust Angst: The Federal Republic of Germany and American Holocaust Memory since the 1970s* (New York, 2016).

31. Some examples include Antony Polonsky, ed., *My Brother's Keeper? Recent Polish Debates on the Holocaust* (London, 1990); Piotr Forecki, *Reconstructing Memory: The Holocaust in Polish Public Debates* (Frankfurt am Main, 2013), 87–133; György Száraz, *Egy előitélet nyomában* (Budapest, 1976); Ferenc Erős, András Kovács, and Katalin Lévai, "Hogyan jöttem rá, hogy zsidó vagyok," *Medvetánc*, nos. 2–3 (1985): 129–144.

32. Samples of this wave of research can be found in Ulrich Herbert, ed., *National Socialist Extermination Policies: Contemporary German Perspectives and Controversies* (New York, 2000), and Michael David-Fox, Peter Holquist, and Alexander M. Martin, eds., *The Holocaust in the East: Local Perpetrators and Soviet Responses* (Pittsburgh, PA, 2014).

33. Marek Kucia, "The Europeanization of Holocaust Memory and Eastern Europe," *East European Politics and Societies and Cultures* 30, no. 1 (February 2016): 97–119.

34. "Elie Wiesel: Acceptance Speech" (December 10, 1986), Nobelprize .org, accessed October 22, 2017, www.nobelprize.org/nobel_prizes/peace /laureates/1986/wiesel-acceptance_en.html.

35. "Anti-Semitic Taunt at Wiesel Talk in Romania," *New York Times*, July 3, 1991; see also Radu Ioanid, "Anti-Semitism and the Treatment of the Holocaust in Postcommunist Romania," in *Anti-Semitism and the Treatment of the Holocaust in Postcommunist Eastern Europe*, ed. Randolph L. Braham (New York, 1994), 159–182.

36. On the rightist press in post-Communist Romania, see Michael Shafir, "Anti-Semitism in the Postcommunist Era," in *The Tragedy of Romanian Jewry*, ed. Randolph L. Braham (New York, 1994), 333–386, citations on 347–348. See also Andrei Pippidi, "Anti-Semitism in Romania after 1989: Facts and Interpretations," in Braham, *Treatment of the Holocaust in Hungary and Romania*,137–166.

37. Michael Shafir, "The Men of the Archangel Revisited: Anti-Semitic Formations among Romania's Communist Intellectuals," *Studies in Comparative Communism* 16, no. 3 (Autumn 1983): 223–243.

38. Dennis Deletant, *Hitler's Forgotten Ally: Ion Antonescu and His Regime, Romania 1940–1944* (Houndmills, Basingstoke, UK, 2006), 130.

39. On the rehabilitation of Antonescu, see Michael Shafir, "Marshal Antonescu's Postcommunist Rehabilitation: *Cui Bono?*," in *The Destruction of Romanian and Ukrainian Jews during the Antonescu Era*, ed. Randolph L. Braham (New York, 1997), 349–410, and Mark Temple, "The Politicization of History: Marshal Antonescu and Romania," *East European Politics and Societies* 10, no. 3 (Fall 1996): 457–503. More generally, see Randolph L. Braham, "Romanian Nationalists and the Holocaust: A Case Study in History Cleansing," *Holocaust and Genocide Studies* 10, no. 3 (Winter 1996): 211–251.

40. Cited in Radu Ioanid, "Romania," in *The World Reacts to the Holocaust*, ed. David S. Wyman (Baltimore, 1996), 225–256, here 248.

41. "Romania Deceives Itself on the Holocaust," *New York Times*, August 27, 1991.

42. "Concurrent Resolution Condemning Resurgent Anti-Semitism and Ethnic Intolerance in Romania," H. Con. Res. 186, 102nd Cong., (1991–1992).

43. Gabriel Andreescu, "Romania," in *Racist Extremism in Central and Eastern Europe*, ed. Cas Mudde (London, 2005), 171–194, here 179–180.

44. The classic text on this is Francis Fukuyama, *The End of History and the Last Man* (New York, 1992).

45. The literature on nationalism and national identity in Eastern Europe written in this vein is vast. For an early influential theoretical work, see Anthony D. Smith, *National Identity* (Reno, NV, 1991). For a widely read account of nationalism after 1989, see Michael Ignatieff, *Blood and Belonging: Journeys into the New Nationalism* (New York, 1994).

46. "Speech Given by Mr. Ion Iliescu, President of Romania, at the Meeting Dedicated to the Holocaust Remembrance Day in Romania, October, 12, 2004," in *Final Report of the International Commission on the Holocaust in Romania* (November 11, 2004), accessed July 15, 2016, www.ushmm.org/m/pdfs/20080226-romania-commission-iliescu-speech.pdf.

47. On the political context of the report, see Ruxandra Cesereanu, "The Final Report on the Holocaust and the Final Report on the Communist Dictatorship in Romania," *East European Politics and Societies* 22, no. 2 (Spring 2008): 270–281.

48. Cited in István Deák, "Anti-Semitism and the Treatment of the Holocaust in Hungary," in Braham, *Anti-Semitism and the Treatment of the Holocaust*, 113–118, here 114–115. On the Csoóri affair, see also András Kovács, *The Stranger at Hand: Antisemitic Prejudices in Post-Communist Hungary* (Leiden, 2011), 8–11. The original text is in Sándor Csoóri, "Nappali hold," *Hitel* 3, no. 18 (September 5, 1990): 4–7.

49. Citations from Deák, "Anti-Semitism," 114–115.

50. On Csoóri, see András Görömbei, *Csoóri Sándor: Monográfia* (Budapest, 2010).

51. Timothy Garton Ash captured the flavor of Hungarian cultural politics in these years, in "The Hungarian Lesson," *New York Review of Books*, December 5, 1985. On the much-debated legacy of the populist-urbanist debate in post-1989 Hungary, see Tamás Fricz, *A népi-urbánus vita tegnap és ma* (Budapest, 1997); Éva Kovács, "Indulatok a népi-urbánus vitában," *2000* 6, no. 8 (1994): 15–22.

52. On the Free Democrats in a regional context, see Michal Kopeček, "Human Rights Facing a National Past: Dissident 'Civic Patriotism' and the Return of History in East-Central Europe, 1968–1989," *Geschichte und Gesellschaft* 38, no. 4 (October–December 2012): 573–602.

53. Cited in Holly Case, "The Holocaust in Regional Perspective: Antisemitism and the Holocaust in Hungary, Romania, and Slovakia," in *Varieties of Antisemitism: History, Ideology, Discourse*, ed. Murray Baumgarten, Peter Kenez, and Peter Thompson (Newark, DE, 2009), 75–92, here 92n87.

54. Shafir, "Between Denial and 'Comparative Trivialization,'" here 109–110.

55. For "Mengele" and "fail to have Europe" citations, see Susan Rubin Suleiman and Éva Forgács, eds., *Contemporary Jewish Writing in Hungary: An Anthology* (Lincoln, NE, 2003), lx; on Kertész, see Magdalena Marsovszky, "Imre Kertész and Hungary Today," in *Imre Kertész and Holocaust Literature*, ed. Louise Olga Vasvári and Steven Tötössy de Zepetnek (West Lafayette, IN, 2005), 148–161, here 153. The Csoóri excerpt is included in László Karsai, ed., *Kirekesztők: Antiszemita írások, 1881–1992* (Budapest, 1992), 158–160.

56. Dean, "Recent French Discourses," 43–85.

57. "A Historical Exchange: Mária Schmidt versus Mária M. Kovács," Hungarian Spectrum, accessed April 15, 2018, http://hungarianspectrum .org/2014/07/20/a-historical-exchange-maria-schmidt-versus-maria-m -kovacs/. Schmidt's essay on the topic was published in the June 26, 2014, issue of the weekly magazine *Heti Válasz*. This was not the first time that Schmidt had taken up these themes. See Mária Schmidt, "'Holocaustok' a huszadik században," in *Egyazon mércével: A visszaperelt történelem* (Budapest, 2003), 10–16, and "The Role of 'The Fight against Anti-Semitism' during the Years of Transition," in *From Totalitarian to Democratic Hungary: Evolution and Transformation, 1990–2000*, ed. Mária Schmidt and László Gy. Tóth (Boulder, CO, 2000), 339–385.

58. Michal Kopeček and Piotr Wciślik, eds., *Thinking Through Transition: Liberal Democracy, Authoritarian Pasts, and Intellectual History in East Central Europe after 1989* (Budapest, 2015).

59. In addition to Cesereanu, "Final Report," see Lavinia Stan, *Transitional Justice in Post-Communist Romania: The Politics of Memory* (Cambridge, 2013), esp. 111–136.

60. "Speech Given by Mr. Ion Iliescu," www.ushmm.org/m/pdfs/20080226 -romania-commission-iliescu-speech.pdf.

61. Timothy Snyder, *Bloodlands: Europe between Hitler and Stalin* (New York, 2010).

62. Jan Tomasz Gross, *Neighbors: The Destruction of the Jewish Community in Jedwabne, Poland* (New York, 2002).

63. Krzystof Persak, "Jedwabne before the Court: Poland's Justice and the Jedwabne Massacre: Investigations and Court Proceedings, 1947–1974," *East European Politics and Societies* 25, no. 3 (August 2011): 410–432.

64. There is a rich literature in English on *Neighbors*, its reception in Poland, and the themes of historical memory that it raises. See, e.g., Anna Bikont, *The Crime and the Silence: Confronting the Massacre of Jews in Wartime Jedwabne*, trans. Alissa Valles (New York, 2015); Marci Shore, "Conversing with Ghosts: Jedwabne, Żydokomuna, and Totalitarianism," *Kritika* 6, no. 2 (Spring 2005): 345–374; Natalia Aleksiun, "Polish Historiography of the Holocaust: Between Silence and Public Debate," *German*

History 22, no. 3 (August 2004): 406–432; and the forum on *Neighbors* in *Slavic Review* 61, no. 3 (Fall 2002).

65. Hanna Świeda-Ziemba, "The Shortsightedness of the 'Cultured,'" reprinted in *The Neighbors Respond: The Controversy over the Jedwabne Massacre in Poland*, ed. Antony Polonsky and Joanna B. Michlic (Princeton, NJ, 2004), 103–113, here 112–113.

66. "Address by President of Poland Aleksander Kwaśniewski at the Ceremonies in Jedwabne Marking the Sixtieth Anniversary of the Jedwabne Tragedy on 10 July 2001," reprinted in Polonsky and Michlic, *The Neighbors Respond*, 130–132, here 131.

67. For a sample of the responses, see Polonsky and Michlic, *The Neighbors Respond*; Ruth Henning, ed., *Die "Jedwabne-Debatte" in polnischen Zeitungen und Zeitschriften* (Potsdam, 2001); and Jacek Borkowicz et al., *Thou Shalt Not Kill: Poles on Jedwabne* (Warsaw, 2001).

68. Gross, *Neighbors*, 92.

69. Antoni Macierewicz, "The Revolution of Nihilism," reprinted in Polonsky and Michlic, *The Neighbors Respond*, 93–102, here 94–98. A leading member of the right-wing populist Law and Justice Party currently in power in Poland, Antoni Macierewicz was appointed minister of national defense in 2015.

70. Tomasz Strzembosz, "'Collaboration Passed over in Silence,' *Rzeczpospolita*, 27 January 2001," in Polonsky and Michlic, *The Neighbors Respond*, 220–237, here 223–227. See also Marek Jan Chodakiewicz, *The Massacre in Jedwabne, July 10, 1941: Before, During and After* (Boulder, CO, 2005)

71. Bogdan Musiał, "The Pogrom in Jedwabne: Critical Remarks about Jan T. Gross's *Neighbors*," in Polonsky and Michlic, *The Neighbors Respond*, 304–344, esp. 327–332.

72. Rafał Pankowski, *The Populist Radical Right in Poland: The Patriots* (London, 2010); David Ost, *The Defeat of Solidarity: Anger and Politics in Postcommunist Europe* (Ithaca, NY, 2005), esp. 60–94.

73. For an exemplary case study, see Geneviéve Zubrzycki, *The Crosses of Auschwitz: Nationalism and Religion in Post-Communist Poland* (Chicago, 2006).

74. Macierewicz, "The Revolution of Nihilism," 94.

75. Joanna Beata Michlic and Małgorzata Melchior, "The Memory of the Holocaust in Post-1989 Poland: Renewal—Its Accomplishments and Its Powerlessness," in *Bringing the Dark Past to Light: The Reception of the Holocaust in Post-Communist Europe*, ed. John-Paul Himka and Joanna Beata Michlic (Lincoln, NE, 2013), 403–450.

Epilogue

1. István I. Mócsy, *The Effects of World War I: The Uprooted: Hungarian Refugees and Their Impact on Hungary's Domestic Politics, 1918–1921* (New York, 1983).

2. Jérôme Tharaud and Jean Tharaud, *Quand Israël est roi* [*When Israel Is King*] (Paris, 1921), 283–291, citations on 283 and 291.

3. There is a vast literature analyzing these debates and the impact of specific interventions on them. Among many works, see Michael Meng, "Silences about Sarrazin's Racism in Contemporary Germany," *Journal of Modern History* 87 (March 2015): 102–135. See also the furor over French author Michel Houellebecq's 2015 novel *Submission*. One critical response: Judith Surkis, "A Muslim Future to Come?," *Public Books*, November 18, 2015, accessed September 10, 2017, www.publicbooks.org/a-muslim-future-to-come.

4. On Kubitschek, see James Angelos, "The Prophet of Germany's New Right," *New York Times Magazine*, October 10, 2017, accessed January 12, 2018, www.nytimes.com/2017/10/10/magazine/the-prophet-of-germanys-new-right.html; Sumi Somaskanda, "A New, New Right Rises in Germany," *Atlantic*, June 22, 2017, accessed January 12, 2018, www.theatlantic.com/international/archive/2017/06/a-new-right-rises-in-germany/529971/.

5. Michael Paulwitz and Götz Kubitschek, *Deutsche Opfer, fremde Täter: Ausländergewalt in Deutschland: Hintergrund-Chronik-Prognose* [German victims, alien perpetrators: Violence by foreigners in Germany: Background, Chronicle, Prognosis] (Schnellroda, 2011).

6. "A vágatlan kötcsei beszéd," *Átlátszó*, September 17, 2015, accessed September 10, 2017, https://vastagbor.atlatszo.hu/2015/09/17/a-vagatlan-kotcsei-beszed/.

7. "Azt akarjuk, hogy az unokáink egy európai kalifátusban éljenek?," *Magyaridők*, September 1, 2015, accessed September 10, 2017, http://

magyaridok.hu/belfold/azt-akarjuk-hogy-az-unokaink-egy-europai-kalifat
usban-eljenek-5035/.

8. David N. Coury, "A Clash of Civilizations? Pegida and the Rise of Cultural Nationalism," *German Politics and Society* 34, no. 4 (Winter 2016): 54–67.

9. Chloe Farand, "Marine Le Pen Launches Presidential Campaign with Hardline Speech," *Independent*, February 5, 2017, accessed September 10, 2017, www.independent.co.uk/news/world/europe/marine-le-pen-front -national-speech-campaign-launch-islamic-fundamentalism-french-elections -a7564051.html.

10. Bruce Pilbeam, "Eurabian Nightmares: American Conservative Discourses and the Islamisation of Europe," *Journal of Transatlantic Studies* 9, no. 2 (June 2011): 151–171.

11. Samuel Moyn, *Christian Human Rights* (Philadelphia, 2015), 137–168.

12. Paul Hanebrink, "Islam, Anti-Communism, and Christian Civilization: The Ottoman Menace in Interwar Hungary," *Austrian History Yearbook* 40 (2009): 114–124; Hans-Georg Betz and Susi Meret, "Revisiting Lepanto: The Political Mobilization against Islam in Contemporary Western Europe," *Patterns of Prejudice* 43, no. 3–4 (2009): 313–334. See also Maureen Healy's forthcoming work on the historical memory of the 1683 Ottoman siege of Vienna.

13. For the text of the speech, see "Remarks by President Trump to the People of Poland," July 6, 2017, accessed September 11, 2017, www .whitehouse.gov/briefings-statements/remarks-president-trump-people -poland/. See also Peter Beinart, "The Racial and Religious Paranoia of Trump's Warsaw Speech," *Atlantic*, July 6, 2017, accessed September 11, 2017, www.theatlantic.com/international/archive/2017/07/trump-speech-poland /532866/.

Acknowledgments

The idea for this book first came to me many years ago, but it has taken me a long time to figure out how to write it. It is a pleasure to thank the friends and colleagues who have been so generous with their advice, insights, helpful criticism, and encouragement.

No one could have better or more supportive colleagues than I do at Rutgers University. Jochen Hellbeck and Belinda Davis generously read and commented on draft chapters. Conversations with Judith Surkis, Seth Koven, Alastair Bellany, Ziva Galili, Bonnie Smith, Temma Kaplan, Jan Kubik, Yael Zerubavel, Nancy Sinkoff, and Jeffrey Shandler helped to sharpen my thinking and opened up intellectual avenues that I had never considered exploring. A History Department faculty brown-bag session gave me the chance to share my work, and I am grateful for the responses of everyone who took part. Similarly, a workshop and conference on contested memories organized at Rutgers by Yael Zerubavel afforded me a wonderful opportunity to think through that aspect of my work.

Early on in this project, a sabbatical leave from Rutgers University helped me to get started. Later, a research leave at the Imre Kertész Kolleg in Jena, Germany, afforded me the luxury of rethinking and reconceptualizing much of what I had done to that point. I am grateful to Joachim von Puttkamer and the staff at the Kolleg for making my time in Jena such a pleasant experience, and to the other fellows who were there with me, for stimulating discussions about my work and many other things besides.

Joyce Seltzer took an interest in this project at its inception and offered sage advice as it took shape. I am grateful for her patience as I took the time to develop the manuscript and for her generosity in reading and commenting on it at several stages. I also want to thank the two readers for Harvard University Press for their extensive, thoughtful, and tremendously helpful responses. Thanks also to Joyce's colleagues for guiding this book to publication and to Julie Hagen for expert copyediting.

I have benefited so much from the intellectual generosity of friends and colleagues who took the time to engage with the larger themes of the work or to point me in the right historiographic direction. I had the pleasure of discussing drafts of several chapters with the Kennebunkport Circle (Eagle Glassheim, Cindy Paces, Melissa Feinberg, and David Frey) in idyllic surroundings, and I look forward to future meetings of the group. Paul Steege invited me to present a chapter at the Philadelphia Area Modern Germany Workshop that he organized. I am grateful to him and to the other participants for a stimulating conversation. Presentations in Regensburg, organized by Ulf Brunnbauer, and in Jena at the Zeitgeschichtliches Kolloquium directed by Norbert Frei were also occasions for tremendously helpful discussions. In addition, numerous friends and colleagues were kind enough to share with me their expertise and insights on specific aspects of this project. I am particularly grateful to Jim Bjork, Jochen Böhler, Holly Case, James Chappel, John Connelly, István Deák, Ben Frommer, Michael Geyer, Árpád von Klimó, the late Mark Pittaway, and Sandrine Sanos. Sam Moyn has been my friend nearly forever, and discussing the issues of this book with him over the years has been one of the greatest pleasures of the entire process. My parents, Wayne and Anneliese Hanebrink, have always taken an interest in what I am working on, and I am thankful for their love and encouragement.

I owe the most to Melissa Feinberg. She read countless drafts of chapters and chapter sections and always saw in all of them the point I was trying to make far more clearly than I was able to express it. Her brilliant and incisive criticism has inspired me and made every part of this book immeasurably better. She has kept me from going down more scholarly rabbit holes than

I can count. Her clear-eyed, wise, and encouraging counsel convinced me on more than one occasion that I was not stuck but simply rethinking the issues of the project in productive ways. Her own work remains a model that I try to emulate. I am grateful, in so many more ways than I can say, for her love and companionship.

Index